JAPAN

HOKKAIDŌ

TOM FAᵀ

T0332127

www.bradtguides.com

Bradt Guides Ltd, UK
The Globe Pequot Press Inc, USA

Bradt GUIDES
TRAVEL TAKEN SERIOUSLY

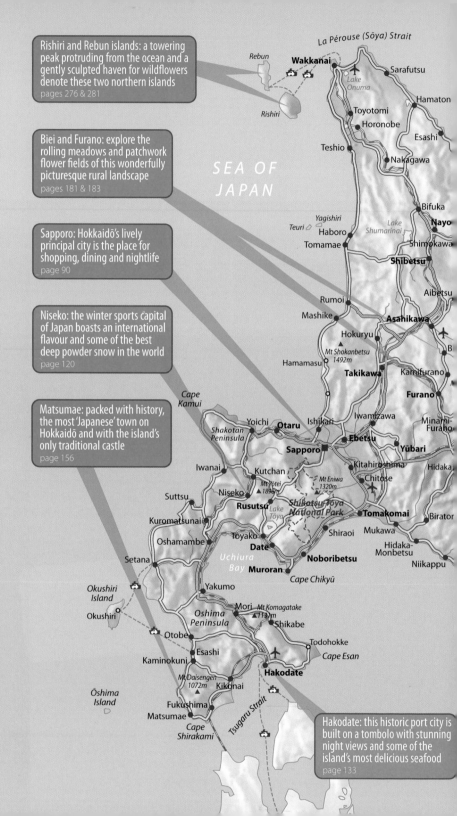

Rishiri and Rebun islands: a towering peak protruding from the ocean and a gently sculpted haven for wildflowers denote these two northern islands
pages 276 & 281

Biei and Furano: explore the rolling meadows and patchwork flower fields of this wonderfully picturesque rural landscape
pages 181 & 183

Sapporo: Hokkaidō's lively principal city is the place for shopping, dining and nightlife
page 90

Niseko: the winter sports capital of Japan boasts an international flavour and some of the best deep powder snow in the world
page 120

Matsumae: packed with history, the most 'Japanese' town on Hokkaidō and with the island's only traditional castle
page 156

Hakodate: this historic port city is built on a tombolo with stunning night views and some of the island's most delicious seafood
page 133

La Pérouse (Sōya) Strait

Rebun

Wakkanai

Lake Onuma

Sarafutsu

Hamaton

Toyotomi

Honorobe

Esashi

Nakagawa

Teshio

Rishiri

SEA OF JAPAN

Bifuka

Nayo

Yagishiri

Teuri

Haboro

Lake Shumarinai

Shimokawa

Shibetsu

Tomamae

Aibetsu

Rumoi

Mashike

Asahikawa

Hokuryu

B

Mt Shokanbetsu 1492m

Hamamasu

Kamifurano

Takikawa

Furano

Cape Kamui

Ishikari

Iwamizawa

Minami-Furano

Yoichi

Otaru

Shakotan Peninsula

Sapporo

Ebetsu

Yūbari

Iwanai

Kutchan

Kitahiroshima

Hidaka

Mt Eniwa 1320m

Chitose

Suttsu

Niseko

Mt Yōtei 1898m

Rusutsu

Shikotsu-Tōya National Park

Tomakomai

Birator

Kuromatsunai

Lake Tōya

Oshamambe

Tōyako

Shiraoi

Mukawa

Date

Setana

Uchiura Bay

Noboribetsu

Hidaka-Monbetsu

Niikappu

Muroran

Cape Chikyū

Okushiri Island

Yakumo

Okushiri

Mori

Mt Komagatake 1131m

Oshima Peninsula

Shikabe

Otobe

Todohokke

Cape Esan

Kaminokuni

Esashi

Ōshima Island

Mt Daisengen 1072m

Kikonai

Hakodate

Fukushima

Matsumae

Cape Shirakami

Tsugaru Strait

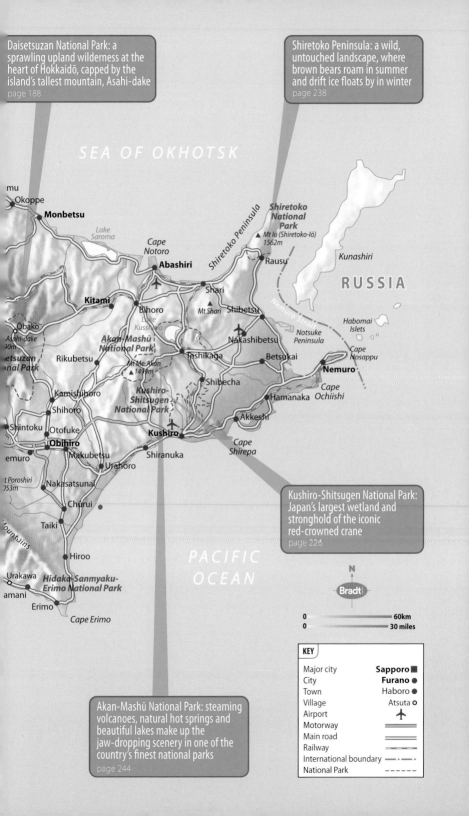

Daisetsuzan National Park: a sprawling upland wilderness at the heart of Hokkaidō, capped by the island's tallest mountain, Asahi-dake
page 188

Shiretoko Peninsula: a wild, untouched landscape, where brown bears roam in summer and drift ice floats by in winter
page 238

SEA OF OKHOTSK

mu
Okoppe
Monbetsu
Lake Saroma
Cape Notoro
Abashiri
Kitami
Bihoro
Lake Kussharo
Shari
Mt Shari
Shibetsu
Akan-Mashū National Park
Teshikaga
Nakashibetsu
Betsukai
Rikubetsu
Mt Me-Akan
▲ 1499m
Shibecha
Kushiro-Shitsugen National Park
Kamishihoro
Hamanaka
Shihoro
Akkeshi
Shintoku
Otofuke
Kushiro
Obihiro
Makubetsu
Shiranuka
Cape Shirepa
emuro
Urahoro
t Poroshiri
053m
Nakasatsunai
Chūrui
Taiki
Hiroo
ountains
Urakawa
Hidaka-Sanmyaku-Erimo National Park
amani
Erimo
Cape Erimo

Shiretoko National Park
▲ Mt Iō (Shiretoko-Iō) 1562m
Rausu
Kunashiri
RUSSIA
Shiretoko Peninsula
Nemuro Strait
Notsuke Peninsula
Habomai Islets
Cape Nosappu
Nemuro
Cape Ochiishi

Asahi-dake
90m
etsuzan
nal Park
Obako

PACIFIC OCEAN

Kushiro-Shitsugen National Park: Japan's largest wetland and stronghold of the iconic red-crowned crane
page 226

Akan-Mashū National Park: steaming volcanoes, natural hot springs and beautiful lakes make up the jaw-dropping scenery in one of the country's finest national parks
page 244

N
Bradt
0   60km
0   30 miles

KEY	
Major city	**Sapporo** ■
City	**Furano** ●
Town	Haboro ●
Village	Atsuta ○
Airport	✈
Motorway	
Main road	
Railway	
International boundary	
National Park	

HOKKAIDŌ
DON'T MISS...

SAPPORO
A green oasis in the heart of Hokkaidō's capital, Ōdōri Park is the venue for many of the city's largest annual events PAGE 101
(S/D)

NATIONAL PARKS
Sensational views, volcanic caldera lakes and hiking trails await in Shikotsu-Tōya, one of six national parks on Hokkaidō
PAGE 126
(SP/D)

WINTER SPORTS
Striking Mount Yōtei is the symbol of Niseko, Hokkaidō's centre for winter sports PAGE 120
(MKP/S)

INDIGENOUS CULTURE
Ainu traditions, such as this marimo (algae) festival on the shores of Lake Akan, are being celebrated once again across the island PAGES 36, 38 & 250
(SS)

WILDLIFE
The island's unique wildlife can be seen at every turn in eastern Hokkaidō. Pictured: Whooper swans on Lake Kussharo PAGES 7, 13 & 249
(OP/D)

HOKKAIDŌ
IN COLOUR

above
(HD/S)
The picturesque old brick warehouses and canals of Otaru draw in the crowds and are a reminder of the city's rich heritage PAGE 114

below
(J/D)
Matsumae Park – home to the only Japanese-style fortification on Hokkaidō – is a prime cherry-blossom-viewing spot in the spring PAGE 157

The rolling meadows and flower fields of Biei and Furano are awash with colour in the summer months PAGES 181 & 183

A ride on the Kurodake Ropeway is one of the best ways to admire the dazzling autumn hues of Sōunkyō Gorge PAGE 192

AUTHOR

Tom Fay (**w** thomasfay.com) grew up in a small village among the green and grassy hills of North Wales, and there developed an appreciation of nature and the outdoors from an early age. After a few years studying medieval history at the University of Manchester, in 2007 he decided to up sticks to the other side of the world to teach English in Osaka, Japan. What started as a temporary adventure developed into a deep-rooted love for the country, and he has been living in and exploring every corner of Japan ever since. He has  also returned to his countryside roots and now resides in a renovated 150-year-old farmhouse among the hills of southern Kyoto.

Over the years Tom has travelled widely around Asia and throughout Japan, writing articles for magazines, newspapers and various websites. He has a particular love for remote and wild places, and so spends much of his time climbing Japan's many mountains, with occasional forays to higher-altitude peaks in the Himalayas. Tom is the main author of *Hiking and Trekking the Japan Alps and Mount Fuji* (Cicerone Press, 2019), has worked on titles for Lonely Planet and Fodor's Travel, and has published his own popular guidebooks *Must-See Japan* and *Secret Japan* (forthcoming).

AUTHOR'S STORY

When I initially started talking to Bradt about possible projects, they had just commissioned their first guidebook to Japan, focused on the balmy subtropical Ryūkyū Islands in the southwest of the archipelago. It soon became obvious that the ideal companion to that title would be a guide to one of my favourite parts of Japan, the much colder and snowier frontier in the far north of the country – and so the idea for this guidebook to Hokkaidō was born.

Having lived in Japan for many years, but not on Hokkaidō itself, I'm in the relatively privileged position of having a familiar knowledge of the language and general ins-and-outs of the country, and yet still get to experience Hokkaidō through the eyes of a visitor every time I go there. Trips to the island always feel like an adventure; cut off from the mainland by the Tsugaru Strait, Hokkaidō is a region with its own unique history, landscapes, climate and wildlife, and feels quite different to the southern realms of the country. While inbound tourism exploded in Japan up until the Covid-19 pandemic (and has now thankfully recovered), Hokkaidō does not tend to feature on most typical tourist itineraries and still feels pretty off the beaten track, despite being the largest of Japan's 47 prefectures and the second largest of the four main islands.

Even when I'm not on Hokkaidō, I find myself constantly dreaming of its open roads, beautiful lakes, mountains and forests; the never-ending coasts; and the produce – outstandingly fresh seafood, fruits and vegetables, creamy sea urchin, spicy soup curry, butter ramen and succulent barbecued lamb. And then there's the snow, humongous powdery white quantities of which bury the entire island for months on end. I hope some of my love for Hokkaidō comes across in these pages, and that this book will also help you to foster a similarly obsessive fascination with Japan's beautiful northernmost outpost.

First edition published May 2024

Bradt Guides Ltd
31a High Street, Chesham, Buckinghamshire, HP5 1BW, England
www.bradtguides.com
Print edition published in the USA by The Globe Pequot Press Inc,
PO Box 480, Guilford, Connecticut 06437-0480

Text copyright © 2024 Tom Fay
Maps copyright © 2024 Bradt Guides Ltd; includes map data ©
OpenStreetMap contributors
Photographs copyright © 2024 Individual photographers (see below)
Project Manager: Susannah Lord
Cover research: Pepi Bluck, Perfect Picture

ISBN: 9781804690994

British Library Cataloguing in Publication Data
A catalogue record for this book is available from the British Library

Photographs Biei Tourism (BT); Dreamstime.com: Areinwald (A/D),
Chinesestudentchengjibing (CS/D), Chu-wen Lin (CL/D), Coconutdreams
(C/D), Jajaladdawan (J/D), Ondřej Prosický (OP/D), Petr Simon (PS/D), Sean
Pavone (SP/D), Seventhmoon (S/D), Tristan Scholze (TS/D); Nature Picture
Library (naturepl.com): David Pike (DP/NPL); Shutterstock.com: 7maru (7M/S),
Agami Photo Agency (APA/S), aiaikawa (A/S), b-hide_the_scene (BTS/S),
CHEN FANGXIANG (CF/S), CHEN_MIN_CHUN (CMC/S), dah_ken (DK/S),
GUDKOV ANDREY (GA/S), hunters-dream (HD/S), Jedsada Kiatpornmongkol
(JK/S), Mayumi.K.Photography (MKP/S), Niels Vos (NV/S), NP27 (NP/S), okimo
(O/S), Ondřej Prosický (OP/S), PaulWong (PW/S), Sean Pavone (SP/S), Teow Cek
Chuan (TCC/S), tkyszk (T/S), zincreative (Z/S); Superstock (SS); Tom Fay (TF).

Front cover Japanese, or red-crowned, crane (*Grus japonensis*) courtship display,
Hokkaidō (DP/NPL)
Back cover, clockwise from top Shirogane Blue Pond (O/S), Sika deer (*Cervus nippon
yesoensis*) (OP/S), drift ice off the Shiretoko Peninsula (Z/S)
Title page, clockwise from top left Ōyunuma pond, Noboribetsu (SP/S), Shirahige
Falls on the Biei River (C/D), Hokkaidō pumpkins (A/D)

Maps David McCutcheon FBCart.S. FRGS
Typeset by Ian Spick, Bradt Guides Ltd
Production managed by Jellyfish Print Solutions; printed in India
Digital conversion by www.dataworks.co.in

Acknowledgements

I'd like to thank, at Bradt Guides, Anna Moores, Claire Strange and Sue Cooper for commissioning and overseeing this project from the start, and for showing great patience throughout the long process; my wonderful editor Susannah Lord for her supreme kindness, efficiency and attention to detail, plus all the other staff at Bradt whose hard work helped make this book a reality. I also thank Jo Davey, author of Bradt's companion guidebook to Okinawa and the Southwest Islands for all the support, useful tidbits, general life musings and Japan-related chat – I'm still amazed at her ability to write a full guidebook despite seemingly jetting off across the globe every other week; Phoenix Scotney at the Hokkaidō Tourism Organization, and all at the Sapporo Tourist Board. Natsumi Wakaki for showing me the sights of Sapporo and answering all of my annoying questions; Mark Brazil (and his wife, Mayumi Brazil) for his valuable insights and expert knowledge; likewise Rob Thompson of HokkaidoWilds for creating such an invaluable resource for outdoor fanatics; Markus Hauser (japanwilds.org) for his extremely helpful mapping assistance; the many native Dōsanko and Hokkaidō locals who provided me with interesting tips, information and warm hospitality as I explored their beautiful island; and, last but not least, my friends and family who have had to put up with me talking almost non-stop about Hokkaidō for the past few years – it's an obsession I just can't seem to shake off.

FEEDBACK REQUEST

At Bradt Guides we're aware that guidebooks start to go out of date on the day they're published – and that you, our readers, are out there in the field doing research of your own. You'll find out before us when a fine new family-run hotel opens or a favourite restaurant changes hands and goes downhill. So why not tell us about your experiences? Contact us on ☎ 01753 893444 or e info@bradtguides.com. We will forward emails to the author who may post updates on the Bradt website at w bradtguides.com/updates. Alternatively, you can add a review of the book to Amazon, or share your adventures with us on social:

🅕 BradtGuides
🆇 BradtGuides & T_in_Japan
🅘 BradtGuides & tomfay.jp

Contents

LIST OF MAPS

Introduction

Hokkaidō has always been seen as somewhat of an outlier; a vast, cold, distant and mysterious island in the far north of Japan; the homeland of the Ainu, a place where winter seems to last almost half the year and brown bears roam wild. Ezo (or Yezo/Yeso/Yesso), as Hokkaidō was once known, differs quite dramatically from the rest of Japan in terms of history, climate and ecology, and the island sits at a unique juncture geographically, culturally and even politically – a kind of halfway house between the mega-cities of central Japan and the great empty wildernesses of the Russian far east. Indeed, Sapporo, Hokkaidō's largest city and the regional capital, is closer to Vladivostok than Tokyo, and the long-running dispute between Japan and Russia over the ownership of the southernmost Kuril Islands – the long island chain that arcs down from Kamchatka and ends almost within touching distance of Hokkaidō's eastern shoreline – has been ongoing since the end of World War II.

But that shouldn't paint a picture of Hokkaidō as some sort of pot-holed battleground between two tussling super-powers – what draws most visitors to Hokkaidō are the beautiful natural landscapes and wide-open spaces that provide a sense of escape from the other much more crowded regions of Japan. In fact, despite encompassing roughly one-fifth of the country's landmass, Hokkaidō is home to only 5% of Japan's total population, so there is plenty of space to escape into. Perhaps for this reason the island has long attracted adventurous souls, bohemians and other people with a spirit of independence. For Japanese people from the mainland, unaccustomed to miles of seemingly unending vistas and rolling farmland, arriving on Hokkaidō may feel like stepping foot in another country.

The Japanese were not the original colonisers of Hokkaidō, however, as they only fully took control of the island as late as the latter half of the 19th century. Before that, Hokkaidō was the stronghold of the Ainu, Japan's indigenous people. But with Japanese expansion across the island, the Ainu, like many native peoples around the world, suffered hardship and discrimination before gradually (and forcefully) being assimilated into Japanese society. Much of their culture and traditions were on the verge of being lost forever, but in recent years the Ainu have finally been recognised by the government as the legitimate indigenous people of Hokkaidō. Although the Ainu population remains low and difficult to substantiate (figures of around 17,000–25,000 are regularly bandied around), it is hoped that the Ainu language, culture and traditions will be seen increasingly as things to cherish and protect.

The name 'Hokkaidō' is comprised of three characters in Japanese: 北 (meaning 'north'), 海 ('sea') and 道 ('road' or 'route'), and so roughly translates to 'northern sea road' or 'northern sea circuit', although the meaning may be even more nuanced than that (page 30). In any case, the name evokes many images for Japanese people – untouched nature, cold and preposterously snowy winters, sprawling expanses, endlessly long, empty, straight roads, bubbling hot springs and steaming volcanoes, bucolic countryside, plus delicious seafood and farm produce. Hokkaidō has long been popular with domestic visitors for these very reasons, and in recent years has seen an increasing number of tourists particularly from other Asian countries, yet it still remains off the main tourist track for the majority of western visitors to Japan.

But the island offers a wealth of attractions, all year round. The warm summers are conducive to hiking, camping, cycling, fishing and road trips, while the cold winters blanket most of Hokkaidō often under metres of snow, providing great opportunities for skiing and snowboarding (both backcountry and piste), ice-floe walks on the Sea of Okhotsk or attending one of the island's spectacular ice festivals. And any time of year is good for wildlife-watching, visiting museums or sampling Hokkaidō's famously fresh produce and sensational seafood. All of which means that one trip simply isn't enough – you'll be drawn, like me, over and over again – with each visit promising different experiences and ever-changing landscapes, owing to the island's transient nature and dramatic contrasts from season to season.

HOW TO USE THIS GUIDE

AUTHOR'S FAVOURITES Finding genuinely characterful accommodation or that unmissable off-the-beaten-track café can be difficult, so the author has chosen a few of his favourite places throughout the country to point you in the right direction. These 'author's favourites' are marked with a ✳.

LISTINGS
Price codes Throughout this guide we have used price codes to indicate the cost of those places to stay and eat listed in the guide. For a key to these price codes, see page 73 for accommodation and page 75 for restaurants.

English menus Restaurants that have an English menu are indicated in the listings with 'EM' at the end of the review.

ADMISSION FEES Unless otherwise stated, admission fees given for attractions and other sites of interest are the standard adult price or, where two prices are given, eg: ¥500/250, these refer to adult/child prices.

MAPS
Keys and symbols Maps include alphabetical keys covering the locations of those places to stay, eat or drink that are featured in the book. Note that regional maps may not show all hotels and restaurants in the area: other establishments may be located in towns shown on the map.

Grids and grid references Several maps use gridlines to allow easy location of sites. Map grid references are listed in square brackets after the name of the place or site of interest in the text, with page number followed by grid number, eg: [95 C3].

Part One

GENERAL INFORMATION

Location Northeast Asia with the Sea of Japan to the west, the Sea of Okhotsk to the north and east, and the Pacific Ocean to the south; Hokkaidō is the northernmost and second largest of Japan's four main islands.

Neighbouring countries The northern tip of Hokkaidō is separated from Sakhalin Island (Russia) by the La Pérouse Strait. In a long-running dispute, Japan claims the four southernmost Kuril Islands off Hokkaidō's eastern coast, but they remain under Russian administration.

Size/area 83,453km^2

Climate Most of the island has a humid continental climate, with warm or hot summers and long, cold, snowy winters.

Status Constitutional monarchy (although Japan has no official head of state)

Population 5.139 million (2023, Ministry of Internal Affairs and Communications). The Ainu (Hokkaidō's indigenous inhabitants) are officially estimated to number around 25,000 (roughly 0.5% of Hokkaidō's population), but these figures are unreliable.

Life expectancy 80.28 years (males), 86.77 years (females)

Capital Sapporo (population 1.96 million)

Other main cities Asahikawa (population 339,000), Hakodate (population 265,000), Kushiro (population 174,000) and Tomakomai (population 172,000)

Economy Agriculture, timber and fishing are key industries, although the biggest sectors are manufacturing and service industries.

GDP US$179 billion (4% of national GDP)

Languages Japanese (main; Japan has no official language), indigenous Ainu language (spoken by few people)

Religion Buddhism (46%) and Shintō (48%), plus Christian (1%) and other religious minorities

Currency Yen (¥/JPY). Banknotes in denominations of 1,000, 2,000, 5,000 and 10,000; coins 1, 5, 10, 50, 100 and 500.

Exchange rate £1 = ¥189, US$1 = ¥150, €1 = ¥162 (February 2024)

National airline Japan Airlines

Regional airline/airport Air Do/New Chitose Airport (IATA: CTS)

International telephone code +81

Time Japan is 9 hours ahead of GMT and does not operate on daylight saving time (it is on Standard Time all year round).

Electrical voltage 100v, 50/60Hz; two-pin plugs

Weights and measures Metric

Flag Japan's national flag has a white background with a crimson-red disc in the centre – officially called the Nisshoki, but commonly known as the Hinomaru ('circle of the sun'). Hokkaidō's flag has a blue background with a seven-point star, red with a white fringe, in the centre.

National anthem 'Kimigayo' ('The Emperor's Reign')

National flower Not designated, but the yellow chrysanthemum is a symbol of the Imperial Family. Hokkaidō's official flower: *hamanasu* or Rugosa rose (*Rosa rugosa*).

National bird *Kiji* or green pheasant (*Phasianus versicolor*). Hokkaido's official bird: *tanchō* or red-crowned crane (*Grus japonensis*).

National sports Sumo, baseball, football

Public holidays See page 78.

1

Background Information

Hokkaidō is the northernmost of Japan's four main islands and has traditionally been divided into four main regions – north (Dōhoku; 道北), east (Dōtō; 道東), central (Dō-ō; 道央) and south (Dōnan; 道南). Sapporo, its capital, is included in the central region, and the nearby Ishikari Plain was where rice cultivation began on the island. The definition of the southern Dōnan region can vary, but always includes the fishtail shaped Oshima Peninsula, and sometimes other areas as far east as Hidaka.

Sapporo is the only real 'big' city on Hokkaidō; even the next largest by population, Asahikawa, feels more like a large provincial town by comparison. The majority of Hokkaidō's small to mid-size towns and cities all have quite a similar vibe and appearance; wide uncongested streets and many shuttered buildings often with a slightly run-down and weather-beaten look, which creates a general small-town sleepy ambiance and adds to the frontier town feeling. In truth, most of these smaller urban areas simply don't have large vibrant populations and so don't tend to have a lot going on, which may strike you most if coming from somewhere lively like Tokyo or Sapporo. But most decent-sized settlements usually offer a few shops, restaurants and places to stay, so you can take a break, refuel and stock up before heading out into wilder and remoter areas.

GEOGRAPHY

The Japanese archipelago lies just to the east of the enormous Eurasian landmass, and stretches over 3,000km in a rough northeast-to-southwest arc. It encompasses a wide range of climates and habitats, ranging from subtropical to subarctic, across nearly 14,000 islands – a figure that jumped from 7,000 after a recent recount – of which around 400 are inhabited. The majority of the country's population of 124 million live in the mostly temperate climes and packed cities in the coastal areas of Honshū, the largest of Japan's four main islands. Hokkaidō is the second largest (followed by Kyūshū then Shikoku), with a total area of 83,424m² and measuring roughly 480km north to south and 500km from its easternmost to westernmost points. Almost double the size of Switzerland, almost equal with Austria, and roughly the same size as the US state of Idaho, it is the 21st largest island in the world (sitting between Ireland and Sakhalin respectively).

Hokkaidō is also the northernmost of Japan's main islands, separated from the mainland of Honshū by the Tsugaru Strait, which is about 20km wide at its narrowest point. Cape Sōya, Hokkaidō's northernmost point, juts up towards the Russian island of Sakhalin, while to the east the island closely bookends the Kuril Island chain (page 234), which sweeps down from the Kamchatka Peninsula in the far east of Russia.

The island has a distinctive angular shape, with long, sweeping coastlines ending at remote peninsulas and, with relatively few large cities, it is Japan's wildest and

As the northernmost of Japan's four main islands, for many Japanese people there is a somewhat romantic notion of Hokkaidō as a distant, wild and unfathomably northern land. Tokyo-born novelist Takeo Arishima wrote works depicting Hokkaidō as a 'frontier' and an 'extremity', while film director Masahiro Kobayashi (who shot a 2003 film there) said 'there's a loneliness and ambiguity to Hokkaidō that cannot be seen elsewhere in Japan'.

In fact, Benten-jima, the small island just off of Hokkaidō's northernmost point of Cape Sōya, is the most northerly land under Japanese control, while the disputed and Russian-administered southern Kuril island of Iturup is claimed by Japan to be its northernmost territory.

Regardless, when living in Japan it is sometimes easy to forget that Hokkaidō actually lies at the same latitude as Rome and New York, neither of which are regarded as particularly extreme northern frontiers. Anyone expecting to catch a glimpse of northern phenomena such as the aurora borealis will be disappointed, although on very rare occasions it has been seen on Hokkaidō (most recently in 2015 and 2023). It is the influence of the nearby Eurasian continental landmass, plus cold ocean currents and Siberian weather fronts which mean that Hokkaidō's climate and ecology share more in common with typically Arctic regions – northern Hokkaidō is classed as taiga (boreal forest), a biome found across the northern regions of Alaska, Canada, Europe and Russia.

least-developed region. Jutting up in the centre of the island are the Daisetsu Mountains, a vast upland wilderness of volcanic mountains, many of which rise to around 2,000m in height making them the tallest peaks on Hokkaidō. Not all of its mountains are volcanic in origin, however – the long Hidaka chain of mountains, which form the backbone of southern Hokkaidō, were created by tectonic uplift (they appear to be rising no more). Away from the highest peaks, there are extensive coniferous and deciduous forests, vast lakes and wetlands, and great rivers such as the Ishikari (Japan's third longest) which meander slowly across the plains out towards the coast. Hokkaidō's flatlands are generally used for intensive agriculture, while many stretches of the coastline are fairly desolate and empty. While around half of Hokkaidō is mountainous, it actually has more extensive flatlands than almost any other region of Japan, most of which have been developed for agriculture.

GEOLOGY

Japan is one of the most geologically active and complex places on earth, and its geography is entirely a result of plate tectonics; the archipelago is situated on the Pacific 'Ring of Fire' in a region where several plates converge, making it one of the most active tectonic zones on earth. The Pacific Plate to the east and the Philippine Plate to the south are subducting below the Amur Plate and the Okhotsk Plates on which most of Japan is bound.

The land that forms Japan probably broke off from the eastern edge of the Rodinia supercontinent some 700 million years ago; and the landmass as we know it today went through various phases of transformation, from continental margin, to the formation of an island arc, and the accretionary complex (the accumulation of materials caused by a continental plate moving beneath another in a process called subduction) of continental plates. The Sea of Japan was formed some 25 million to 15 million years ago by such subduction. Japan's oldest known basement (or foundation) rocks are granite and gneisses in central Honshū; these are overlain by younger sedimentary and metamorphic rocks.

Hokkaidō (and most of northern Honshū) sits on the Okhotsk Plate, under which the Pacific Plate to the east is subducting. Japan has four main geological domains, and Hokkaidō belongs to two of them: the Kuril and eastern Hokkaidō Arc, which stretches for 1,000km from Kamchatka to the eastern third of Hokkaidō, with a central collision zone which formed the Hidaka Mountains; and the Hokkaidō–Honshū Arc to which the other two thirds of the island belong. Accordingly, Hokkaidō also has five main geological belts; the island's underlying rocks were formed by the subduction of oceanic plates, but because of all the complex processes going on, we can find a wide range of rock types all over Hokkaidō, ranging from deep-sea sediments, ophiolites, metamorphic rocks and basalt.

VOLCANOES Plate tectonics are the reason for the extensive mountain ranges and numerous volcanoes which are spread right across Japan, with the formation of volcanic belts (or arcs) usually situated parallel and close to plate boundaries. Volcanic activity is evident across Hokkaidō, in its impressive steam and sulphur vents, bubbling hot springs, classic-shaped volcanoes (both active and dormant), gaping calderas and picturesque crater lakes. There are currently 110 active volcanoes in the country with almost a quarter of these found on Hokkaidō, one of Japan's literal volcanic hotspots. Mount Usu on the rim of the Tōya Caldera is one of the most frequently erupting volcanoes in Japan, with recent eruptions in 1910, 1943–45, 1977 and 2000. The 1929 eruption of Mount Hokkaidō-Komagatake in southwest Hokkaidō is one of the largest (when measured by material ejected) eruptions in Japan in the past century. The Kussharo Caldera in eastern Hokkaidō is Japan's largest caldera – measuring 26km by 20km, it was formed by an almighty eruption approximately 400,000 years ago.

EARTHQUAKES Japan's ceaseless tectonic activity also results in frequent earthquakes and the potential for devastating tsunamis. Earthquakes are recorded every day in Japan (and account for about 10% of all earthquake activity in the world), although most of them are too small to notice. The most powerful earthquake in the country's modern recorded history occurred on 11 March 2011 in the Tōhoku region of northeastern Japan – it registered 9.0 on the Richter scale and the resultant tsunami caused widespread devastation and the loss of around 20,000 lives, along with the meltdown of three reactors at the Fukushima Daiichi nuclear power plant. The earthquake was felt quite strongly on Hokkaidō, with the tsunami hitting the coasts and creating waves of up to 3.5m high at Erimo on the island's southern tip. Many harbours along Hokkaidō's southern and eastern coasts were denuded by water and some aquaculture farms were rendered unusable, but there was nothing like the devastation and almost 40m-high watermarks recorded in some parts of Tōhoku. Hokkaidō has been subject to its own earthquake and tsunami disasters, however, the most notable being the Okushiri earthquake in July 1993, which caused a devastating tsunami and the loss of 230 lives (page 168).

Japan's intense geological activity does have a more pleasant side effect, though – the formation of geothermally heated hot springs, which can be found right across the country. These naturally heated and mineral-rich waters have created Japan's deep and culturally embedded *onsen* (hot-spring bath) tradition. Other geothermal curiosities include steam vents, sulphurous fumaroles, geysers and bubbling mud pools, examples of which can all be found on Hokkaidō.

CLIMATE

Hokkaidō is known in Japan for its distinctive climate – bordering the northern limits of the temperate zone and the southern limit of the subarctic, the average annual temperature is quite cool (around 9°C in Sapporo, compared with Tokyo's 16°C) and the seasons are well defined, with summer and winter contrasting quite dramatically. Much of the island is part of the humid continental climate zone, while the far north of Hokkaidō falls into the taiga biome, which is characterised by coniferous forests.

Hokkaidō winters (December to February) are infamous for extremely cold and snowy weather, caused by two opposing pressure systems – the Siberian High, an area of stable high pressure which develops over the Eurasian Continent, and the Aleutian Low, which hovers around the North Pacific. Bitterly cold northwesterly winds are drawn in from Russia, picking up moisture from the Sea of Japan, which is then dumped as heavy snowfall when it hits the mountains of Hokkaidō. As the air loses its moisture over the mountains, most places on their eastern, leeward side and along the Pacific coast of Hokkaidō receive much less snowfall. The temperature in Sapporo averages about -5°C between December and February, but in inland areas it frequently drops to below -20°C, and drift ice brings additional cooling to eastern Hokkaidō.

Western and northern Hokkaidō (the Sea of Japan side) are the snowiest parts of the island, and in a typical winter Sapporo sees over 6m of snowfall from late November to March (*hatsuyuki*, 初雪, or 'first snowfall' usually occurs around mid-October to mid-November). The city receives its heaviest snow in December, January and February, with a negligible amount in the shoulder months of October and April. Eastern and southern Hokkaidō receive significantly less annual snowfall (down to 1.8m on the Pacific coast), but most of the island is nevertheless blanketed white for four months (December to March), and mountainous areas for at least six months of the year. Most rivers on Hokkaidō freeze throughout the winter.

Even though the island is buried in snow for many months, apart from the occasional wild snowstorm which disrupts everything for a day or two, life in winter pretty much continues as usual – trains generally run on time, vehicles ply the ice-covered roads with their winter tyres, and people spend many mornings shovelling snow from driveways and pavements. You may notice that lots of buildings have a ladder running halfway up one wall; these are to provide easy access to the roof for snow removal (where it can pile up dangerously if left to accumulate).

Spring (April to May) is short but pleasant in much of Hokkaidō, as the snow begins to melt and temperatures gradually warm up; Sapporo's daily average temperature increases from 7.3°C in April to 13.4°C in May. Evenings and early mornings tend to be chilly still, and while the lowlands will be clear of snow, the mountains will still be covered. Anticyclonic systems bring the sunniest weather of the year in May.

In June and July, much of Japan experiences *tsuyu* (梅雨), the Japanese rainy season, when the warm air mass from the North Pacific and southeast Asia moves northwards and meets the body of colder air from Siberia, causing a band of clouds and unsettled weather to form and settle over the south of the country. While much of Japan is soaked and steamed during this early summer period, by virtue of being that further bit north, Hokkaidō generally avoids the worst of the rain and humidity (although residents still say that this is a bit of a myth and that the island still bears the outer brunt of the rainy front). But likely on account of global warming, even the predictable nature of rainy season seems to be changing (2022 saw the official end of rainy season before the end of June in Tokyo, the earliest since records began), and Hokkaidō may not be able to avoid it for much longer if the rainy band is regularly pushed further north.

Rainy season comes to an end around late July when the North Pacific High pushes northwards across the entire country, bringing warm and sunny conditions to Hokkaidō. Summers on Hokkaidō are said to be much more bearable than in southern Japan, with less of the stifling heat and humidity that envelops much of the country in late July and throughout August, but in recent years even Hokkaidō has suffered from bouts of oppressive summer heat. Temperatures often reach over 30°C, and the Foehn phenomenon can bring hot temperatures to the generally cool Sea of Okhotsk coast. Hokkaidō's southeastern coastline is regularly smothered in thick ocean fog during the summer – this is due to moist southerly air being cooled by the cold Oyashio Current which flows down Hokkaidō's eastern seaboard.

Autumn (September to early November) comes early to Hokkaidō, with the first hint of changing foliage as soon as late August or early September on the island's higher peaks. More typically you can expect to see the autumn colours at their best around early to mid-October, with popular leaf-viewing spots such as Sōunkyō Onsen attracting droves of visitors. Late September is usually harvest time in agricultural areas, while along the coast you may spot bright red swathes of coral grass around coastal lagoons. Autumn brings cooling temperatures; Sapporo goes from an average of 19°C in September, down to 12°C in October and 5°C by November. The first snow tends to fall in late October, or as early as the beginning of September on the very highest mountains, signalling that winter is once again on its way.

Although precipitation varies depending on the region, Hokkaidō is generally driest from around April to June, with annual rainfall peaking in August and September as a result of the activity of various weather fronts. But a little like Great Britain, the island is always subject to rain showers, so it's a good idea to pack rainwear or a folding umbrella whatever the season.

Sapporo gets 1,750 hours of sunshine per year, with May being the sunniest month (199hrs) and December the least (87hrs). As there is no daylight saving, the evenings draw in early even in summer – in late June the sun rises at about 04.00 and sets at 19.00. At the end of December there are 9 hours of sunlight a day, with sunrise at about 07.00 and sunset at 16.00.

The Japan Meteorological Agency publishes detailed English-language forecasts on their website (**w** jma.go.jp).

NATURAL HISTORY AND CONSERVATION

The Japanese archipelago stretches across many climatic zones, from subtropical to subarctic, and so supports a wide range of habitats and boasts an incredibly varied biodiversity. Many endemic species can be found here. Thanks to the biogeographical boundary which is signified by Blakiston's Line (page 8), Hokkaidō's flora and fauna differs quite significantly from those found in the rest of Japan.

FAUNA
Mammals Much of Hokkaidō's mammalian fauna is unique in Japan; while 21 species occur on both sides of the strait, 19 species are found only on Hokkaidō but

not further south. On the contrary, some mammals resident on Honshū but not found on Hokkaidō include wild boar, Asiatic black bears, Japanese macaques and the Japanese serow.

Brown bear Hokkaidō's (and indeed Japan's) largest and most impressive mammal is the Ezo brown bear (*Ursus arctos yesoensis*), simply known as *higuma* (ヒグマ) in Japanese. It is a subspecies of the Ussuri brown bear, with others in the family including the relatively widespread Eurasian brown bear and the fearsome grizzly bear of North America. Ussuri brown bears are also found in the Russian Far East, on Sakhalin and on the southern Kuril Islands, and are one of the larger brown bear subspecies. They are entirely absent from the rest of Japan, where the smaller Asiatic black bear roams instead.

Males can grow to about 2m (when standing on hind legs) and weigh 150–400kg, while females are slightly smaller, reaching 1.5m and 100–200kg. They are omnivorous, subsisting on a diet of insects, plants, small animals, berries, nuts and fish. To survive Hokkaidō's harsh winter, brown bears fatten up over the summer and early autumn, retreating to a quiet den to begin hibernation, which lasts from roughly December until late March. Females give birth to one or two cubs in their winter den and then accompany them for the first year or so of their lives, while males live more solitary lives.

Brown bears can be found from coastal lowlands to mountain tops, favouring mixed deciduous and coniferous forests and alpine grasslands, but due to habitat

BLAKISTON'S LINE

Thomas Wright Blakiston (1832–91) was a British merchant and naturalist who lived in Japan from 1861 to 1884, mostly in Hakodate. He spent much of his time collecting natural history specimens from all over Japan, shipping them back to Britain, and in collaboration with Henry Pryer (an entomologist living in Yokohama) published the ground-breaking *Catalogue of the Birds of Japan* – all of which greatly increased Western knowledge of Japanese flora and fauna. Blakiston was also the first person to recognise that there was a great deal of disparity between the fauna of Hokkaidō, which was more closely related to that of northern Asia, and that of Honshū, which shared more in common with the fauna of southern Asia.

Blakiston's Line is a zoo-geographical boundary which lies between Hokkaidō and Honshū along the Tsugaru Strait. In the past, land bridges once connected Japan to the Asian subcontinent both to the north and south, allowing species to colonise the archipelago. It is not known exactly when these land bridges existed, but probably between 26,000 and 18,000 years ago, around the time of the last ice age. While relatively narrow, the Tsugaru Strait is much deeper than the strait that separates Honshū from the Korean Peninsula, and so Hokkaidō and Honshū were probably cut off from each other much earlier, creating a large ecological divide.

Some species that occur on both sides of the line, such as the red fox, possibly have much more ancient distribution origins, or occur so widely that they were able to colonise Japan from both the north and south.

Blakiston's Line was first used as a term by John Milne in a questions session after Blakiston presented his evidence to the Asiatic Society of Japan in Tokyo in 1883. A monument to Blakiston can be seen on Mount Hakodate.

AVOIDING BEAR ENCOUNTERS

Bears are usually very shy animals and generally keep away from humans at all costs. In fact, you are very unlikely to encounter or even see any hint of a bear while out hiking or cycling, but even so, when in bear country it is best to take a few sensible precautions.

MAKE NOISE To avoid startling a bear, most Japanese hikers carry a bear bell (known as a *suzu*). The bell can be attached to your rucksack – and the ringing alerts any bears (and all other wildlife) of your presence, giving them ample chance to scarper. In areas where the sound of cascading water may drown out the gentle chime of a small bear bell, then it may be worth carrying a whistle.

DON'T APPROACH If you see a bear, slowly and calmly return the way you came, allowing the bear a clear escape route. Don't run (as that will only encourage a bear to pursue) or make any sudden movements or noises while backing away. Talking calmly in low tones may help to identify yourself as a human and not prey. Don't climb a tree as bears can climb too. Mothers with cubs are especially protective and should not be approached.

BEAR SPRAY In remote areas with relatively dense or substantial bear populations (such as the Shiretoko Peninsula or Hidaka Mountains), you may want to carry bear spray to use as a last resort in the rare case of an aggressive encounter. It is not possible to take bear spray on a plane, but it can be bought online (try w amazon.co.jp) and delivered to your accommodation on Hokkaidō – don't forget that you'll need a harness too for quick access. Alternatively, since it's not cheap to buy (around ¥10,000 a bottle), bear spray can be rented via w asahikawaride.com/bearspray-rentals-eng, and is sometimes available to rent for a small fee from visitor centres near popular trailheads, with the canister to be returned after the hike.

DON'T LEAVE FOOD AROUND Bears have an excellent sense of smell, so be sure not to leave any food or litter on trails or at camp. A small number of campsites have food storage boxes, so do store your supplies in one overnight if available. If wild or stealth camping in remote areas, it's probably wise to cook away from the tent and – although not at all a common practice in Japan as it is in bear country in North America – for peace of mind at night, store food by hanging it in a tree.

interference and persecution they are now mostly found in mountainous areas far away from human activity. In recent years, however, their numbers do seem to have been increasing, and there have been well-publicised incidents of bears entering populated areas (including the suburbs of Sapporo). But owing to a few notorious historical bear-encounter incidents, the threat of brown bears has been somewhat overplayed by a fear-induced public. In truth, brown bears are shy creatures and your chances of meeting one are very slim. Even in the highest-density bear population areas – the Shiretoko Peninsula and the Daisetsu and Hidaka mountains – the chances of a bear encounter are low, and the risk of injury or death from a bear attack is unlikely in the extreme (though it is still wise to take precautions; see above). Giant hornets pose a much more pertinent threat.

THE EZO WOLF

Once fairly widespread on Hokkaidō, the Ezo or Hokkaidō wolf (*Canis lupus hattai*) was an island subspecies of the grey wolf which ranged across coastal northeast Asia. It preyed primarily on deer and was known to the Ainu as Horkew Kamuy – the howling deity of the forest. Some Ainu groups even believed that they themselves derived from the union of a white wolf and a goddess.

Despite living alongside the Ainu in relative harmony for centuries, it was during the stark upheaval of the Meiji era that, as the Japanese colonised and pushed further into Hokkaidō, wolves were hunted and then systematically exterminated (often using poisoned bait) in order to protect livestock on the growing number of ranches and farms. As the human population of Hokkaidō increased, deer numbers dwindled, and wolves (and possibly also bears) increasingly took farm animals. An Ohio rancher named Edwin Dun (page 35) was hired in 1873 as an advisor for the Kaitakushi (Hokkaidō Development Agency) and oversaw the extermination campaign, starting in the burgeoning horse-breeding region of southern Hokkaidō. The Kaitakushi also introduced an island-wide bounty system for wolf kills, with Ainu hunters rewarded for their skills and expertise. These governmental policies were so successful, that in the space of a few decades wolves were completely wiped out, with the last wolf on Hokkaidō being killed in 1896.

The Ezo wolf was more closely related to the wolves of North America than to the Japanese wolf (*Canis lulpus hodophilax*), a smaller subspecies of wolf found in Japan, which ranged across Honshū, Shikoku and Kyūshū, and was descended from a much older lineage of Siberian wolves from the Asian subcontinent. The Japanese wolf was also sadly hunted to extinction around the beginning of the 20th century, though there are rumours that it has somehow managed to cling on to this day deep in the mountains of central Japan.

By contrast, for the native Ainu the brown bear is known as Kimun Kamuy – the deity of the mountains. The Ainu hunted bears for their fur and meat, but they also revered them as gods; even the young bears captured for sacrifice in the Iomante ceremony were treated with great respect before their passage back to the spirit world (page 42).

Japanese deer Also known as the Sika deer, the Japanese deer (*Cervus nippon yesoensis*) is the most commonly seen large mammal on Hokkaidō, with the Hokkaidō subspecies (Yezo or Ezo deer) the largest of its kind in Japan – stags can weigh up to 130kg (females are generally much smaller). These deer subsist on a diet of plants such as leafy herbs, grasses and other vegetation, but may resort to eating tree bark when the snow is deep. Deer can be found in forests, mountains, marshlands and agricultural areas, and are regularly encountered crossing roads (particularly at dawn and dusk), making them a significant traffic hazard in some areas. Indeed, in recent decades deer numbers have been on the increase significantly throughout much of Japan, and their destructive eating habits have caused loss of vegetation and devastation to habitats in many regions. Hokkaidō's official deer-hunting season runs from 1 October to 31 March, but it doesn't seem to have impacted much on deer numbers. This is in stark contrast to the late

19th century when deer were almost hunted to extinction on Hokkaidō; in 1892 the government even banned deer hunting temporarily.

Red fox Unlike the red fox that can be found throughout much of Japan, where it is mostly nocturnal and shy, the slightly larger Hokkaidō subspecies, the Ezo red fox (*Vulpes vulpes schrencki*), is mostly diurnal and so is frequently spotted in the middle of the day. Like other foxes, they are opportunistic scavengers and should not be approached if encountered, especially as those on Hokkaidō are known sometimes to harbour *Echinococcus* tapeworms, the parasitic larvae of which can infect humans and on very rare occasions lead to fatalities (this is usually by drinking from fox-contaminated water; page 59).

Sable A relation of stoats, weasels, badgers and martens, the sable (*Martes zibellina*) is a nimble and aggressive predator which can hunt down animals larger than itself, both on the ground and up in trees. It has a thick, creamy-coloured winter coat, a bushy tail, white fur on its face, and small black eyes and nose. In winter, it preys on rodents living beneath the snow, but will also feed on invertebrates in the summer, plus fruits, nuts and seeds when available. Males can measure up to 67cm in length and weigh 1.5kg, with females slightly smaller. They are often solitary and can be found in mixed deciduous and coniferous woods in both lowlands and up to the treeline.

Japanese pika Also known as the northern pika, the Japanese pika (*Ochotona hyperborea*), a rabbit-like relict species from the Ice Age, can be found living among the jumbles of rock in the high mountains of central Hokkaidō (namely the Daisetsu and Hidaka ranges). Alpine zone specialists, these small brownish creatures measure just 13–19cm in length and have short tails and ears, helping them to blend in with their surroundings. In fact, before you see one, you are much more likely to hear one, as pika are famed for their high-pitched whistle-like cries. Remarkably hardy, they are active throughout the year. Hokkaidō is the southern limit of their range in east Asia.

Siberian chipmunk The Siberian chipmunk (*Eutamias sibiricus*), a small terrestrial squirrel, with a long, bushy tail almost as long as its body, can be found throughout Hokkaidō and is especially active during warm summer days when it can be seen darting through low-lying brush and along woodland floors. Subsisting mostly on a diet of seeds, berries, nuts, buds and fungi, it beds down for winter in late October and emerges in April, when it will feed to restore body mass and mate, with females giving birth to a litter of three to seven young, which will remain close to their mother until it is time to hibernate once again.

Siberian flying squirrel As sunlight fades in the forest, the Siberian flying squirrel (*Pteromys volans*) – a big-eyed, greyish-to-white boreal species – becomes active up in the treetops, hunting for leaves, seeds, flowers and nuts, leaping and gliding from bough to bough, using the membrane between its outstretched limbs as a kind of parachute. Widespread throughout Hokkaidō but not found anywhere else in Japan, the Siberian flying squirrel prefers old forests with a mix of conifers and deciduous trees, often making its nest in holes chiselled by woodpeckers.

Birds Hokkaidō is a birder's paradise. Home to a number of endemic and rare species, it provides a key stopover and seasonal retreat for migratory species from as far away as Australasia and the Russian northeast. The avifauna of Hokkaidō generally has more in common with northern regions such as Sakhalin than with southern Japan, and the island is the southern limit for many northern species such as the white-tailed eagle, Blakiston's fish owl and spectacled guillemot. But Hokkaidō is also the northern limit for numerous southern species, including the Japanese accentor and Japanese wagtail.

Red-crowned crane The red-crowned crane (*Grus japonensis*), or *tanchō-zuru*, is the only crane species resident in Japan – others are just temporary visitors. Deified by the Ainu, who know them by the name Sarurun Kamuy, the god of the marshes, these cranes are the official mascot and de facto symbol of Hokkaidō. They are said to symbolise longevity and happiness and have been a popular subject in Japanese art for centuries.

Once spread more widely across the country, the red-crowned crane was hunted almost to extinction, with only around 30 individuals remaining in its stronghold of the Kushiro wetlands by the early 20th century. But thanks to conservation efforts, it numbers around 2,000 today, and its range has spread both west and north.

Standing about 1.5m tall, with a wingspan of 2.4m, sporting white and black plumage and a dash of red on the crown, these are impressive and graceful birds, especially when spotted engaging in winter courtship dances in the falling snow – a huge draw to the Kushiro wetlands for nature photographers. During the summer the birds build large nests on the ground in which the females lay two white eggs; in the tall wetland reeds, both the birds and their nests tend to be well hidden.

Steller's sea eagle Steller's sea eagle (*Haliaeetus pelagicus*) is one of the most impressive-looking raptors in the world and Japan's largest bird of prey. This giant fish-hunting eagle has a wingspan of up to 2.5m and boasts a striking black-and-white patterned plumage and huge orange bill and talons. Natives of the Kamchatka Peninsula and northern areas around the Sea of Okhotsk, Steller's sea eagles fly south in the winter and between November and March can be found in eastern Hokkaidō, where they forage for fish and nest along the coast, river mouths and lakes. In fact, eastern Hokkaidō is one of the best places in the world to see these birds up close, often spotted perching on floating sea ice around the Shiretoko Peninsula or hunting fish at Lake Fūren further to the south.

White-tailed eagle Almost as impressive as Steller's sea eagle, the white-tailed eagle (*Haliaeetus albicilla*) with a wingspan of 1.9–2.4m is the second largest bird of prey in Japan. This raptor can be seen year-round, often soaring in the sky above coastal and forested regions as it hunts for food including fish, smaller birds and carrion.

Blakiston's fish owl The largest owl species in the world, the magnificent Blakiston's fish owl (*Bubo blakistoni*) is revered by the Ainu as Kotan-kor-kamuy, the deity and protector of the village, as it often lived close to traditional Ainu settlements in riverside forests where fish were plentiful. This is a bird that likes to nest in large ancient trees, but as these sites have become increasingly sparse, this secretive predator is now very rarely spotted on Hokkaidō, although it does manage to cling on in a few mature deep-growth forests in eastern regions.

Black-eared kite Known as *tonbi* in Japanese, the black-eared kite (*Milvus lineatus*) is the most widespread and commonly seen bird of prey in Japan by far, and can be found in a wide range of habitats from inland plains to coastal towns, including over roads. Its impressive size and dark silhouette make it easy to spot as it soars overhead searching and swooping for roadkill or any small morsels to scavenge. In some areas the kites are seen as a nuisance as they have been known to snatch food from people.

Long-tailed tit Called *Shima enaga* locally, the adorable long-tailed tit (*Aegithalos caudatus japonicus*) has become one of the unofficial mascots of Hokkaidō in recent years. Sometimes nicknamed 'snow fairies' and known as *Upas cir* (snow birds) to the Ainu, these tiny fluffy birds look like little balls of cotton with their white plumage contrasting strikingly against their dark eyes. They feed mostly on insects and tree sap, and can be spotted year-round flitting among the trees in forests and parks throughout the island.

Seabirds Found in great colonies on the tiny island of Teuri on Hokkaidō's northwest, the **rhinoceros auklet** (*Cerorhinca monocerata*) ranges widely across the North Pacific. Their name derives from the birds' distinctive bill, which grows a brightly coloured orange outer sheath and a horn-like extension at the base during the early summer breeding season, after which it is shed. Clumsy in flight, these endearing puffin-like seabirds feed on fish during twilight hours, before returning to shore and crash-landing close to their nests to feed their young.

Despite its name, the **common guillemot** (*Uria aalge*) is now a rare sight on Hokkaidō, although the distinctive **spectacled guillemot** (*Cepphus carbo*) is endemic to the Sea of Okhotsk, while the **tufted puffin** (*Fratercula cirrhata*), with its colourful bill, is critically endangered in Japan and restricted to a few islands near the Nemuro Peninsula. Harbours can be good places to spot various species including gulls, cormorants, sea ducks, grebes, divers and auks.

Other birds In the forests you can see a wide range of woodpecker species – the largest is the **black woodpecker** (*Dryocopus martius*), a designated national treasure and endangered species. The smallest is the **Japanese pygmy woodpecker** (*Yungipicus kizuki*); patterned brown and white, it lives in woodlands, gardens and parks.

Rivers are home to **brown dippers** (*Cinclus pallasii*), a wren-like bird which prefers clear and fast-flowing waters; the monotone **crested kingfisher** (*Megaceryle lugubris*) with its Mohican-style crest; and the unmistakable **common kingfisher** (*Alcedo atthis*), with its bright blue and orange plumage, a summer visitor. **Whooper swans** (*Cygnus cygnus*) are common winter visitors to northern parts of Hokkaidō, where they gather in large numbers around frozen lakes and rivers.

Reptiles and amphibians
The Japanese archipelago has an abundance of reptile and amphibian species, but in the cooler climes of Hokkaidō their numbers are more limited. In marshes and wetlands you may come across the **Hokkaidō brown frog** (*Rana pirica*), **Japanese tree frog** (*Hyla japonica*) and **Siberian salamander** (*Salamandrella keyserlingii*), all of which are adapted to colder temperatures.

A couple of the more commonly seen reptile species include the **Japanese pit viper** (*Gloydius blomhoffii*), or *mamushi*, which is found across the country and is one of Japan's most venomous snakes. It is a small, stocky, beige and brown snake, with adults rarely exceeding 80cm in length and, despite its fearsome reputation, is actually extremely shy and retiring, using its camouflage to hide among leaf litter and vegetation. Bites are rarely fatal (approx 10 people die per year), but medical attention

1

Hokkaidō offers great regional and seasonal diversity, and so wildlife watchers are spoilt for choice. Wildflowers, birds, butterflies, dragonflies and mammals – whatever your interest, there is so much to see here.

Wherever you explore, there are numerous red fox, Japanese deer, and *tanuki* (raccoon dog) – they may appear at the roadside (or even in the road) at any time. Watch out too in mixed forest for the widespread and quite common Eurasian red squirrel, and at dusk you may be lucky to glimpse a Siberian flying squirrel. In the agricultural fields of eastern Hokkaidō the crepuscular mountain hare is sometimes to be seen – along with deer and foxes – and in winter the snow-covered fields are peppered with their tracks.

In the high, central, Daisetsu Mountains, and other montane areas, summer hikers will delight in the array of alpine flowers and may spot Asiatic chipmunk, northern pika and brown bear – though the Shiretoko Peninsula in the northeast offers the very best chances of bear sightings both from land and from coast-hugging boat trips from Utoro or Aidomari.

Various inshore boat trips now offer fantastic wildlife-watching experiences. Around Teuri Island, off Hokkaidō's west coast, you can go out to watch the multitudes of burrow-breeding rhinoceros auklets. An array of whale-watching excursions now depart from various ports including Abashiri and Rausu, giving access to the rich waters of the Sea of Okhotsk and the Nemuro Channel, and providing opportunities to see, each in their season, fin whale, northern minke whale, sperm whale, orca, Pacific white-sided dolphin, Dall's porpoise and harbour porpoise; as well as Steller's sea lion and northern fur, harbour and spotted seals. In winter, there are fantastic opportunities to watch sea eagles from boats leaving Rausu harbour and heading out into the Nemuro Channel. Steller's sea eagle and white-tailed sea eagle are both common here in winter, having migrated to Hokkaidō from the Russian Far East.

From ports in the Nemuro region, in the southeast, nature cruises now offer winter and summer trips to the tip of the Nemuro Peninsula or around offshore islets. Here, seabird watching can be exciting. Even sightings of migratory albatrosses are possible – species such as black-footed, Laysan and the rare short-tailed, all visitors from their breeding areas further south in the North Pacific. Additionally, large numbers of short-tailed shearwaters, which breed in the antipodes and then migrate thousands of kilometres to reach the North Pacific, Bering Sea and Sea of Okhotsk, may be encountered in rafts on the water. Rhinoceros auklet is abundant here too, while there are lesser numbers of murrelets and even, occasionally, tufted puffin. Close to the Nemuro Peninsula's offshore islands, the once locally extinct sea otter population is increasing and chances of sighting them during a nature cruise are now good. From shore, by scanning carefully with binoculars, you might see sea otters also at Cape Nosappu, and especially so at Cape Kiritappu.

Being patient, ever watchful, and moving slowly and quietly is the key to successful wildlife watching wherever you are in the world – including on and around Hokkaidō.

For details on where to see red-crowned crane, see page 230.

should be sought immediately if you do happen to be bitten by one. On Hokkaidō you may also come across the **Japanese ratsnake** (*Elaphe climacophora*); known as *aodaisho* in Japanese, this mottled green serpent is one of Japan's largest snakes with adults reaching 1–2m in length, but is completely harmless and non-venomous.

Marine life The waters around Hokkaidō are rich in marine life and, depending on the season, you will be able to see **cetaceans** such as fin whale (*Balaenoptera physalus*), orca (*Orcinus orca*), sperm whale (*Physeter macrosephalus*), Pacific white-sided dolphin (*Lagenorhynchus obliquidens*) and northern minke whale (*Balaenoptera acutorostrata*). The Shiretoko Peninsula, Nemuro Peninsula and Muroran are particularly good areas for marine wildlife spotting.

Sea otters (*Enhydra lutris*), measuring up to 110cm long and weighing as much as 45kg, used to be hunted in this region for fur. Once more widespread, they can now be seen off the Shiretoko and Nemuro peninsulas in eastern Hokkaidō as the Kuril Island population seems to be extending its range southwards.

Seal species include **Steller's sea lion** (*Eumetopias jubatus*) and **Japanese harbour seals** (*Phoca vitulina*). The biggest population of harbour seals in Japan is at Cape Erimo in southern Hokkaidō, where young pups can be seen around May and June.

FLORA One of the highlights of a summer visit to Hokkaidō is admiring the colourful wildflowers dotted here and there, with orange lilies, yellow lupins, purple irises and pink wild roses among the many varieties on show during the main blooming season from June to August. Coastal marshes and brackish lakes are home to swathes of common glasswort and grasses which turn crimson as autumn draws in.

Forests in western Hokkaidō are broadleaf deciduous, while much of the rest of the island is boreal subarctic evergreen coniferous forest. Woodland species include spruce, birch, fir, oak, elm and pine in mountain areas, while stands of larch (native to other parts of Japan) form windbreaks in agricultural regions. Knee- to waist-high stone (or dwarf) pine is common at the highest elevations on Honshū, but can be found much lower down on Hokkaidō.

Much of the forest floor and roadsides are covered in species of dwarf bamboo (known as *sasa* in Japanese), which tends to grow between 2m and 3m tall and has dense leaves that tend to suppress the growth of other species. You may also spot along roadsides large herbaceous perennials or 'megaherbs' such as Asian skunk cabbage (*Lysichiton camtschatcensis*) – one of the first flowers to emerge after the snow melts – and Japanese butterbur (*Petasites japonicus*), which has leaves as large as umbrellas. Giant knotweed (*Fallopia sachalinensis*) is of course ubiquitous, and likely familiar to many as an invasive alien species in their home country.

ANIMAL WELFARE Japan is seen as an animal-loving nation, especially regarding those creatures considered *kawaii* or 'cute'; but there is an odd juxtaposition between attitudes towards these over-pampered 'cute' animals and many animals kept in captivity in Japan's zoos and wildlife parks. Conditions tend to lag some distance behind those of many Western countries (though not as far as in many other parts of Asia), with small concrete enclosures the norm rather than the exception and evidence of neglect or abuse. Hokkaidō is home to a number of bear parks, which are mostly depressing and awful, and visits to these should be avoided. One exception, however, is Bear Mountain – Bear Research Centre in Sahoro where rescued native brown bears are free to roam around a large naturalistic forest enclosure.

1

Animal cafés, where customers can pet cats, dogs, rabbits and other creatures while enjoying a cup of coffee, are popular in the big cities, but the effects of constant human interaction under bright lights on reclusive animals such as owls and reptiles rarely seem to be considered.

NATIONAL PARKS The first national parks were established in Japan in 1934, and there are now a total of 35 spread across the country. These regions are designated, managed and protected by the government and, similar to national parks in the UK, can include settlements, industrial and privately owned land. Japan also has a plethora of quasi-national parks and nature preserves (prefectural natural parks) which are managed by the local prefectural governments. There are currently six national parks on Hokkaidō (with a new one slated for 2024), which together with quasi-national parks and nature preserves comprise about 10% of the island's total area.

Rishiri-Rebun-Sarobetsu National Park (Land area: 212km²) Japan's northernmost national park encompasses the two small islands of Rishiri and Rebun, plus the coastal dunes and subarctic moorlands of Sarobetsu right at the northern tip of Hokkaidō. See page 276.

Shiretoko National Park (Land area: 386km²) A 70km-long peninsula in the northeast of Hokkaidō, Shiretoko National Park is regarded as one of Japan's last wildernesses. Famous for its large and dense population of brown bears, drifting ice floes from Siberia collect along its northern shores during the winter. See page 238.

Akan-Mashū National Park (Land area: 905km²) Established in 1934, this national park is home to active volcanoes, forests, hot springs and some of the world's clearest lakes. It is the only place in Japan where you can find marimo (large green algae balls). See page 244.

Kushiro-Shitsugen National Park (Land area: 269km²) Japan's largest wetland, Kushiro-Shitsugen in eastern Hokkaidō is the best place to see the red-crowned crane (page 12), a species brought back from the edge of extinction in the early 20th century. See page 226.

Daisetsuzan National Park (Land area: 2,268km²) The largest national park in Japan, Daisetsuzan is a remote and mountainous wilderness area in the centre of Hokkaidō. It offers excellent hiking, including short or multi-day treks amid its landscape of steaming calderas and summer snow patches. See page 188.

Shikotsu-Tōya National Park (Land area: 993km²) Centred around the two caldera lakes of Shikotsu and Tōya, this national park is popular due to its easy access and proximity to Sapporo; great for camping, hiking and kayaking. See page 126.

Hidaka-Sanmyaku Erimo National Park (Land area: 1,034km²) Hidaka-Sanmyaku Erimo, comprising the wild and remote Hidaka Mountains and windswept Cape Erimo in southeast Hokkaidō , is set to be Japan's newest national park sometime in 2024. See page 200.

Abashiri Quasi-National Park (Land area: 373km²) Abashiri comprises numerous lakes and coastline along the Sea of Okhotsk in northeast Hokkaidō. See page 255.

Akkeshi-Kiritappu-Konbumori Quasi-National Park (Land area: 415km²)

Established in 2021, this park in eastern Hokkaidō covers three non-contiguous coastal areas, and includes wetlands, lakes, forests, islands and marine environments. See page 231.

Shokanbetsu-Teuri-Yagishiri Quasi-National Park (Land area: 436km²) This

park includes Shokanbetsu, a mountainous range on the west coast of Hokkaidō, and the two small islands of Teuri and Yagishiri. See page 287.

Niseko-Shakotan-Otaru Kaigan Quasi-National Park (Land area: 190km²)

Located in western Hokkaidō, this park includes parts of the Shakotan Peninsula and the Niseko volcanic group. See page 118.

Ōnuma Quasi-National Park (Land area: 91km²) Ōnuma, situated north of

Hakodate, encompasses the volcanic Mount Komagatake and nearby lakes Ōnuma and Konuma. See page 150.

PALAEONTOLOGY AND ARCHAEOLOGY

Hokkaidō's palaeontological history includes some of Japan's most significant prehistoric finds, and many are displayed in the small regional museums dotted around the island. Giant ammonites from the Cretaceous period (approx 100 million to 65 million years ago) have been unearthed around Nakagawa, Yūbari and Mukawa, making this central region of Hokkaidō the most prolific place for ammonite discoveries in Japan. Other discoveries on Hokkaidō include numerous plesiosaur, and the celebrated Mukawa dinosaur, a new species of hadrosaurid (or duck-billed dinosaur) – at 8m long, this is the largest dinosaur skeleton ever found in Japan.

One of Hokkaidō's most celebrated finds is the complete skeleton of a large semi-aquatic mammal, *Desmostylus,* dating back 14 million years, found at Utanobori near Esashi in north Hokkaidō. Sea cow fossils from around 12 million to 2.5 million years ago have also been unearthed, in Sapporo and Takikawa, and are evidence of a warm sea. Hokkaidō is the only place in Japan where both Naumann elephants and woolly mammoths could both be found following successive periods of cooling and warming around the Ice Age; the elephants crossing from a southern land bridge around 120,000 years ago, and the mammoths from Sakhalin between 45,000 and 20,000 years ago. It is believed that people from the north followed the mammoths across the Sakhalin land bridge around 30,000 years ago and so became the first human residents of Hokkaidō.

The island is rich in archaeological treasures, with the earliest stone tools dating from around the end of the Palaeolithic or Stone Age (30,000–12,000 years ago). At various sites around Hokkaidō, but notably in the obsidian-rich Shiritaki area of the northeast, versatile microblades were produced in vast quantities – this technology was probably introduced from Siberia (via Sakhalin). As the climate warmed and the Ice Age ended, the Jōmon era (14,000–300BCE became a period of significant advancements in pottery, weaponry and handicrafts as the populace moved to more sedentary lifestyles and bigger communities, and the first pottery finds on Hokkaidō date from this time, while in coastal regions there are numerous examples of early to middle Jōmon period shell mounds. At the Menashidomari Ruins in northern Hokkaidō, as well as at many other sites, artefacts and pit dwellings of the Okhotsk culture have been unearthed, while faithful reconstructions of later Ainu houses and *kotan* (villages) are to be found all over Hokkaidō.

ANCIENT HISTORY Palaeolithic stone tools dating from 30000BCE have been discovered in Japan, and these are the earliest human traces in the archipelago. Around this time the islands of Japan were still connected to continental Asia by a land bridge, but as glaciers melted at the end of the last ice age (approx 12000BCE) the sea level rose and Japan was separated from the rest of Asia, allowing a new culture to develop. The people of the **Jōmon period** (14000–300BCE) are considered Japan's earliest natives. They were predominantly hunter-gatherers, organised into groups or tribes, who practised some early forms of agriculture, and their development of pottery (some of the oldest in the world) signals that these foragers had begun a more sedentary lifestyle; they went on to create more intricate pottery figures and vessels, typically characterised by their unique imprinted cord-markings, to which the name Jōmon refers. The Jōmon used stone tools to craft and hunt, and thanks to the warming environment, southern Japan in particular became a resource-rich place for the people to flourish. They also lived as far north as Hokkaidō, and many Jōmon sites have been discovered across the island.

The **Yayoi period** (roughly 300BCE–CE250) followed and superseded the Jōmon period in most of Japan. It was initiated by an influx of immigrants to Kyūshū from continental Asia – most notably the Korean Peninsula – whose influence quickly spread across much of the country, although not as far as Hokkaidō. The Yayoi period is significant for a number of reasons, not least due to its introduction to Japan of intensive rice cultivation, allowing the Yayoi population to swiftly increase and overcome (and also mix with) the Jōmon people. Other advancements included new pottery styles, metalworking, weaving and silk production, glasswork, the construction of more permanent dwellings and the development of new social classes.

During the Yayoi period, tribes organised themselves into kingdoms, and the end of the period saw the emergence of one of the most significant figures in early Japanese history, Himiko (CE170–248), the queen of Wakoku (the oldest known reference to Japan in ancient Chinese texts). Little is known about her true identity or even her domain, as she was curiously not mentioned in any early Japanese writings. She is associated with shamanistic practices and using sorcery to commune with new emerging deities, including Amaterasu (the goddess of the sun), one of the major deities of Shintō and mythological ancestress of the imperial family. Shintō, the so-called indigenous religion of Japan with its polytheistic and animistic traits, probably has its roots in the Yayoi period.

The Yayoi's influence did not extend across the entire archipelago, however. On Hokkaidō, where the climate was too cold for Yayoi rice paddy farming, the Jōmon were succeeded instead by the Okhotsk and Epi-Jōmon (or Zoku-Jōmon) cultures.

The Okhotsk people lived in northeastern Hokkaidō, Sakhalin and the Kuril Islands from around the 5th to the 9th century; they were hunter-gatherers who fished and made extensive use of marine resources – early Western observers referred to them as the 'pit-dwellers' owing to archaeological findings of their sunken pit houses. The Okhotsk shared numerous similarities with other northern peoples such as the Nivkh and Sami, and passed on many parts of their culture to the later Ainu, including bear worship.

The **Epi-Jōmon** (340BCE–CE700) on the other hand were based in northern Tōhoku as well as much of Hokkaidō, and their culture can be seen as a continuation of Jōmon period traditions, running parallel to the Yayoi-era advancements which were taking place in southern and western Japan.

Back in western Honshū, where the roots of imperial Japan were beginning to take shape following the reign of Himiko, the **Kofun period** (around CE250–538) was beginning. Himiko had been honoured with an elaborate tomb after her death, and her successors continued this new tradition of tomb building. Yamato Province (in present-day Nara, in south-central Honshū) developed as the centre of power for this newly emerging state and line of imperial rulers, many of whom were buried in enormous keyhole-shaped burial mounds known as *kofun* (the largest examples of which can still be seen around the Kansai region); even in death these tombs acted as symbols of their occupants' impressive power and wealth. The Kofun period saw the Yamato rulers extend their reach across much of central and western Japan, sometimes by military conquest, but more often by coercing local leaders to accept privileged positions in their government.

CLASSICAL JAPAN During the **Asuka period** (CE538–710), there were many political, artistic and social transformations centred around the imperial court in Yamato Province. Some changes originated from the continent such as Chinese-inspired administrative practices, and Buddhism arrived in Japan from one of the Three Kingdoms of Korea. The succession of powerful Yamato rulers led to them being seen no longer as controllers of the sacred, but as gods themselves.

In the CE580s, the powerful aristocratic and Buddhist-adherent Sogo clan controlled the government, with Prince Shōtoku, who served as regent under Empress Suiko (his aunt), going on to become the de facto leader of Japan from CE594 to 622. Inspired by Buddha's teachings, Shōtoku established a centralised government and promoted Buddhism throughout his reign (his CE615 commentary of the *Three Sutras* is regarded as the first Japanese-language text, making him the oldest-known Japanese writer). In a letter in CE607 to Emperor Wang of the Sui Dynasty in China, Shōtoku made the earliest-discovered reference to Japan as 'the land of the rising sun', and within a few decades the kingdom of Wakoku came to be known as Nihon (meaning 'originating from the sun'), the modern name for Japan. Shōtoku commissioned the Buddhist temple of Horyu-ji, which was completed in CE607 and is now the world's oldest standing wooden structure.

In CE645 the Sogo clan was overthrown in a coup and the new government led by Emperor Kōtoku introduced the Taika Reforms. Based on the governmental structure of China, the reforms (which took place over many years) aimed to bring greater centralisation and strengthen the power of the imperial court, setting the foundations for governance for centuries to come.

The following periods, covering five centuries, were formative years for Japan's imperial line during an era of conflict and administrative and judicial upheaval. Marking the beginning of the **Nara period**, in CE710 the government established a new capital at Heijō-kyō (modern-day Nara), modelled on the capital of the Chinese Tang Dynasty, Chang'an. During this short period (CE710–94), Japan suffered a number of natural disasters, famines, droughts and diseases, including an outbreak of smallpox in CE735–37 which killed a quarter of the population. Emperor Shōmu (CE724–49) feared it was due to his lack of piousness and so instructed the government to promote Buddhism further, including the building of the magnificent temple Tōdai-ji (in Nara). The first two books ever produced in Japan, the *Kojiki* and the *Nihon Shoki*, were also written in this period – they include accounts of early Japan and tales of how the imperial line was descended from the gods. The latter years of the century saw the compilation of the highly revered *Man'yōshū* – a mammoth tome containing 20 volumes and around 4,500 *waka* poems.

It is probably around the 7th century CE that on Hokkaidō, the Okhotsk and Epi-Jōmon likely began to merge with the Satsumon culture, and this gradual blending eventually resulted with the emergence of the Ainu culture around the 13th century. The **Heian period** (CE794–1185), the last of the classical era, followed the relocation of the capital to Heian-kyō (Kyoto). The Chinese-style centralised government introduced in the Nara period gradually began to lose its grip on authority owing to the increased influence of *shōen*. These private and tax-free estates began to undermine the economic power of the emperor and led to the growth of powerful local clans (which were to become the dominant feature of the medieval period).

By around the mid 9th century, the imperial court was dominated by regents of the Fujiwara family, who married off their daughters to heirs of the imperial line, culminating in the reign of Michinaga Fujiwara (CE995–1027), the most powerful face of the Fujiwara era. Eventually the family's dominance of the court waned as more non-Fujiwara-backed emperors came to the fore, notably with Shirakawa who succeeded to the throne in 1072. He is mostly remembered for setting a new precedent, abdicating the throne in 1086 to form a cloister government (*insei*), which dissolved him of the burdens of family and ceremonial duties, but allowed him still extensive power as a retired emperor to counter the influence of the waning Fujiwara regent.

The Heian period was characterised by a refined courtly culture with all its social intricacies. The famous 11th-century novel *The Tale of Genji* is a remarkable account of courtly life. Buddhism continued to flourish with esoteric sects such as Shingon Buddhism developing formal rites and practices which mirrored court rituals. The True Pure Land sect, which encouraged a pure and simple faith in Buddha Amida, also offered solace to a populace that saw increasing local strife and military conflict as the period went on. These disturbances eventually reached the capital in 1156, as soldiers of the Taira and Minamoto clans battled for rival claimants of the throne. The Taira emerged victorious and thereafter held a vestige of power in the court until 1185.

FEUDAL/MEDIEVAL JAPAN The medieval period in Japan is generally considered to span 1185–1603, and is known as an era of long civil wars and the upending of the aristocracy by a new samurai class, with the power of emperors waning and the rise of shōgun military rulers – their shōgunate administrations were known as the *bakufu*. A new and enduring class system based on profession developed, and Japan was dragged into increased international prominence as it defended itself against the Mongols in the late 13th century, and later attempted two unsuccessful invasions of Korea at the end of the period in 1592 and 1597.

The **Kamakura period** (1185–1333) began with Minamoto no Yorimoto's defeat of the Taira clan at the Battle of Dannoura in 1185, the last event of the Genpei War 1180–85. The powerful Minamoto and Taira clans had by now become bitter rivals constantly vying for the throne, but with this victory the Minamoto clan seized control and ruled from their base at Kamakura, near Edo (Tokyo). Yorimoto became Japan's first shōgun (military dictator) in 1192 – a significant development as this shifted power away from the emperor and imperial court for the first time in written records. The emperor still remained in place back in Heian-kyō (Kyoto), but his powers were mostly ceremonial as there was no competing with the shōgunate warlord's vast army.

Yorimoto ruled until his death in 1199, but it was Yorimoto's wife, Masako Hōjō, and her father, Tokimasa Hōjō, who went on to seize power and shift influence to the Hōjō clan. They also introduced a new position of shōgun regent, which changed the face of politics until the Meiji era, as it was now the regent who exerted the real power, with the shōgun more of a puppet. Owing to the rise of these powerful regional warlords, society became structured around the feudal relationship between lords and vassals, with the shōgun giving land in return for military service. When a shōgun had many estates to oversee, he would sometimes entrust them to a steward (*jito*), a man or woman with loyalty to the shōgun who would manage and collect taxes, taking some of the bounty and becoming powerful in their own right. Jito descendants often became the *daimyō* (feudal landlords) who rose to prominence in the latter medieval period.

There were advancements in farming (better tools, fertilisers and strains of hardier rice), and trade grew with neighbouring countries, particularly China. But the Kamakura shōgunate faced its biggest challenge in the form of two attempted invasions by Mongol forces in the years 1274 and 1281; both invasions ultimately failed as a result of samurai resistance, poorly built Mongol boats and logistical issues, plus the effects of two typhoons (this is where the Japanese word *kamikaze*, meaning 'divine wind', originates from). In anticipation of a third foreign invasion (which never came), the government invested in a huge standing army, with the high cost of this weakening the regime.

During this time, Hokkaidō was known as Ezo-ga-shima (Ezo Island) or Ezo-chi (Ezo region). Ezo roughly translates as 'savages' and probably refers originally to people of the Satsumon culture, who were later superseded by the Ainu. The Kamakura shōgunate had controlled all of Japan except Hokkaidō – that was still the land of the Emishi and was considered *kegai no chi* (place beyond control of the state) or *iiki* (foreign region). But it was during this period that exiles from the mainland first started to be sent to Hokkaidō.

The Kamakura era was brought to an end by various uprisings. First, the **Kenmu Restoration** (1333–36) was a short-lived return to imperial rule by the once-exiled Emperor Go-Daigo, who with the aid of some powerful samurai toppled the now unpopular Hōjō shōgunate. But the emperor soon fell out of favour with his own supporters (and much of the populace) because of various policy failures, such as not protecting the rights of tenants and workers and, perhaps most importantly, undervaluing his warrior-class supporters. A rift had also developed between Go-Daigo and Takauji Ashikaga, the powerful samurai army commander who had helped the emperor to first seize power after Go-Daigo refused Takauji's request to be made shōgun; Takauji went on to overcome the imperial government (and other rebels with an eye on the throne) to establish the Ashikaga shōgunate in Kyoto's Muromachi district in 1338.

The **Muromachi period** (1338–1568; also sometimes known as the Ashikaga period) was a time of much civil conflict, as the succession of Ashikaga shōguns struggled to maintain control and order over the regional warlords (daimyō) who constructed castles around the country; Buddhist populist revolts also undermined any central authority.

This era also overlaps with the Sengoku (Warring States) period, which started with the Ōnin War of 1467–77 – a tussle for succession claims that nearly obliterated Kyoto. This was followed by a century of near-constant civil war, which saw the building of many new castles and fortifications across the feuding country, with the bloodshed and brutality affecting ordinary people and not just warlords and militants.

But despite all the unrest of this period, there was increased trade with the Ming Dynasty of China, and as a result culture flourished in many areas, including art,

Samurai were privileged members of the medieval warrior class who appeared from around the 12th century and had an influence on Japanese politics, culture and society, until they were eventually replaced by a more modern conscript army after the Meiji Restoration in the 1330s. They intimidated with their intricate plated armour, faceguards, helmets with crests or horns, and the wielding of *katana* – the traditional curved-blade Japanese sword. The main duty of the samurai was to give loyal service to their lord – indeed the original meaning of the word 'samurai' is something like 'to serve'. A code of conduct, known as *bushido* (the way of the warrior), developed over the centuries, prizing honour above all else; disgrace and shame were to be avoided at all costs, and insults would be avenged. Cutting off the head (and later displaying it) of a battlefield opponent was a source of pride for many samurai. But the samurai were also supposed to show compassion to those oppressed. Suicide (known as *sepukku* or sometimes *hara-kiri*) was more honourable than surrendering and was often carried out in brutal fashion – a samurai would disembowel himself and then have his head cut off by an aide. By the time of the relatively peaceful Edo period, they were more often engaged in managing daimyō estates than engaging in battle. Samurai who became lordless were known as *rōnin* and they sometimes caused trouble as roaming brigands.

tea ceremony, literature and architecture. The newly emergent (and later much-celebrated) Muromachi culture was a result of the mingling of courtly, samurai and Zen Buddhism influences.

Japanese colonisers began to move to Ezo (Hokkaidō) in ever-greater numbers from around the mid 14th century, although even by then they had already established fishing and trading posts on the Oshima Peninsula. Accordingly, this region was sometimes called Ningenchi or 'human land', while the rest of the island (which still belonged to the Ainu) was known as Ezochi, 'barbarian land' or 'land of savages'. At that time the Ando clan was in control of Japanese-occupied areas of Hokkaidō and administered 12 garrisons along the southern coast of the Oshima Peninsula – from current-day Hakodate, out west to Kaminokuni – which functioned as trading posts between the Japanese and Ainu. The Ainu coveted Japanese goods such as sake, rice, metal and lacquerware, which they traded for pelts and other items, but as time went on the Japanese began to exert their power more, resulting in unfair deals and growing Ainu resentment.

Despite some minor unrest and occasional fracases between the natives and occupiers, there wasn't too much in the way of significant conflict on the peninsula until Koshamain's War in 1457, an Ainu uprising led by Ainu chief Koshamain. It began with a trade dispute over a sword, when a Japanese blacksmith murdered a young Ainu customer with the very same blade after the buyer complained about the price and quality of the item. Koshamain led groups of infuriated Ainu to ransack ten of the 12 Japanese garrisons, burning many of them to the ground. One fort led by a young samurai named Nobuhiro Takeda managed to fend off the attacks however – he then led a counterattack against the Ainu forces, and after many bloody battles, Koshamain and his sons were killed, and any chance of a wider Ainu uprising was quelled. Impressed by his achievement, the locally powerful Kakizaki family invited Takeda to officially join them (a fairly common occurrence in samurai families), and he eventually rose to head of the clan, and would go on to rule Japanese-controlled Ezo in place of the Ando clan.

In 1516 the Kakizaki were granted rights to tax ships arriving and leaving Hokkaidō, which helped to consolidate their power, although there were still occasional skirmishes with the native Ainu. The Kakizaki clan tried to implement fairer rules to avoid further conflicts – they would go on to change their name to Matsumae and control the southern part of Hokkaidō for the next 200 years.

Meanwhile, further south, Portuguese traders became the first Europeans to visit Japan when they arrived in Kyūshū in 1543. They brought firearms (which proved popular with the feudal warlords) and introduced Christianity.

The **Azuchi-Momoyama period** (1568–1600) was the final chapter of the Warring States era and the medieval period, and began with the powerful and egotistical warlord Nobunaga Oda marching into Kyoto in 1568 to ordain Yoshiaki Ashikaga as the last Ashikaga shōgun. By 1573, however, Nobunaga had gained enough power and support to expel Yoshiaki from Kyoto, while also seeing off pressure from rival warlords and Buddhist monasteries – the latter had become rich, powerful and capable of fielding armies themselves. Nobunaga did not take the title of shōgun, but sometimes ruled with brutality, his disdain for Buddhist rebels demonstrated most famously when in 1571 he destroyed the temple complex at Enryaku-ji on Mount Hiei near Kyoto. He confiscated all weaponry held by the peasantry in 1576, but it was tough policies such as this that allowed Nobunaga to set the wheels in motion for the unification of the country – indeed, he is regarded as the first of three 'great unifiers' of Japan.

Nobunaga's power was not to last, however; in 1582 he was betrayed and suffered an attempted assassination which forced him to commit *seppuku* (suicide). One of his loyal generals, Hideyoshi Toyotomi, became regent and took the reins of power two weeks later – the second 'great unifier' of Japan is famed for the construction of Osaka Castle. In 1590, Hideyoshi bestowed the Kakizaki (later Matsumae) clan the right to rule southern Hokkaidō as a march fief – a borderland which they were required to defend from the 'barbarian' Ainu hordes to the north.

In his later years, Hideyoshi became increasingly paranoid and power-hungry, launching failed attempts at a Korean invasion before his death (from illness) in 1598. On his deathbed, he entrusted one of his generals, Ieyasu Tokugawa, to oversee the succession of his young son Hideyori, but Ieyasu quickly broke the promise, and a few years later went to war with Hideyori's forces at the famous Battle of Sekigahara in 1600. The emperor named Ieyasu as shōgun in 1603, and in a massive break with tradition, Ieyasu decided to set up government in his stronghold out east, in the small castle town of Edo (now Tokyo).

THE EDO AND MATSUMAE ERA After the constant feuds of the medieval age, the **Edo period** (1603–1868) was an age of relative peace under the rule of the Tokugawa dynasty. Ieyasu levied tight control by redistributing land among the daimyō who had been most loyal to him, and they were also required to spend every second year in Edo (Tokyo), which was not only a financial burden (ensuring they didn't overreach their power) but kept them under the close influence of the shōgunate.

Initially the Tokugawa regime promoted foreign trade, establishing relations with the English and Dutch, but perceiving a growing threat from outside influences, the shōgunate soon embarked upon a policy of *sakoku*, or the 'locking of the country'. Suppression and persecution of Christianity had already started around 1614 – this was followed with further clamping down by forbidding travel outside Japan in 1633, and then strictly limiting foreign trade a few years later, while all foreign books were banned and foreigners expelled. While Japan had entered its isolationist era, domestic trade and agricultural production steadily flourished, much of the land was at peace, and the samurai and upper echelons of society could devote time to literature, philosophy and culture. During the **Genroku era** (1688–1703) in particular, new art forms such as *kabuki* and *ukiyo-e* developed.

The Edo period was also a time of increasing change on Hokkaidō. The Matsumae clan governed a small area around Ezo's southern tip, which they called Wajinchi or 'Japanese Land'. Because of the climatic conditions, the Japanese were unable to grow rice easily on Hokkaidō, and so unlike daimyō in other regions who gained their wealth from agriculture, the Matsumae relied on trade with the Ainu to subsist. The Matsumae operated trading posts across much of Hokkaidō's southern coast, trading their rice, sake, metal and lacquerware for Ainu fish and animal pelts. The 12 old Japanese garrisons on the Oshima Peninsula gradually fell out of use and were abandoned, but in 1606 Matsumae Castle (then known as Fukuyama Castle and the only Japanese-style castle on Hokkaidō) was constructed, and the town of Matsumae became the region's main centre of trade and governance for the next 200 years.

Although the Tokugawa shōgunate had closed off Japan, it was not entirely isolated – they allowed a small amount of foreign trade strictly on their own terms, namely through four trading posts: Tsushima for trade with Korea; Satsuma for trade with Ryukyu kingdom; Nagasaki for trade with Chinese and Dutch; and, lastly, Matsumae for trade with the Ainu.

Through the regional governance of the Matsumae clan, the Tokugawa shōgunate sought to implement the gradual colonisation of southern Hokkaidō by increasing, controlling and necessitating trade with Ainu, and in other ways such as providing the Ainu with medical assistance for measles and smallpox (brought in by the

SHAKUSHAIN'S WAR (1669–72)

This Ainu uprising has its roots in the Ainu experience at the hands of Japanese colonisers during the mid 1600s. Until around the early 17th century, the Ainu had been living in relative peace alongside the small pockets of Japanese traders, with some Ainu families even doing rather well, trading their fish and furs for lacquerware, swords, metalware, sake and rice. But this began to change from around 1631, when gold was discovered on Hokkaidō, leading to an influx of Japanese miners and the establishment of new mining camps in previously Ainu-only areas, with little policing from the Matsumae clan.

Things got worse in 1644, when the shōgunate granted Matsumae exclusive trading rights on Hokkaidō – up until then, the Ainu had been free to trade with various daimyō (feudal lords) and fetch the best prices, but now they had to accept the Matsumae trading post offers, or nothing. The Japanese also started netting salmon at the mouths of rivers before the fish could swim upstream to spawning grounds where the Ainu usually caught them. This combination of lower prices and fewer resources sparked competition and fighting between various Ainu groups, until some communities in south and eastern Hokkaidō formed two larger opposing groups under the leadership of two strong rival chiefs, named Shakushain and Onibishi.

In a long-running feud, Shakushain attacked Onibishi forces at a Japanese mining camp. In so doing, he not only defeated his rival but also effectively waged war with the Japanese. Rallying together other Ainu tribes, possibly numbering up to 3,000 men, Shakushain went on the offensive (until now, most Ainu fighters had

Japanese colonisers) and encouraging Japanese language use. The late 17th and early 18th centuries saw the start of *basho ukeoi*, a contract labour system in which Ainu became seasonal workers and merchants from Osaka and Omi employed Ainu to catch fish, which were then dried and shipped south. Hokkaidō's economy became largely dependent upon trade between the Japanese, Ainu and some foreign merchants, and during the Matsumae era (around 1600–1800) the fishing ports of Matsumae, Esashi and Hakodate, collectively known as the 'Matsumae Sanso', were said to have more combined wealth than Edo (Tokyo) at that time.

It wasn't all peaceful, however, as minor outbreaks of unrest did occur between the Japanese and Ainu, with the largest battle on the island an uprising of Ainu communities in Shakushain's War of 1669 (see opposite).

As the decades rolled on, the Tokugawa shōgunate became more concerned about protecting its northern borders, as encounters with Russian vessels were becoming more common, and the Matsumae clan was not deemed totally trustworthy. So the shōgunate sought to gather more information about the lands to the north, and this began the first serious Japanese explorations of Hokkaidō and beyond.

Tokunai Mogami (1755–1836) was a samurai and geographer who explored and mapped hitherto uncharted areas of Hokkaidō, Sakhalin and some of the Kuril Islands in an expedition in 1785–86. He also compiled an early Ainu–Japanese dictionary, but it was his trip reports that helped to inform the Tokugawa shōgunate of the geography (and potential threats) that lay to the north.

A couple of decades later, in 1808, Rinzō Mamiya (1775–1844) – an explorer best known for mapping Sakhalin (then known as Karafuto) – departed with his assistant Denjūrō Matsuda from Wakkanai. The pair split up to explore both the west and east coasts of Sakhalin, and when they met up at its northernmost

been involved solely in defensive skirmishes), attacking mining camps, Matsumae trading forts and Japanese merchant ships all along the coasts of Hokkaidō in a hitherto unseen large-scale and well-coordinated Ainu offensive. More than 270 Japanese were killed and 19 merchant ships destroyed as panic spread among Hokkaidō's resident Japanese population; it is said only about 20 Japanese people outside the enclave of Matsumae and its castle survived.

Matsumae leaders reported the uprising to Edo (Tokyo) and summoned help from nearby daimyō, bolstering soldier numbers from an initial 80 to almost 700. Ainu and Japanese forces met some distance away from Matsumae at a place called Kunnui, and, though the Japanese party was small, their muskets proved too much for the Ainu with only their poison-tipped arrows, forcing the Ainu to retreat. As more soldiers arrived from the mainland, Ainu forts and canoes were destroyed and by October Shakushain had surrendered. Although Shakushain and his forces clearly represented no real threat to Japanese dominion on Hokkaidō now, at a drinking party to celebrate an end to the war and new-found peace in Ezo, the unarmed Shakushain and three Ainu generals were murdered by a Matsumae samurai.

It took another three years for the Japanese to fully quell all Ainu revolts, after which Matsumae expanded their trading posts on Hokkaidō and forced the Ainu into swearing allegiance to them. The Ainu did manage to make some minor gains in this peace treaty, being guaranteed a degree of autonomy in their lands and a slight concession on their trading rates, though, arguably, it sealed their fate for the centuries of persecution and assimilation which were to come.

THE GODPARENT OF HOKKAIDŌ: TAKESHIRŌ MATSUURA

Born into a samurai family in Ise Province (now Mie Prefecture), Takeshirō Matsuura (1818–88) was a fascinating individual with a wide range of interests and esoteric pursuits – an explorer, writer, cartographer, painter and priest among many other things, it was his forays as a young man to unexplored regions of Ezo (Hokkaidō) which led to the first accurate mapping of the island.

During extensive travels around Japan in his early years, Matsuura heard tales of Ezo and Karafuto (Sakhalin), and so in 1844 travelled north, where he was halted at the Tsugaru Strait due to restrictions placed by the Matsumae Domain. The following year he tried again, disguising himself as a merchant and travelling around Ezo for seven months, enlisting Ainu guides to aid him. The following year he came back again, but he continued northwards to Karafuto, which he mapped for the first time, before returning south and exploring more of Hokkaidō. In 1849, he returned to the island for a third time, covering regions he had not set foot in before, making notes and maps while also studying the Ainu language and growing increasingly aware of the plight of the Ainu and their unfair treatment by the Matsumae Domain.

Matsuura's next visit, seven years later, was under the instruction of the *bafuku* (government), who valued his knowledge and experience and requested him to compile further details on Ezo's geography. Over the next three years he would make three more visits, completing a circuit of the island, followed the full courses of the Ishikari and Teshio rivers, and explored the island's interior, all while documenting the island's physical and human geography and suggesting areas ripe for development.

Following the Meiji Restoration and the establishment of the Hokkaidō Development Commission in 1869, he was appointed to find a new name for the island – he originally conceived the name 'Hokkaidō' during his 24 days exploring the Teshio River where he was inspired by tales told by local Ainu in Otoineppu. On account of this, and his clear interest in the island and the lot of its native people, Matsuura is sometimes referred to as the 'godparent of Hokkaidō'. In his later years he continued to travel, climbed mountains (including Mount Fuji), collected rocks and artwork, and chose to live in a tiny tatami-mat sized room for the final two years of his life. He became sick from meningitis in 1888 and soon died of a brain haemorrhage – a series of 69 markers, located in places Matsuura visited across Hokkaidō, were erected in his honour in 2018.

point, they were able to confirm that it was in fact an island, and not connected to the Asian continent (although they had in fact unknowingly been beaten to this discovery by the French explorer Jean François de La Pérouse in 1787). The Strait of Tartary, which separates Sakhalin from the mainland, is still called the Mamiya-kaikyō (Mamiya Strait) in Japan.

The last serious Ainu rebellion was the 1789 Menashi-Kunashir Battle, between Ainu and Japanese on the Shiretoko Peninsula – its origins are a little murky, but possibly involve a bottle of poisoned sake being given to the Ainu in a loyalty ceremony and some other shady dealings by Japanese traders; it resulted in the deaths of more than 70 *wajin* (Japanese), who then executed 37 Ainu and arrested many others.

Towards the end of the Tokugawa era the government came under increasing pressure both at home and from abroad. Higher taxes and famines led to unrest among the population, while the merchant class grew ever more powerful, and corruption and incompetence became rife within the government. Russian traders tried to establish contact with Japanese ports, but were firmly rejected – in fact, suspecting illicit trade with Russians and other violations, the government seized control of Ezo from the Matsumae in 1802 and established Hakodate as the main power base in the region.

By the first half of the 19th century, the Ainu population had also been greatly reduced (from around 80,000 in the 18th century, to around 15,000 by 1868), not only due to introduced diseases such as smallpox, but because Ainu families were broken up as the men were deported to work for Tokugawa merchants and Ainu women were sometimes forced to marry Japanese men.

Other European nations and the Americans also tried to push Japan into opening up for trade, but it wasn't until 1854 that Commodore Perry's famous 'black ships' arrived in Hakodate and drove the Japanese (under the threat of force) to open up the ports of Shimoda and Hakodate to American trading vessels. This proved to be a big turning point for Japan, as it was agreed that five ports in total would open up for international trade – the country from then on began to see a gradual influx of Western goods and ideas which would eventually hasten the demise of the Tokugawa regime.

The 260-year reign of the Tokugawa government came to an end with the Boshin War (sometimes known as the Japanese Revolution or Japanese Civil War) in 1868–69. A coalition of nobles and samurai, unhappy with how the government handled the opening of Japan, seized control of the Imperial Court and garnered the support of the young emperor Meiji. The reigning shōgun Yoshinobu Tokugawa abdicated and handed power over to the emperor, and following a number of skirmishes which culminated in the surrender of Edo (Tokyo), the remaining Tokugawa forces and those loyal to the regime retreated north, eventually holding out on Hokkaidō until losing the Battle of Hakodate (page 138), the last stage of the war and the point at which power was fully ceded to the new Meiji regime.

POST-MEIJI RESTORATION The Meiji era began with imperial power being transferred to Emperor Meiji, who moved from Kyoto to Tokyo to set up a new government. This new regime introduced enormous reforms in many areas: feudal lords had to return their lands to the emperor; the strict social classes of the Tokugawa period were abolished – with samurai losing many of their privileges; and changes to education, military, industry, science, government, banking, infrastructure and business were instigated, either by sending Japanese officials abroad to study Western advancements, or by bringing in foreign experts to help modernise the country from within.

The newly formed government also sought full control of Ezo (both to dissuade Russian interest and to control trade), renaming it Hokkaidō and encouraging more Japanese to settle there, especially those involved in agriculture and fishing. The government established the Kaitakushi or Hokkaidō Colonisation Commission to develop the island. They had a ten-year plan with a budget of 1 million yen per year (an enormous amount considering the national budget was 50 million a year). The Meiji government saw Hokkaidō as an experimental ground for modernisation. It focused on productivity and more efficient agriculture (wiping out wolves etc), and brought in foreign advisers such as American Edwin Dun (page 35) to oversee development of livestock industry on the island – a huge shift from Japan's rice-growing past.

The Kaitakushi was in charge of administering Hokkaidō from 1869 to 1881, encouraging settlers, and developing industries and infrastructure. It was a colonial atmosphere, with the aim of assimilating Hokkaidō fully into Japan, and the island population increased dramatically from around 67,000 in 1870 to 427,000 by 1890.

In 1875, Japan and Russia signed the Treaty for the Exchange of Sakhalin for the Kuril Islands, and many Ainu were displaced from southern Sakhalin to Hokkaidō. But epidemics ravaged the population – the Kuril Islands Ainu were wiped out entirely after being regrouped (on an island off the coast of Hokkaidō) for national security reasons, as the Japanese government feared that some of these Ainu who had converted to Orthodox Christianity would serve as spies for the Russians based in the Kurils.

Up until now, the centre of trade and local government on Hokkaidō had been Matsumae and then Hakodate, but the Kaitakushi decided to create a more centrally located capital. Despite the disadvantage of not being on the coast, Sapporo was chosen for its location on the Ishikari River, close to flat and potentially fertile lands. The once-small Ainu village grew quickly, and the Kaitakushi enlisted the help of ex-samurai military farmer colonists called the *tondenhei* (see opposite) to help develop and, if necessary, defend Hokkaidō from other nations (namely imperial Russia), with the first soldier-agriculturist villages established in Sapporo from around 1875, and then later spreading to other parts of the island. The city became the official capital of Hokkaidō in 1886.

Sapporo Agricultural College (later to become Hokkaidō University), established in 1876 and run by American William S Clark, played a significant role in the island's development, with English classes, the teaching of new ideas and the provision of training for colonial officials. In order to recruit the best students (and to help lure them to a new institution in a faraway undeveloped colony), the college provided government stipends and guaranteed Kaitakushi jobs after graduation.

In stark contrast, however, to the promotion of Hokkaidō as a land of opportunity and independence, prisoners and felons were also brought in large numbers as disposable labour. Mining was also developed, and convicts used for hard labour and road construction. But, as more settlers arrived, there was a growing fear of prison escapes and the negative effects of ex-convicts on society, so from 1894 convicts were no longer allowed to settle on the island after serving their sentences.

Due to increasing humanitarian concerns, prison labour was eventually superseded by prison camps known as *dokōbeya*, where contractors from the mainland brought cheap labourers to Hokkaidō (often press-ganged Chinese or Koreans) to live in filthy prison-like spaces and work long, hard hours for meagre reward. It was said that, once in the camp, no-one would make it out alive.

Life and conditions were tough for many of these early settlers, especially as some had little to no farming experience, but the most determined eventually prevailed. Farmers had to learn to grow and subsist on potatoes and millet (and other northern crops) instead of rice (although new hardier strains of rice were developed later).

As more Japanese moved to Hokkaidō for fishing and agriculture, the Kaitakushi opened up the fisheries, resulting in the growth of coastal fishing settlements, although some lived there only seasonally. Herring was the main industry and peaked in spring followed by *konbu*, then trout and salmon in summer and autumn, and cuttlefish and shellfish in winter. Most herring was used for making fertilisers for Honshū's rice farmers. The industry for sea otter skin also boomed (especially around the Kurils) at the end of the 19th century, driving the animals to near extinction. Overfishing almost caused the demise of the main herring industry in the early 20th century.

Coal mining (and to a lesser degree sulphur mining) was also a pioneering industry, in the late 19th century, with early mines developed at Horonai and Yūbari and the Sorachi region becoming a major coal-producing area; both northern Kyūshū and Hokkaidō were said to have Japan's best coalfields (the nation's last coal mine in Kushiro (eastern Hokkaidō) closed in 2002).

In 1882 the first railway on Hokkaidō between Otaru, Sapporo and Horonai was built (but used for coal) – it was in fact only the third railway line to be built in Japan. Better roads were also beginning to be developed but progress was slow, ultimately hindering development of the island. Horse-drawn sleighs (based on earlier Russian designs) were introduced on Hokkaidō for winter use.

TONDENHEI: HOKKAIDŌ'S MILITARY SETTLER COLONISTS

After acceding power in 1868, the Meiji government sought to colonise and incorporate both Hokkaidō and Karafuto (southern Sakhalin) as fully fledged territories of Japan, particularly in light of the perceived threat from imperial Russia. Establishing settlements, industry and infrastructure in these relatively virgin lands however proved to be quite a challenge, and so in the early days the government decided to recruit a number of former samurai families who were now effectively unemployed and landless after their feudal lords had opposed the incoming Meiji regime. These military settler colonists were known as the *tondenhei* and were tasked with helping to develop, populate and if necessary, defend Hokkaidō and Karafuto.

The first of these settlers arrived on Hokkaidō in 1875 and consisted of a group of almost 200 former samurai and their extended families. They settled in the Kotoni district of Sapporo, and within about two years more than 2,000 tondenhei families had arrived to start new lives on the island. Each newly established village numbered a troop of about 200 families, and the government gave each soldier a cold-weather uniform and a 3.5ha parcel of land to use for farming, with a pre-built wooden house (called a *heioku*), which, while basic, was generally better than the homes of ordinary folk. Coming from milder southern climes, many settlers struggled in Hokkaidō's harsh winters when they would perform most of their military duties. Summers were for farming, of which many samurai had little direct experience, especially when it came to growing northern crops such as potatoes, millet and beans. The tondenhei had to observe strict living regulations, getting up and working at fixed times, and along with military training and farming, they were engaged in the construction of roads and waterways.

Tondenhei recruits later included common folk, as well as ex-samurai, and together they played a key role in the early development of Sapporo, as well as other settlements along the Ishikari River and north as far as Asahikawa, together with some military colonies near ports in the south and east of the island too. In total it is estimated that more than 7,000 tondenhei families relocated and helped establish about 40 villages on Hokkaidō before the system was abolished in 1904. Today, a few humble tondenhei properties can still be seen around Sapporo, standing as small monuments to the people who helped found the city.

Until the Meiji Restoration in 1868 – which signified the end of feudal Japan and the first big step on the nation's road to modernisation – Hokkaidō was known as Ezo, meaning 'foreigner', in reference to the Ainu people who inhabited that northern region (along with Sakhalin and the Kuril Islands). The Japanese often referred to the island as Ezo-chi (foreign-land). Up until that time Japanese influence on the island extended only as far as a few settlements on its southern coast, but the newly installed Meiji government sought to gain complete control of the island, especially in the face of a perceived increasing threat of Russian advances. The Japanese explorer and 'godparent of Hokkaidō', Takeshirō Matsuura (1818–88; page 26), who had visited Ezo numerous times, suggested six new names for the island, with the government settling on Hokkaidō (北海道) in 1869 to signal the start of the island's new era as an official part of the Japanese nation.

'Hokkaidō' roughly translates to 'northern sea route'. However, the last character, '道' (dō), can be interpreted in a number of ways. Some suggest that, instead of the more common reading of 'road' or 'route', it could actually refer to 'the way' (as in shodō, 書道, 'the way of writing' for example), hereby symbolising 'the way' of the new Meiji regime. Others have argued that it may actually derive from an old Chinese Tang-dynasty term for an administrative division or province, and so should be thought of more in those terms than as a passage for travel.

Japanese people born and raised on Hokkaidō are sometimes referred to as 'Dōsanko' (道産子), a name that derives from Hokkaidō's native horse, the Hokkaidō pony, or dōsanko as it is also commonly known. It is a strong and mild-mannered breed capable of withstanding the island's harsh climate – not unlike Hokkaidō's equally hardy human residents perhaps.

In regards to the Ainu, government policy sought to transform them from 'backward' hunter-gatherers into small-scale farmers, especially with the Hokkaidō Former Aborigine Protection Act (1899), which 'provided' Ainu families with 5ha parcels of land for farming, further breaking down their traditional ways and increasing servitude to the state. The act's main purpose was one of assimilation, its main policies being to grant land to Ainu who wished to engage in agriculture, as well as providing elementary schools for Ainu children; and through this the Ainu would be assimilated into the Japanese way of life and culture, effectively wiping out their own.

Following the disposal act of 1897, by the 1920s almost all state-owned land on Hokkaidō was ceded to wealthy merchants, aristocrats and statesmen who acquired large estates on which tenant-farmers worked for their landlords, a far cry from the original vision of Hokkaidō as a land of self-supported farmers. This period also saw the largest influx of immigrants to Hokkaidō, but also large-scale emigration, as Japan expanded its empire in Taiwan, Korea, Manchuria and Karafuto, with Hokkaidō becoming a stopping-off point for emigrants to these new lands (Karafuto in particular).

Various wars took place in this period, including the Seinan War (or Satsuma Rebellion, a revolt in 1877 of disaffected samurai), the Sino-Japanese War (1894–95) and the Russo-Japanese War (1904–05), with Hokkaidō's tondenhei drafted to fight in all of them. At the end of the Russo-Japanese War, Russia ceded the southern half of Sakhalin to Japan, and many Ainu returned there (before being expelled in 1945 and returning to Hokkaidō; these were the last Ainu on Sakhalin).

Japan went on to annex Korea in 1910, and these military victories caused a rise in nationalistic sentiment and gave Japan increasing confidence on the world stage. In 1912, Emperor Meiji died, bringing an end to this hugely transformative era.

TAISHŌ AND WARTIME The **Taishō period** (1912–26) was a period of rule under Emperor Taishō, a sickly man, which prompted a shift from oligarchic rule to the Imperial Diet of Japan and the democratic parties. In World War I, Japan joined the Allied powers, but played only a minor role.

In 1920, the first national census counted 2,359,183 people on Hokkaidō, an increase of about 2 million since the start of the Meiji era. However, by the early 20th century, the once-important herring fishing industry (used chiefly to make fish oil and fertiliser), which had long sustained fishing communities around the southwestern coast of Hokkaidō, was on the brink of collapse, mainly as a result of overfishing – this risked pulling large swathes of the population into economic hardship.

After World War I, Japan's economic situation worsened, with the Great Kantō Earthquake in 1923 (which devastated Tokyo and killed thousands) and the worldwide depression of 1929 only compounding matters. In 1926 the Shōwa era began with the ascension of Hirohito, and his reign (which lasted until 1989) would go on to be the longest of any Japanese emperor.

The worst disaster on Hokkaidō during the prewar decades was the Great Hakodate Fire of 1934 – the city had been ravaged by numerous fires since its founding (due to high winds), but this was worst of all, with 23,000 homes destroyed and more than 2,000 deaths; 917 of these were caused by drowning in the harbour as they tried to escape the flames.

During the 1930s, the depression meant that hundreds of thousands of Hokkaidō's poorest people were just barely surviving, with some resorting to eating herring dregs usually used for fertiliser or weeds. The situation was exasperated in some years by crop failures, and in 1938 a herring shortage caused destitution for fishermen. Some people emigrated to Manchuria – which was annexed by Japan in 1931 – or Brazil.

In 1937, the second Sino-Japanese War broke out, with Japanese forces occupying almost the entire coast of China and committing untold atrocities on the native population, most famously during the six-week-long Nanjing Massacre. China never completely surrendered, however, with low-scale battles rumbling on until 1945.

World War II In 1940 Japan occupied French Indochina (Vietnam) and joined the Axis powers. The USA and Great Britain retaliated with an oil boycott, and owing to the resulting oil shortages Japan decided to capture the oil-rich Dutch East Indies (Indonesia), bringing it into more direct conflict with the Allies. In December 1941, Japan attacked Pearl Harbor along with other American bases and British colonies in the Pacific region. The turning point of the Pacific War was the battle of Midway in June 1942, from when the Allied forces began to win back territories lost to the Japanese, followed by air raids over Japan in 1944. In spring 1945, US forces invaded Okinawa in one of the war's bloodiest battles.

Hokkaidō and northern Honshū were bombed by American aircraft on 15 and 16 July, right at the end of World War II; most of the island's bigger cities were targeted, with the air raids destroying not only factories and industrial infrastructure but some civilian residences too. Eight of the 12 railway car ferries and many smaller ships that carried coal from Hokkaidō to Honshū were sunk; this reduced the amount of coal shipped to the mainland by 80%, greatly affecting Japan's factory output – this military operation is often said to be the single most effective air attack of the Pacific War. Although the island received comparatively little war damage, about 2,900 people on Hokkaidō lost their lives over those two nights.

By the end of World War II, thousands of Korean and Chinese had been forcefully brought to Japan, with perhaps half of them sent to Hokkaidō to work in the coal mines and for other physical labour. On 27 July 1945, the Allied powers requested Japan to surrender in the Potsdam Declaration, but it took until the USA dropped atomic bombs on Hiroshima and Nagasaki on 6 and 9 August (plus the Soviet Union joining the war against Japan on 8 August) before Emperor Shōwa surrendered on 14 August, bringing an end to the conflict. About 800,000 Japanese civilians and 2 million Japanese soldiers died during the war.

POST-WORLD WAR II AND MODERN JAPAN In the peace treaty signed with the Allies in 1951, Japan renounced its claims on Sakhalin and the Kuril Islands, although Russia and Japan never signed a peace treaty themselves, and Japan claims to this day that the Russian occupation of the southernmost Kurils is illegal. Japan also had to give up its territorial claims in China and Korea, and while the emperor was retained as the ceremonial head of state, he no longer wielded any power or could be thought of as divine. Under General Douglas MacArthur, Japan was occupied by American forces until 1952 (and until 1972 in Okinawa), with a new constitution that renounced Japan's right to have a standing army, although a 1951 security treaty (which still stands to this day) means that Japan falls under US military protection.

Hokkaidō played an important role in Japan's post-war recovery, with its coal mines, food and timber resources vital for a nation struggling to rebuild. The American occupation of Japan meant that many US airbases were located on the island, and these became of strategic importance especially during the Cold War tensions between the USSR and the West. The most famous Cold War incident on Hokkaidō was the shooting down of Korean Airlines Flight 007 on 1 September 1983. The plane had veered off course over the Sea of Okhotsk during its flight from New York to Seoul, and four Soviet interceptor planes shot it down, killing 269 people on board, with remains and wreckage washing up on Hokkaidō.

In the decades leading up to that event, Japan had begun to embark on a remarkable upward spiral of economic growth – starting in 1955 when the Liberal Democratic Party came to power. The 1960s saw the country's GDP grow year after year, with the 1964 Tokyo Olympics seeming to signify Japan's recovery and arrival as a significant power on the world stage. The boom years reached a crescendo by the late 1980s (known as the 'bubble years') coinciding with the beginning of the **Heisei era** (1989–2019) when Emperor Akihito ascended to the throne in 1989. This year marked one of the largest economic growth spurts in Japan's history.

Just two years later, however, the economy crashed, bringing an end to the 'bubble years', and starting an economic slump from which, some would argue, Japan has never really recovered.

1995   The country was further rocked in early 1995 by two events: the Great Hanshin Earthquake, which destroyed large parts of Kobe and killed more than 6,000 people; and the infamous sarin gas attack by doomsday cult Aum Shinrikyo on the Tokyo subway which claimed 13 lives.

1997	The Hokkaidō Former Aborigines Protection Act was finally abolished, so ending 98 years of official government policy to subjugate Ainu culture. Then, in December of the same year, 192 countries agreed to the Kyoto Protocol to regulate greenhouse gas emissions, which at the time was seen as a landmark international treaty.
2002	Japan jointly hosted the FIFA World Cup with South Korea – the first time the tournament had been held outside of Europe or the Americas.
2004	Another big earthquake in Niigata killed 52 people and injured hundreds.
2007	Prime Minister Abe Shinzo resigned suddenly (but would take the same office for a second time in 2012).
2010	Japan's population hit an all-time peak of 128 million, but from then started a steady decline which shows no sign of abating.
2011	11 March saw Japan's worst natural disaster of modern times. The Great East Japan Earthquake struck off the coast of Tōhoku, causing a tsunami which killed thousands and setting off a nuclear crisis at a power plant in Fukushima Prefecture.
2019	Emperor Akihito abdicated and his son, Crown Prince Naruhito, ascended the throne, signalling the start of the **Reiwa era**, while inbound tourism to the country boomed.
2020–present	Japan was due to host its second summer Olympics in 2020, but due to the Covid-19 pandemic borders closed and the event was postponed a year (and held with no spectators), with much public unease about the expense and evident corruption it all entailed. Hokkaidō had one of the highest rates of transmission in the first year of the pandemic, and while Japan never officially went into lockdown like many other countries, its borders stayed closed and its citizens remained masked for far longer than many other nations, although tourist numbers are now returning close to pre-pandemic levels.

GOVERNMENT AND POLITICS

Japan has a constitutional monarchy – the emperor is head of the imperial family, serves as head of state and is a symbol of the nation. Since World War II, however, the role has become mostly ceremonial, and the emperor has no real influence on the government or politics.

The modern-day constitution came into being in 1947 and is based on three basic principles: sovereignty of the people, respect for human rights and the renunciation of war. The government is divided into three branches: legislative (the Diet), executive (the Cabinet), and judicial (the courts). The National Diet is Japan's parliament and is divided into the 465-seat House of Representatives (lower house) and the 248-seat House of Councillors (upper house). Diet members are elected by the Japanese people, with a system similar to the UK's in that Diet members elect a prime minister from among themselves, as opposed to a president elected by the citizens. The prime minster forms and leads a cabinet comprising members of state who may be appointed or dismissed at any time, and the prime minister can serve for a term of up to four years, with no limit on how many terms they can serve.

The conservative and nationalist-leaning Liberal Democratic Party (LDP) is the current ruling party and has been in almost continuous power since its formation in 1955. All Japanese citizens from the age of 18 years are eligible to vote in elections.

HOKKAIDŌ'S ADMINISTRATIVE REGIONS By some distance Hokkaidō is the largest prefecture by area in Japan (it is over five times larger than Iwate, the next largest), and so for administrative purposes is split further into 14 sub-prefectures (支庁, *shichō*). As in the rest of Japan, localities are subdivided into cities (市, *shi*), towns (町, *chō*) and villages (村, *mura*), meaning that sometimes even rather rural-looking communities can confusingly be classed as 'city' if they happen to fall under that jurisdiction.

ECONOMY

Japan has the third largest economy in the world (after the USA and China), with Tokyo alone comprising some 19% (around US$976 billion) of the national GDP. By contrast, Hokkaidō contributes about 3.5%. The regional GDP of Hokkaidō

Edwin Dun was a rancher from Ohio who was brought over to help develop Hokkaidō's agricultural industry; he became known as the 'father of Hokkaidō agriculture'. Arriving in Tokyo in 1873, he first began teaching at the new agricultural school there before moving to Sapporo to live and work from 1876 to 1883, setting up horse ranches, a dairy farm (with facilities for producing butter and cheese), experimenting with crops and constructing Hokkaidō's first horseracing track. He also helped establish a brewery, which would eventually become the producer of the now famous Sapporo Beer. One major blot on his legacy, however, is that it was he who encouraged the government to push forth with their policy of eradicating wolves from Hokkaidō (page 10). Dun married two Japanese women (not concurrently), and continued his involvement with Japan, eventually settling in Tokyo and working as a diplomat before his death in 1931, aged 82.

Known as the father of Hokkaidō's railroads, **Joseph Crawford** arrived on Hokkaidō in 1878 to carry out surveys and plans for the first railways on the island. His engineering skills were widely acclaimed, especially regarding the construction of the Otaru–Sapporo line with its difficult cliff section between Otaru and Zenibako – he was also involved with the crucial Horonai–Sapporo line used for transporting coal which opened in 1882. His achievements were recognised by the Japanese government, which awarded him the Order of the Rising Sun in 1881.

William Smith Clark came to Hokkaidō in 1876 as an educator hired by the Japanese government, principally to teach new farming techniques at the Sapporo Agricultural College (later to become Hokkaidō University). However, during his short tenure (only eight months) he encouraged his students to flourish in a range of other subjects and pursuits too, teaching them English literature, psychology and economics, while shunning the establishment's rules and regulations and demanding that his students simply 'be gentlemen'. His parting words of 'Boys, be ambitious!' left an indelible mark on the college and many of its most esteemed graduates, and is a motto known nationwide still to this day.

is ¥18.2 trillion, with the service industry making up the largest sector (29.2% of GDP), followed by wholesale and retail trade (13.2%). The island's manufacturing industry is dominated by food, chemical and transportation equipment production. Hokkaidō's traditional main industries of farming, fishing and forestry make up only 3.3% of its GDP, but this is significantly higher than the 0.8% for the sector in Japan as a whole. These days tourism is playing a more significant role in the island's economy.

Hokkaidō has long been known as the 'breadbasket of Japan' and is a vital contributor to the nation's food supply, producing 20% of all Japan's food output. The island's rich soils and climate make it an ideal crop-growing and livestock-rearing region; it is so productive in fact that it is one of Japan's few food self-sufficient prefectures, with a food surplus and self-sufficiency ratio often over 200% (Japan as a whole has a food deficit, with a ratio of around 38% in 2021).

Rice was impossible to grow until the late 19th century, when new hardy strains were developed; Hokkaidō is now the second largest rice-growing prefecture in Japan. The island is also effectively Japan's sole producer of beetroot, and the number one prefecture for producing potatoes, sweetcorn, onions, wheat, barley, carrots, daikon

(Japanese white radish), asparagus, broccoli, pumpkins and yams, while also ranking high for tomatoes, garlic, soybeans and many other crops. It produces 54% of Japan's dairy output, and 19% of its beef. On any road or cycling trip through Hokkaidō's agricultural landscapes you'll pass by fields of vegetables, rice, buckwheat (for making soba noodles), canola and wheat, and unlike most other regions of Japan, there is a high chance of seeing livestock out in the open fields during the milder months.

PEOPLE

The population of Japan is about 124 million, and while often considered a homogenous nation (the Japanese government for a long time, and until recently, claimed that Japan was a 'mono-ethnic nation'), there are some notable minority cultures. Japanese people refer to themselves as *nihon-jin* (日本人), and the modern Japanese census records nationality, rather than ethnicity. At the end of 2022, a record high 3 million foreigners were living in Japan, including students and temporary workers. The largest non-Japanese minority in the country is Chinese (about 760,000), followed by Vietnamese (490,000) and Koreans (410,000). About 35,000 foreigners are registered as living on Hokkaidō.

JAPANESE About 98% of Japan's population is ethnically Japanese – this east Asian group probably owes its origins to a mixture of Jōmon, Kofun and Yayoi peoples, who then later developed into the Yamato Japanese, or Wajin as they called themselves (the hegemonic ethnicity of Japan). Recent genetic studies seem to indicate that modern Japanese people can trace more than 90% of their genome back to the Yayoi people, with this group being closely related to people of the Korean peninsula and the Han-Chinese.

Despite being the home of the indigenous Ainu (page 36), the population of Hokkaidō is now predominantly Japanese, although, thanks to the thorough colonisation and assimilation of the Ainu during the Meiji period, it is very difficult to know the percentage of people who may have some Ainu ancestry. Along with the merchants, fishermen, labourers and officials who first colonised Hokkaidō, a sizeable proportion of the early Japanese population there was made up of convicts and ex-convicts, having been sent there in many cases to do manual work, with many becoming fishermen after their sentence was up.

AINU The Ainu are the indigenous people of the lands around the Sea of Okhotsk, and were once fairly widespread from Kamchatka, Sakhalin, the Kuril Islands, Hokkaidō and parts of northern Honshū, although most of those populations were eventually wiped out or subjugated by Russian or Japanese influences. Hokkaidō (then known as Ezo) was the homeland of the Ainu from the 12th century onwards, and they outnumbered Japanese people there until the 1800s, but now they constitute a very small percentage of Hokkaidō's population, with those identifying as Ainu perhaps numbering around 20,000. The number of people with Ainu blood could be much higher, however (perhaps upwards of 200,000) – owing to the comprehensive Meiji-era policy of assimilation with the Japanese, many people of Ainu descent either hid or were totally unaware of their heritage.

In the Ainu language, the word 'Ainu' means 'human', although some Ainu people prefer to be called Utari, meaning 'comrade' or 'people'. The Ainu called their homeland Ainu Mosir, which simply means 'earth'.

The Ainu's origins are murky, but they were probably an ancestral mix of the earlier Jōmon and later Epi-Jōmon (1st–7th century) and Okhotsk (6th–11th century) cultures. The Ainu were once said to be descended from dogs, although this creation myth was probably propagated by the Japanese rather than the Ainu themselves. Ainu of pure descent (who are now practically non-existent in number) had notably different physical characteristics to the ethnic Japanese, with stouter, hairier bodies, darker complexions, thick wavy hair and sometimes bluish or greenish eyes. Ainu men typically had long dark beards, and women often had a broad band tattoo around the mouth, and banded patterns on their hands and arms up to the elbow. Early European visitors speculated that the Ainu may have been a lost Caucasian tribe, but evidence seems to indicate that the Ainu (and their Jōmon ancestors) share a common deep link with other North Pacific peoples of the Russian Far East and northwestern America.

On Hokkaidō there were at least five major regional groups, which archaeologists claim were distinguishable by language, burial customs and other practices. These were: Shumukuru, Menashikuru, Ishikari, Uchiura and Sōya.

LANGUAGE

JAPANESE The Japanese language is spoken by the roughly 126 million natives of Japan, and by a few emigrant groups of people with Japanese ancestry living further afield, most notably in Brazil and Hawaii. Little is known about the language's early origins; Chinese documents from around the 3rd century recorded some Japanese words, but the first texts written in Old Japanese didn't appear until the 8th century. The standard form of Japanese is called *hyōjungo*; originating from the higher-class neighbourhoods of Tokyo, it is the form taught in schools and is used in all official communications and mass media.

See page 289 for more details on Japanese alphabets, grammar and pronunciation.

HOKKAIDŌ-BEN Each region of Japan has its own unique variation of spoken (and written) Japanese or dialect known as *-ben* (a well-known example being Osaka-ben, the dialect of Osaka). Hokkaidō is no different, although unsurprisingly for a big place there are also regional variations on Hokkaidō itself. As early and subsequent Japanese settlers came from various parts of the country, they each brought with them local variations in language, resulting in a mix of dialects. So, in Hokkaidō-ben people say *shibareru* ('to freeze' or 'freezing cold'), which has origins in the Tōhoku dialect; and *waya* (meaning 'terrible', 'messy' or 'no good'), which comes from western Japan. Some linguists have questioned whether Hokkaidō-ben can really be considered a dialect at all, partly because it may simply be a fairly recent mishmash of other regional dialects, and in truth, compared with some other regional dialects, Hokkaidō-ben doesn't deviate too far from standard Japanese in vocabulary and accent. But it is widely said that coastal areas of Hokkaidō have a stronger Tōhoku influence, and the Oshima Peninsula even has its own regional variation, Hama-kotoba (seashore speech). Sapporo's dialect is regarded as close to standard Japanese.

AINU The Ainu language (most correctly referred to as Hokkaidō Ainu) is part of a small language family that is a real linguistic enigma. Categorised as a language isolate with no known relatives, Ainu was traditionally spoken by the people of Hokkaidō, Sakhalin and the Kuril Islands; the Sakhalin and Kuril variants are now extinct, and on Hokkaidō only a handful of elderly people still speak Ainu fluently. When Ainu was more widely spoken on Hokkaidō, there were numerous local

1

variants and dialects; the Sōya dialect of northern Hokkaidō had similarities with Sakhalin Ainu for example.

Ainu most likely has its origins with the Neolithic Jōmon people who preceded the Ainu in northern Japan and probably spoke a proto-Ainu language. It is

TRADITIONAL WAYS OF THE AINU

The Ainu were said to be a gentle, courteous people who prized bravery and courage above all else. They would greet people by waving their hands towards their face and the men by stroking their beards. Dance and song were an important aspect of Ainu custom, and they crafted their own musical instruments. Families all lived under one roof, and the elderly were respected and treated with kindness.

Ainu settlements (known as *kotan*) consisted of huts (*cise*), always built in a line and constructed on wooden frames, with thatched roofs and walls made from reeds and other grasses. Some homes would also have outdoor storehouses and a bear cage (for housing a young bear until its sacrifice in the bear ceremony; page 42). Graveyards were always separate from the village. Traditionally, each Ainu village had a chief, who exercised authority and appointed a suitable successor (not necessarily his son). He approved all marriages, settled disputes and chose the site of new huts. Criminals were judged by a panel of community members, with beatings rather than imprisonment meted out as punishment.

Two main meals would be eaten each day, with breakfast often being the remains of the previous evening's dinner. Food consisted of fresh, dried and salted fish, fresh and dried venison and bear meat, seaweed, millet, wild vegetables, roots and berries, and mushrooms, with everything often all mixed into a stew – unlike the Japanese, the Ainu never ate raw fish or meat.

Traditionally hunter-gatherers and fishermen, by the 1800s the Ainu were growing millet (instead of rice), pumpkins, potatoes, onions and tobacco. Many also kept dogs and horses. Over time, the Ainu traded increasingly with the Japanese for rice, lacquerware, metals and sake – sake was highly prized and drunk frequently, including as a salutation to the Ainu deities.

Women seemed to have worked hard – they sewed, weaved, split bark (used for making clothing), chopped wood, collected water, ground millet and cultivated the soil. Men hunted – with bows (using poisoned arrows), spears and traps – fished, built houses and often played with their children.

An Ainu woman couldn't marry unless she was tattooed. Tattooing would be started from childhood – a knife would be used to mark the skin, into which soot would be rubbed and a few days later washed with a concoction containing bark. The process would be repeated every year until the girl was 15 or 16 and considered an adult. Polygamy was not common, and usually only permitted for chiefs, or if a man's wife couldn't bear a child.

Ainu clothing was originally made from animal furs, with some items even made from salmon skin. During the winter, deer pelts would be used for clothing and shoes because of their waterproof properties, and superior warmth compared with bear hides. From around the 13th century, threads of tree bark were used to make cloth for clothing. And as the Ainu began to trade, they obtained cotton and started developing distinctive embroidered patterns as decoration. Females would also wear large hoop earrings and necklaces.

About 80% of the place names on Hokkaidō have Ainu language origins, and this includes settlements, mountains, rivers and other landforms. The Ainu names tended to be descriptive rather than overly poetic, and were later directly adopted into Japanese, retaining almost the same sounds and giving many place names on Hokkaidō the unique flavour we still see today. Sapporo, for example, originates from the Ainu Satporopet (dry-big-river), Otaru was Otaornai (river-through-sandy-beach) and Noboribetsu comes from Nupurpet (which has been translated as river-of-deep-colour). Some of the more commonly seen place name components of Ainu origin on Hokkaidō include pet (*betsu*) or nay (*nai*) meaning 'river', poro (*horo/boro*) which translates to 'large' or 'many', and *nupuri* which signifies 'mountain'.

interesting to note that some Ainu words resemble those of several other northeast Asian languages such as Nivkh and the Mongolic languages, although how exactly they are connected remains a mystery. It has also been suggested that the Emishi people of northern Honshū may have spoken Ainu, as some place names in that region appear to retain Ainu elements (eg: the –*be* element in 'Kurobe', a famous river in Toyama Prefecture).

Ainu is traditionally an oral language; it originally had no written form, with history, folklore and stories passed down from generation to generation in speech and song, including the epic *Yukar*, Ainu hero-sagas. When Ainu later came to be transcribed it tended to be in the Latin alphabet, or now more commonly in a modified form of katakana (page 289).

As the Japanese sought to colonise Hokkaidō during the Meiji era, new policies attempted to assimilate and 'civilise' the Ainu people, including the teaching of Japanese in schools, meaning that both the Ainu language and culture were gradually marginalised and pushed close to the point of extinction. In part due to historical persecution, the number of people who identify as Ainu is disputed and it is difficult to obtain accurate data about the current number of Ainu speakers; a 2017 survey by the Hokkaidō Prefectural Government put the number as 13,118, and it is likely that only a very tiny percentage of those people would have any practical working knowledge of the language.

In June 2008, the Japanese government finally recognised Ainu as a legitimate indigenous language, and efforts have been made by authorities, community groups and citizens to encourage more people to speak and learn it. In 2009, UNESCO listed Ainu as an endangered language. The government has since established the Council for Ainu Policy Promotion, and in 2019 passed the (ever-so-slightly wordy) Act Promoting Measures to Achieve a Society in which the Pride of Ainu People is Respected, with the aim to increase nationwide understanding and respect for Ainu culture, and multiculturalism more broadly.

Some of the initiatives include announcements in Ainu on some bus routes in the town of Biratori, where around 80% of residents have Ainu roots – new words that had to be created for the announcements include *kampiop* (seat pocket) and *tumamkauspe* (poster). Another more long-term project headed by the Cultural Affairs Agency has been recording and archiving Ainu speech, for academic research, language-learning and posterity. Thousands of hours of analogue recordings have already been digitised, and include interviews, oral narratives and folklore, with some recordings from the former Ainu Museum at Shiraoi.

Hokkaidō's Ainu Association (founded in 1946) runs free language courses for Ainu and Japanese people in various regions of Hokkaidō. Recent decades have also seen a modest proliferation of Ainu-language dictionaries and books, and the 1997 law for the protection and promotion of Ainu culture actively sought to facilitate language instruction, with the Foundation for Ainu Culture (w ff-ainu.or.jp/web/English/index.html) offering Ainu classes for adults, children and teachers. Its website is a useful resource for those wanting to know more about Ainu culture.

Since 1987 there have been Ainu conversation lessons broadcast on the radio, with accompanying textbooks available for listeners. But interest in the language has increased in recent times thanks to the efforts of enthusiastic individuals. A student of Ainu heritage at Keio University, Maya Sekine, set up The Sito Channel (*sito* is a type of grain-based Ainu dumpling), a YouTube channel offering lessons on conversational Ainu covering a range of topics – it has proved popular with people from all over Japan and even abroad. (see ▶ @user-sg7qz4sh8p)

Many years earlier in April 2001, the prominent Ainu activist (and first Ainu parliamentary member) Shigeru Kayano financed FM Pipaushi, which aired an Ainu-language radio show two Sundays a month. For details of an Ainu-language newspaper, see page 85.

In 2022, the 700-page *Handbook of the Ainu Language* was published by De Gruyter and the National Institute for Japanese Language and Linguistics; compiled by numerous language experts over the course of many years, it is the most comprehensive English-language resource on the subject, and will hopefully help preserve knowledge of Ainu and encourage future study.

RELIGION

Religion in Japan is less rigidly defined or practised than it is in many other countries, and many Japanese people don't necessarily label themselves as religious at all, while still following a mix of traditions and spiritual rituals that derive from the two main religions, Shintō and Buddhism, in a combination known as *shinbutsu-shūgō*. Up until 1945, shinbutsu-shūgō was the official state religion. Few people nowadays follow strict religious doctrines in their daily lives, but common practices familiar to most include respecting ancestors at shrines and private home altars, and visiting Shintō shrines to commemorate major life events such as weddings and births (funerals tend to take place at Buddhist temples), where people also often go to pray for health, luck or wealth.

SHINTŌ Regarded as the indigenous religion of Japan, Shintō (which literally means 'the way of the gods') dates from around the early 8th century, although the seeds of pan-deity worship were probably set in the earlier Yayoi period. It works on the polytheistic belief that *kami* (gods or spirits) exist everywhere and inhabit all aspects of nature, such as rocks, rivers, trees and mountains. They can also inhabit objects and lifeforms (both inanimate and living) and can manifest as forces such as wind, plague and earthquakes. Kami can be summoned at shrines by dance or music. In Shintō, purity is revered above all else, hence the cleaning of hands (and mouth) at a shrine, and some rites involving fire, a purifying force. *Torii* gates signify the entrance to a Shintō shrine, while the *honden* (main hall) is where the kami are enshrined – toss a coin into a collection box and summon the deities by pulling on a rope to ring the gong; then pray, clap twice, bow and back away from the shrine, before bowing once more at the gate as you leave.

The Meiji government made Shintō the state religion and encouraged citizens to worship the emperor as a kami. In some ways, it is difficult to classify Shintō as a religion as it has no central authority, nor any holy books or doctrine; even the job of a *kannushi* (Shintō priest, though even 'priest' is a misnomer) is not to instruct but rather to mediate between people and the spirits found in nature. Following Japan's defeat in World War II, Shintō was separated from the state, but certain Shintō practices, such as praying at a shrine – be it for success in love, work or examinations, or to usher in the new year – still pervade society today.

BUDDHISM Buddhism originated in India and then spread to China and Korea via the Silk Road more than 2,000 years ago; from there it made its way to Japan around the mid 6th century. Japanese Buddhism (known as Bukkyō) has a long and deep history, but it stems from the Mahāyāna (Great Vehicle) tradition, which teaches that anyone (not just monks) can achieve salvation during their lifetime. Prince Shōtoku (CE574–622) is credited with first promoting Buddhism in Japan, and over the centuries various sects developed, the most famous being Zen Buddhism, which introduced the concept of seated meditation (*zazen*). Other sects include Shingon (which shares similarities with Tibetan Buddhism) and the Pure Land sect, which has the most followers. Common to and revered in all sects of Japanese Buddhism is Kannon, a deity who embodies mercy and compassion.

The growth of Buddhism in Japan was possibly helped by the fact that it fitted quite seamlessly alongside Shintō, with some Buddhist deities being seen as the other face of a Shintō one. Over time Shintō and Buddhist practices became so intertwined that it can sometimes be difficult to unravel them. Some Buddhist traditions are associated with the afterlife, and so practices at funerals and the summer festival of Obon – when the spirits of departed ancestors return and families gather at gravestones to greet them – are adhered to even by non-believers.

AINU BELIEFS The Ainu had animistic beliefs more akin to Shintō than a typical religion. They attached great reverence to nature and physical places (the sun, moon, mountains, rivers, trees), while living entities were often perceived as gods (*kamuy*). The Ainu believed in two planes of existence: the human world, Ainu Mosir; and the spirit world, Kamuy Mosir, which was inhabited by the deities. But the deities also manifested themselves in the bodies of certain animals such as Blakiston's fish owl, known as Kotan kor Kamuy (the god of the village), and especially the brown bear, known as Kimun Kamuy (the god of the mountains), revered by the Ainu and to whom they paid homage in the Iomante bear ceremony, arguably the closest the Ainu ever came to 'worship' (page 42).

A significant difference between Ainu beliefs and Shintō is that the *kamuy* sent gifts to the Ainu. These gifts could be good or bad, depending on how they were received. The bear, for example, was a deity in ursine form, and so even bears captured for sacrificial slaughter would be treated with kindness and respect until their death. If humans were not respectful of nature, then the *wen-kamuy* (evil gods) could wreak havoc, sending floods or other natural disasters to the human realm. In this way, the Ainu, their spiritual beliefs and the natural world were all deeply intertwined.

The Ainu have very few frivolous symbols of religiosity such as temples or priests, and their 'religious' objects consist of simple sticks, called *inaw*, made from peeled, whittled wood, with the shavings flailing down and outwards in decorative curls – they would have been seen often in Ainu homes, along riverbanks and at mountain passes, and were thrown into rivers by boatmen at dangerous places. Decorated

Perhaps one of the most infamous, and controversial, aspects of Ainu culture is the Iomante (sometimes written Iyomante), or bear ceremony. The Ainu depended on bears for their fur and meat, but also revered them as deities – referring to them as Kimun Kamuy. The bear ceremony was a way to obtain physical gifts from the animal before sending it back to the spirit world.

It started with the capture of a bear cub – perhaps after its mother was killed in a hunt – then nurtured in the chief's or sub-chief's home (there are even tales of them being suckled by the women). As the bear grew it was kept in a wooden cage outside and fed until autumn of the following year when it was time for the Iomante. Customs varied from region to region, but generally involved gathering in an atmosphere of festive revelry, with plenty of drink, feasting, and the men dancing.

The sacrifice itself is difficult to sugarcoat – the bear would be tied to a post and then shot with bamboo arrows, the men rushing forwards to draw blood in brutal bludgeoning fashion (drawing blood was said to bring good luck). Finally, the bear would be decapitated, its head put on a pole and weapons offered to it; then the body divided and the meat shared among the villagers, followed by feasting, drinking and utterings of thanks to the bear deity after the releasing of its spirit.

Even before the Former Aborigines Act was passed in 1899, so-called primitive displays of Ainu culture such as this were outlawed by the government. The ceremony is no longer practised, though black-and-white footage still exists of one of the last-known bear ceremonies.

wooden prayer sticks (*ikupasuy*) and lacquer bowls (*taki*) were used in prayer and during libation ceremonies to the deities. With no doctrine or strict religious 'rules' to follow, drinking sake was never prohibited; in fact, it was often encouraged as a libation and a 'religious' act.

CHRISTIANITY Christianity in Japan is not as widespread as in other regions of east Asia (notably South Korea), but nevertheless about 1.9 million people profess to belong to the faith (about 1.5% of the population).

Christianity has an interesting and eventful history in Japan. It was introduced in 1549 towards the end of the tumultuous Warring States period (1467–1568), when the Spanish Jesuit priest Francis Xavier arrived on a Portuguese Catholic mission to spread Christianity in Asia. Arriving first in Kagoshima, the missionaries were welcomed by the ruling daimyōs, as Portuguese traders had already been doing business there since 1543. The first Japanese Christian convert, a man named Anjirō (who Xavier had met a couple of years earlier in Malaysia), accompanied the missionaries as an interpreter, although initially it was a struggle to convert the locals because many of them were already Buddhist or Shintō practitioners. Over the following years, however, thousands of people in Kyūshū converted, from lowly peasants to reigning lords, with around 100,000 converts to the new religion by the 1570s, and Nagasaki became the centre of Japanese Catholicism. But within a few decades of its arrival, Christianity was outlawed by Hideyoshi Toyotomi, who banished missionaries from Kyūshū in 1587 as he sought to exert more power in the region. The oppression went up a notch in 1597, when 26 foreign and Japanese Catholics – later to become known as the 'Twenty-six

Martyrs of Japan' – were arrested, tortured, mutilated and finally executed by public crucifixion in Nagasaki; a stark warning that Christianity would no longer be tolerated. Under the succeeding Tokugawa government there was a further tightening of the stance against Christianity, as the shōgunate claimed that the religion was responsible for undermining the authorities and encouraging anti-establishment behaviour. Following a rebellion on the Shimabara Peninsula in the late 1630s, thousands of Christians were executed and a full ban on the religion was enforced. For the next 260 years, Christianity in Japan was strictly prohibited, although small pockets of 'hidden Christians' continued to practise their religion in secret. Some Christian communities initially moved to Hokkaidō to escape persecution, but the Tokugawa shōgunate eventually managed to track them down.

The Meiji Restoration of 1868 brought a wealth of changes to Japan which included much more freedom of religion, and so the number of Christian followers started slowly to increase once again. Trappist monks who moved to Hokkaidō from southern Japan established the first monastery in the country at Tōbetsu in 1896.

Although Christianity remains a minor religion in Japan, Christian-style weddings in a faux church or chapel (sometimes presided over by a Westerner dressed as a vicar) have become popular in recent years, often instead of or in addition to a traditional Shintō wedding ceremony. Christmas is not a public holiday in Japan, although it is celebrated in a commercial and secular fashion, with Christmas Eve being seen as a romantic time for couples. Easter is not marked in any significant way at all.

EDUCATION

Japanese citizens are entitled to 12 years of education: the first six years in elementary school (6–12 years old), followed by three years in junior high school (12–15 years old), and a further three years in senior high school (15–18 years old). Attendance is compulsory until the end of junior high, although the majority continue on to complete their studies until the age of 18. The academic year, like the financial year, runs from April to March, with a summer vacation in August, a shorter winter vacation from late December to early January, and a spring vacation from mid-March to the beginning of April.

Many students attend after-hours cram schools called *juku* – this is usually to brush up on weaker subjects or to study intensely for college or university entrance examinations, which usually require extra tutelage to pass. Some students participate in school clubs, which, especially in the case of sports clubs such as baseball or basketball, can be all-consuming and take up almost all available free time after school, at weekends and holidays for students and teachers alike.

CULTURE

Japan has an extremely rich cultural heritage, especially in terms of the arts. Literature, poetry, painting, dance, tea ceremony and drama have been refined over many centuries, and still are held in high esteem in society today.

With its much shorter history in terms of Japanese influence, Hokkaidō has few regionally specific contributions, although recent years have seen a proliferation of artists, musicians and film-makers celebrate all that is unique about Hokkaidō; while Ainu culture and customs have intriguingly deep roots but have not yet reached a wider world audience – hopefully this will change over time.

1

From around the beginning of the Meiji period, with the start of the government's concerted effort to develop and open up Hokkaidō, we begin to see Hokkaidō featured more prominently in Japanese literature. Of course, the Ainu had their own rich tradition of legends and folklore going back hundreds of years, but as theirs is an almost entirely oral history, little was recorded or transcribed until relatively recently.

Among celebrated Japanese literature of the early Meiji era, author and poet Doppo Kunikida (1871–1908) saw Hokkaidō as a land of freedom and independence. Fellow author Hōmei Iwano (1873–1920) wrote in his work *Hōrō* that 'Hokkaidō feels like a foreign country'. Indeed, many works of Japanese literature featuring Hokkaidō focused on its 'otherness' and difference to the rest of Japan, often in terms of climate; while novelist Takeo Arishima (1878–1923) described it as a place where the wild, primordial side of humans can be displayed, an unsubtle reference perhaps to the traditions of the indigenous Ainu. Arishima is sometimes described as the father of Hokkaidō literature, with many of his works such as *Kain no Matsuei* (*Descendants of Cain*) set on Hokkaidō and depicting people struggling against the power of nature. Later writers also tackled Hokkaidō's colonial tensions, with Hokkaidō-born modernist author Sei Itō (1905–69) imbuing his works with the uneasy dichotomy of coloniser and colonised.

FILM AND TELEVISION *Ainu Mosir* is a 2020 Netflix drama set in contemporary Hokkaidō about a 14-year-old boy of Ainu heritage seeking a spiritual connection with his recently deceased father, while also trying to make sense of his own identity.

Hokkaidō is also the setting for the popular historical manga and accompanying anime titled *Golden Kamuy*. The story takes place after the Russo-Japanese war of 1904–05, as the main protagonist and veteran of the war, Saichi Sugimoto, goes on a quest to find a huge treasure trove of Ainu gold, helped by a young Ainu girl called Asirpa. An English-language translation of the manga is available, and a live-action film adaptation of the story came out in early 2024.

Older Japanese viewers will recall a very famous television drama from the 1980s called *Kita-no-kuni-kara* (*From the Northern Country*), which was set in Furano (page 187).

ARCHITECTURE Wood has long been the staple building material for traditional buildings in Japan, and this is the case on Hokkaidō too, despite the island's much shorter history as a fully fledged Japanese region. The early pioneer houses, trading posts and much grander herring mansions were all constructed from wood, with examples still surviving in some places. Traditional Ainu homes were regarded as basic by contemporary accounts, but some were impressive in scale and craftsmanship, and all were built to withstand Hokkaidō's brutal winters. With the influx of foreign advisors and traders during Hokkaidō's colonisation period, some notable buildings in Hakodate, Otaru and Sapporo, for example, were constructed in Western styles and from new materials such as stone and brick, while Russian Orthodox churches and their like stood in great contrast to the more traditional Japanese shrines and temples.

In the countryside, Hokkaidō's farms tend to be spread out (unlike in the rest of Japan where even farmers tend to live clustered together) and in appearance resemble the farmsteads of America or Europe much more closely than they do standard Japanese ones – think white-and-red clapboard farmhouses and barns.

Modern Japanese buildings tend to favour form and function over style, with Japanese homes often compact and packed tightly together; on Hokkaidō there is far more space to play with and so properties tend to cover a larger footprint – they also often look slightly more Western in style. One typical feature of Hokkaidō homes which is not so common in other regions of Japan is the front porch, which provides an extra level of insulation from the cold and is useful for changing footwear, clothes and gear without getting snow inside the house.

Hokkaidō's towns and cities are fairly uniform in appearance and with a few exceptions, are architecturally uninteresting. Partly due to the harsh winter conditions and a declining population, many structures on Hokkaidō have a rather weather-beaten look about them, but this somehow adds to the slightly bleak frontier charm of the island.

SPORTS

Japan is a nation of sports fans and, despite being snow-covered for a good portion of the year, Hokkaidō plays its part in the country's vibrant sports scene.

BASEBALL Baseball is the national sport and one whose popularity shows little sign of abating now that superstar Shōhei Ōtani is making waves over in America – in fact, he started his professional career with the Hokkaidō Nippon-Ham Fighters. They are based in Kitahiroshima, a small city just outside of Sapporo, and compete in the six-team Pacific League; there is also a six-team Central League, and following the conclusion of each regular season (which lasts from around late March to October and consists of about 140 games), the top three teams in each league go on to play in the Climax Series to determine which team from each of the Central and Pacific leagues will face off for the championship in the Japan Series.

FOOTBALL Soccer is only a little less popular than baseball; the J-League is Japan's top-flight professional league and is divided into three divisions (J1, J2, J3). From 2024, J1 has 20 competing teams, with the season running from early March to early December – Hokkaidō Consadole Sapporo is the island's sole representative. The men's national team is nicknamed the 'Samurai Blue' and is consistently among the highest-ranked Asian teams; similarly, the women's national team – nicknamed 'Nadeshiko Japan' (named after a flower supposed to signify the ideal Japanese woman) – was the first Asian team to win the World Cup in 2011.

WINTER SPORTS Skiing and snowboarding are immensely popular pastimes in Japan, with an estimated 500-plus ski resorts spread across the country (mostly in central and northern regions). After Sapporo hosted the Winter Olympics in 1972 (and it may be gearing up for another future bid), there was a skiing boom which lasted until the economic bubble collapsed in the late 1980s, forcing the closure of many resorts. But the 1998 Nagano Winter Olympics kick-started the industry again, with foreigners finally discovering Japan's (and Hokkaidō's in particular) incredible snow – the country has since hosted numerous international winter sports events and competitions. Other than skiing and snowboarding, Hokkaidō is a base for others sports such as speed skating and curling, while figure skating is a remarkably popular spectator sport throughout Japan.

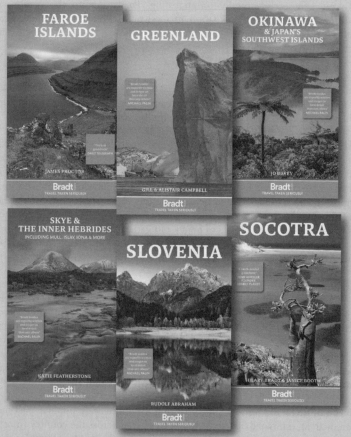

2

Practical Information

WHEN TO VISIT

In Japan generally, and on Hokkaidō in particular, the seasons are distinct and dictate everything – winters are long, cold and snowy, and summers can be (like the rest of Japan) uncomfortably hot and humid, though Hokkaidō tends to be a bit less stiflingly hot and sticky than other parts of the country. In spring the cherry blossoms bloom here later than anywhere else, and conversely the autumn colours arrive much earlier. As such, the activities and sights on offer depend entirely on when you plan to visit – the popular resort village of Niseko, for instance, is a bustling centre for skiers and snowboarders during the winter months, but in the summer is comparatively quiet and offers more sedate activities such as hiking and camping.

SPRING A short but pleasant season, running only from April to May, spring is famous for *hanami* (cherry-blossom viewing; page 48), one of the most anticipated events on the calendar. In the spring, daytime temperatures start to edge gradually towards warm and comfortable, but bring clothing suitable for chilly weather. Eastern Hokkaidō in particular can still remain cold late into the season.

SUMMER At the beginning of summer, from around June to mid-July, most of Japan experiences the rainy season (*tsuyu*), when daily rain showers and storms are a likely occurrence. It is often said that this wet weather front doesn't reach as far north as Hokkaidō and that the island experiences no rainy season, but local residents will tell you that even here this period does tend to be greyer and rainier than usual.

However, when the real heat and humidity of high summer finally kicks in, Hokkaidō does usually remain a fair bit cooler and less humid than more southerly regions of Japan – many Japanese people head to Hokkaidō for their summer vacations to escape the brutal heat and humidity down south. This is the peak season for hiking, camping, cycling and other outdoor activities, with the colourful flower fields of Furano a major draw; elsewhere you can see lush green pastures and alpine flowers in full bloom if you venture into the mountains. At this latitude, summer days are nowhere near as long as in the UK, for example; expect it to be dark by around 19.00, and as there is no daylight saving, the sun rises early too, at around 04.00.

AUTUMN Autumn (early September to early November) arrives earlier on Hokkaidō than anywhere else in the country, and so is the first place Japanese people can indulge in *kōyō* (autumn leaf viewing), another national pastime which borders on obsession. In the high altitudes of Daisetsuzan and other places, the leaves first begin to turn as early as late August or early September, but more generally you can expect peak autumn colours around mid-October. Typhoons, which sometimes

Literally meaning 'flower viewing', *hanami* is a national pastime in the spring, when people of all ages go to parks and outdoor spots to admire, photograph and picnic under the velvety pink and white blossoms of the cherry (*sakura*) trees. The custom dates back centuries (though probably started with an appreciation of the earlier-to-bloom and longer-lasting plum (*ume*) trees), with the fleeting beauty of the cherry blossom seen as something to be cherished. The first flowering to peak plumage can take as little as a week, with the trees soon shedding their blossom in a snowfall of petals, the whole spectacle rarely lasting more than a fortnight. Popular spots hold special light-up events and stalls sell festival snacks, while families, friends and work colleagues hold *hanami* parties, setting out tarpaulins to sit on and a spread of food and drink – it's one of the rare occasions when people let their hair down in public, and is often a good chance to make new friends.

On Hokkaidō the blooms are usually a month or so later than in Tokyo or Osaka – in Sapporo the cherry blossoms start to bloom around late April to early May, peaking a week later. Popular viewing spots in the city include Maruyama Park and Hokkaidō Shrine, and Makomanai and Moerenuma parks; there are also a few cherry trees dotted around Ōdōri Park. Almost all small towns and cities have an area for viewing blossoms, but some of the most popular spots around Hokkaidō outside of Sapporo include Matsumae Castle, Asahiyama Park in Asahikawa, Hakodate and Goryōkaku parks in Hakodate, Oniushi Park in Mori, Noboribetsu Cherry Blossom Road and the 7km-long Nijūkken Road in Shinhidaka Town.

The Japan Meteorological Corporation publishes an official cherry blossom forecast for the entire country from around January, which is updated regularly as the peak approaches – it is available at various places online in English (try **w** japan-guide.com/sakura).

batter the more southerly reaches of Japan during the summer and autumn, tend mostly to fizzle out before reaching Hokkaidō and so are not usually a major issue, although deluges of heavy rain do present a flood and landslide risk.

WINTER Unlike many other regions of Japan, winter (mid-November to late March) is one of the prime tourist windows on Hokkaidō, thanks to the guaranteed cold weather and the abundance of high-quality powder snow. Most of Hokkaidō is blanketed with snow from around December to late March (with snow lying much later in central areas and at higher elevations). City streets, main roads and pavements are often completely covered in compacted snow and ice – even in the centre of Sapporo – so it is important to take great care when walking anywhere or driving (page 69). Trains, buses and flights can be disrupted if the weather is particularly bad. It goes without saying that it tends to be bitingly cold outside, so you should wear warm clothes and footwear suitable for walking in snow (page 62).

HIGHLIGHTS

Hokkaidō is (rightly) seen as Japan's go-to place for outdoor enthusiasts and nature lovers (see opposite), but there are a great deal of other interesting attractions around the island too, from art or history to food, so you don't need to be a super fit or rugged outdoors type to find plenty to enjoy.

NATURE AND THE OUTDOORS TOP SIX
Kushiro-Shitsugen National Park Japan's largest wetland region offers fantastic birdwatching and kayaking; the winter courtship dance of the red-crowned crane is an iconic image of Hokkaidō.

Lake Mashū One of the most picturesque lakes in Japan, Mashū is a large volcanic crater lake with deep clear waters, zero signs of human interference and jaw-dropping viewpoints from the steep and high crater rim.

Mount Asahi-dake Hokkaidō's tallest peak is located within the beautiful Daisetsuzan National Park; a ropeway allows for a relatively short and straightforward climb in summer, with views of steaming fumaroles and untamed wilderness, while winter draws backcountry enthusiasts.

Mount Tokachi-dake Located in the southwest corner of Daisetsuzan, the Tokachi-dake volcanic group is a startling landscape of smouldering calderas and seared Mordor-esque vistas, crisscrossed by trails perfect for one- or two-day treks.

Rishiri and Rebun islands A visit to these two small islands in the far north of Hokkaidō is well worth the effort. Rishiri is dominated by its 1,700m peak which rises directly from the sea, while more gently sculpted Rebun has a beautiful rugged coastline and hills of wildflower meadows.

Shiretoko Peninsula A UNESCO World Heritage Site and wildlife haven, this remote peninsula offers hiking and nature cruises, plus a good chance of spotting a brown bear or two.

CULTURAL AND MANMADE ATTRACTIONS TOP SIX
Abashiri Prison Museum Established in 1890 and opened as a museum in 1983, the 25 brilliantly preserved historical buildings are the oldest existing wooden penological buildings in the world.

Hakodate A foodie city crammed with history, famous views and fabulous seafood – for *uni* (sea urchin), *ika* (squid) and *kani* (crab) lovers, there are few places better.

Historical Village of Hokkaidō This fascinating open-air museum showcases more than 50 kinds of building (both replicas and originals) from throughout the history of Hokkaidō, including farmhouses, shops, governing offices and schools.

Nibutani Ainu Culture Museum This is arguably the best Ainu museum on Hokkaidō, situated deep in the countryside of the Hidaka region, one of the Ainu's traditional heartlands.

Sapporo TV Tower This iconic landmark stands at the very heart of the city, at the eastern end of Ōdōri Park; views across the city and out towards the mountains are wonderful in clear weather.

Snow festivals Marvel at the impressive snow and ice sculptures at one of Hokkaidō's winter snow festivals. Sapporo and Asahikawa are the most famous, but smaller festivals are held in other places too.

SUGGESTED ITINERARIES

Hokkaidō is a large place (by Japanese standards), so unless you are staying for three to four weeks or longer it is almost impossible to see everything on the island during one trip. Itineraries and activities will also depend greatly on when you visit, with many places difficult to reach and some facilities closed during the height of winter.

If you are visiting Hokkaidō in winter, then be aware that rail, road and plane delays or cancellations are a distinct possibility due to the weather, so always try to avoid tight travel connections. It's often a good idea to factor in an extra day or two for disruptions.

HOKKAIDŌ HIGHLIGHTS TOUR Allow at least 12 days (but preferably longer), and start by spending two days and a night in **Sapporo** (perhaps with a side trip to Otaru), then head over to picturesque **Furano** for a couple of days. Allow one full day to ride the Asahidake Ropeway and sample the splendour of **Daisetsuzan National Park** (summer or autumn). Then head east – in winter you can take an icebreaker cruise from Abashiri; in the summer cruise or hike at the **Shiretoko Peninsula**. After a day or two, head south via **Akan-Mashū National Park** for volcanoes, lakes, hot springs and Ainu culture; then if you're a nature lover continue to **Kushiro-Shitsugen National Park** for a spot of wildlife watching. Make your way back west via **Obihiro** and the **Tokachi Plain**, and aim to spend a few days exploring western Hokkaidō – **Shikotsu-Tōya National Park, Noboribetsu Onsen** and **Niseko** all have appeal whatever the season. From there it is a short hop to New Chitose Airport, or, if time allows, make your way down to **Hakodate** for outstanding seafood and night views. From Hakodate you can make your way to Honshū and Tokyo on the Shinkansen (bullet train).

A LONG WEEKEND Flights from various Japanese cities to New Chitose Airport take an hour or two, so it is perfectly viable to pop up to Hokkaidō for a couple of days. You could opt to spend a weekend mainly eating and drinking in **Sapporo**, sampling the city's great ramen, soup curry, *jingisukan* (barbecued lamb), seafood and beer, and perhaps taking in the views from nearby **Mount Moiwa**, or wandering around the art installations of **Moerenuma Park**. The pleasant harbour town of **Otaru** is only 30 minutes away by train too. If visiting in winter then there is the **Sapporo Snow Festival** in early February, or you can head directly to the slopes for world-class skiing at **Niseko** (there are seasonal buses directly to and from the airport for skiers). **Hakodate** at the southern tip of the island also makes for a good weekend getaway, especially with its direct rail links to northern Honshū and Tokyo. There is plenty to see and do around Hakodate, and its seafood is not to be missed.

ONE WEEK With limited time, it's best to focus on one region. Some options for summer and winter seasons are suggested.

In summer In the summer it's worth spending as much time as possible in Hokkaidō's magnificent outdoors, so after flying in to New Chitose you could spend a day or two exploring nearby **Shikotsu-Tōya National Park**. Alternatively, head up to see the colourful flower fields of **Furano** and **Biei**, and then strap on your hiking boots and hit the shorter trails of **Daisetsuzan National Park**. Self-drivers will have even more options – head west to enjoy the spectacular **Shakotan Peninsula**, southeast to discover the Ainu heartlands amid the remote **Hidaka Mountains** and **Cape Erimo**, or push further east to explore the volcanoes and lakes of **Akan-Mashū National Park**.

In winter During the winter, you could catch the **Sapporo Snow Festival** before spending a few days on the slopes at **Niseko** or **Furano** – wallowing in a steaming outdoor hot spring surrounded by snow is something of a winter must-do. Or you could instead head to eastern Hokkaidō and take an **icebreaker cruise**, walk on floating **drift ice**, or do a spot of **birdwatching**. Eastern Hokkaidō's Japanese cranes and Steller's sea eagles are at the top of many twitchers' wish lists.

TWO WEEKS

In summer In the summer take a day or two to enjoy the sights and tastes of **Sapporo**, and then any of the one-week itinerary suggestions. But with an extra seven days to play with (and your own set of wheels) you could conceivably do a decent loop of the island (or the **Hokkaidō Highlights Tour**; see opposite) to see a few different regions. Consider heading up to the far north of Hokkaidō, and catching a boat from the quasi-frontier town of **Wakkanai** to the two nearby islands. **Rishiri Island** offers fantastic hiking, while **Rebun Island** is a flower lover's paradise; both have outstanding seafood (don't miss the sea urchin). Or head way out east to the UNESCO World Heritage-listed **Shiretoko Peninsula** to discover a world where sea eagles swoop and brown bears roam, while whales, orcas and dolphins dance in the icy waters along the coast. Keen cyclists could opt for a cycling tour, or well-equipped hikers could try one of Hokkaidō's fantastic multi-day treks such as the **Daisetsuzan Grand Traverse**.

In winter During the winter you can spend literally days out on the slopes at Hokkaidō's best **winter sports resorts**. This can be mixed up with excursions to the bigger cities: **Sapporo**, **Asahikawa** and **Hakodate** all have their own winter charms. You could also head to eastern Hokkaidō to see the **drift ice** and **birdlife**, but factor in the long travel times – it takes almost a full day to travel across the island, and possibly longer depending on the weather.

HOKKAIDŌ GRAND TOUR (3+ weeks) With three weeks or more to play with, you can consider a fairly comprehensive tour of the island, with enough time for excursions to a couple of the smaller islands. Self-driving gives you much more freedom, but most places are reachable with a little planning if you are reliant on public transport (especially during the summer). A winter grand tour is also a fabulous adventure, with plenty of scope for various snow-related activities. But do take into consideration that delays, cancellations and changes to travel plans are likely in adverse weather conditions, so having a loose, rather than a strictly regimented schedule, may work best.

CHASING SPRING'S CHERRY BLOSSOMS The cherry trees bloom later on Hokkaidō than anywhere else in Japan, peaking around late April to early May, so if you time it right you could spend a week or two following the blooms across the island. At the far southern end of Hokkaidō, **Matsumae Castle** is one of the best places to see the *sakura*, with its thousands of trees and a month-long cherry-blossom festival. It's then a quick jaunt up the coast to **Hakodate**, where the fortress of Goryōkaku looks resplendent in pink. It's another hour or so north past Mount Komagatake to **Mori** and the sea of blossoms at Oniushi Park. Both **Sapporo** and **Otaru** have lovely *sakura* spots, and if you venture over to the rolling landscapes of central Hokkaidō you can marvel at other spring wonders – the deep purple Shibazakura of Takinoue Park, and the stunning floral displays at Kamiyubetsu Tulip Park – all under the backdrop of distant snow-capped peaks.

A WEEK OF AUTUMN COLOUR During the autumn peak in mid to late October, **Sapporo** has some good leaf-viewing spots: Nakajima Park and Hokkaidō University's Gingko Avenue are particularly popular. But you'll want to head out of the city to see Hokkaidō's most impressive autumn hues. The wooded gorges of nearby **Jōzankei Onsen** become a riot of colour, while **Shikotsu-Tōya National Park** offers a wealth of autumnal possibilities if you have your own wheels. If you're on Hokkaidō at the beginning of the season then it's best to head further north; the peaks of **Daisetsuzan** have Japan's first autumn colours from early September, and neighbouring **Sōunkyō Onsen** is jaw-droppingly gorgeous a few weeks later.

CYCLING TRIPS With its long, mostly empty and well-maintained roads, Hokkaidō is a cyclist's dream, and there are an almost limitless number of possibilities for short and long cycle tours, whether it be gliding along from town to town on national routes, or exploring the island's plethora of rough and wild gravel forestry tracks (page 72). You would probably need at least three weeks to do a thorough circuit of the island, but even with only a few days to spare you could explore a particular region: follow the coastal roads around the Oshima Peninsula (and Ōshima Island) in southwest Hokkaidō, tour the rolling fields and farmland of central Furano and/ or Tokachi, or follow the scenic coast roads up to Wakkanai in the far north. But you can't really go wrong wherever you end up cycling on Hokkaidō, as almost every corner of the prefecture is great for exploring by bike. Mid-July to early September is the summer cycling season.

See page 71 for more, general, information on cycling on Hokkaidō.

TOURIST INFORMATION

The Japan National Tourism Organisation (**w** jnto.go.jp) promotes the country as a travel destination, with worldwide regional offices and websites aimed at inbound foreign visitors (**w** japan.travel/en/uk is specifically for visitors from the UK). Japan's national parks are administered by the Ministry of the Environment (**w** env.go.jp/en/nature/nps/park) but you can find information specifically for foreign visitors at **w** japan.travel/national-parks. Most train stations have a tourist information centre (観光案内所, *kankō-annai-jō*) either inside or very close by; they are a good place to pick up English-language maps, pamphlets and bus schedules, and the larger ones will usually have some English-speaking staff who can help with any query and may be able to assist with booking tours, activities and accommodation.

TOUR OPERATORS

Many Hokkaidō-specific tours and guides have a focus on nature or the outdoors, so if these are your main interests, then a good tour guide can provide the detailed knowledge and logistics for a great trip. They can also make travel arrangements for exploring the island, especially if you don't have a car, and ensure everything goes smoothly.

The Japanese companies listed below cover several regions, although many of them cover activities across various parts of Hokkaidō. The **Hokkaidō Mountain Guide Association** (**w** hmga.org) has a list of English-speaking local expert guides on its website.

AUSTRALIA

Wendy Wu Tours w wendywutours.com. au. Specialist Asian country tour operator, with all-inclusive trips which include the international airfares.

JAPAN

Adventure Hokkaido w adventure-hokkaido. com. Company offering group hiking, cycling & adventurous nature tours across Hokkaidō's national parks & scenic areas.

Go Hokkaido w go-hokkaido.com. An agency specialising in road trips, they offer guided private bus & car tours all over the island, plus a campervan rental service.

H2O Adventure w h2o-a.jp. Outfitter focusing on kayak, sea-kayak, rafting & SUP-board half-day tours.

Hokkaido Nature Tours w hokkaidonaturetours. com. Specialises in private & customisable 1- or 2-day tours across Hokkaidō during all seasons; longer trips available too.

Japan Nature Guides w japannatureguides. com. Hokkaidō-based owner & tour guide Mark Brazil is the foremost English-speaking authority on Japan's wildlife. His company offers birding & nature tours across the country.

Kawanoko Rafting w kawanoko.jp. Expert-led & reasonably priced rafting tours around Minami-Furano & Tomamu in central Hokkaidō; pick-ups & gear provided.

Mountain Flow w mountain-flow.com. Company run by fully certified & English-speaking female hiking & skiing guide, Michiko Aoki.

Niseko Outdoor Centre w noc-hokkaido.jp. Niseko-based operator offering guided canoeing, fishing, snowshoeing, skiing & trekking trips, plus other indoor activities.

Nomad w hokkaido-nomad.co.jp. Well-known local travel agency specialising in adventure & off-the-beaten-track destinations (previously including Sakhalin).

Picchio Wildlife Research Center w picchio. co.jp. Lots of short eco tours around the Shiretoko Peninsula.

Travel Hokkaido w yourtravelhokkaido. com. Provides trip-planning & guiding services for a range of experiences, with a focus on sustainable travel.

Travel Local w travellocal.com. A UK-based website where you can book direct with selected local travel companies, allowing you to communicate with an expert ground operator without having to go through a 3rd party travel operator or agent. Your booking with the local company has full financial protection, but note that travel to the destination is not included. Member of ABTA, ASTA.

UK

Inside Japan w insidejapantours.com. Small group & self-guided tours highlighting Japan's natural & cultural wonders.

Walk Japan w walkjapan.com. Organises guided & self-guided multi-day walking tours through some of Japan's most scenic & historic regions.

USA AND CANADA

All Japan Tours w alljapantours.com. Long-running Japan specialists offering group & private tours, including many on Hokkaidō.

Japan Deluxe Tours w japandeluxetours.com. Group & custom tours of Japan's main sights.

RED TAPE

Nationals of 68 countries and territories including the UK, USA, Canada, Australia, Hong Kong, Ireland, Korea and New Zealand, plus most European nationals are issued a temporary visitor visa upon arrival in Japan, allowing them to stay for 90 days. Upon entry to the country, all non-Japanese passport holders have their photographs and fingerprints taken. Citizens of the UK, Ireland, Germany, Switzerland and some other countries may extend their temporary visitor visa once for another 90 days, but must apply at a regional immigration bureau before the first one expires.

Nationals of more than 20 countries, including the UK, Australia, Canada, Ireland and New Zealand are eligible for working-holiday visas; applicants must be between 18 and 30 years old (or 18 and 25 for some countries) and the visa is valid for one year. Check **w** www.mofa.go.jp/j_info/visit/w_holiday/index.html for more.

For a list of **embassies and consulates** in Japan, see **w** mofa.go.jp/about/emb_cons/mofaserv.html.

CUSTOMS All passengers entering Japan must submit a Customs Declaration Form, which is usually handed out before landing and can be filled out on the plane prior to arrival. Visitors are permitted to bring three bottles of alcohol (760ml in volume per bottle), 200 cigarettes or 50 cigars, two ounces of perfume, currency up to a value of ¥1,000,000, and goods for personal use not exceeding ¥200,000 in value. Anything over these limits must be declared. Forbidden items are much the same as for many countries (drugs, firearms, explosives, pornography). For more information, see **w** customs.go.jp/english.

GETTING THERE AND AWAY

BY AIR Most visitors arrive in Japan at either Narita International Airport (near Tokyo) or Kansai International Airport (which serves Osaka/Kyoto), with other international gateways including Haneda (Tokyo), Nagoya, Fukuoka, Naha (Okinawa) and New Chitose (Sapporo). The majority of international flights arriving at New Chitose are from neighbouring Asian countries, so chances are you'll need to catch a connecting flight to Hokkaidō if flying into Japan from abroad.

Only ANA, British Airways and Japan Airlines fly directly from the UK (Heathrow) to Tokyo (Narita); all other airlines require a transfer. Other major airlines fly internationally to either Tokyo (Narita or Haneda) or Osaka (Kansai International Airport), from where you can transfer for flights to Hokkaidō.

Japanese airlines

Air Do **w** airdo.jp. Hokkaidō's regional airline, flying to & from Tokyo (Haneda), Kobe, Nagoya, Sendai & Fukuoka.

ANA **w** ana.co.jp. ANA (All Nippon Airways) operates routes between Hokkaidō & Tokyo, Osaka (Itami & Kansai), Kobe, Nagoya, Aomori, Akita, Sendai, Niigata, Fukushima, Toyama, Komatsu, Shizuoka, Okayama, Hiroshima & Fukuoka.

Fuji Dream Airlines **w** fujidream.co.jp. Regional airline with minor routes to & from Yamagata, Shinshu-Matsumoto & Shizuoka.

Ibex **w** ibexair.co.jp. Small airline with 1 route between Hokkaidō & Sendai.

Japan Airlines **w** jal.co.jp/uk/en. Japan's flag carrier & largest airline has routes to & from Tokyo (Haneda), Osaka (Itami & Kansai), Nagoya, Aomori, Iwate-Hanamaki, Akita, Sendai, Yamagata, Niigata, Shinshu-Matsumoto, Shizuoka, Izumo, Tokushima, Hiroshima & Fukuoka.

Jetstar **w** jetstar.com. Low-cost airline flying between Tokyo (Narita), Osaka (Kansai) & Hokkaidō.

Peach **w** flypeach.com. Budget airline operating routes to Tokyo (Narita), Osaka (Kansai), Nagoya, Sendai, Fukuoka & Okinawa.

Skymark **w** skymark.co.jp. Low-cost airline operating out of Tokyo (Haneda), also with routes to Hokkaidō from Kobe, Nagoya & Ibaraki.

Spring Japan **w** en.ch.com. Budget airline based at Tokyo (Narita).

Main airports Japan's fifth busiest and Hokkaidō's largest airport, **Sapporo New Chitose Airport** (新千歳空港, Shin Chitose kūkō; CTS; **w** new-chitose-airport. jp) is the main gateway to the island. It lies about 50km southeast of Sapporo and handles both domestic and a small number of international flights, with the flight corridor to Tokyo Haneda said to be the second busiest in the world in terms of passenger numbers. The airport opened in 1988 to replace the adjacent Chitose Airport, which now functions solely as an airbase for the Japan Air Self-Defence

2

Force, although they are both connected by taxiways and share the same air traffic control.

New Chitose is a well-equipped airport with two terminals (domestic and international), a 188-room hotel, a cinema, on-site hot-spring baths, plus plenty of shops and restaurants flaunting Hokkaidō's most famous wares. Transitting through the airport is usually quick and easy.

Sapporo Okadama Airport (丘珠空港; OKD; w okadama-airport.co.jp), also known as Sapporo Airfield, is much smaller and closer to the city, handling domestic turboprop flights to locations around Hokkaidō and a handful of other Japanese cities.

Airport transfers

By train JR Hokkaidō (w jrhokkaido.co.jp) runs the fast and regular Rapid Airport service which connects the airport to JR Sapporo Station (and Otaru); trains run roughly every 15 minutes, take around 40 minutes and cost ¥1,150 (non-reserved). It is a six-car train, with five of the carriages being non-reserved; only car 4 is for reserved seating, which costs an extra ¥530 and has more storage space for luggage. The JR (Japan Railways) information desk (◷ 08.30–19.00) near the ticket gates has English-speaking staff who can help with buying tickets and passes, activating your JR Pass (page 66) and all travel queries.

By bus There are regular limousine buses between the airport and various places in Sapporo including JR Sapporo Station, Nakajima Park and some popular city centre hotels. Two companies run services: Hokuto Kotsu and Hokkaidō Chūō Bus, but the fare is the same for both at ¥1,100. Buses between the airport and JR Sapporo Station take around 1 hour 20 minutes. Tickets can be purchased from the bus counter or bus ticket vending machines at the airport's bus terminals.

By road Car rental company counters are located on the first floor of the domestic terminal. If you rent a car from the airport, it takes around 1 hour to reach Sapporo and costs ¥1,330 in highway toll fees. A taxi from the airport to Sapporo is expensive at around ¥15,000–18,000.

BY TRAIN Since 1988, Hokkaidō has been connected to the mainland by rail following the opening of the Seikan Tunnel which passes beneath the Tsugaru Strait, and it is now possible to take the Shinkansen all the way from Tokyo to the current terminus of the Hokkaidō Shinkansen Line at Shin-Hakodate-Hokuto (4hrs; ¥23,630). Shinkansen trains run from JR Shin-Hakodate-Hokuto Station to JR Shin-Aomori Station on the mainland in about an hour, stopping a couple of times in between, and the 23km portion which passes beneath the seabed makes it one of the longest undersea tunnels in the world. The Hokkaidō Shinkansen Line will eventually be extended to Sapporo and will include a stop at Kuchan (Niseko) – the line is scheduled to be completed by 2031.

BY SEA The traditional way to reach Hokkaidō was by boat, and it is a relaxing way to visit the island if you have some time on your hands. There are numerous daily sailings between Aomori, the nearest big city on the mainland, and Hakodate (3hrs 40mins), plus one from Aomori to Muroran (7hrs), as well as two daily ferries from Oma (1hr 30mins), a small town at the very northern tip of Honshū.

There are also longer-distance ferries to and from Hokkaidō from much further afield in Japan; they usually have a choice of private or shared cabins or communal tatami rooms for sleeping, plus karaoke rooms, cafeterias and a bathhouse. Routes include Hachinohe–Tomakomai (8hrs), Maizuru–Otaru (20hrs), Niigata–Otaru (18hrs) and Nagoya/Sendai–Tomakomai (40hrs), which is Japan's longest ferry route, with a brief stop at Sendai midway (15hrs). Prices vary depending on season, ticket class and oil price, so it's best to check online. A summer ferry service used to run between Wakkanai and Sakhalin, but due to various geopolitical events that service is no longer in operation.

Seikan Ferry w seikan-ferry.co.jp   **Tsugaru Kaikyo Ferry** w tsugarukaikyo.co.jp
Taiheiyo Ferry w taiheiyo-ferry.co.jp

HEALTH *with Dr Daniel Campion*

Japan is a healthy and safe country by any standards, though the usual precautions should be considered and you should always take out adequate insurance before travelling.

PREPARATIONS No specific **vaccinations** are required for visiting Japan, although travellers should ensure they are up to date on all routine vaccinations, including seasonal influenza for those at higher risk. If you are planning to spend significant time (more than a month) in rural areas, you might consider getting vaccinated for Japanese encephalitis, a rare but sometimes fatal disease spread by mosquitoes. However, most human cases of Japanese encephalitis involve pig farms in the west of the country, and none has been recorded on Hokkaidō. A related tick-borne encephalitis virus has also been reported on the island, albeit very rarely – see below. Travellers at very high risk of tick exposure may wish to consider vaccination. Rabies has not been reported in pets or terrestrial wild animals in Japan, but bats may carry rabies-like viruses. Rabies vaccination before travel is recommended only for travellers at highest risk, such as people working directly with wildlife.

Be aware that bringing certain **medications** into Japan is strictly prohibited, especially anything containing Amphetamine or Methamphetamine. Commonly used inhalers and some over-the-counter decongestant medications such as Actifed, Sudafed and Vicks inhalers all contain stimulants banned in Japan (see w ncd.mhlw.go.jp/dl_data/keitai/list.pdf).

Prolonged immobility on long-haul flights can result in **deep-vein thrombosis** (DVT), which can be dangerous if the clot travels to the lungs to cause pulmonary embolus. The risk increases with age, and is higher in obese or pregnant travellers, heavy smokers, those taller than 6ft/1.8m or shorter than 5ft/1.5m, and anybody with a history of clots, recent major operation or varicose veins surgery, cancer, a stroke or heart disease. If any of these criteria apply, consult a doctor before you travel.

Travel clinics and health information A full list of current travel clinic websites worldwide is available on w istm.org. For other journey preparation information, consult w travelhealthpro.org.uk (UK) or w wwwnc.cdc.gov/travel (USA). All advice found online should be used in conjunction with expert advice received prior to or during travel.

MEDICAL PROBLEMS
Tick- and insect-borne diseases There is the small risk of contracting serious and potentially life-threatening diseases such as Lyme disease or tick-borne encephalitis from ticks in Japan. Avoiding tick bites is the best way to mitigate the risk, so if

2

Ticks should ideally be removed complete, and as soon as possible, to reduce the chance of infection. You can use special tick tweezers, which can be bought in good travel shops; or failing this, with your fingernails, grasp the tick as close to your body as possible, and pull it away steadily and firmly at right angles to your skin without jerking or twisting. Applying irritants (eg: Olbas oil) or lit cigarettes is to be discouraged as a means of removal since they can cause the ticks to regurgitate and therefore increase the risk of disease. Once the tick is removed, if possible douse the wound with alcohol (any spirit will do), soap and water, or iodine. If you are travelling with small children, remember to check their heads, and particularly behind the ears, for ticks. Spreading redness around the bite and/or fever and/or aching joints after a tick bite imply that you have an infection that requires antibiotic treatment. In this case seek medical advice.

walking in forests or grasslands, try to cover exposed areas of skin and check your body for ticks after any hike or outdoor activity. If found, they should be removed as soon as possible – see above for advice. Although the risk of Japanese encephalitis is very low on Hokkaidō, mosquito bites can be an irritant during the mild summer months. It's worth packing an insect repellent containing the active ingredients DEET, icaridin, 3-ethlyaminopropionate (IR3535) or eucalyptus citriodora oil.

Hornet stings The Japanese giant hornet (known in Japanese as *O-suzume-bachi*, the 'giant sparrow bee') is one of the world's largest hornet species, which has gained notoriety in recent years following its introduction to foreign shores – in the USA they are slightly unfairly known as 'murder hornets'. It is by far Japan's most dangerous animal and is said to be responsible for 30–50 deaths a year, a figure much higher than that for fatalities from bear attacks or snake bites. The giant hornet's sting delivers intense pain and can sometimes lead to anaphylactic shock and coma. They are said to be drawn to the colour black, so when outdoors try to avoid wearing that colour. If you do encounter a hornet, keep calm and don't flap your hands about. Although these insects are aggressive, the chances are they won't sting (unless you're threatening the nest). In the case of a sting, place the wound under running water and seek medical attention.

Rabies Rabies is a deadly disease but, as explained on page 57, most travellers are at very low risk: terrestrial rabies was eliminated from Japan 60 years ago. Bats, however, could potentially still carry rabies-like viruses. Bites or scratches from bats can usually be felt, but the small wounds may be hard to see. Rabies is preventable with timely post-exposure treatment. After any contact with a bat (even if a bite or scratch was uncertain), wash the wound thoroughly and seek medical advice.

MEDICAL TREATMENT All cities and decent-sized towns have hospitals or medical clinics, but doctors and nurses will not necessarily speak much English. **Local clinics** (called *kurinikku*, クリニック; or *naika*, 内科) accept walk-ins and are good for minor ailments and non-emergencies, but they may keep irregular hours and tend to be closed in the afternoons.

Pharmacies are known as '*doragu suto-a*' (drug stores) or *ya-kyoku* (薬局), and offer a wide range of medicines and treatments, though don't expect to see many familiar names or brands. (They are also often a good place to shop for cheap snacks, drinks and daily essentials.) Big drugstore chains with branches on Hokkaidō include Matsumoto Kiyoshi (マツモトキヨシ薬局), Sapporo Drug Store (サツドラ), Daikoku Drug (ダイコクドラッグ), Sun Drug (サンドラッグ), Tsuruha Drug (ツルハドラッグ) and Kokumin (コクミン). Dosages and strength tend to be on the low side compared with Western medicine, so it's wise to bring your regular medication from home (if not restricted; page 57).

The **cost** of medical care is relatively low, especially compared with the USA. Japanese-issued health insurance covers most of the costs for residents; travellers will have to pay for treatment (carry cash, as credit cards are not always accepted) and then (if insured) apply for reimbursement from the travel insurance company at a later date.

DRINKING WATER Tap water in Japan is generally perfectly safe to drink. But at some rural campsites and restrooms there may be signs (usually in Japanese) warning not to drink the tap water, so, if in doubt, err on the side of caution. Campers and hikers should filter or boil all water gathered at natural sources due to the risk of infection from the Echinococcus parasite which can be found in contaminated water (see below).

FACE MASKS Even before the Covid-19 pandemic it was common for Japanese people to wear face masks on public transport and when out and about, either to stop the spread of colds and viruses, for hay fever or to avoid breathing in airborne particles from dust which occasionally blows over from the Asian mainland. While staff in many establishments continue to wear masks, travellers are not obliged to do so.

PUBLIC TOILETS Japan has plenty of clean and free public toilets, often with a choice of Western-style or squat-style; high-tech toilets with bidet features and

BOILING AND FILTERING WATER TO AVOID ECHINOCOCCOSIS

Echinococcosis is a serious parasite-borne disease carried by foxes and which has a 90% fatality rate in humans if left untreated. It is caused by ingesting water (or wild plants) contaminated with the faeces of foxes infected by the Echinococcus tapeworm (thought to be up to 40% of all foxes on Hokkaidō). Once inside the body, the tapeworm's tiny eggs hatch into larvae which get into the bloodstream and make their way to various organs, typically the liver for the strain of worm most commonly found on Hokkaidō. The larvae cause tumours which, if not removed, lead to almost certain death, and symptoms take a long time to develop – between five and ten years – by which time the damage may already be done. This disease is found in many Northern Hemisphere countries, but Hokkaidō is the only place in Japan where the risk is notable.

Thankfully, the disease is easy to avoid if you follow good hygiene and water-boiling practices when out in the wilds. The most important rule to follow is to boil (at 100°C for 1min, or 60°C for 10mins) or filter all water collected from natural water sources (including rivers, springs, snow melt, etc) before drinking, and also make sure to wash your hands as regularly as possible and clean any collected wild plants if intended for consumption.

a multitude of buttons are common. Toilet paper is almost always provided, but in more rural locations there may be no soap or hand towels, so it's a good idea to carry a handkerchief or small towel for drying and a small bottle of hand sanitiser.

SAFETY

Japan is one of the world's safest countries for visitors. People often walk alone at night, leave their laptops unattended in cafés, and if you do lose something valuable there is a high chance it will be returned, handed in somewhere, or found exactly where you left it. Cases of pickpocketing, assaults or robberies are extremely rare, although umbrellas and bicycles are said to be the most commonly stolen items. In the larger cities, however, groping and sexual assaults are a hazard for women, especially on tightly packed commuter trains, so caution is advised. Don't hesitate to alert station staff if you experience or witness this type of behaviour.

NATURAL HAZARDS Hokkaidō (and almost the whole of Japan) is subject to various natural hazards. **Earthquakes** can cause death, injury and damage; although buildings may shake considerably, most modern-built ones are fairly resistant. It is the associated threat of tsunamis which can be even more devastating (as was the case in Tohoku on 11 March 2011).

Volcanoes are constantly monitored, and the authorities will limit access if there is a perceived imminent threat; but that doesn't rule out the chance of a sudden unexpected eruption (such as the one at Mount Norikura in central Honshū which killed more than 60 hikers in 2014). There are 20 volcanoes on Hokkaidō listed as active at present.

Typhoons are a mostly seasonal hazard; they generally occur from around July to October and make landfall a handful of times a year. While they tend to affect the south and west of the country the worst, Hokkaidō still gets hit by the tail end of them as they travel northwards. Typhoons can result in heavy rain, flooding, strong winds and landslides (even if they are downgraded to tropical storm status), and they often severely disrupt transport for a day or two.

POLICE The police in Japan (✆110) deal arguably less frequently with serious crime than their counterparts in many other countries; instead they can often be seen waiting in their cars to catch unsuspecting speeders, or be stationed at a *koban* (police box) to assist with lost items and offering directions. It is a legal requirement always to carry your passport (or resident card), as the police are known (and have the right) occasionally to stop foreigners and ask them for identification. The police also have substantial powers to detain a suspect without charge for up to 48 hours, which can be extended to ten days (plus a further ten days) if a judge can be swayed. If you do find yourself on the wrong side of the law, then it's best to request help from your embassy and insist on an interpreter.

DRUGS Japan has an extremely tough stance on drugs. There are long prison sentences and hefty fines even for first-time recreational users; drug smugglers face life imprisonment (not the death penalty as in many other Asian countries). Methamphetamines are said to be the most widely used drug in Japan, and possession of even a small amount of cannabis can result in a five-year prison sentence. Also be aware that some common non-prescription medicines from abroad are banned in Japan. Bringing prescribed medications for personal use also has restrictions; see w mhlw.go.jp/english/policy/health-medical/pharmeauticals/01.html for details.

WOMEN TRAVELLERS

Hokkaidō (and Japan in general) is generally a very safe place for women, although sexual assaults are a common enough occurrence on public transport in the larger cities that there are women-only carriages in the likes of Tokyo and Osaka. On Hokkaidō there is probably less risk, but female travellers should still take the usual precautions as they would anywhere else, especially when walking around drinking districts or if alone at night.

TRAVELLING WITH A DISABILITY

In Japan, large train stations, shopping malls and popular attractions have lifts, access ramps and accessible toilet facilities for wheelchair users, and staff at train stations will help you on and off trains with a movable ramp. Some higher-end hotels have accessible rooms (known as 'barrier-free'). However, many restaurants, hotels and shops can be too cramped for wheelchair users, and especially in smaller cities and rural areas on Hokkaidō pavements are not always in good condition.

The **Accessible Japan** (w accessible-japan.com) and **Barrier Free Japan** (w barrierfreejapan.com) websites offer lots of good information for travellers with a disability. In addition, the UK's **gov.uk** website (w gov.uk/government/publications/disabled-travellers/disability-and-travel-abroad) has a downloadable guide giving general advice and practical information for travellers with a disability (and their companions) preparing for overseas travel. The **Society for Accessible Travel and Hospitality** (w sath.org) also provides some general information.

LGBTQIA+ TRAVELLERS

Travellers are unlikely to experience any discrimination in Japan; homosexuality is legal, although Japan is the only G7 nation that does not have legal protection for same-sex unions, and many keep their relationships discreet in a country where public outward displays of affection are not common regardless of sexual orientation.

Sapporo has a small but vibrant gay and lesbian scene, plus an annual Pride parade (w sprrainbowpride.com). Most of the city's small number of gay bars are located in or around the No 6. G ビル (formerly known as the SA Building) in the southwest part of Susukino, about three blocks west and four south of the main junction.

TRAVELLING WITH CHILDREN

Japan is for the most part a great place to travel with kids, and Hokkaidō in particular is great for active families who enjoy hiking, camping, nature, skiing, snowboarding and general snowy or outdoor activities.

Most hotels can usually provide a cot for an additional fee, and *ryokan* and *minshuku* are usually quite accommodating of families with children, although young (and not so young) fussy eaters may struggle with the traditional breakfasts. When eating out, family restaurants such as Gusto, Saizeriya and Royal Host have kids' meals and semi-familiar Western-style dishes; food courts in shopping malls are another good option. Larger cities and train stations have facilities for nappy-changing and feeding, but don't expect much out in the more provincial areas. Pharmacies are the best place to find nappies, wipes and baby food.

Children under the age of six can travel on trains (including the Shinkansen) for free, while those between the ages of 6 and 11 can ride for half the adult fare. Many museums and attractions are free for children up until about junior-high-school age (13 years old), or have discounted entry for under 18s. At the onsen, boys up to the age of about eight or nine may enter the female baths with their mother or female guardian; the same applies to fathers and daughters, though it's less common.

WHAT TO TAKE

You can buy pretty much everything you would ever need in Japan, and so it's best to pack as light as possible to make travelling easier; even in big cities such as Sapporo you can end up doing a fair amount of walking between train stations and hotels, and using public transport while lugging big heavy suitcases is not much fun.

It may be difficult to buy clothing and footwear for larger (or even almost average Western) frames in Japan, however, so pack accordingly. You should always bring a warm layer or two even if visiting in the summer, as Hokkaidō, more so than other regions of Japan, can still get chilly at times. If visiting in the winter, you will need plenty of warm layers and suitable winter weather gear (see below). Shoes that are easy to slip on and off can save a lot of hassle in Japan, as you may be required to remove your shoes at some restaurants, ryokan and temples or shrines.

ELECTRICITY Japan has two electricity frequencies – 50hz in eastern Japan (which includes Tokyo, Tōhoku and Hokkaidō) and 60hz in western Japan (Kyoto, Osaka, Hiroshima) – but almost all equipment works at both frequencies.

The voltage in Japan is 100V, which is less than most of Europe and America. Electronic devices from abroad will work fine (apart from heating appliances such as hair irons, unless they are international), but if you buy electronic items in Japan

PACKING FOR HOKKAIDŌ IN WINTER

Hokkaidō is famed for its cold and snowy winters, so if visiting between late November and late March you will need to pack accordingly. A good warm winter jacket is essential – preferably one that is wind and rain (or at least splash) proof and has a hood. Materials which allow snow to be brushed off easily make you less likely to get wet and cold. Thermal clothing is great for outdoors, but inside buildings and on public transport it is usually well heated, so it's a good idea to wear layers which can be easily put on/removed as and when needed. Other useful winter garments include a warm hat, scarf/neck warmer, earmuffs, gloves (preferably more than one pair) and a few pairs of wool socks. Footwear is very important, as even city streets tend to be snow and ice covered – think insulated waterproof boots that will keep snow away from your feet. On Hokkaidō you can buy snowshoes with built-in spikes on the soles to help with grip on the icy streets, or there are non-slip covers for your existing shoes if you find you are slipping and sliding everywhere.

for use abroad, you will need to check that they will work at higher voltages. Plugs are American-style, with two parallel flat prongs. Adaptors can be bought in large electronic stores and at major airports.

MAPS In the age of smartphones, Google Maps and satellite navigation, the halcyon days of relying on paper maps and road atlases for a trip are now mostly long gone. That said, tourist information centres offer free English-language regional and sightseeing maps which can be useful and are often worth picking up. For bikers and cyclists, the Hokkaidō Touring Mapple map book (ツーリングマップル北海道), available in bookshops and online, is an excellent Japanese resource, as it even includes forestry roads.

In terms of smartphone apps, Maps.me is very useful for navigating when there is no Wi-Fi – download the maps for Hokkaidō before heading out. Hikers may want to check out an app called Yamap, which has maps and trail reports for almost every Japanese mountain, although free accounts are restricted to only two downloadable maps per month. An excellent online resource is the Hokkaido Wilds website (w hokkaidowilds.org), which offers an ever-increasing selection of high-quality and free downloadable maps for backcountry ski routes and other outdoor activities.

MONEY

The unit of currency in Japan is the Japanese yen (¥). Banknotes come in denominations of ¥10,000, ¥5,000, ¥2,000 (these are rare) and ¥1,000, and coins in denominations of ¥500, ¥100, ¥50, ¥10, ¥5 and ¥1. It is always a good idea to carry some coins for using at vending machines (except ¥5 and ¥1 coins which are not accepted) and on buses (which do not offer change).

Your best bet for **changing money** into other currencies is at major airports, large banks, post offices, hotels and at some large train stations. There are some currency exchange services dotted around Sapporo; operated by MUFG, the World Currency Shop in Sapporo (ワールドカレンシーショップ札幌店; ⊕ 10.00–13.00 & 14.15–17.00 Mon–Fri) offers good rates and service. However, you'll probably receive the best exchange rate when simply withdrawing cash from an ATM.

The easiest place to withdraw money in Japan for visitors is often at a 7-Eleven convenience store; their Seven Bank **ATMs** have an English-language option and accept foreign-issued credit and debit cards, plus most stores are open 24/7. Other convenience stores may have ATMs too. Another option is the post office: Japan Post Bank ATMs can be found inside all post offices and at some train stations, and they also have English instructions and accept foreign cards. The main drawback is that the ATM may only be accessible for slightly longer than the post office's opening hours. The withdrawal limit is ¥100,000 per transaction at Seven Bank ATMs, and ¥50,000 at Japan Post Bank machines.

Japan is often said to be a cash-based society, but these days this is certainly changing as most hotels, restaurants, shops and attractions in the bigger cities take credit and debit cards for payment, with Visa and MasterCard the most commonly accepted. But small, older establishments and many places in more rural regions may only accept cold hard cash, so it is always a good idea to carry as much as you think you'll need for those trips outside the main urban areas.

TAX REFUNDS Japan has a tax-exemption policy for tourists, with the 8% or 10% VAT on consumer and consumable goods refundable at the point of purchase; you will need to buy from a store displaying the red-and-white 'Tax-free shop' logo

2

(larger stores will often have a dedicated desk), and present your passport when paying; you may also have to fill out a small form. The tax refund can only be applied to items or multiple items in a single transaction with a minimum purchase amount of ¥5,000.

BUDGETING

Japan isn't nearly as expensive for travellers as it used to be, especially with the weak yen and numerous affordable dining options, and with some careful planning and a bit of knowledge it is possible to make your money go a long way.

CHEAP Business hotels offer affordable, small rooms in convenient locations, but if you want to go even cheaper then capsule hotels and hostels can be half to a third of the price. Camping and using onsen to freshen up reduces accommodation costs to the bare minimum. You can fill yourself up at *shokudō* and noodle restaurants for little more than ¥1,000; lunchtime is cheaper than dinner at higher-end places. Convenience stores sell *bentō* boxes, cup noodles, sandwiches and rice balls for meals at a pinch, but supermarkets and grocery stores often have similar items at slightly cheaper prices; hit the shops in the early evening for sometimes heavy discounts on food-to-go.

Buses are generally cheaper than taking the train over long distances; night buses save on accommodation too.

MID-RANGE A budget of around ¥15,000 per day allows you to stay in comfortable accommodation, eat a good meal for dinner and lunch and still have a bit left for train rides and attractions.

LUXURY Joining custom tours will take the hassle out of travel, and allow you to see and experience things that will only elevate your trip. If money is no real object, then you can splash out on high-end hotels, ryokan and ski lodges, and in Sapporo in particular there are no end of fine restaurants and swanky bars to enjoy.

TIPPING There is no tipping culture in Japan at all, which makes completing most transactions incredibly straightforward. In fact, if you do leave someone a tip, they are more likely to chase you down the street to return it rather than accept it. But if you do insist that someone's kind service merits something, then it is perhaps best to offer a small gift instead of money, though it may be accepted reluctantly (but gratefully).

There is one exception to this non-tipping rule, however: when staying at a very high-end ryokan, it is sometimes customary, though not obligatory, to leave a tip (called *kokorozuke*) for the serving lady (*nakai-san*) who leads you to your room, serves you dinner, sets out the futon, clears up, etc. At high-end properties guests are assigned one person to attend to all their needs for the duration of their stay, and so it is not uncommon to give a small sum of money (perhaps a few thousand yen), neatly wrapped in tissue paper or possibly placed in an envelope, and handed to them at a discreet and opportune moment towards the end of the stay.

GETTING AROUND

Japan is an easy country to explore for foreign travellers, owing to its superb and reliable transport infrastructure, dutifully helpful staff and the kindness of locals.

Trains and stations usually have plenty of English signage and announcements, especially in the bigger cities.

BY TRAIN Japan's railway network is famously punctual, and extensive, with around 70% of train lines in the country operated by JR (Japan Railways). JR Hokkaidō (w jrhokkaido.co.jp) operates all of the railways on the island; their website has plenty of useful information on routes, timetables, rail passes and service status updates. The railway network on Hokkaidō was once far more extensive than it is today, but due to dwindling passenger numbers, many lines and stations have been shut down over the years. Hokkaidō's harsh winter weather and frequently deep snow means that trains are delayed sometimes, but locomotives are equipped with massive snowploughs to help carve a way through snowfalls which would otherwise bring the entire network to a complete standstill in most other countries.

Train types There are many types of trains in Japan, but they usually fall into the following categories: local (普通, *futsū*), the slowest trains which stop at all stations; **rapid** (快速, *kaisoku*), faster trains, which skip the smaller stations; **express** (急行, *kyūkō*), which stop ever fewer times than rapid trains and may require an extra seating fee; the confusingly named **limited express** (特急, *tokyū*), which are the fastest of all, stopping at major stations and which require an extra seating fee; and **bullet trains** (新幹線, *shinkansen*), which are operated by JR but run on their own network, and can reach speeds of over 300km/h. Currently the Shinkansen Line runs only as far as Hakodate in southern Hokkaidō, but will eventually be extended to Sapporo.

There are also sightseeing or special **seasonal trains**, which operate in scenic areas such as Furano/Biei and Kushiro-Shitsugen National Park – reservations are recommended.

Tickets Tickets for short journeys on local trains can be purchased at ticket vending machines – find your destination station on the information board and note its corresponding fare (or check how much the fare is online), put your money in the machine and select the correct fare from the options listed. For longer-distance trains you can sometimes purchase tickets from a ticket machine, but if in doubt, it's best to go to the JR Ticket Counter (みどりの窓口, *midori-no-madoguchi*); reserved seat tickets can also be purchased there. Some ticket machines have an English-language function.

Note that the first-class/business-class green seat and gran class (on the Shinkansen) are considerably more expensive than regular tickets. The cheaper non-reserved and standard reserved seat prices are quoted in this guide.

Luggage Most large stations have lifts for passengers with mobility problems, and for those travelling with pushchairs and heavy luggage; they also often have lockers of varying sizes in which you can store baggage, usually costing between ¥300 and ¥800 per day for a maximum of three days. Don't expect such luxuries at smaller stations, however.

BY AIR Flying can be a time-efficient way to reach the furthest corners of Hokkaidō. Daily (and some seasonal) flights with ANA and Japan Airlines connect New Chitose Airport to Hakodate (35mins), Kushiro (45mins), Memanbetsu (45mins), Nakashibetsu (50mins), Wakkanai (55mins) and Rishiri (55mins). Fuji Dream Airlines and Japan Airlines operate some regional routes to and from Sapporo's Okadama Airport, including Kushiro (45mins), Hakodate (40mins),

Practical Information GETTING AROUND

2

A wide range of discount rail passes are available in Japan, the most popular of which is undoubtedly the **JR Rail Pass** (w japanrailpass.net). This useful pass allows for unlimited and nationwide travel on all JR trains (including express trains and all but Nozomi and Mizuho classes of Shinkansen), JR buses and even some ferries. Unlike the Hokkaidō-specific passes, it is also valid for the Hokkaidō Shinkansen. Passes are available for 7-, 14- and 21-day durations (¥50,000/80,000/100,000), with a Green Pass for travelling in the business-class 'green' train carriages.

The JR Rail Pass is only available for foreign travellers with a 'Temporary Visitor' stamp in their passport, and should be bought up to three months in advance, before arriving in Japan, from an authorised travel agency. You will receive an 'exchange order' which should be taken along with your passport to a JR Travel Service Centre (located at Narita, Haneda and Kansai Airports and at most major train stations), where you can obtain your rail pass. At that time you can choose to activate your pass immediately or set it for a later date (which may be convenient if you plan to stay put for a few days). Once activated, the pass allows you to travel freely on any non-reserved trains and for reserved seats you can make reservations at any midori-no-madoguchi ('green window' ticket counter). To use the JR Rail Pass, just insert it into the slot like a regular ticket when passing through a ticket gate.

In October 2023, the JR Rail Pass saw a substantial price increase (of about 66%), so it is now not the bargain it once was, but is still a good investment if you intend to travel extensively around Japan. Note that the JR Rail Pass can be used on the Hokkaidō Shinkansen (but requires a seat reservation).

Region-specific passes are available for almost all parts of Japan, and Hokkaidō is no different. The **Hokkaidō Rail Pass** (w jrhokkaido.co.jp/global/english/ticket/railpass/index) allows for unlimited travel on all JR Hokkaidō lines, but is not valid for the Hokkaidō Shinkansen. It is valid for both non-reserved and reserved seats (for seat reservations, you must get a reserved seat ticket before boarding the train, either online or at the station ticket counter). It can also be used for travel on JR Hokkaidō buses. There are two types of Hokkaidō Rail Pass: five-day (adult/child ¥19,000/9,500) and seven-day (adult/child ¥25,000/12,500). Similar to the JR Pass,

---

Memanbetsu (45mins), Okushiri (30mins) and Rishiri (50mins). See page 55 for these airlines' websites.

BY BUS Buses run between all of Hokkaidō's main cities and to pretty much every corner of the island, including some surprisingly remote locations. Much like the trains, they tend to run on time; check bus terminals and tourist information centres for English-language bus timetables.

Long-distance highway buses (*kosoku-basu*) and **night buses** are often the cheapest way to travel far and wide, and connect most of Hokkaidō's main cities. Many buses have Wi-Fi and toilets and are fairly comfortable, and night buses can save you a night's accommodation fee too. Willer Express (w willerexpress.com/en) offers online reservations and has a good-value Japan Bus Pass for durations of three, five or seven days' use. Other useful websites include w japanbusonline.com and w kosokubus.com, which allow online reservations for many different bus routes and companies in Japan. Large bus terminals and tourist information centres can provide English-language information on routes, schedules and fares.

these can be used by foreign visitors only (with a 'Temporary Visitor' stamp in their passport), and can be purchased up to three months in advance at a travel agency in your country of origin (see website for listings). You will receive an 'exchange order' which can be exchanged for a rail pass at a designated counter when you arrive on Hokkaidō. You can also purchase one online (w eki-net.com/en/jreast-train-reservation/top/index), or at a designated counter when you arrive in Japan, although for both of these methods the cost is ¥1,000 (¥500 for children) more. Designated counters can be found at the following stations: New Chitose Airport, Abashiri, Asahikawa, Hakodate, Kushiro, Noboribetsu, Obihiro, Sapporo and Shin-Hakodate-Hokuto. The pass is also available at Narita and Haneda airports, and many of Tokyo's larger stations.

Two other useful regional passes for foreign visitors are available on Hokkaidō, but both are valid for non-reserved seats only. The **Sapporo-Noboribetsu Area Pass** (¥8,000/4,000) is a four-day pass offering unlimited rides on JR trains between New Chitose Airport, Sapporo, Otaru and Noboribetsu and is available from the ticket counters at New Chitose Airport, Sapporo and Noboribetsu stations. The **Sapporo-Furano Area Pass** (¥9,000/4,500) is a four-day pass for unlimited travel on JR trains between New Chitose Airport, Sapporo, Otaru, Furano, Biei and Asahikawa. It can be purchased from the ticket counters at New Chitose Airport, Sapporo and Asahikawa stations.

IC cards are prepaid travel cards for use on trains, subways, buses and trams in metropolitan areas, and each big city has its own variation (such as Kitaca, Pasmo, Suica and Icoca), but they can all be used nationwide in any other metropolitan area interchangeably. Sapporo's IC card is called Sapica and can be used for trains, buses and the subway in the Sapporo area, but not anywhere else on Hokkaidō. IC cards are available from any ticket vending machine in the city and require a ¥500 deposit; this can be refunded at the end of your trip by returning the card to a JR ticket window. IC cards are very simple to use: simply top up the card with funds at a ticket machine, then place it over the reader at ticket gates to pass through (or swipe near the door on buses and trams). Some convenience stores and vending machines also accept IC cards as a form of payment.

Local **city buses** can be good and affordable ways to see places on the edge of town, but they are not always completely tourist friendly – check the local bus terminal or tourist information centre for English-language bus schedules and more detailed information.

Particularly popular with domestic visitors, many bus companies operate **tour buses** throughout Hokkaidō, and these can often be a very efficient and cost-effective way to see a number of sights in a particular region. HIS (w his-j.com; in English) is one of Japan's largest travel operators, offering a variety of tours. Alternatively, ask at tourist information centres for the latest tours and more up-to-date information, or check the websites of the regional bus operators listed in each chapter.

BY CAR Driving in Japan is fairly straightforward and driving on Hokkaidō in particular can be a pure joy owing to its many wide, open roads, pleasant scenery and relatively little traffic. Cars drive on the left and most place names on road signs are also written in English. Japanese drivers are mostly very law-abiding, although Hokkaidō does have the highest ratio of traffic accident fatalities in

Japan – this is likely due to speeding on rural roads and the sometimes adverse weather conditions. The rich abundance of wildlife can also cause problems for road users; collisions with wildlife such as deer is a particular problem, especially on the eastern end of the island.

Car hire You must apply for an international driver's license before coming to Japan if you want to rent a car. Two of the most popular car rental companies are Hertz (w hertz.com) and Toyota Rent a Car (w rent.toyota.co.jp/en), which have many offices around the country, usually conveniently located at airports or near train stations. It's worth checking online for local car rental companies, too. Prices vary depending on the type and size of vehicle, but expect around ¥5,000 per day for compact cars and up to ¥15,000 for large cars, more for vans; note that rates often increase during peak seasons. Cars are usually expected to be returned with a full tank of petrol.

Most rental cars are equipped with a satnav, but it may be worth double-checking that it has an English-language function. It is sometimes easiest to enter your destination's phone number when operating it. Cars will come equipped with snow tyres during the winter.

Road rules Hokkaidō has more traffic accidents than anywhere else in Japan, mostly due to speeding on the enticingly long and empty roads and the frequently adverse winter weather. Usual road rules must be followed; the Japan Automobile Federation (JAF; w english.jaf.or.jp) publishes a *Rules of the Road* guidebook in English, available in print and e-book form (see the website for details), which drivers will find useful. Some basic rules worth remembering are: that vehicles drive on the left; red lights always mean 'stop', although a green arrow means you can turn in that direction; and always come to a complete stop at a railway crossing and look both ways and ahead before proceeding. See w hokkaido.japandrive.com for useful driving tips and information specific to Hokkaidō.

When there are no **speed limit** signs or markings, the maximum speed is 60km/h on ordinary roads and 100km/h on expressways. Seat belts should be worn by all occupants of the vehicle, and children under six years old must use a child seat

UNIQUE ROADSIDE INFRASTRUCTURE

While driving around Hokkaidō, you may notice various roadside infrastructures which are not so common in the rest of Japan.

Almost all roads are lined with red-and-white poles at regular intervals along the roadside – these mark the edge of the road, which is very useful for navigation in winter whiteouts. In other places you may spot taller poles which arch over and have red-and-white arrows pointing downwards to mark the edge of the asphalt; they sometimes have solar-powered flashing lights to make them more noticeable in bad weather.

In places where snow frequently builds up and drifts across the road, there are sturdy snow fences to keep the snow at bay, or sometimes roads pass through concrete tunnels which allow vehicles to move through areas where large snowdrifts are common. You may also spot huge metal snow gates next to the road – these are usually kept open, but in severe winter conditions they may be used to close off a road when the authorities are literally too snowed under to keep the route clear.

GENERAL

- The best time for driving on Hokkaidō is May to October if you want to avoid snow.
- Watch your speed on seemingly empty roads; Hokkaidō has a high rate of road traffic accidents.
- Be cautious of wildlife (particularly deer), a common cause of accidents.
- Signposts usually have English, but signs warning of road-closures (通行止, *tsūkōdome*) tend to be in Japanese.
- Petrol stations and convenience stores tend to close around 19.00–20.00, especially in small countryside towns.

IN WINTER

- Check the weather beforehand, and if possible, delay your journey if bad weather is expected.
- Drive slowly on ice or snow-covered roads, keeping a greater distance than usual between the next vehicle and yourself.
- On icy roads apply the brakes gently to avoid the wheels locking; if the wheels lock then ease off the brakes and reapply again slowly. For cars with ABS (anti-lock brake system), keep firm pressure on the brakes to activate the function.
- Avoid sudden or rapid acceleration and deceleration as this may cause the car to spin out of control.
- Always pack snacks, warm drinks and extra warm clothing for emergency use, and keep the fuel tank from running low.
- Keep the exhaust pipe clear of snow (a blocked pipe can cause carbon monoxide poisoning if the engine is running).

(available for a small extra fee from rental agencies). Be aware that Japan has some of the strictest drink-drive laws in the world: you are considered over the limit if you have over 0.15ml of alcohol in 1 litre of breath, so drivers effectively should not drink anything before getting behind the wheel.

Road types There are various types of road on Hokkaidō. In addition to those described below, there are also a plethora of smaller local roads, farm roads, etc, but be aware that these minor roads may not be accessible at all in winter.

Expressways (高速道路, *kōsoku-dōro*) are the network of high-speed toll roads found across Japan. They are designated by green signs with an 'E' for 'expressway' (or 'C' for 'circular' in some other regions of Japan), followed by a number (eg: E5). They tend to be two- or four-laned with a default maximum speed limit of 100km/h, or an absolute maximum of 120km/h in some variable-speed locations. Slow vehicles (such as mopeds and bicycles) unable to reach 50km/h are prohibited from using expressways.

Be warned that expressway **tolls** are expensive. There are some sections of toll-free expressway, but otherwise tolls are paid by taking a ticket at entry to the expressway and paying at a booth or machine when exiting. The ETC (Electronic Toll Collection) card system allows cars with it installed to pay and pass through toll gates automatically. At toll gates, head through the automatic 'ETC' gates only if your vehicle is equipped with an ETC card (check to see if one is included with your rental); otherwise, enter and exit toll roads using the general (一般, *ippan*) gates, where you can collect the ticket or pay the fee. Tolls are generally calculated on distance travelled (approx ¥25 yen/km) and size of the vehicle, plus a ¥150 terminal charge. This makes toll fees in Japan quite expensive compared with those in other countries – the standard toll for a small car travelling the 125km between Sapporo and Asahikawa, for example, is around ¥3,380. There is usually a 30% discount if travelling late at night (midnight–04.00) or during holidays and weekends.

There is a Hokkaidō Expressway Pass (w en.driveplaza.com/drawari/hokkaido_expass) available only to foreign visitors, though, which allows unlimited use of Hokkaidō's expressways for a flat rate, which may save you money if you intend to drive fairly long distances over multiple days.

National Highway Routes (国道, *kokudō*) are indicated by blue signs with a two- or three-digit number, and these make up the vast majority of main roads on Hokkaidō. The speed limit is usually around 50–60km/h (30–40km/h in urban areas), and outside of the cities there is usually very little congestion.

Forestry roads (林道, *rindou*) slice through some of Hokkaidō's wildest and most remote country but are not generally recommended for most typical road vehicles as they usually have rough, gravel surfaces and are rarely well maintained. They can offer good opportunities for adventure for cyclists with rugged tyres and appropriate outdoor gear (page 72).

Roadside service stations

Literally meaning 'road station', *michi-no-eki* (道の駅) are a staple of road travel on Hokkaidō (with more than 120, it has the most of any prefecture) and sometimes offer much more than merely a place to rest for weary drivers. At the very minimum, michi-no-eki offer free parking and clean toilets open 24/7 throughout the year, and usually there are vending machines selling hot and cold drinks. Most have restaurants offering nourishing and local speciality dishes, plus shops selling fresh regional produce and souvenirs, and many have information on nearby sights of interest; a few also have showers and onsen for freshening up.

While all in Japanese, the website w michi-no-eki.jp has details of every service station on Hokkaidō, as well as others across Japan.

BY TAXI Taxis in Japan are trustworthy and reliable, although not cheap (but you don't need to tip). They can be found at taxi ranks outside major stations, department stores and some hotels, and in the bigger cities you can usually hail one on the street. When you see an oncoming taxi, look for the small light on the passenger side: green means it is already occupied, but red means vacant. At night, available taxis will often have a sign lit up on their roof too. There will usually be a base fare, which quickly increases depending on distance travelled, and many companies add an extra surcharge (up to 20–25%) between around 22.00 and 05.00. There are three standard taxi sizes in Japan: small (小型, *kogata*), medium (中型, *chūgata*) and large (大型, *ōgata*), and fares are higher for larger vehicles. But most standard taxis (which can carry up to four passengers) are the small type. In winter many taxis are equipped with snowboard and ski roof racks.

Drivers don't necessarily speak any English at all, so have your destination written down in Japanese. Cash and credit cards are generally accepted for payment. While taxis are numerous in the bigger cities, don't expect such luck when venturing further afield – you'll have to either book one ahead of time or call a local taxi company upon arrival at a local train station (phone numbers are often listed at the station; English is rarely spoken).

BY BIKE Cycling tours and bike-packing trips are fabulous ways to explore Hokkaidō at your own pace (see page 72 for cycle tour operators). Although the harsh winters up here do take their toll on surfaces more than anywhere else in Japan, roads are generally smooth and well maintained. Traffic tends to be quiet, scenic coastal roads almost beg to be explored on two wheels, and many stretches of long, flat tarmac pass through bucolic farmland and picturesque farmsteads. The best choice of accommodation may be mostly limited to major settlements, but there are minshuku, pensions, rider houses and rural hot-spring hotels in many backwater locations, and if you have a tent then the numerous campsites and michi-no-eki dotted around the island extend your options immensely; onsen offer a place for cyclists to take a bath, freshen up and often grab a meal.

Road bikes will cope with all standard routes, while rougher forestry roads (page 72) require bicycles built for rugged terrain. There are a few dedicated cycling lanes on Hokkaidō, although the usually wide and empty normal roads mean that contending with heavy traffic is rarely an issue. Tunnels, however, are numerous and cycling through them occasionally nerve-wracking – the narrower older ones tend to have very little in the way of a shoulder or pavement for cyclists or pedestrians, and truck drivers aren't especially known for their caution, even in polite and courteous Japan.

In road traffic law, bicycles are considered 'light vehicles' and so cyclists must follow all standard road rules (including not drinking and riding). In cities it is common for people to cycle along pavements and not wear a helmet, although both are technically prohibited (but very rarely enforced). If taking a bicycle on the train, you will have to partially dismantle it and carry it in a bike bag.

Early May to mid-November is the best time for cycling (although midsummer is increasingly uncomfortably hot and humid); go before or after those dates and you will likely have to contend with snow. Bear in mind that the sun is strong at these latitudes, so wear sunscreen even on overcast days. Winter bike tours on a 'fat tire' bike are feasible, if you (and your bike) can handle the deep snow, extreme cold and more limited facilities.

Websites with useful information on cycling routes include: w cycle-hokkaido.jp, w hokkaidowilds.org and w hokkaido.cci.or.jp/cycletourism-hokkaido/guidebook/HCT_pamphlet_e.pdf.

NATIONAL CYCLE ROUTE: TOKAPUCHI 400

Japan's National Cycle Routes are government-endorsed cycling routes in areas of great scenery which have provisions, facilities and accommodation options for cyclists along the way. The Tokapuchi 400 was selected as the first (and so far, only) National Cycle Route on Hokkaidō – this 403km route starts and ends in the city of Obihiro and loops in a figure of eight, taking in the scenic farmland of the Tokachi Plain plus the lakes and foothills of Daisetsuzan National Park, including a climb up to the Mikuni Pass, Hokkaidō's highest road pass. Cycle stations at each designated section of the route offer year-round bike rentals, repairs, maps and rest spaces, and blue-and-white road markings signify the route. If that all sounds a bit much, then it is possible to do shorter-length sections such as the 96km Panorama Course and the 91km Garden Course. The tourist information centre in Obihiro (page 209) is a good place to go to get started.

2

Known as *rindou* (林道), Hokkaidō's gravel forestry roads crisscross some of the island's most impenetrable terrain, and can offer almost limitless adventure for well-equipped and self-sufficient cyclists with a robust pair of wheels. Some of these tracks can offer a smooth ride and serve as useful links between places, while others may be rough and all but impassable, especially as they can often be damaged, washed out, blocked by fallen trees and broken bridges or be completely overgrown. Some roads damaged by recent typhoons have not yet been (and may never be) repaired. Try to get local, up-to-date information beforehand; just because a track is marked on a map there is no guarantee that it will be rideable.

Keep an eye out for signs saying 直行止 (no-through pass) as there will likely be no way to proceed down the road ahead. Also bear in mind that, if you get into trouble, you could well be out of mobile phone range and many hours from help. And speaking of bears, when travelling on these remote tracks through the woods, it's wise to attach a bear bell to your bicycle, and take necessary precautions if wild camping (page 74). Having said all that, forestry roads are a great way to really get away from it all and explore Hokkaidō's wild interior deeply.

Cycling tour operators

Adventure Hokkaido
w adventure-hokkaido.com
Cycling Tours Japan w cyclingtoursjapan.com

Journey into Japan w journeyintojapan.com
Oka Tours w okatours.com

BY FERRY Ferries connect mainland Hokkaidō to some of the smaller outlying islands. Up in the north, Rishiri and Rebun can be reached from Wakkanai by Heartland Ferry (w heartlandferry.jp); the same company also operates ferries to Okushiri from the port of Esashi in southwest Hokkaidō. Ferries to the tiny islands of Teuri and Yagishiri are operated by Haboro Enkai Ferry (w haboro-enkai.com).

ON FOOT Walking around towns and cities is usually no problem on Hokkaidō, but it can be quite gruelling for long distances along straight, empty roads or when it gets hilly. Outside of urban areas there are very few pavements.

While **hitchhiking** is not common in Japan, foreign travellers sometimes report success, with drivers being known to go well out of their way to help someone get from A to B. You'll probably have more luck on well-travelled countryside roads, where passers-by may take the most pity on your situation. As in all countries, however, use your common sense when getting into a stranger's car, and offer some money for fuel when saying your goodbyes (it will probably be refused).

ACCOMMODATION

Accommodation on Hokkaidō comes in many guises, and generally the bigger the town or city the more options there will be. It is usually best to book ahead if possible, as smaller places with more limited options may become fully booked during popular periods. These days credit cards are accepted in most hotels, but cash is king everywhere else, especially outside of the major settlements. Not all guesthouses can be booked online; in those cases, you may be able to email, or more likely call. Hotels, ryokan and minshuku often include dinner and breakfast plans, but usually have a cheaper room-only (no meals) option – this is called *sudomari* (素泊まり) in Japanese.

Some useful websites for Japan-specific bookings are: w jalan.net, a popular discount accommodation website, useable in English; w japaneseinngroup.com, for bookings in ryokan and small inns; w japanican.com, a site run by JTB, one of Japan's biggest travel agencies.

HOSTELS Hokkaidō has numerous hostels (ホステル) catering to not only young backpackers and students but more mature clientèle too. Hostels may offer dorm-style bunks, capsule-style compartments, partitioned private rooms and sometimes even small guestrooms. Japan Youth Hostel (w jyh.or.jp) lists their network of properties, but there are many independent establishments too.

HOTELS The larger cities have many hotels (ホテル) to choose from, but in rural areas you may be limited to fairly dated or basic business-style hotels near the centre of town, or possibly a more expensive resort or hot-spring hotel further out in the sticks. Hostel-style hotels with shared bathrooms, kitchens and toilets are usually the cheapest options, running from around ¥2,500 to ¥5,000 per person. Capsule hotels, with bed-sized compartments and shared facilities can be found here and there on Hokkaidō, and are priced similar to hostels.

Business hotels are the next level up and cost between ¥5,000 and ¥10,000 per night for a single room; they can vary from clean, modern and comfortable to dusty and dated, with scuff marks on walls and the lingering stale whiff of old cigarettes – expect compact rooms and tiny en-suite bathrooms.

Hot-spring hotels can range from relatively affordable to expensive – upwards (sometimes significantly) of ¥10,000 per person per night for sure – but dinner and breakfast may well be included, as well as unlimited use of the hot-spring baths. Hokkaidō also has some higher-end hotels, mainly in Sapporo and resort areas.

RYOKAN *Ryokan* (旅館) – Japanese-style inns – are traditional and generally old-fashioned establishments where you can expect a high level of hospitality and exquisite food. Unlike in other parts of Japan, Hokkaidō lacks many authentic, truly old, generation-spanning ryokan, but there are plenty of small family-run establishments and bigger ryokan-style hot-spring resorts. Ryokan tend to be pricey – typically from around ¥14,000 to ¥30,000 per person per night, but this usually always includes a lavish multi-course evening meal and full Japanese breakfast, often served in your room. Most ryokans also have their own hot-spring baths.

MINSHUKU *Minshuku* (民宿) are the Japanese equivalent of a family-run bed and breakfast, often akin to a no-frills ryokan in more simple, homely surroundings.

ACCOMMODATION PRICE CODES

Prices are based on the cost of a double room per night.

Luxury	$$$$$	over ¥20,000
Upmarket	$$$$	¥10,000–20,000
Mid-range	$$$	¥6,000–10,000
Budget	$$	¥4,000–6,000
Shoestring	$	less than ¥4,000

Rooms can be Western-style, or more typically with tatami flooring and futons to sleep on, and there is usually the option of dinner (expect excellent seafood in coastal areas). In smaller towns, minshuku may be the only form of accommodation and they don't always allow online booking; a Japanese speaker may be required to call instead. Prices tend to range from ¥6,000 to ¥10,000 per person per night.

PENSIONS Almost the same as a minshuku, and generally with a Japanese take on Western style, pensions (ペンション) are most often found in ski resorts and rural areas on Hokkaidō.

RIDER HOUSES A Hokkaidō speciality – although they are sometimes found in other prefectures – rider houses (ライダーハウス) are cheap and super-basic accommodations which pop up at roadside locations during the warmer summer months, specifically targeting bikers and cyclists touring the island. You'll get a space to sleep, some shared facilities and that's about it, with prices ranging from around ¥800 to ¥2,000 per person per night. The website (w hatinosu.net/house) has a map and information about rider houses around Japan.

CAMPING Hokkaidō is a great place for camping (キャンプ場), with a plethora of managed campgrounds dotted around the island. Prices range from free up to about ¥2,000 per person, with ¥500 around the average. Facilities tend to be basic, with perhaps a covered washing-up area and toilets, but not much else. Some of the fanciest grounds may have coin-operated showers (usually ¥100–300 for 10mins), but they are generally rare. Instead, most campgrounds are located very or fairly close to onsen, where you can bathe, freshen up and perhaps even grab a light meal.

Auto-camping is the Japanese term for car or RV camping, and these grounds tend to be the most expensive but may have the most luxurious facilities.

Campsites don't need to be booked in advance, but on busy summer weekends you may have to squeeze your tent in a space mere inches away from fellow campers, especially at the most popular grounds within a couple of hours of Sapporo. Almost all campsites close completely for winter.

Wild or stealth camping is also a viable option on Hokkaidō – although the official word is that camping should only be at designated campgrounds, camping anywhere inconspicuously is generally not frowned upon, as long as you keep noise down and leave without a trace. Good locations include parks, michi-no-eki and beaches. There will often be public toilets and perhaps even drinking water available. If camping wild in genuinely remote areas, then take sensible precautions to avoid attracting bears (an unlikely, but nevertheless possible risk), such as cooking away from your tent and storing food in a bag hung in a tree some distance away.

Check w japancamp.jp for some campsite listings (in Japanese).

EATING AND DRINKING

Japan takes its food very seriously, and Hokkaidō's fertile fields grow a staggering variety of fruits and vegetables which often make their way into dishes when in season – signature Hokkaidō crops include asparagus (especially from May to June), succulent sweetcorn (*tomorokoshi* or *tokibi* in the Hokkaidō dialect) and potatoes (*jagaimo*).

Food is closely linked with the seasons – spring means *takenoko* (bamboo shoots) and *sansai* (wild mountain vegetables); summer is a time for *reimen* (cold ramen), *uni* (sea urchin) and *unagi* (conger eel); autumn brings *sanma* (Pacific saury) and *matsutake* mushrooms; winter is the time for *nabe* (hot pot) and *oden* (stewed items in a *dashi* broth), but many dishes can be eaten throughout the year.

As Japan's dairy farm capital, Hokkaidō naturally offers the best selection of dairy products in the country – think soft cheeses, fresh yoghurts, creamy butter and of course, milk.

With far more on offer than just sushi or ramen, you can be dining on refined multi-course *kaiseki* (Japanese haute cuisine) dishes at one establishment, while next door they are swilling beer and eating grilled chicken gizzards at a smoky hole-in-the-wall *yakitori* joint.

The traditional Japanese breakfast is often served at ryokan and minshuku and consists of rice, miso soup and an assortment of items usually including tofu, a piece of cooked fish, *nattō* (fermented beans) and *tsukemono* (Japanese pickles), but most hotels will have pastries, coffee and more Western-style fare.

The best restaurants tend to specialise in one thing – be it sushi (寿司), ramen (ラーメン) or *yakitori* (焼鳥; charcoal-grilled chicken), but there are other more general options too. *Shokudō* (食堂) are casual, affordable restaurants with a wide choice of dishes (mostly Japanese or Japan-style Western) including *katsu-karē* (rice topped with fried pork cutlet and curry), *ebi-katsu* (fried breaded prawns) and *hambāgu* (meat patty served with rice), with meals typically served as a set, called *teishoku* (定食), and these restaurants are often found near train stations or in shopping malls.

Izakaya (居酒屋) are the equivalent of Japanese pubs, where both food and drinks are ordered together; they range from cheap, lively chains with multi-lingual tablet style menus, to old-fashioned family-run establishments with not a lick of English spoken or written. *Izakayas* are a good place to sample a range of dishes (everything from sashimi and fried chicken to chips and Caesar salad) and soak in some authentic Japanese atmosphere.

When dining out, staff will likely greet you with '*Irasshaimase*' ('Welcome') and ask you '*Nan-mei sama?*' ('How many people?') which you can just answer by using your fingers (as most Japanese people do). Once seated you will often be given an *o-shibori* (hot or cold towel) and a cup of water or tea. If there is no English menu and you are willing to try anything, ask '*O-susume wa nan desu ka?*' ('What do you recommend?'), or in slightly higher-end restaurants you can plump for *omakase* (the chef's choice). Before tucking into your food, you can say '*Itadakimasu*' ('I humbly receive', but closer in meaning to 'bon appetit'), and when leaving the restaurant or going up to pay the bill you can say '*Gochisōsama-deshita*' ('Thank you for the meal').

HOKKAIDŌ SPECIALITIES The island's *meibutsu* (local specialities) are many and varied, and it would be remiss not to sample at least a few of them during any trip.

Savoury dishes Probably Hokkaidō's most famous speciality and similar to *yakiniku* (Japanese BBQ), ***jingisukan*** (ジンギスカン) is grilled lamb or mutton usually cooked over charcoal on a dome-shaped hotplate said to resemble the helmet of Genghis Khan (Jingisukan being the Japanese reading of the famous warlord's name). Sheep are not commonly reared in other parts of Japan, so their meat is very much a regional delicacy. The hotplate is at your table, so you cook the meat yourself; the lamb is typically placed at the top of the griddle, allowing the juices to flow down the sides, and onions, pumpkin, bean sprouts and other vegetables are added to the mix. You can find jingisukan restaurants all over Hokkaidō. But beware, some establishments can be a little smoky and can leave your clothes smelling quite flavoursome – you'll sometimes be given a paper bib to offer some protection.

Soup curry (スープカレー) is said to have been invented in Sapporo in the 1970s and has now spread right across the island. It consists of a large bowl of a thin, smooth, curry-flavoured soup packed with various vegetables and some meat (typically chicken), but non-meat options are usually available; you can choose just how spicy you would like to have it too. It is a relatively healthy and affordable meal which is well suited to Hokkaidō's cold winters.

One of Japan's most popular dishes, **ramen** (ラーメン) consists of Chinese-style wheat noodles served in a broth, usually made from either a pork- or chicken-based stock (or sometimes fish, vegetable, beef, seaweed or any combination) and flavoured with miso, soy or salt. Ramen can be topped with almost anything, but common items include braised pork (*chāshū*), dried seaweed (*nori*), bamboo shoots (*menma*) and sliced green onions. ***Tonkotsu*** (豚骨/とんこつ) is a commonly seen and deep, rich pork bone broth ramen with origins in Kyūshū.

Each of Hokkaidō's three main cities are known for a particular type of ramen; in Sapporo it is *miso ramen* (味噌ラーメン), Asahikawa has *shōyu ramen* (醤油ラーメン; soy-sauce based broth), and Hakodate is famous for the lighter *shio ramen* (塩ラーメン; salt-seasoned broth). The two Hokkaidō staples of butter and sweetcorn are often optional ramen toppings too.

Japan is of course well known for its **seafood**, and Hokkaidō is regarded as one of the best places in Japan to find it, mainly due to its cool currents and clean waters which are home to a rich variety and abundance of marine life. The island's seafood markets offer freshly caught produce almost straight off the boat. While most seafood can be obtained year-round, the best of each type is seasonal. As a general rule, spring is the season for *botan ebi* (sweet prawns); summer treats include *uni* (sea urchin) and *hotate* (scallops); autumn offers *maguro* (tuna) and *ikura* (salmon roe); and winter is the time for *kani* (crab) and *ika* (squid).

There are numerous ways to enjoy seafood; sushi (寿司) is raw fish on vinegared rice, while sashimi (刺身) is simply thin slices of raw fish – both tend to be eaten by dipping them in soy sauce with perhaps a dollop of wasabi. *Kaisendon* (海鮮丼) – this is a popular dish in restaurants at Hokkaidō's ubiquitous morning markets – is a bowl of rice topped with a mix (or your choice) of raw fish and shellfish, a good way to sample a number of items in one go.

Perhaps less appealing, and actually not very common or easy to find, **bear meat** (熊肉, *kuma-niku*) is sometimes seen in tinned and curried form in some souvenir shops.

Sweets and desserts

Purin (プリン) is a popular crème caramel custard dessert. Ice cream (or soft-cream) is a ubiquitous summer treat. Be aware that not all white-coloured ones are vanilla; sometimes they will be 'milk' flavour. Lavender ice cream

CRABS ON HOKKAIDŌ

Walk around any Hokkaidō seafood market and you won't fail to notice the impressive selection of crustaceans for sale – while not usually practical to buy and cook yourself, restaurants offer them in various delicious and easy-to-consume forms. Each species varies slightly in flavour and texture, and usually it is during their peak season when you will find the largest and tastiest individuals.

HANASAKI CRAB So named because it turns bright red like a flower (*hana* in Japanese) when boiled, hanasaki crab (*hanasakigani*) has a very hard, thorny shell and on Hokkaidō is caught mainly off the coast of Nemuro. The best season for this species is from May to August, when they are sometimes referred to as *natsugani* (*natsu* meaning 'summer').

HAIRY CRAB Smaller than most other varieties, hairy crabs (*kegani*) have a shell covered in hairs and are the most common species landed on Hokkaidō; they are available throughout the year, with the peak season varying depending on location. They don't contain a lot of meat, but their innards are rich and tasty.

KING CRAB A large species with a spiny shell and long meat-filled legs, the red king crab (*tarabagani*) is caught mainly in the Sea of Okhotsk, and November to February is the peak season, although they are available fresh and frozen all year round. The closely related and similar-looking brown crab (*ibaragani*) and blue crab (*aburagani*) live in deeper waters and are sold only in frozen form.

SNOW CRAB The snow crab (*zuwaigani*) has slender legs and is best eaten from March to July – the meat is quite juicy and sweet and can be eaten raw as sashimi; its innards (called *kani-miso*) are also delicious.

is a floral-tinged speciality which can be sampled in the Furano region, while in recent years Sapporo has developed a sophisticated after-dinner parfait culture which makes the most of the island's excellent ice cream and other produce.

Hokkaidō is the home to some well-known chocolate and biscuit makers and brands. One of the most famous is Royce, which produces a popular chocolate-covered potato chip snack, while Shiroi Kobito is a thin and buttery sandwich biscuit filled with sweet white chocolate. Both make good gifts for people from other regions of Japan.

A more traditional sweet is *bekomochi* (べこ餅), a rice cake made from rice flour and sugar, often sculpted into the shape of a leaf and two-tone (white and brown), though can be more colourful too. They were originally made to celebrate Boy's Day (now known as Children's Day) and are popular especially in southern Hokkaidō and northern Tōhoku.

DRINKS *Sake* (often also referred to as *nihonshu* in Japan) is a Japanese rice wine made by fermenting rice that has been polished to remove the bran; it comes in many varieties and can be served hot or cold. *Shōchū* is a similarly strong distilled alcohol typically made from rice, barley, buckwheat or potatoes. **Beer** is the most popular alcoholic beverage in Japan, however, with four Japanese brands (Asahi, Kirin, Sapporo, Suntory) dominating the market, although regional craft beers have been on the increase in the last decade or so. At an izakaya ask for a *nama-bīru* (draft beer) – they usually come in medium (*chū*) and small (*shō*) glass sizes; bottled beer is called *bin-bīru*. Japanese **whiskies** are now regarded as some of the most high-quality liquors in the world, with the best-known distilleries being Suntory, Yamazaki and Nikka (the latter of which was founded on Hokkaidō). Japanese **wines** have been improving steadily over the years, and are now perfectly palatable – there are notable and award-winning wineries on Hokkaidō in Ikeda, Yoichi and on Okushiri Island.

A quick browse in the drinks section of any convenience store on Hokkaidō and you will discover bottles of Gua–ana. This **soft drink** originating in Brazil was introduced to Japan in the 1950s but failed to catch on. Apart from on Hokkaidō, where it is common, it is now rarely seen anywhere else in the country. It tastes a bit like a mix of aniseed, medicine, cola and root beer. Another Hokkaidō-only soft drink is Ribbon Napolin, an orange-coloured fizzy soda with a unique flavour which has been in production since 1911.

PUBLIC HOLIDAYS AND FESTIVALS

Japan is a hard-working country, but there are also a lot of public holidays spread throughout the year – these are worth factoring into your travel plans as many people make the most of some rare time off work to go travelling, and so places tend to be more crowded. The biggest holiday is Golden Week, a succession of public holidays from the end of April into the first week of May – expect increased hotel rates, very busy transport links and big crowds at tourist spots.

It may also be a good idea to avoid travelling during O-bon, an almost week-long holiday in mid-August for commemorating ancestors and a time when many Japanese people return to their hometowns or take trips, meaning transport and accommodation options can be much busier (and more expensive) than usual. Some businesses close during this period too. When national holidays fall on a Sunday, they are sometimes celebrated on the following Monday.

For details of local festivals, see destination chapters.

1 January	New Year's Day
January, second Monday	Coming of Age Day
11 February	National Foundation Day
24 February	Emperor's Birthday
Around 20 March	Vernal Equinox Day
29 April	Shōwa Day
3 May	Constitution Memorial Day
4 May	Greenery Day
5 May	Children's Day
July, third Monday	Marine Day
11 August	Mountain Day
13–16 August	O-bon
September, third Monday	Respect for the Aged Day
Around 23 September	Autumnal Equinox Day
October, second Monday	Health and Sports Day
3 November	Culture Day
23 November	Labour Thanksgiving Day

SHOPPING

Sapporo offers all the shopping you could ever want, with fancy designer brand stores, multi-floor shopping malls, boutique speciality shops and rough-around-the-edges markets. The old-fashioned Tanukikoji shopping arcade is a fine example of a traditional *shōtengai* (商店街; covered shopping street) which are still to be found across most of Japan – though many are sadly suffering with increasingly shuttered shop fronts in the face of competition from modern shopping centres. Hokkaidō's smaller cities offer a more limited choice of shops and amenities, but convenience stores (see below) can be found in even the smallest backwater settlements and sell a good selection of snacks, drinks and essential items.

Local souvenirs, known as *omiyage* (お土産), can be found in gift shops all over the land, and gift-buying for friends, family and co-workers is close to a required duty for any trip-going Japanese person. These small gifts are usually edible, neatly packaged in attractive boxes and showcase a place's speciality or unique characteristic. On Hokkaidō there are also many roadside stores and farmshops selling locally produced fruits, vegetables, dairy products, sweets, breads and cakes, while michi-no-eki (page 70) also tend to offer regional produce.

CONVENIENCE STORES Japan is the land of convenience stores; known as *konbini*, there are estimated to be around 50,000 across the country. They can be found on almost every other block in the cities and at various spots way out in the countryside too. They sell everything from bento-box lunches and snacks, to stationery, sunscreen and basic clothing. But they are more than just shops: at most konbinis

WHERE TO SHOP FOR OUTDOOR GEAR

Japan has plenty of outdoor stores to cater for the country's many outdoor enthusiasts, and they tend to stock a good mix of Western brands along with some Japanese ones, though prices can be expensive. If you are larger framed or have big feet, then it may be a struggle to find clothing and footwear that fits, so try to source those items before travelling. Arguably the most popular outdoor brand in Japan is Mont-Bell; they have shops in almost every large city, including two in central Sapporo. Popular general outdoor stockists include Ishii Sports (石井スポーツ; ICI Sports) and Kōjitsusansō (好日山荘), both with branches in Sapporo which sell almost any item you could need. Shūgakusō (秀岳荘; w shugakuso.com) is a Hokkaidō-only outdoor retailer with a few stores in Sapporo and one in Asahikawa. About 15 minutes' walk southeast of JR Sapporo Station is Sapporo Factory, a large shopping mall where you can find many popular outdoor retailers including the aforementioned Mont-Bell and Kōjitsusansō, along with more familiar stores such as Mammut, The North Face, Columbia and Arc'Teryx.

Remember that it is prohibited to take gas canisters on a plane; if you're flying into New Chitose Airport and plan on heading straight out into the wilds, you may find it useful to know that you can buy Iwatani gas canisters (medium and large sizes) at Snow Shop (スノーショプ), located on the second floor of the terminal building. The canisters are not actually on display; you'll have to ask the staff, and they cost slightly more than ones in outdoor shops. Useful if you don't have time to head into Sapporo though.

you can also pay your utility bills, buy concert tickets and ship things. They also have ATMs and toilets and are often open 24/7. In Hokkaidō's convenience stores you can also fill up your flask with hot water for free; great for keeping topped up with tea or coffee all day.

Lawson, 7-Eleven, Family Mart and Daily Yamazaki have the most stores across the country, but on Hokkaidō you will also find Seicomart – the name comes from 'seiko', meaning 'success'. Curiously it also has a few branches in Ibaraki and Saitama prefectures, but is found nowhere else in Japan. Seicomart tends to have a bit more of a local vibe than the bigger nationwide chains, and many of its stores are not open all night long. The same company also runs ハマナス (Hamanasu), another chain of Hokkaidō-only local convenience stores, most easily distinguishable by its pink logo if you can't read the Japanese branding.

ENTERTAINMENT AND NIGHTLIFE

Much like in most of Japan, the people of Hokkaidō spend their free time in a variety of ways, from watching television and browsing social media, to visiting art galleries and museums, both of which are fairly abundant on Hokkaidō. Outdoorsy types are of course well catered for, with hiking, camping, skiing, snowboarding and canoeing all readily available.

Pachinko is a bafflingly noisy cross between pinball and slot machines, and a relatively popular pastime with certain sections of society who seem to enjoy the low-stakes passive gambling inside the garish pachinko parlours which are often dotted about on the edge of towns. **Karaoke** has much broader appeal, with private rooms and usually a decent smattering of English songs, while more old-fashioned karaoke bars can be found in entertainment districts.

The best **nightlife** is found only in the bigger cities, and even then the likes of Asahikawa and Hakodate can seem mostly very quiet at night outside the aforementioned entertainment districts, where touts or young women on the street try to lure customers to girls' bars and other 'adult entertainment' venues.

In terms of **music and film**, Hokkaidō has a number of small festivals and event spaces – keep an eye out for flyers and posters in tourist information centres and michi-no-eki. Also check out the Ainu musicians trying to foster connections with people through their music, such as Oki Dub Ainu Band (w tonkori.com) or Marewrew (**f**).

OUTDOOR ACTIVITIES

CANOEING, KAYAKING AND RAFTING Between spring and autumn, Hokkaidō's pristine waterways make for some of the best river, lake and sea excursions in the whole of Japan, but unless you know what you're doing and have all your own equipment, you'll probably need to join a guided tour. There are some rental companies for experienced hobbyists.

CYCLING Hokkaidō is one of Japan's prime cycling destinations, with miles of well-maintained and empty tarmac flanked by glorious scenery, with numerous roadside stops and accommodation options, making the island perfect for road biking and bicycle touring. The much rougher and remoter interior forestry roads offer potential for much wilder two-wheeled adventuring. The Tokapuchi 400 is a National Cycling Route in the Tokachi region of eastern/southern Hokkaidō (page 71).

FISHING Fishing is a relatively popular pastime on Hokkaidō, and some harbours have places offering fishing boat trips and gear rental (although don't expect much English to be spoken). Rivers and lakes offer good fishing; *wakasagi* (Japanese smelt) is a small fish common to lakes and estuaries in northern Honshū and Hokkaidō and is a popular choice for ice-fishing in the winter – after being caught, it is often made into tempura and eaten on the spot. Some local outdoor operators run fishing and ice-fishing trips conducted in English.

HIKING Said to be over 70% mountainous, Japan is a dream destination for hikers, with easy access to a plethora of well-maintained trails spread all over the country, and courses suitable for all levels, from short, gentle nature walks for beginners all the way up to strenuous multi-day treks for hardened veterans. Hokkaidō doesn't disappoint in this respect and boasts some of the finest hiking in the country, including jaunts up active and dormant volcanoes (Mount Asahi-dake, Mount Yōtei, Mount Meakan), walks through vibrant wildflower meadows (Rebun Island, Mount Furano) and remote wilderness treks (Daisetsuzan Grand Traverse, Shiretoko Traverse) among many others.

The main hiking season on Hokkaidō is from around July to October when trails should mostly be snow-free. Suitable footwear is a must, and be sure to dress in layers and bring suitable warm and waterproof clothing as conditions can be very changeable in the mountains – the higher peaks can be cold even during the height of summer. As you would do anywhere when heading into wild and sometimes

HYAKUMEIZAN: JAPAN'S 100 FAMOUS MOUNTAINS

Familiar to most serious Japanese hikers, the *hyakumeizan*, or '100 famous mountains of Japan' is a list of the 100 most celebrated peaks across the country, ranging from Hokkaidō in the north all the way down to the island of Yakushima south of Kyūshū. The list was devised by the fabled writer and mountaineer Kyūya Fukuda, who started composing articles about the Japanese mountains which he regarded as particularly notable; this resulted in the publication of his seminal book *Nihon Hyakumeizan*, in 1964. The mountains Fukada chose were all ones he had climbed himself and his selection based on a number of factors including: historical merit; cultural, literary or physical stature; and uniqueness of form. They were not selected necessarily for their height, although the vast majority of peaks on the list are over 1,500m tall. Even though the list was purely subjective, it quickly captured the attention of mountain climbers across the country, and has now become the de facto list for Japan's most eager peak baggers. The current record for climbing all 100 mountains is a startling 33 days, set in 2014.

By its very nature, however, the hyakumeizan left out many additional notable mountains, so experts have subsequently drawn up further lists, including Japan's 200 (and 300) famous mountains, and more esoteric ones such as Japan's 100 famous flower mountains.

Nine of Hokkaidō's mountains are listed as hyakumeizan, and as the list ranks all 100 mountains in order of latitude from north to south, Hokkaidō makes up the first nine listings of the book. In numerical order they are: (1) Rishiri-dake; (2) Rausu-dake; (3) Shari-dake; (4) Meakan-dake; (5) Asahi-dake; (6) Tomuraushi-yama; (7) Tokachi-dake; (8) Poroshiri-dake; and (9) Yōtei-zan.

remote terrain, carefully research the route before any hike, download maps on to your phone (Yamap is probably the best hiking app in Japan) and preferably take a paper map and compass as backup – the Yama-to-kōgen (山と高原) series of hiking maps published by Shobunsha are the best and most detailed maps around, with maps 1 to 3 covering most of the main trails on Hokkaidō; they contain very little English, but clearly show trail times and are relatively easy to use if you can pick out some of the kanji. They are available in hiking stores, large bookshops and online.

Be sure to carry enough food and water for the duration (factor in emergencies too) and always tell someone about your plans. On Hokkaidō, many areas encourage hikers to carry (and use) portable toilet bags, to help keep the delicate mountain ecosystems as pristine as possible. No permits are necessary for hiking anywhere in Japan, but it is wise to submit a hiking plan in a *tozan-posuto* (postbox-like climbing register) if there is one at the trailhead. Bear bells are carried by most hikers on Hokkaidō to avoid surprise encounters with brown bears (page 9), and although the chance of an encounter is extremely rare, in notable brown bear hotspots it is probably a good idea to carry bear spray too. Don't forget to boil or filter your drinking water to avoid the parasite-borne disease echinococcosis, another Hokkaidō-specific hazard (page 59).

There are not so many truly long-distance hiking trails on Hokkaidō or in Japan in general – the 1,000km Michinoku Coastal Trail is one of the longest, although there are plans to create an even longer Hokkaidō Nature Trail eventually, and a new long-distance hiking course in eastern Hokkaidō is due for completion in 2024. Places like the Japan Alps in central Honshū have well-developed networks of mountain huts, but on Hokkaidō most mountain huts and refuges are maintained by volunteers and have much more basic facilities. During the summer hiking season some may have a warden present, but no food or bedding is provided, so you must be self-sufficient. Most huts have a water source and camping area close by. Some have toilets and a few even a wood stove, but it is always a good idea to bring your own portable toilet bag. The fee is generally around ¥1,500–2,000 per person per night. It is possible to use the huts outside of the main summer season, although you may have to dig through metres of snow to gain access. It goes without saying that you should leave a hut just as clean as (or even cleaner than) when you find it.

HOT SPRINGS Japan has thousands of geothermally heated *onsen* (hot springs) spread right across the archipelago, and wallowing in a spring-fed bath is not only a

ONSEN ETIQUETTE

Hot-spring baths can be a little intimidating for first timers, but there is actually not a lot to it. First, be sure to enter the correct bath and changing room – it's 男 for men, and 女 for women. These characters will usually be printed on the *noren* (curtains) hanging in front of the door. In the changing area, take off all your clothes and put them in the locker or basket. You can take a small towel into the bathing area, where you should first wash your body and hair using the showers or washbowls, being careful to rinse off all soap and shampoo. Rinse off the stool if you used one to sit on. You can then enter the bath, keeping splashing to a minimum, and don't dunk your head in. The small towel is used to dry off a bit before re-entering the changing area, and while bathing you can keep it either folded at the side of the bath, or balanced on top of your head like a seasoned onsen pro.

Hokkaidō is blessed with such fantastic snow conditions that there are numerous excellent ski areas spread right across the island. The following may not be as big or flashy as the more famous resorts such as those in Niseko or Furano, but they can be cheaper and quieter alternatives for your powder fix.

Asarigawa Onsen Ski Resort
w asari-ski.com. Superb little resort close to Otaru, used mostly by locals.

Hakugindai Ski Resort
w makubetsu-ski.com. Small hill with nice wide runs & rarely crowded, on the edge of the Tokachi Plain in southeast Hokkaidō.

Iwanai Resort w iwanairesort.com. Fantastic deep powder, ocean views, cat skiing & friendly atmosphere make this excellent resort one of Hokkaidō's fast-rising stars.

Kamui Ski Links w kamui-skilinks.com. Largest ski resort in the Asahikawa region but rarely too crowded, about 20km (30mins) drive from the city centre.

Kokusetsu Horotachi
w dankejapan.co.jp/horotachi.html. Small ski area in northern Hokkaidō with only 1 lift, but cheap & lots of snow.

Nayoro Piyashiri w nayoro.co.jp. Small resort which claims to have the highest-quality snow in Japan, with 3 lifts & a good variety of courses.

Pippu Ski Resort w town.pippu. hokkaido.jp/ski/top.html. Nice, small & quiet ski area in the Furano region, so great powder guaranteed.

national pastime but something that is intrinsic to Japanese culture. Baths range from luxurious hot-spring resorts to rustic bathhouses to mere open-air pools out in the middle of nature, and most (although not all) are gender segregated. Bathers do not (usually) wear any clothing, and while it can be a bit uncomfortable getting naked in front of strangers (and perhaps even more so your friends and family!), the onsen is a great social leveller, where everyone is equal. Many ryokan (traditional Japanese inns) have their own hot springs, and the fanciest ones of all have private hot-spring baths in the guestrooms. Many onsen pride themselves on the healing nature of their waters, which can vary greatly by mineral content, acidity, salinity and colour.

Hot-spring resorts can pop up around popular hot springs, with numerous ryokan and more Western-style hotels (also with their own hot-spring baths) to choose from. Non-staying guests can usually use the baths during the daytime – this is called *higaeri-onsen* (日帰り温泉) and tends to cost between ¥500 and ¥2,000. Towels are usually available to rent or buy if you don't have your own.

Outdoor or open-air hot springs are called *rotenburo* (露天風呂; many ryokan will have both indoor and outdoor options) and these can often offer wonderful views – sitting in a piping-hot outdoor bath surrounded by the deep snow of a Hokkaidō winter should be experienced at least once. Wild onsen can be found along river valleys, halfway up mountains and on the shores of beaches and lakes all over Hokkaidō; often nothing more than a small open-air pool, these sites tend to be free, have no facilities and have mixed bathing, so swimsuits are optional.

You may find entry to some onsen a bit tricky if you have tattoos – this is because of historical associations with the *yakuza* – but attitudes are slowly changing and many bathhouses have a relaxed policy, although some may ask you to cover up small tattoos with a plaster; the strictest onsen refuse entry full stop.

Also keep a lookout for *ashiyu* (足湯; foot baths) in some onsen towns – at these shallow baths, which are free to use, you can just sit down and dip your feet in. *Sentō* (銭湯), cheap, no-frills public baths which generally just use heated water (not sourced from a natural hot spring, unless in an onsen town), can be found in some neighbourhoods.

WINTER SPORTS Japan is world-famous for its powder snow (hence the moniker 'Japow!'), and Hokkaidō is home to arguably the biggest and best dumps in the whole of the country, with a long winter sports season lasting from around December to April. The Niseko and Furano regions attract the most visitors searching for fresh powder, but there are good small ski resorts across the island (although fewer in eastern Hokkaidō). Snowshoeing can be done almost anywhere there is snow, and more specialised winter activities include husky racing, snow-mobiling and ice-floe walking – check local operators for guided tours in these and other winter activities.

Some useful websites for Hokkaidō's winter sports scene and Japan in general include w snowjapan.com and w skiing-hokkaido.com.

PHOTOGRAPHY

Japan is a country of photographers, from serious camera aficionados lugging around expensive tripods and heavy kit to selfie snappers documenting everything on their smartphones. Many people enjoy taking pictures of food, natural phenomena showcasing the seasons (flowers, leaves) and Japan's many ubiquitous 'cute' things. Doing the two-fingered 'peace' sign seems to be almost mandatory when having your photo taken.

Japan has a wealth of extremely photogenic locations, both natural and manmade. Photography is permitted in the grounds of most temples and shrines, but taking pictures of deities, sacred relics and depictions of the Buddha is prohibited, and photography around inner sanctum buildings is usually not allowed – look out for signs.

The use of drones is strictly prohibited in many areas, including over centres of population, at most famous landmarks and attractions, near airports and other sensitive locations and also within all national parks. Also, all drones over 100g must be registered and a small fee paid before use; see w mlit.go.jp/koku/drone/en.

OPENING TIMES

Most **banks** are open from 09.00 to 15.00 Monday to Friday, and are closed at weekends and on national holidays. ATMs usually have longer opening hours and are available at weekends, although most machines in Japanese banks don't accept foreign cards. The largest domestic banks are Japan Post, Mizuho, Mitsubishi UFJ Bank, Mitsui Sumitomo and Resona.

Small **post offices** are typically open Monday to Friday from 09.00 to 17.00, and are closed at weekends and on national holidays; the largest city branches (such as Sapporo Chūō Office) may keep longer hours and also be open on Saturdays and Sundays. Even the smallest towns and many villages have a post office operated by Japan Post, usually open from 09.00 to 17.00 Monday to Friday – they are distinguished by a red 'T' symbol with a bar across the top (T̄) on a white background. Post office ATMs may only be accessible for slightly longer than opening hours.

Be aware that many **museums** are closed on Mondays, or the following day if the Monday happens to be a national holiday. Large **shops** and department stores are typically open from around 10.00 to 20.00, seven days a week, and are also open on most national holidays (apart from around New Year). Smaller shops in more provincial areas will tend to have shorter business hours.

Many shops, restaurants and businesses close around the New Year period, which can be from as early as 30 December to as late as 6 January – during this time, transport still runs and accommodation remains open, but rates may increase slightly.

MEDIA AND COMMUNICATIONS

NEWSPAPERS AND MAGAZINES The most popular daily Japanese-language newspapers are the left-leaning *Mainichi Shimbun* and *Asahi Shimbun*, along with the more conservative *Yomiuri Shimbun*, *Sankei Shimbun* and *Nikkei Shimbun*. The *Hokkaidō Shimbun* (**w** hokkaido-np.co.jp) is the main regional news provider.

Hokkaidō Magazine KAI (**w** kai-hokkaido.com) is an online magazine with articles covering various topics related to Hokkaidō.

Alternative-language press The *Japan Times* is the nation's largest and oldest English-language daily newspaper; it can be bought from some kiosks at major airports and train stations, plus at some convenience stores, news-stands and large bookshops. The *Asahi Shimbun* (**w** asahi.com/ajw) has an English-language website. *Outdoor Japan* (**w** outdoorjapan.com) is a website and magazine focused on adventure travel around Japan.

The *Ainu Times* (**w** otarunay.at-ninja.jp) is an Ainu-language newspaper and the only dedicated Ainu-language publication in the world. First published in March 1997 with four editions annually, it now runs just two or three times a year. The paper is written by a dedicated group of about ten people, mostly in their 50s to 70s, and is published by the Ainugo Pen Club, a small organisation established by Shiro Kayano, director of the Kayano Shigeru Nibutani Ainu Museum in the town of Nibutani, and the newspaper's founder. The news is printed entirely in Ainu, in both the Roman alphabet and katakana, and is also available in an e-book format (a Japanese translation is available as well). At its peak the newspaper had many hundreds of subscribers (including some overseas), but that number has steadily dwindled (to around 80 at the time of writing). Contact the Kayano Shigeru Nibutani Ainu Museum for details on subscriptions and for other inquiries.

TELEVISION AND RADIO Japan has dozens of television stations, both national and regional. NHK is the public service broadcaster (equivalent to the BBC in the UK) with the TV licence helping to subsidise it (for which non-payment is generally not punished in Japan). The most popular TV channels are NHK G, TV Asahi, Nippon TV, TBS and Fuji TV. Some modern hotels have cable TV with a selection of international channels, or smart TVs for a wider choice of viewing options.

Japan has many regional radio broadcasters offering a mix of talk shows, music and news. NHK World-Japan radio service broadcasts in 17 languages and is also available to listen to on a free app.

TELEPHONE Public phones, though not as commons as they once were, can be found around train and bus stations. Local calls are possible from any public phone and cost ¥10 per minute, but international calls are limited to certain ones (usually grey coloured) and cost ¥100 for less than a minute. Most phones accept coins, and telephone cards which are sold at convenience stores and kiosks.

Mobile phones Prepaid data-only SIM cards for unlocked smartphones can be bought at the arrivals hall at New Chitose Airport and other major airports, and also from some large electronic retailers such as BIC Camera. Sakura Mobile (w sakuramobile.jp), IIJmio (w t.iijmio.jp/en/index.html) and Softbank (w softbank.jp/en/mobile/special/prepaid-sim-for-travel/en) offer affordable tourist SIM cards which can be pre-ordered in advance.

INTERNET Nearly all hotels and guesthouses have free Wi-Fi, and you can also find it at airports, train stations, restaurants and many other hotspots, although less so in rural regions. Check w japanfreewifi.com to search for local Wi-Fi spots.

Many Japanese websites can be slightly clunky and have no English-language option, but there are a number of workarounds you can use. Probably easiest of all is Google Translate (w google.translate.com); simply click on the website tab and paste the website URL for a generally useable (if not always perfect) translation. Browsers such as Chrome and Firefox have their own translating functions and add-ons too.

Renting a **pocket Wi-Fi** router is the best way to stay connected during your travels. You can arrange to pick one up at the airport or your hotel, and then simply pop it in a prepaid envelope and drop it in a post box or leave at a collection point before leaving the country. Japan Wireless (w japan-wireless.com) offers affordable and easy-to-use plans with unlimited data, but other providers such as Ninja WiFi (w ninjawifi.com) and CDJapan (w rental.cdjapan.co.jp/index_en_jpy_7.html) are available too. The same companies also tend to offer prepaid SIM cards which are useful if your phone is unlocked.

COURIER SERVICES AND LUGGAGE FORWARDING To limit the burden of lugging heavy or bulky luggage around, some visitors make use of the relatively affordable and very useful door-to-door delivery service known as *takuhaibin* (宅配便), or *takkyubin* as it is often called. Goods including suitcases, large parcels and ski/golf equipment can be dropped off and sent from luggage counters at airports and train stations, some convenience stores or directly between hotels (ask at the front desk whether they can arrange this for you), with delivery usually by the next day (longer if shipping from one end of the country to the other).

Yamato are the forerunners of this service and offer a reliable and efficient 'hands-free' luggage-forwarding service (w global-yamato.com/en/hands-free-travel), while other alternatives include Sagawa Express (w sagawa-exp.co.jp) and Japan Post.

CULTURAL ETIQUETTE

The Japanese are famously polite and rule-abiding; and social interactions reflect various levels of formality depending on seniority and standing. Foreigners are not really expected to follow or even know much about any of this, however. As long as you are friendly and polite, no offence is likely to be taken if you do unknowingly commit a faux pas.

SPEAKING JAPANESE Most Japanese people will assume you don't speak any Japanese, but will be delighted if you make any effort with the language at all. Expect to be showered with praise of '*nihongo jōzu!*' ('your Japanese is great!'), even if you manage only to splutter out a word or two. It is customary to say *Itadakimasu* (roughly meaning 'I humbly receive') before starting a meal and *Gochisōsamadeshita*

('Thank you for the meal') after finishing. Most Japanese people refer to others by their surname, adding the honorific suffix *-san* at the end, eg: Yamada-san.

MEETING AND GREETING People greet each other by bowing – a long, deep bow bending from the waist being very formal, while a small nod is much more casual. Shaking hands is not so common. Other physical forms of greeting such as hugging and kissing are rare, even among close friends and family.

BUSINESS Age and status are very important in Japanese business culture – and life in general – with relationships based on a hierarchical system of *senpai* (seniors) and *kōhai* (juniors). Relationships are often key when it comes to doing business too, with a preference for building trust and familiarity before striking a deal. Modesty and humility are also highly valued.

Almost every professional, from salaried company employee to freelance entrepreneur, carries a set of their own personalised business cards known as *meishi*. These are exchanged during the initial meeting and greeting with new business associates, and should be given and received in both hands, and then placed face up on the desk in front of you (if there is one). Shaking hands is not typical, but exceptions may be made in international business dealings.

SHOES Take off your shoes when entering a building with a raised floor at the *genkan* (entrance); often indoor slippers will be provided, otherwise it's fine to walk indoors in your socks or barefoot. Outdoor shoes should never be worn when stepping on to tatami mats. Use the toilet slippers if provided in a bathroom, but don't forget to take them off when you leave!

DRESS Apart from on special occasions when kimono and the more casual *yukata* are worn, fashion in Japan is much as you will find in other places around the world. That being said, the careful observer may notice that in some respects Japan has an ever-so-slightly conservative approach to clothing and street fashion. Women mostly avoid anything low-cut or exposing much skin on the upper body (so expect stares if you dress that way), but conversely extremely short skirts are not an uncommon sight in the cities of an evening. Figure-hugging clothing is generally not the norm, and yoga-pant-style leggings tend to be worn only while engaging in sporting activities. Even in the sweltering heat of summer, many people wear full-length trousers instead of shorts. But generally Western-style fashion is ubiquitous, and tourists of course are free to wear whatever they want, although use common sense when visiting shrines and temples.

EATING AND DRINKING Eating while walking is traditionally frowned upon. But slurping some foods (especially noodles) is not only OK, but actively encouraged! Do not stab food with your **chopsticks**, as this is considered very uncouth. Also do not pass food from person to person using chopsticks or stand them upright in your food – both are practices associated with funerals. When not in use, chopsticks should be placed on a chopstick holder, or arranged neatly side by side on your plate or bowl.

OUT AND ABOUT Japanese people are generally rule-abiding, and will often wait at pedestrian crossings until the light turns green even if the street is narrow and there is zero road traffic. It is considered poor etiquette to speak too loudly in public areas and on public transport; as with any country, don't cut into queues. Owing to decades-old counter-terrorism measures there are few public litter bins in Japan; carry a bag for your rubbish and dispose of it later (convenience stores often have bins you can use too).

TIPPING AND BARTERING There is no tipping culture in Japan, apart from on a few very rare occasions (page 64). Bartering for a better price is not the done thing in almost any circumstance.

TRAVELLING POSITIVELY

Carrying your own pair of reusable chopsticks means you can refuse disposable chopsticks at the supermarket or convenience store check-out – say *ohashi wa kekō desu* ('I don't need chopsticks'); the same goes for plastic bags – (*fukuro wa kekō desu* ('I don't need a plastic bag').

Japan is the land of convenience stores and vending machines, so the temptation to buy bottled drinks is huge. However, you can cut down on single-use PET bottle usage by carrying your own drinks bottle – the Mymizu app (w mymizu.co) shows you where you can find free water-refill spots all across the country (and beyond). If you do buy a plastic PET bottle be sure to dispose of it in the correct bin; rubbish tends to be separated into paper/burnable, plastic, glass and cans, and PET bottles.

Lastly, support local businesses and establishments where possible, especially in the more provincial and rural regions. **WWOOF Japan** (w wwoofjapan.com), part of the WWOOF (World Wide Opportunities on Organic Farms) network, can arrange for you to work and stay on an organic farm for free after registering online and paying the yearly membership of ¥5,500.

Part Two

THE GUIDE

3

Sapporo

Sapporo (札幌) is the regional capital of Hokkaidō and the fifth largest city in Japan, with a population of 1.9 million. Serving as the administrative and economic centre of the island, this bustling city is home to over a third of Hokkaidō's population, though it has a slightly more relaxed feeling than most of Japan's other heaving mega-cities. Its wide streets and pavements are rarely crowded to bursting point, and yet Sapporo still has all the flashing neon lights, tall buildings, beguiling backstreets and fabulous eateries that you would expect of a sprawling Japanese metropolis. In the summer it can get hot, but less stifling than the concrete cookers of Tokyo and Osaka, while in winter the entire city is transformed into a startlingly winter wonderland, with regular snow flurries, ice-encrusted streets, and snow piled up higher than your head along pavements and roadsides. What is most remarkable is that, despite the massive snowfalls and sub-zero temperatures – which would grind most other big cities around the world to a complete standstill – Sapporo and its residents just get on with things and life carries on pretty much as normal, whatever the conditions. Perhaps it is due to this spirit and the friendly nature of the locals that the city always seems to be gearing up for a party, with the big summertime

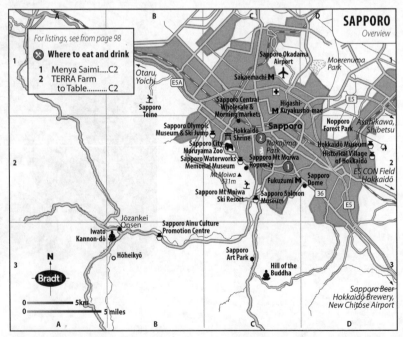

beer and *yosakoi* dance festivals and the wintertime *yuki-matsuri* (snow festival) in particular drawing millions of visitors every year.

Hemmed in by mountains to the west, and rolling plains to the east, Sapporo is blessed with nature right on its doorstep, and hiking and skiing is possible even within the city limits. While Sapporo's suburbs stretch north and eastwards for miles, the city centre is fairly compact and perfectly walkable, with some further-out attractions reachable by subway, bus or tram (streetcar). Susukino is the city's lively central area and main dining and entertainment district, and although Sapporo is not rammed with historic sights or famous tourist attractions, there is more than enough to do and explore to happily while away a couple of days. Its fairly central location and good road and rail links to all the far-flung corners of Hokkaidō make Sapporo an excellent hub for accessing the rest of the island. New Chitose Airport is the main gateway to Hokkaidō for most visitors and is located 40km southeast of Sapporo, with regular train and bus services connecting the airport to the city. What's more, by 2031 Sapporo will also finally become the northern terminus for Hokkaidō's Shinkansen Line, meaning it will be possible to take direct bullet trains to and from Tokyo and beyond.

HISTORY

The city of Sapporo began life as a small Ainu village in the Ishikari Valley called Satsuporo, roughly meaning 'a river running through a reed-filled plain', and by 1857, two Japanese families were living there. In 1866 the Kaitakushi sent Kametaro Otomo, an official with experience of establishing pioneer farms, to the area, encouraging many more families to move there. Soon after, the Sōsei Canal was constructed through what is now central Sapporo. Some of the most successful early crops grown in the region were onions.

As part of the Kaitakushi's plan to rename and develop Ezo, they also wanted to establish a new, more centrally located capital than Hakodate. Despite not being on the coast, Sapporo was chosen for its promise as an agricultural centre, with the canal providing irrigation, drinking water and a transport link for early settlers. The canal was later superseded by the railway to Otaru (Sapporo's nearest seaport), and today a highway runs along either side of it. The city was planned in 1869 by Shima Yoshitake to be laid out in a grid system, inspired by Kyoto (but reminiscent of some American cities). The long strip of Ōdōri Park, which bisects the city north to south, was designed as a firebreak, with government buildings on the north side, business and entertainment districts to the south (and industry mostly to the east).

In 1871, Sapporo became the official capital of Hokkaidō, with Sapporo Shrine established in today's Maruyama Park at the western edge of the city. At that time, the tiny city had fewer than 700 residents and much of the land was still densely wooded. But already by 1874 the population had swelled to more than 2,000, with most new residents arriving from Tokyo, brought to Sapporo to work in factories being built along the Toyohira River as the Kaitakushi founded new industries.

In 1872, work began on a road connecting Sapporo to Hakodate (still Hokkaidō's main commercial centre and biggest port), via Chitose and Tomakomai. The road didn't actually go directly all the way to Hakodate at that time, but instead to the port at Muroran; a well-established sea route between Muroran and Mori made up part of the journey, negating the need to develop a long land passage over the difficult terrain encircling the vast Uchiura Bay. The road was completed within a year but was often damaged by floods and spring thaw.

William Smith Clark arrived in Sapporo in 1876 to open Sapporo Agricultural College (later to become Hokkaidō University), a key component in the city's development. In the same year a brewery was opened thanks to the discovery of native hops growing on Hokkaidō and the local climate being conducive to the growth of barley. Sapporo Beer was the first beverage produced, in 1877, and although they sold the factory to a private firm in 1886, the label today still features the red star of the Kaitakushi.

Around 1875–76 the first group of tondenhei (page 29) arrived and settled in the Kotoni district of Sapporo. Numbering around 200, these ex-samurai families were brought to colonise and also defend, if necessary, these frontier lands, and in the following years more (many from Kyūshū and Shikoku) established other villages around the Sapporo area. The city was officially renamed Sapporo-ku (Sapporo Ward) in 1880, and in the same year the railway from Otaru to Sapporo became operational. By 1888 the Western-style and red-bricked Hokkaidō Government Office building had been constructed, and around that time the last tondenhei group arrived to settle in the city.

As the 20th century began, Sapporo still remained smaller than Otaru and Hakodate. Poet Takuboku Ishikawa (1886–1912) visited Sapporo in 1907 and described it as 'a big country town', quiet, full of trees and with Western-style houses lined up sparsely. In 1909 the first section of the tram line was opened, and by 1918 it was electrified – at its peak in 1958 the network had 11 routes and was 25km long, but was reduced to three lines by the 1970s (which have now been combined into the singular circular route that remains today).

In 1922 Sapporo officially became a city, with its population having grown to more than 100,000. A decade later it was chosen as host of the 1940 Winter Olympics, although this was cancelled on account of the start of the Second Sino-Japanese War in 1937.

The city was bombed by US aircraft right at the end of World War II, though most of its infrastructure remained undamaged. During the American occupation, US forces set up Camp Crawford in the Makomanai district at the southern end of the city. Sapporo became one of the fastest-growing cities in Japan during the post-war decades; its population reached 1 million by 1970, just over a century after its formation.

Sapporo hosted the 1972 Winter Olympics, the first time the event was to be held in Asia. In the years leading up to the event, massive improvements were made to the city's infrastructure; the first subway line north of Tokyo was built, and Chitose Airport was upgraded to handle international flights. Another sporting event, the 2002 FIFA World Cup, brought further attention to the city, with three games hosted at the newly built Sapporo Dome, which is now home to Sapporo's football and baseball teams. Much more recently, the marathon and race-walking events of the delayed 2020 Tokyo Olympics were held in Sapporo, thanks to its cooler climate.

GETTING THERE AND AWAY

BY AIR The main gateway to Hokkaidō for the vast majority of visitors is **New Chitose Airport** [map, page 110], which is located 50km southeast of Sapporo. There are numerous daily flights to Tokyo, Osaka and other Japanese cities, plus a number of international destinations. JR Hokkaidō runs the fast and regular Rapid Airport service which connects the New Chitose to JR Sapporo Station (and Otaru); trains run roughly every 15 minutes, take around 40 minutes and cost ¥1,150 (non-reserved). It is a six-carriage train, with five of the carriages being non-reserved; only car 4 is for reserved seating, which costs an extra ¥530 and has more storage space for luggage.

There are regular limousine buses between the airport and various places in Sapporo including JR Sapporo Station, Nakajima Park and some popular central area hotels. Two companies, Hokuto Kotsu and Hokkaidō Chuo Bus, run these services but the fare is the same for both (¥1,100). Buses between the airport and JR Sapporo Station take around 1 hour 20 minutes.

It takes around an hour to reach Sapporo if self-driving with costs of ¥1,330 in highway toll fees. A taxi from the airport to Sapporo is expensive at around ¥15,000–18,000.

Sapporo Okadama Airport [90 D1] is much smaller and closer to the city, handling domestic flights to locations around Hokkaidō and a handful of other Japanese cities. There are buses from central Sapporo which take around 30 minutes and cost ¥700. The closest station is Sakaemachi Station [90 C1] on the Toho subway line, from where it is a 20-minute walk or 5-minute bus ride (¥350; services roughly every hour) to the airport. Okadama Airport is 20 minutes by car or taxi (roughly ¥3,000) from JR Sapporo Station.

BY TRAIN JR Sapporo Station [95 D1] is the city's main train station and transportation hub, with trains to places both near and far away. Daily limited express trains connect Sapporo to most of Hokkaidō's major cities: Asahikawa (1hr 30mins; ¥5,220), Hakodate (4hrs; ¥9,440), Kushiro (4hrs 30mins; ¥9,990), Abashiri (5hrs 30mins; ¥10,540) and Wakkanai (5hrs; ¥11,090). It is even possible to reach Sapporo from Tokyo by train by taking the Shinkansen to the line's current northern terminus at Shin-Hakodate-Hokuto (4hrs), and then transferring to the limited express Hokuto train (3hrs 30mins) for the final leg to Sapporo. The total price is around ¥27,000, so it is usually cheaper (and much quicker) to fly, although the entire train journey is covered by the JR Pass. All being well, Sapporo will finally become the northern terminus of the Hokkaidō Shinkansen Line when construction on the long-running project reaches its completion in 2030.

BY ROAD The E5 expressway is the main toll road in and out of the city if heading southeast for New Chitose Airport and beyond. It also links northeast to Asahikawa and as far north as Shibetsu. The E5A is a toll road running northwest from Sapporo to Otaru and Yoichi. Near the city centre there are many traffic lights so progress can be slow, but once out of the city, all roads are usually uncongested.

ORIENTATION

Sapporo was built on a grid system, which means that navigation can be both straightforward and confusing, as many streets look alike. Starting from JR Sapporo Station, most people will exit south for the main city sights, hotels and dining districts.

Ekimae-dōri (駅前通り; Rte 36) is one of the city's main thoroughfares and runs directly south from the station (above the Namboku subway line). A large underground street (colloquially known as Chi-ka-ho) runs for 520m in the same direction from the station to centrally located Ōdōri Park [95 C3] and Ōdōri subway station [95 D3]. It takes about 10 minutes to walk its length, and it is a popular thoroughfare particularly in the winter. There is a free Wi-Fi service and various spots with tables and chairs to rest, so it makes for a convenient refuge at any time. Ōdōri Park cuts east–west across the centre of town, with the red-and-white Eiffel Tower-esque Sapporo TV Tower [95 D3] at the park's eastern edge providing a useful landmark. It is from the tower where all addresses on the grid system emanate, with streets named *kita* (north), *minami* (south), *higashi* (east) or *nishi* (west), and numbers indicating blocks, for example: Kita 2 Nishi 3 is two blocks north and three blocks west of the TV tower. A few blocks south of Ōdōri Park is Susukino, Sapporo's lively entertainment and dining district – the main landmark is the famous Susukino crossroads on Ekimae-dōri [95 D4], lit up at night by massive colourful billboards on the surrounding buildings, like a mini Times Square. It is roughly 20 minutes' walk there from JR Sapporo Station, and is a stop on the subway and tram lines.

Of the other Sapporo landmarks, Hokkaidō University [95 B1] can be found northwest of JR Sapporo Station, and Sapporo Beer Museum (page 103) is 2km northeast. Central Sapporo is nice for strolling as the streets and pavements are wide and uncluttered, and there's plenty of English signage, but don't expect to get anywhere in a hurry as the many traffic lights and pedestrian crossings can make journeys a little stop-start.

GETTING AROUND

Despite Sapporo's overall size, the city centre is relatively compact and fairly easy to get around on foot, while buses, subway lines and trams are useful for reaching points of interest further out.

BY TRAIN AND SUBWAY Japanese Rail runs local trains which serve stations just outside the centre of the city and the suburbs.

Sapporo has a subway (w city.sapporo.jp/st/english/routemap.html) with three lines: the Namboku Line (green) runs north to south through the city, the Tozai Line (orange) runs east to west, and the Toho Line (blue) follows a less defined north–south route on the east side of the city. All three lines connect at Ōdōri Station in the heart of the city, while the Namboku and Toho lines also have stops at JR Sapporo Station. Subway trains operate between about 06.00 and 23.00. The ticket machines have English-language instructions, and the fare chart above the machines shows how much to pay for each stop. Fares range from ¥210 to ¥380 for adults, and half that price for children. The One Day Ticket (¥830/420) is available from the ticket machines and it allows unlimited rides for a day – good value if

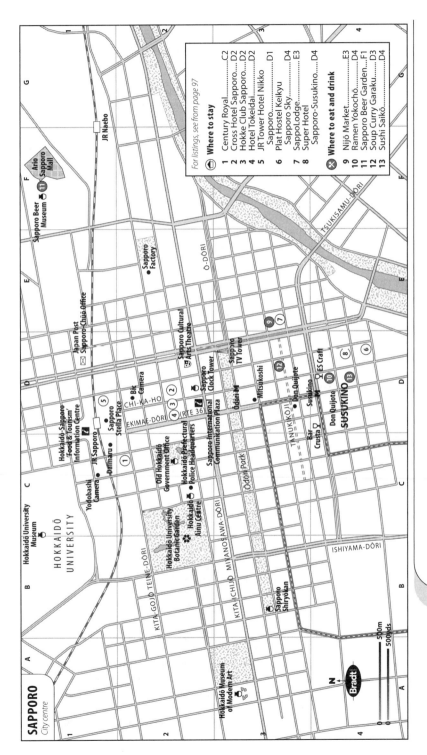

SAPPORO
City centre

Sapporo GETTING AROUND

3

95

you plan to use the subway a lot. A cheaper version called the Donchika Ticket (¥520/260) is available at weekends and on national holidays. Prepaid IC cards (page 67) can also be used for the subway.

BY BUS Sapporo has a comprehensive and easy-to-use bus network servicing almost anywhere you'd want to visit in the city. Three companies, all with fares at a similar price, service the main bus routes: Hokkaido Chūō Bus, JR Hokkaidō Bus and Jotetsu Bus. Fares are calculated based on the number of stops travelled, although most fares within the city limits are around ¥210 for adults and ¥110 for children. Bus 88 is a particularly useful one as it connects JR Sapporo Station with Sapporo Beer Garden, Ōdōri Park and the Clock Tower – catch it near the south exit of the station.

JR Sapporo Station is the central hub for all buses; there are major bus stops directly outside the north exit, on the streets across from the south side of the station. Sapporo Station Bus Terminal is undergoing redevelopment until 2028, but a temporary bus terminal is located outside the station's south exit. You can also catch sightseeing and long-distance highway buses from there too. Prepaid IC cards or cash can be used to pay your bus fare.

BY TRAM The Sapporo Streetcar (Sapporo Shinden) is a tram system which runs in a loop around the city's Chuo ward, with many stops close to subway stations. Trams run at roughly 7-minute intervals during the day and operate from about 06.00 to 23.00. The full loop has 24 stops and is 8.9km long, running from the central Ōdōri area towards Mount Moiwa and back – it takes about 55 minutes to ride the complete circuit. There is a flat fare for a single journey – ¥200/100 for adults/children and free for children aged under six. Pay with cash, an IC card or a One-Day Streetcar Pass as you exit the tram. Passes cost ¥500/250 for adults/children and entitle you to unlimited rides on the tram for 24 hours. The Dōsanko Pass (¥370) is a cheaper version for use at weekends and on holidays – both passes are available to buy on the trams themselves or from ticket counters at certain subway stations (such as Ōdōri, Susukino, Nakajima-koen).

The trams can even be rented out for parties three months in advance, but you'll need a Japanese speaker to go through the process by telephone (☏ 011 551 3944).

BY BIKE Sapporo's flat streets are good for cycling and the city has a handy bike-share scheme called Porocle (w porocle.jp). It allows you to borrow and return electric-assisted bikes at any of the 50 or so ports dotted around the city, making it a good way to get around. A one-day pass costs ¥1,650 and can be bought online, at a tourist office or at some hotels. If you can read Japanese, then you can also buy one at a convenience store for a small discount. Repeat users should register as a member, for which you need a mobile number and a passport; this can also be done online. The scheme operates from May to mid-November (very few people cycle in the winter generally when the streets are caked in snow and ice).

BY TAXI Fares start at ¥670 for the first (very specific) 1,463m, but then rise ¥80 for every 276m after that. Most companies add a 20% surcharge between 22.00 and 05.00. Some drivers can speak a little English, but don't count on it – having your destination written down helps. Most taxis accept credit cards, as well as cash. Taxi ranks can be found outside JR Sapporo Station and some of the major hotels, otherwise feel free to wave one down on the street if the little light on the passenger side is red (confusingly, green means it's occupied); at night a glowing light on the roof means the taxi is vacant.

TOURIST INFORMATION

Your first port of call should be the excellent **Hokkaidō-Sapporo 'Food & Tourism' Information Centre** [95 D1] (北海道さっぽろ「食と観光」情報館; ⏱ 08.30–20.00 daily), located on the ground-floor west concourse (near the north exit) of JR Sapporo Station. This large facility has an information desk with English-speaking staff who will be able to help you with almost anything, from seasonal events and package tours to hotel availability, plus you can obtain pamphlets, maps and other information about sightseeing spots in Sapporo and all across Hokkaidō. There is also a currency exchange, ATM, a charging station and a JR information desk for assistance with trains, tickets, timetables and rail passes.

The **Sapporo International Communication Plaza** [95 D2] (札幌国際プラザ; w plaza-sapporo.or.jp; ⏱ 09.30–17.00 Mon–Fri, closed hols) is situated directly opposite the Clock Tower, near Ōdōri Station (exit 16). The friendly staff offer help with almost any query, and the centre has many English-language resources for both foreign visitors and residents.

WHERE TO STAY

Sapporo has plenty of good accommodation options, and staff at most hotels will usually speak at least rudimentary English. Book well in advance for the Snow Festival, the summer season and holiday weekends as prices increase dramatically. The listings that follow are all within the convenient JR Sapporo Station–Susukino central corridor.

LUXURY AND UPMARKET

JR Tower Hotel Nikko Sapporo [95 D1] JRタワーホテル日航札幌; Kita 5-jō, Nishi 2-chōme 5; 📞011 251 2222; w jrhotels.co.jp/tower. This high-end hotel right above the station has its own hot-spring baths & guestrooms. While slightly on the small side, the rooms offer sensational city views. Service is of the highest calibre. **$$$$$**

Century Royal Hotel [95 C2] センチュリーロイヤルホテル; Kita 5-jō, Nishi 5-chōme 2; 📞011 221 3001; w cr-hotel.com. Near the train station, this hotel was probably once one of the city's fanciest with (still) the only revolving restaurant on Hokkaidō & exemplary service, but rooms feel a tad cramped & dated. **$$$$**

Cross Hotel Sapporo [95 D2] クロスホテル札幌; Kita 2-jō, Nishi 2-chōme 2–3; 📞011 272 0010; w crosshotel.com/sapporo. Understated chic & fresh vibes, plus its convenient central location make this a good choice as a base in the city. Extra points for the friendly staff & night views from the rooftop onsen. **$$$$**

MID-RANGE

Hokke Club Sapporo [95 D2] ホテル法華クラブ札幌; Kita 2-jō, Nishi 3-chōme; 📞011 221

2141; w hokke.co.jp. Comfortable, clean rooms, right in the heart of the city between JR Sapporo Station & Ōdōri Park. The optional b/fast, although a little pricey, is excellent & sets you up well for the day. **$$$**

Super Hotel Sapporo-Susukino [95 D4] スーパーホテル札幌すすきの; Minami 6-jō, Nishi 2-chōme 8-1; 📞011 521 9000; w superhoteljapan. com/en. Reasonably priced & in an excellent location for enjoying the bustle of Susukino; rooms are basic & compact but seal out the sound. **$$$**

BUDGET AND SHOESTRING

Hotel Tokeidai [95 D2] ホテル時計台; Kita 2-jō, Nishi 3-chōme 1-35; 📞011 241 3676; w hoteltokeidai.co.jp. Cheap & cheerful hotel with a visceral Shōwa-era vibe in regard to its décor & fittings, although remarkably there is Wi-Fi. Rooms & beds are comfortable enough, & no smaller than those in more expensive properties. **$$**

Plat Hostel Keikyu Sapporo Sky [95 D4] プラットホテルケイキュウサッポロスカイ; Minami 7-jō, Nishi 2-2-14; 📞011 596 9792; w plat-hostel-keikyu.com/en/hostel/sapporo-sky. Modern & spotless rooms at the quieter end of Susukino, within a short walk of the subway station & a

nearby onsen. The mix of private & dormitory rooms all have en-suite showers & toilets. **$$**
SappoLodge [95 E3] サッポロッジ; Minami 5-jō, Higashi 1-chōme 1-4; ☎011 211 4314; w sappolodge.com. The owner of this wooden mountain hut masquerading as an inner-city

guesthouse is a friendly outdoor guide full of interesting stories. Rooms are private or dorm-style bunks. It can be a bit noisy until the bar winds down, but a good place to hang for 'outdoors' chat. **$**

✖ WHERE TO EAT AND DRINK

Sapporo is arguably one of Japan's great food cities, as most of Hokkaidō's fabulous array of produce finds its way here in some form or another. The city is well known for its beer and ramen; and soup curry, said to have been invented in Sapporo during the 1970s, is another one of the city's soul foods. One of Sapporo's unique, and relatively new, food culture aspects, which is sure to please anyone with a sweet tooth, is going to eat parfaits during the evening (often after eating dinner and/or drinking).

The lively Susukino district is the best place to head for its multitude of dining options, but you will find good eateries and drinking spots all over the city. One of Susukino's most popular haunts for hungry visitors is **Ramen Yokochō** [95 D4] (ラーメン横丁; Minami 5 Nishi 3, 8), a narrow back alley crammed with tiny ramen shops – most are open until late and you may have to queue at dinnertime, but the wait is rarely too long. It can be found two blocks southeast of the main junction.

If seafood is more your thing, then **Nijō Market** [95 E3] (二条市場, Nijō Ichiba; Minami 3 Higashi, 1-Chōme/2-Chōme w nijomarket.com) should be your first stop; this centrally located market attracts lots of tourists yet still retains an authentic feel, with numerous stalls offering crab, sea urchin and salmon roe among other ocean delicacies. It also houses some excellent seafood restaurants, generally open from around 07.00 until mid afternoon, but it goes without saying that the earlier you go, the fresher and better (and restaurants may sell out of some items later on).

Sushi Saikō [95 D4] 鮨西光; Chūō-ku, Minami 6-jō Nishi 3-chōme 6-6; ☎011 511 1544; w sushisaikou.com; ⊕ 17.30–23.00 Mon–Fri, 11.00–23.00 Sat, closed hols. Hokkaidō is the right place to find fresh seafood, and this tiny restaurant tucked away in Susukino serves possibly the best sushi in all of Sapporo. This is high-end stuff & with only 10 counter seats, & the attention to detail & hospitality is second-to-none. The chef's choice omakase course is not cheap (around ¥20,000 pp) but you will struggle to find a better sushi experience anywhere else. Make a reservation by phone or online. **$$$$$**
Sapporo Beer Garden [95 F1] サッポロビール園; Higashi-ku, Kita 7-jō Higashi 9-2-10; ☎0120 150 550; ⊕ 11.30–21.00 daily. After touring the Sapporo Beer Museum, head next door to this German-style Kessel beerhall to feast on all-you-can-eat *jingisukan* (BBQ lamb) & a smattering of veggies, all washed down with flagons of cold, smooth, golden Sapporo Beer. Reasonably priced

at ¥5,280 for 2hrs of unlimited food & drink; reservations recommended; other restaurants on site too. EM. **$$$$**
Soup Curry Garaku [95 D3] スープカレーGARAKU; Chūō-ku, Okumura Bldg B1; ☎011 233 5568; ⊕ 11.30–15.30 & 17.00–21.00 daily. There are many soup curry restaurants to choose from in this city, but this place just a few blocks south of Ōdōri Park is undoubtedly one of the best – their classic dish is a slow-cooked chicken thigh soup curry, but other meat & vegetable options are available. A multitude of toppings & spice levels allow you to really go wild. EM. **$$$**
TERRA Farm to Table [90 C2] Chūō-ku, Minami 9-jō Nishi 2-chōme 2-10; ☎011 512 3547; ⊕ 07.00–22.00 daily. Lovely light & airy greenery-filled restaurant located on the ground floor of Hotel Mystays Premier Sapporo Park. It focuses on locally sourced & organic ingredients, with plenty of tasty vegetarian & vegan options on the menu.

Their flavoursome b/fast galettes served in a skillet are a great way to start the day. EM. $$$
✴ **Menya Saimi** [90 C2] 麺屋彩未; Misono 10-jō, 5-chōme 3-12; ☎ 011 820 6511; ◷ 11.00–15.15 Tue–Thu, 11.00–15.15 & 17.00–19.30 Fri–Sun. Out in the eastern suburbs of the city, this legendary ramen shop is worth making the pilgrimage for. The signature *miso ramen* is served with a touch of ginger which makes the bowl just sing. There is always a queue, so get there as early as possible. $$

ENTERTAINMENT AND NIGHTLIFE

Sapporo is well endowed with concert halls and cinemas, while Susukino is northern Japan's liveliest entertainment district and absolutely packed to the rafters with bars, clubs and drinking holes – half the fun is discovering a new favourite place for yourself!

BARS
Bar Crusta [95 D4] Chūō-ku, Minami-4 Nishi 5-8, F45 Bldg, 6F; ◷ 18.00–midnight Tue–Fri, 16.00–midnight Sat–Sun. Intimate 6th-floor bar with a wide selection of cocktails, whiskies and gins, all served in a quiet ambience with soothing background tones of classical jazz. Cocktail-master Shōji-san is talented, extremely affable & speaks a little English.
ES Craft [95 D4] ESクラフト; Chūō-ku, Minami-4 Nishi 3-2-1, N-Place 1F; ◷ 18.00–03.00 daily. Warm & welcoming craft beer bar close to the centre of Susukino, with a proper pub-like counter, surprisingly fancy food & a timed all-you-can-drink course. Can get a little smoky.

THEATRE
Sapporo Cultural Arts Theatre [95 D2] 札幌市民交流プラザ; Chūō-ku, 1-1; **w** sapporo-community-plaza.jp/theater.html; ◷ ticket window 10.00–19.00 daily. Large modern multi-floor complex for community events & well-known touring productions; the 2,000-plus-seater Hitaru Theatre has excellent acoustics & regularly hosts concerts, plays & musicals.

SHOPPING

JR Sapporo Station is the main hub for serious shoppers. Huge department stores such as Daimaru [95 C1] and Sapporo Stella Place [95 D1] are accessible directly from the station; if you're looking for electronics, then either head to the large Yodobashi Camera [95 C1] store just west of the station or try Bic Camera [95 D2] just to the east.

On the south side of Ōdōri Park is Mitsukoshi [95 D3], a high-end department store, while continuing south along Ekimae-dōri (Route 36) to Susukino you'll come across two branches of Don Quijote [95 C4] (the 'Mega' one is the bigger of the two), the famous nationwide discount store, which sells everything from groceries, to toys, cosmetics and clothing plus a fair amount of tat. If you're up at the Sapporo Beer Museum and have time and the inclination for shopping, then the Ario Sapporo Mall [95 F1] next door has three storeys of stores and restaurants to peruse.

For a more traditional shopping experience, stroll over to **Tanukikōji** [95 D3] (狸小路商店街; Minami 2 Nishi 3, 1-7-Chōme; **w** tanukikoji.or.jp), a covered shopping street five blocks south of Ōdōri Park and stretching east to west for seven blocks; along it you can find a whole variety of stores, restaurants and cafés. Its popularity has seemingly waned in recent years and some parts feel a bit dated, but it's a good place to get a taste of the atmosphere of yesteryear – exploring some of the adjacent backstreets may reward you with more Shōwa-era vibes, and lead to the discovery of all manner of quirky independent shops and bars.

For more up-to-date convenience, **Sapporo Factory** [95 E2] (Kita 2 Higashi 4, 1-2; w sapporofactory.jp; ⊕ 10.00–20.00 daily) is an enormous shopping mall inside a converted beer factory, about 15 minutes' walk southeast from JR Sapporo Station. As well as all the usual types of shops and restaurants, it has a comprehensive collection of outdoor specialist stores such as Mont-Bell, The North Face, Columbia, Mammut and many others, so is the place to go if you're in need of hiking, camping or snow gear. It also has an IMAX cinema and an excellent food court.

If your shopping is centred more on your stomach, **Sapporo Central Wholesale Market** [90 C2] (札幌市中央卸売市場; Kita 12 Nishi 20, 2-1; w sapporo-market. gr.jp; ⊕ 05.00–16.00 Mon–Sat, closed hols & most Weds) can be found a little distance west of JR Sapporo Station (a 10min walk from Nijuyonken subway station or 15mins from JR Soen Station); it is Hokkaidō's largest wholesale market, with lively vendors selling fresh seafood and produce from all over the island. There is an early-morning fish auction which a limited number of tourists can see, but reservations must be made by phone (or fax!) two days in advance – not a straightforward process.

Instead, head to the adjacent **Sapporo Morning Market** [90 C2] (さっぽろ朝市; Kita 12 Nishi 20, 1-20; w asaichi-maruka.jp; ⊕ 05.00–11.00 Mon–Tue & Thu–Sat,) to gawp at the baffling array of seafood – get there early as it begins to shut up shop by mid morning. There are a handful of tiny restaurants on the premises too. Probably the best place actually to eat seafood (other than Nijō Market; page 98) is a block to the south at **Sapporo Curb Market** (札幌場外市場, Sapporo jōgai-ichiba; Kita 11 Nishi 21, 2-3; w jyogaishijyo.com; ⊕ 06.00–17.00 daily), where numerous establishments selling crab and other wares make up this 'outer' market, and open just as the wholesale 'inner' market is finishing up (restaurants open from 07.00) – here you'll find Sapporo's freshest sushi and *kaisendon* (seafood rice bowls).

SPORTS

Sapporo's **football** (soccer) team is called Hokkaidō Consadole Sapporo and they play in J-League 1. The season runs from February to the beginning of December and home games are mostly at the metallic, cavernous and completely roof-covered **Sapporo Dome** [90 D2] (札幌ドーム; 1 Hitsujigaoka, Toyohira-ku; w sapporo-dome.co.jp). It was built for the 2002 World Cup, has a capacity of 41,000 and is fitted with a retractable grass pitch. Occasionally games are played at the less impressive Sapporo Atsubetsu Stadium. The dome is a 10–15-minute walk from Fukuzumi Station at the end of the Tōhō subway line; matchday tickets usually range in price from ¥2,500 to ¥5,000 and can be bought online (w consadole-sapporo.jp). Japanese football crowds are generally very enthusiastic but polite at the same time.

The city's **baseball** team is the Hokkaidō Nippon Ham Fighters. They compete in the Pacific League and play most of their home games at the **ES CON Field Hokkaidō** [90 D2] (エスコンフィールドHokkaidō; w hkdballpark.com), which is actually located about 25km out of town in Kitahiroshima. Their custom-built and architecturally impressive stadium was opened only in 2023 – before that the team used to play at the all-purpose Sapporo Dome. The season runs from the end of March to mid-October, with about 60 home games per year – tickets cost from around ¥2,000 to ¥3,500 via w fighters.co.jp/ticket, and are worth a punt just to experience the stadium and lively fandom even if you have no knowledge of the sport. The baseball field is a 25-minute walk from JR Kitahiroshima Station, with shuttle buses even on non-game days.

The **Hokkaidō Marathon** (w hokkaido-marathon.com) takes place in Sapporo in late August and is the only major marathon in Japan held during the summer, taking advantage of the city's slightly milder climate.

OTHER PRACTICALITIES

Sapporo has lots of banks, and branches capable of exchanging currency will have a sign or counter saying so, usually in English.

Emergency Relief Centre Sapporo ✆7119, 011 272 7119. A multi-lingual 24hr health hotline.
Sapporo Higashi Tokushukai Hospital [90 C1] ✆011 722 1110; w higashi-tokushukai.or.jp/la_en; ☉ 24hrs daily

Hokkaidō Prefectural Police Headquarters [95 C2] Kita 2-jō Nishi 4-chōme; ✆011 251 0110
Japan Post Sapporo-Chūō Office [95 D1] Higashi 1-chōme-2-1 Kita 6-jō; ☉ 09.00–20.00 Mon–Fri, 09.00–18.00 Sat, 09.00–17.00 Sun & hols

WHAT TO SEE AND DO

CENTRAL SAPPORO Compared with some of Japan's other big cities, Sapporo doesn't have a huge number of sights or attractions, but there is still plenty to do beyond eating, drinking and shopping, and as the central area is relatively compact, most places of interest can be reached on foot from JR Sapporo Station.

Sapporo Clock Tower [95 D2] (札幌市時計台, Sapporo-shi Tokeidai; Kita 1 Nishi 2; w sapporoshi tokeidai.jp; ☉ 08.45–17.10 daily; ¥200/free) A famous Sapporo landmark, 10 minutes' walk directly south of JR Sapporo Station, this small and quaint church-like building was constructed in 1878 as a drill hall for students of Sapporo Agricultural College (now Hokkaidō University), although these days it stands out in complete juxtaposition to the modern tower blocks surrounding it. Inside there are photographs and documents explaining the city's history, but despite (or perhaps because of) its fame, it is sometimes regarded as one of Japan's most underwhelming attractions! But it's still worth a visit if passing by.

Ōdōri Park [95 C3] (大通公園; Ōdōri Kōen) The green heart of the city, Ōdōri Park stretches for 1.5km east to west and is the site of many events throughout the year, most notably the Sapporo Snow Festival held every February (page 102), but it is a lovely place to stroll in the warmer months, with green lawns, flowerbeds and some interesting sculptures. The park can be reached in 10 minutes walking south from JR Sapporo Station; it also has its own stop on the Tōhō and Namboku subway lines.

At the park's eastern end stands the **Sapporo TV Tower** [95 D3] (札幌テレビ塔; w tv-tower.co.jp; ☉ 09.00–22.00 daily; ¥1,000/500). Constructed in 1956 (making it two years older than Tokyo Tower), this iconic Sapporo landmark looks a bit like the Eiffel Tower but, at just a touch under 150m tall, is half the size of its Parisian cousin. On the first three floors there are restaurants, shops and a tourist information centre; the basement level has a food court and is connected to the Aurora Town underground shopping street. From the observation deck near the top, but accessed from the third floor, it is possible to look out over most of the city and across to the distant mountains at the city's edge.

At the western end of the park, **Sapporo Shiryōkan** [95 B3] (札幌市資料館; Ōdōri-Nishi 13; w s-shiryokan.jp; ☉ 09.00–19.00 daily; free), a beautiful grand stone building dating to 1926, was the former Sapporo Court of Appeals, but now

The Sapporo Snow Festival (さっぽろ雪まつり, Sapporo Yuki-Matsuri; w snowfes.com) is a popular winter festival and one of Japan's biggest annual events. Held in Sapporo for seven days during early February, across three sites, the festival's main attractions are the large and intricate snow and ice sculptures crafted by a mixture of international teams and locals – themes change every year, but usually include life-size replicas of famous buildings and landmarks as well as pop culture characters, and the spectacle brings in millions of visitors from both within Japan and abroad. The festival began in 1950 when some local schoolchildren built six statues in Ōdōri Park, and from those humble origins it gradually grew into the mammoth event of today.

The main event is at Ōdōri Park, where you can see dozens of large snow sculptures lit up until 22.00; in Susukino some streets are closed off to traffic to make way for about 100 intricate ice sculptures which are also lit up at night; and the Tsu Dome site – a little out of the city centre, but there are shuttle buses from Ōdōri Park and JR Sapporo Station (or it's a 15-minute walk from Sakaemachi Station – has snow slides, sculptures and a family atmosphere, running only until about 17.00. Entry at all three sites is free, and in Ōdōri Park there are plentiful food and drink stalls to add to the festive fun.

functions as a local museum documenting the history of the city through old photos and various displays, with snippets of explanations in English. The original courtroom looks just as it did back in the day.

Old Hokkaidō Government Office [95 C2] (北海道庁旧本庁舎 / 赤れんが庁舎; Kita 3 Nishi 6; w pref.hokkaido.lg.jp/foreign/english.html; ⊕ 08.45–18.00 daily; free) Nicknamed Akarenga (meaning 'red bricks'), this grand red-brick building dating to 1888 now has a small museum inside, but you can probably afford to skip that and just stroll around the gardens and admire the architecture instead. The building is closed for renovations until March 2025, but the gardens are still open. It is a 5-minute walk south and west from JR Sapporo Station.

Hokkaidō University Botanic Garden [95 B2] (北海道大学植物園; Kita 3 Nishi 8; w hokudai.ac.jp/fsc/bg; ⊕ May–Oct 09.00–16.30, Nov–Apr 10.00–15.30 daily; ¥420/300, greenhouse only (winter) ¥120) These spacious and pretty gardens are home to more than 5,000 varieties of plants, greenhouses and a number of historic buildings, including a small but very interesting Northern Peoples (Ainu) Museum (北方民族資料室), which showcases the indigenous cultures of northern Asia such as the Ainu and Nivkh of Sakhalin. The highlight is a harrowing but fascinating early Shōwa-era film of an Iomante bear ceremony filmed in Asahikawa in 1935. In another building, which happens to be Hokkaidō's oldest museum, is a stuffed husky called Taro who was a survivor of a 1958 Antarctic expedition, made famous in the Disney film *Eight Below* (2006). The gardens are a 10-minute walk west of JR Sapporo Station, and only the greenhouse is open during the winter period.

Hokkaidō Ainu Centre [95 C2] (北海道立アイヌ総合センター; Kita 2 Nishi 7, Kaderu 2, 7 Bldg, Fl 7; w ainu-assn.or.jp/center.html; ⊕ 09.00–17.00 daily; free) Just across from the southeast corner of the botanical garden, this small facility on the

seventh floor of the ugly Kaderu 2.7 Building is run by the Hokkaidō Ainu Association and contains a small collection of artefacts with a smattering of labels in English.

Hokkaidō University Museum
[95 C1] (北海道大学総合博物館; Kita 10 Nishi 8; w museum.hokudai.ac.jp; ⏲ 10.00–17.00 daily; free) Located among the ginkgo avenues and greenery of the grounds of Hokkaidō University, this brilliant museum houses more than 4 million specimens, fossils and artefacts charting the human and natural history of Hokkaidō, making it a good place to spend a couple of hours on a rainy day. The on-site café sells excellent soft-serve ice cream.

Hokkaidō Museum of Modern Art
[95 A3] (北海道立近代美術館; Kita 1 Nishi 17; w artmuseum.pref.hokkaido.lg.jp/knb; ⏲ 09.30–17.00 daily; ¥510/250) Opened in 1977, this relatively small museum houses a collection of Japanese and international art, with some English explanations, and has ever-changing special exhibitions (additional fees apply), so check online for updates. The second-floor rest space has large windows and pleasant park views. There are combined discount tickets for the **Migishi Kōtarō Museum** (北海道立三岸好太郎美術館) next door, which showcases work by the Hokkaidō-born artist and is worth a look if you like landscapes and abstract paintings.

Sapporo Beer Museum
[95 F1] (サッポロビール博物館; Kita 7 Higashi 9, 1-1; w sapporobeer.jp/akajim/brewery/s_museum; ⏲ 11.00–18.00 Tue–Sun; free) Originally constructed as a sugar factory, dating to 1879, the magnificent brick brewery is the home of Japan's seminal beer, and here you can learn a little about its rich history and the beer-making process. Beer was brewed here from 1903 until 1965, when operations were moved elsewhere (page 104) and it was converted into a museum. Free tours – with a smidgen of English spoken, but supplemented with an English-language pamphlet – last about half an hour, and you can taste a selection of beverages for a fee. The ¥1,000 premium tour includes beer tasting (reserve a place online). Connected to the museum are a number of restaurants, including an enormous German-style beerhall where you can fill yourself up with all-you-can-eat *jingisu-kan* lamb and lashings of beer.

The museum is about a 10-minute walk from JR Naebo Station, or 10 minutes from Higashi-Kuyakusho-mae subway station. You can also catch the regular #88 'Loop Factory Line' bus (¥210) from Ōdōri Station or from the south side of JR Sapporo Station.

Nakajima Park
[90 C2] (中島公園; w sapporo-park.or.jp/nakajima; ⏲ 24hrs daily) Another of the city's green havens, this large park about 10 minutes' walk south of Susukino has many grassy and wooded corners, a literature museum, concert hall, a boating lake (with rental boats), and an Edo-era teahouse relocated here in 1919 and which now sits in its own Japanese-style gardens. The striking white-and-ultramarine blue Western-style building called **Hōhei-kan** (豊平館; w s-hoheikan.jp; ⏲ 09.00–17.00 daily; ¥300/free) west of the lake is a registered important cultural property; it dates to 1880 and was first used as a hotel by the imperial family during their trips to Sapporo, before it was relocated here from close to Ōdōri Park in 1958.

SAPPORO OUTSKIRTS There are a number of attractions on the edge of and just outside the city, most with good public transport links. Sapporo City Maruyama Zoo is on the west side of Maruyama Park.

The name Sapporo is synonymous with 'beer' for drinkers around the world, and if you're in the city during the summer then you can join the crowds of happy imbibers during the almost month-long Sapporo Beer Festival (w sapporo.travel/en/event/event-list/sapporo_summer_festival) which takes place in July and August. It began as part of the Sapporo Summer Festival in the late 1950s and is centred around Ōdōri Park, where every block becomes a *biergarten* for a Japanese beer company, with foreign beers and microbrews at the periphery and the flagship Sapporo Beer slap bang in the centre. Last orders are at 21.00.

Sapporo Beer is Japan's oldest beer brand, and it began life as one of the early state-endorsed enterprises of the Kaitakushi (Hokkaidō Development Commission). Seibei Nakagawa, the original brew master, spent two years studying brewing techniques in Germany before starting the Kaitakushi Brewery in 1876 (the original premises is now the Sapporo Factory shopping mall), with the first beer, the red-and-black-labelled Sapporo Reisi Beer, going on sale the following year. Sapporo Beer is now available in three main varieties: Sapporo Black Label, Sapporo Lager and Sapporo Classic, the latter being extremely hard to come by outside of Hokkaidō. The red star symbol of the Kaitakushi became the trademark star of Sapporo Beer and is ubiquitous still today.

The main Sapporo Beer brewery on Hokkaidō is not actually in Sapporo anymore – rather it is in the city of Eniwa not far from New Chitose Airport. The **Sapporo Beer Hokkaidō Brewery** [90 D3] (サッポロビール北海道工場; Sapporo Bi-ru Hokkaidō Kōjō; w sapporobeer.jp/akajim/brewery/akajima; ⊕ 10.10–16.00 Wed–Sun; free) is open to the public, with free 60-minute tours including tasting (conducted in Japanese; online reservation necessary), a beer shop and a restaurant. It is a 50-minute drive from Sapporo, or a short walk from JR Sapporo-Beer-Teien Station.

Hokkaidō Shrine [90 C2] (北海道神宮; Hokkaidō-Jingu; w hokkaidojingu. or.jp) Situated in the vast and forested Maruyama Park, Hokkaidō's most impressive shrine, built in 1871, is approached by passing through a massive *torii* gate and along a gravel path to the inner sanctum. Locals still come here for weddings and other ceremonies, and the whole place has a quiet and mystical air, which is equally beguiling when blanketed in winter snow. The park and shrine are a 10-minute walk from Maruyama-kōen subway station. A hiking trail (20mins) leads through the park to the mini 225m summit of Mount Maruyama (円山), from where there are expansive views of the city.

Sapporo Olympic Museum [90 C2] (札幌オリンピックミュージアム; Miyanomori 1274; w sapporo-olympicmuseum.jp; ⊕ May–Oct 09.00–18.00 daily, Nov–Apr 09.30–17.00 daily; ¥600/free) Built to commemorate the 1972 Winter Olympics held here in Sapporo, this museum is surprisingly engaging even if you're not a huge winter sports fan. Along with all the expected Winter Olympics paraphernalia, interactive simulations allow you to experience the exhilarating rush of a ski jump or bobsleigh. Most impressive of all is the nearby **Ōkurayama Ski Jump Stadium** [90 C2] (大倉山ジャンプ競技場; w okurayama-jump.jp; ⊕ May–Jun & Oct 08.30–18.00 daily, Jul–Sep 08.30–21.00 daily, Nov–Apr 09.00–17.00 daily;

lift ¥1,000, combination ticket with museum ¥1,300). The observatory at the top can be reached by chairlift, from where the height and steepness of the 90m run is mildly terrifying.

To reach both the museum and ski jump, take a No. 14 bus (10mins; ¥210) from Maruyama Bus Terminal (near Maruyama-kōen subway station) to Ōkurayama-kyōgijo-iriguchi (大倉山ジャンプ競技場) bus stop, from where it is a 10-minute uphill walk.

Mount Moiwa [90 C2] A well-known mountain at the southern end of the city, Mount Moiwa (藻岩山; 531m) has two main attractions. The **Sapporo Mount Moiwa Ropeway** [90 C2] (もいわ山ロープウェイ; w mt-moiwa.jp; ⏱ 10.30–22.00 daily; ¥2,100/1,050 return combined with cable car) on the north side of the peak whisks visitors up to an observatory at the top, from where there are sweeping panoramic views of the city – the outdoor deck is particularly popular at night; there is a restaurant too.

On the southern slopes of the mountain is **Sapporo Mount Moiwa Ski Resort** [90 C2] (札幌藻岩山スキー場; w rinyu.co.jp), a family-friendly ski resort (no snowboarding allowed) right on the edge of the city, yet one that rarely gets too busy. It offers scenic sunset views and enough runs to keep both beginners and experts happy. During the season, a free shuttle bus service operates from Makomanai subway station.

Sapporo Waterworks Memorial Museum [90 C2] (札幌市水道記念館; Fushimi 4-6-17; w swsa.jp/museum; ⏱ May–mid-Nov 09.30–16.30 daily; free) Japan likes its quirky and niche museums, and this is Sapporo's take on the theme, a museum dedicated entirely to the city's water-related infrastructure, with interactive exhibits. Explanations are predominantly in Japanese, but the fountains in the park outside are great fun for kids to splash around in during the summer. The museum is just north of Mount Moiwa Ropeway lower station.

Sapporo Salmon Museum [90 C2] (札幌市豊平川さけ科学館; Makomanai Park 2-1; w salmon-museum.jp; ⏱ 09.15–16.45 Tue–Sun; free) Come to this small, well-appointed facility on the banks of the Toyohira River to learn all about the conservation efforts surrounding the island's native salmon. There are salmon at all stages of development on display in large tanks, along with other fish and reptiles, and enough English to get the gist of what's going on. The surrounding parklands are nice for a stroll too. To get there by public transport, take a Jōtetsu bus from Makomanai Station (25mins; ¥410) and get off at Makomanai-kyōgijo-mae (真駒内競技場前) bus stop.

Moerenuma Park [90 D1] (モエレ沼公園, Moerenuma-kōen; w moerenumapark.jp; ⏱ 07.00–22.00 daily; free) Out on the northeast edge of the city, this glorious and delightful fusion of art and nature was designed by Japanese-American sculptor Isamu Noguchi; it had a long gestation period, however, as construction began in 1982 but wasn't completed until 2005, with Noguchi passing away before seeing his vision realised in full. The enormous park incorporates mini-grass hills to clamber up, fountains and fun water features, an iconic glass pyramid, and of course some intriguing sculptures. Get there by taking a No. 69 or No. 79 bus (25mins; ¥210) from Kanjō-dōri-higashi subway station to Moerenuma-kōen higashi-guchi (モエレ沼公園東口). Self-drivers can get there in about 20 minutes from central Sapporo.

Historical Village of Hokkaidō [90 D2] (野外博物館　北海道開拓の村, Hokkaidō Kaitaku-no-mura; Atsubetsu, Konopporo 50-1; w kaitaku.or.jp; ⊕ May–Sep 09.00–17.00 Tue–Sun, Oct–Apr 09.00–16.30 Tue–Sun; ¥800/600) A must-see attraction if you're interested in history, this huge open-air museum contains about 60 original Meiji- and Taishō-era buildings (and a few recreations) relocated from all over Hokkaidō, including pioneer homes, stately wooden herring mansions, farmyards, shops and medical practices. You can wander inside most of the buildings, which are evocatively decked out just as they'd have looked over 100 years ago during the island's key developmental phase. An English-language guide is available at the ticket counter. The village is located on the edge of the enormous and fairly wild **Nopporo Forest Park** [90 D2] and can be reached by taking a train to JR Shinrin-kōen Station – from there it is a 20-minute walk, or there are buses (5mins; ¥210) which also run from JR Shin-Sapporo Station.

Hokkaidō Museum [90 D2] (北海道博物館; Atsubetsu, Konopporo 53-2; w hm.pref.hokkaido.lg.jp; ⊕ May–Sep 09.30–17.00 Tue–Sun, Oct–Apr 09.30–16.30 Tue–Sun; ¥600/300) Located a short 10-minute walk from the historical village, this museum covers in great depth the human and natural histories of the island through a varied multitude of exhibits, from prehistoric animal bones, to Ainu implements and machinery relating to Hokkaidō's industrial and farming heritage. Free audio-guides help explain many of the finer points, and while interesting, the displays are functional rather than flashy. There is a discounted ticket for combined admission to the museum and Historical Village of Hokkaidō.

FURTHER AFIELD

Jōzankei Onsen [90 B3] (定山渓温泉; w jozankei.jp) A popular getaway for Sapporoites, this small hot-spring town is tucked away in an idyllic valley about 45 minutes' drive southeast of the capital. During the autumn the hills turn red and gold, but it makes for a pleasant retreat at any time of year. There is not actually a great deal to do in town other than relax in one of the many hot-spring hotels dotted around, but there are some free footbaths, and **Iwato Kannon-dō** [90 B3] (岩戸観音堂; ⊕ 07.00–20.00 daily; ¥300). This unique temple – most of it is underground – was built for roadworkers killed during the construction of a nearby tunnel, and its 120m-long underground passage is lined with 33 statues of the Buddhist deity of compassion, Kannon. If you're in town in late January to early February, then don't miss the evening spectacle of 1,000 snow lanterns made by locals in the grounds of Jōzankei Shrine (定山渓神社). From JR Sapporo Station take Jōtetsu bus No. 7 or No. 8 for Jōzankei Onsen (75mins; ¥790).

A little to the east before reaching the town if coming from Sapporo, it is worth stopping off at **Sapporo Ainu Culture Promotion Centre** [90 B3] (札幌市アイヌ文化交流センター; ⊕ 08.45–22.00 daily; ¥200/100), an excellent small facility where you can handle many of the items on display, watch subtitled films on Ainu culture, and there is enough English to ensure you learn something. The grounds also have beautiful recreations of traditional Ainu homes.

Finally, just a short drive south of town is **Hōheikyō** [90 B3] (豊平峡温泉; w hoheikyo.co.jp; ⊕ 10.00–22.30 daily; ¥1,000/500), a traditional hot-spring bathhouse with stupendously picturesque outdoor baths. Often said to be Hokkaidō's greatest hot spring, the adjoining restaurant bizarrely specialises in Indian curry with supposedly the 'world's best naan' (it is very good!). There is a free shuttle bus service to the onsen from Makomanai Station (see website for details), otherwise it is a 50-minute drive from Sapporo.

Sapporo Art Park [90 C3] (札幌芸術の森, Sapporo Geijutsu-no-mori; w artpark.or.jp; ◷ 09.45–17.00 daily; free, ¥700 for sculpture garden) About half an hour's drive south of Sapporo, this sprawling site is home to Sapporo Art Museum, the wonderful Sapporo Sculpture Garden, artists' workshops, a buffet restaurant and numerous temporary and permanent events and exhibitions. It is a lovely place to spend half a day wandering freely. By public transport, it is a 15-minute (¥290) Chūō bus ride from Makomanai Station, south of the city – get off at either Geijutsu-no-mori-iriguchi (芸術の森入口) or Geijutsu-no-mori-centre (芸術の森センター) bus stops. Self-drivers will have to pay ¥500 for parking.

A 6km drive south of the art park is **Makomanai Takino Cemetery** (◷ 08.45–16.00 daily; free); while a graveyard might not sound like much of a tourist spot, this one is unique because it contains artwork by the famous modernist architect Tadao Ando. The centrepiece is the **Hill of the Buddha** [90 C3], where a tunnel leads to a 13.5m-tall sitting Buddha statue cocooned within a circular, open-topped hill covered with 150,000 lavender plants – the statue was actually already there before Ando created the rotunda around it. Other quirky sights around the grounds include rows of 10m-tall Moai statues and a replica of Stonehenge – locals seem a little bemused by the whole enterprise, but it certainly draws in tourists by the bus load.

Sapporo Teine [90 B1] (サッポロテイネ; w sapporo-teine.com/snow; ◷ early Dec–late Mar) Heading north out of the city towards Otaru, this is the largest ski resort in the immediate vicinity of Sapporo. It offers tremendous views out over the Sea of Japan and the city, and you know its slopes must be good as they hosted slalom events during the 1972 Winter Olympics. There are runs for all levels, including some backcountry options for experts. Access couldn't be easier too: trains from Sapporo to JR Teine take only 15 minutes, from where buses (16mins; ¥380) leave the south exit taking you direct to the resort. During the summertime there is hiking to the 1,000m mountain summit, and Sapporo Teine Golf Club has three tricky but incredibly scenic nine-hole courses.

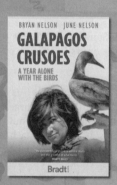

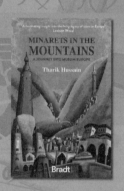
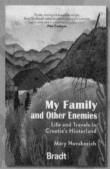

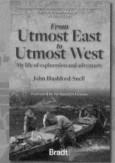

4

Western Hokkaidō

The western region of Hokkaidō covers much of the three sub-prefectures of Ishikari, Shiribeshi and Iburi, and in some ways it represents the best of Hokkaidō in microcosm – there are verdant forests and shapely mountains, volcanic lakes and steaming calderas, rugged peninsulas and hot-spring retreats, plus numerous significant cultural and historic sites; the bright lights of Sapporo are just on the doorstep too. This region also sees some of the heaviest snowfall in all of Hokkaidō due to the influence of the Sea of Japan, and the winter resorts of Niseko, Hirafu and Rusutsu are considered some of the best in the world owing to the quality and quantity of their powder.

It is also a region well connected by transport, with New Chitose Airport to the east, a couple of long-distance ferry ports on the Sea of Japan and Pacific coasts, and the final section of Hokkaidō's long-awaited Shinkansen Line will eventually pass through here on its way to Sapporo by the end of the decade. Because of its proximity to the airport and Hokkaidō's capital, this western region welcomes many visitors throughout the year, and if you have only a short time to spend on Hokkaidō, then it is an obvious choice for exploration and for getting a taste of the island's natural beauty, with plenty to see and do.

OTARU

A popular and easy day trip just 30 minutes northwest of Sapporo, Otaru (小樽; population 115,000) is a small, historic port city, with a still bustling harbour and a nostalgic central area. Hemmed in between mountains and the sea, Otaru is perhaps best known for its harbour side canal lined by large Taishō-era warehouses, with the

Western Hokkaidō   OTARU

4

MAJOR FESTIVALS IN WESTERN HOKKAIDŌ

Noboribetsu Hot Water ('Naked Man') Festival (登別温泉湯まつり, Noboribetsu Onsen Yu-Matsuri) **w** noboribetsu-spa.jp/en/spot/spot1003; 3–4 February

Otaru Snow Light Path Festival (Lantern Festival) See page 115

Hokkai Sōran (Fireworks) Festival (北海ソーラン 祭り; Hokkai Sōran Matsuri) Early July

Shakotan Fire Festival (積丹火祭り / 天狗の火ぐくり, Shakotan Hi-Matsuri/Tenguno-hi-gukuri) **w** kanko-shakotan.jp/en/events; 5–6 July

Kutchan Potato Festival (くっちゃんじゃが祭り, Kutchan Jaga-Matsuri) **w** town.kutchan.hokkaido.jp/tourism/jaga-matsuri; early August

Niseko Autumn Food Festival (ニセコオータムフードフェスティバル, Niseko Ōtamu Fūdo Fesutibaru) **f** niseko.autumn.fes; mid-September

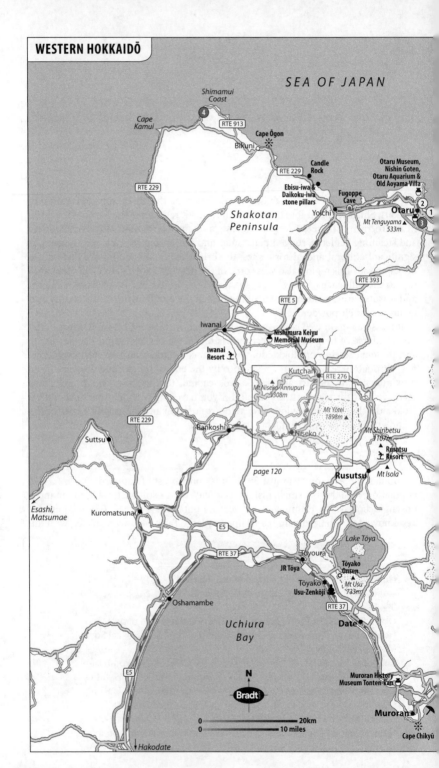

WESTERN HOKKAIDŌ

SEA OF JAPAN

Shimamui
Coast

Cape
Kamui

RTE 913

Cape Ōgon

Bikuni

RTE 229

Candle
Rock

Otaru Museum,
Nishin Goten,
Otaru Aquarium &
Old Aoyama Villa

RTE 229

Ebisu-iwa &
Daikoku-iwa
stone pillars

Fugoppe
Cave

Shakotan
Peninsula

Yoichi

Otaru

Mt Tenguyama
533m

RTE 393

RTE 5

Iwanai

Nishimura Keiyu
Memorial Museum

Iwanai
Resort

Kutchan

RTE 276

Mt Niseko Annupuri
1308m

Mt Yōtei
1898m

Mt Shiribetsu
1107m

RTE 229

Rankoshi

Niseko

Rusutsu
Resort

Suttsu

page 120

Rusutsu

Mt Isola

Esashi,
Matsumae

Kuromatsunai

E5

Lake Tōya

RTE 37

Tōyoura

Tōyako
Onsen

JR Tōya

Mt Usu
733m

Tōyako
Usu-Zenkōji

RTE 37

Oshamambe

Date

Uchiura
Bay

Muroran History
Museum Tonten-kan

E5

N

Muroran

Bradt

0 ——————— 20km
0 ——————— 10 miles

Cape Chikyū

Hakodate

110

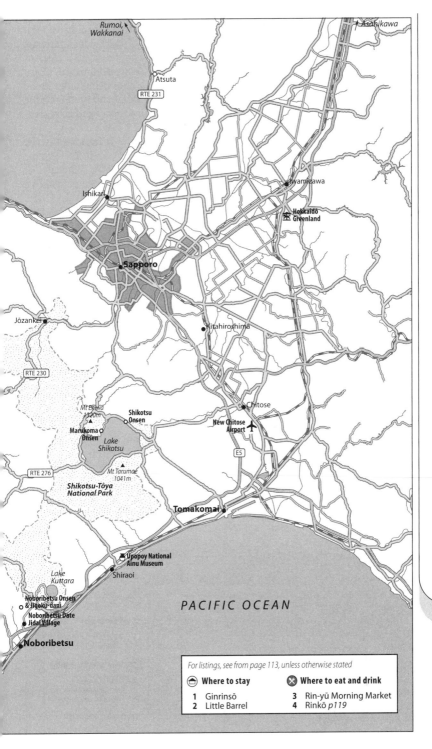

For listings, see from page 113, unless otherwise stated

◉ **Where to stay**

1 Ginrinsō
2 Little Barrel

⊗ **Where to eat and drink**

3 Rin-yū Morning Market
4 Rinkō *p119*

whole area lit up beautifully in winter during the famous lantern festival (page 115). Otaru was for a time the major trade and financial hub of Hokkaidō, and many interesting Western-style buildings remain in the city giving the streets a pleasant old-fashioned charm. After its importance as a trading centre diminished, Otaru became more known as a tourist destination, and many of the old buildings in the downtown Sakaimachi district have been converted into shops and museums; the city has also built a curious niche for itself as a hub for music boxes and glass art.

HISTORY There have been humans living in the Otaru area for at least 8,000 years, starting with the Jōmon and then later the Ainu. The name Otaru originates from the Ainu Ota-or-nay, which means 'river that flows through a sandy beach', although that in fact refers to a place further along the coast where the Matsumae clan developed a trading post – this was later moved to the more sheltered location of present-day Otaru, bringing the name with it. But even before the Matsumae period, the very first Japanese settlers had arrived in the area much earlier, around the end of the 16th century.

Otaru started as a small fishing settlement based around the herring industry, which peaked with a yield of 100,000 tonnes in 1897, a Japanese record during a period nicknamed 'the herring rush'. The population also boomed around this time, up to 60,000 from about 1,000 over 30 years. The herring was mostly ground up and used as fertiliser for the cotton and indigo trade, or made into oil for lamps, with only about 10% used for consumption. The herring industry made Otaru one of the richest cities in Japan for a time, and it was also an important centre for overseas trade, notably with Sakhalin and China. The *kitamaebune* ('northbound ships') sailed from as far afield as Osaka for herring and other commodities, and Otaru developed as an increasingly wealthy financial hub. Despite its inland location, Sapporo was selected as the regional capital and so Otaru was chosen as the city's main port and sea link, although there were some concerns about its shallow harbour and poor winter weather.

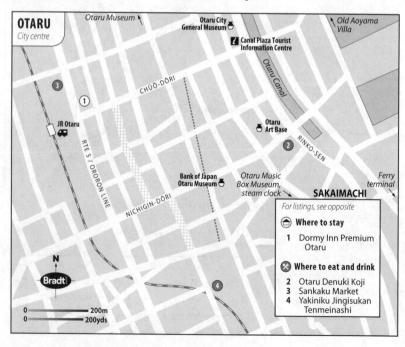

Construction of a railway soon became a priority and it was completed in 1880, with trains taking 2–3 hours to ply the 35km route to Sapporo (and onwards to the coal mines of Horonai), though the track was often damaged by storms. Otaru's canal was built in the early 1920s to allow barges to bring goods from ships anchored in the harbour to the warehouses, and Otaru's wealth soared, with trading company offices and banks popping up a few blocks from the waterfront in what was dubbed the 'Wall Street of the North'. Eventually, however, the herring industry collapsed as a result of overfishing and Otaru's docks were extended out into the deep water, and so the canal fell out of use.

Other hardships befell the city too. In December 1924 there was an accidental explosion near Temiya Station during the unloading of a ship's cargo of explosives – it left a huge 3m-wide crater, caused an intense fire which destroyed warehouses, shops and 1,000 houses, sank boats in the harbour and claimed 120 lives, with many more injured. During World War I, Otaru was the site of a prisoner-of-war camp, and was then bombed by American naval aircraft towards the very end of the conflict in July 1945. As other large ports such as Tomakomai grew into the ascendancy, and with the collapse of the coal mining industry from around the 1950s, Otaru became less vital as a trading and transport post, but its charming and well-preserved period atmosphere means that tourism now plays a key role in the lifeblood of this storied city.

GETTING THERE AND AROUND

By train Multiple trains run every hour from Sapporo on the JR Hakodate Main Line, with a choice of rapid (30mins; ¥750) or local (45mins; ¥750). There are about two trains an hour direct to New Chitose Airport (70mins; ¥1,910) via Sapporo.

By bus Most of Otaru's attractions are in walkable distance of the station, apart from the ones further north such as the herring mansions, which can be reached by bus (25mins; ¥240) from JR Otaru Station. There are also special Otaru Stroller tourist buses which connect all of the cities' sights for the same flat rate (¥240), or you can buy a one-day bus pass for ¥800.

By road Expressway E5A connects Sapporo and Otaru (45mins), or avoiding tolls you can take Route 5 (1hr).

By ferry Shin Nihonkai (w snf.jp) runs long-distance ferry services to Niigata (16hrs; ¥7,500–12,300) and Maizuru (20hrs; ¥11,000–20,000); prices vary depending on season and class. The ferry terminal is about 10 minutes' drive from JR Otaru Station.

TOURIST INFORMATION The **Canal Plaza Tourist Information Centre** (小樽市観光物産プラザ / 運河プラザ; ⊕ 09.00–18.00 daily) is in a big brick warehouse at the end of the main street, down from the station and opposite the canal; it has a good information desk, plus a souvenir shop and resting space if you're feeling weary.

WHERE TO STAY Map, page 110, unless otherwise stated

Ginrinsō 銀鱗荘; Sakura 1-chōme 1; ☎0134 547010; w ginrinsou.com/en. This grand old hot-spring lodge, perched on a bluff overlooking the sea, has tatami-floored guestrooms, & boasts splendid views, private hot springs & an ocean-side bathhouse with resplendent indoor & outdoor baths. It's always worth splurging for 1 night in a ryokan & this is as good as any. **$$$$$**

Dormy Inn Premium Otaru [map, opposite] ドーミーイン小樽; 3-9-1 Inahō; ☎0134 215489;

w hotespa.net/dormyinn/english. A busy hotel but in an excellent location across from the station & Sankaku Market, also within walking distance of Otaru's main tourist spots. Rooms are comfortable, if a little on the small side, & there are budget capsule pods if you really have no need for space. Great b/fast, free ramen, coffee & snacks, & a big indoor bathhouse for guests. **$$$**

Little Barrel リトルバレル; Hanazono 3-chōme, 4-17; \0902 816 2808; w littlebarrel. site. An utterly charming European-style period guesthouse, with beautiful, cosy, clean rooms. Kind staff add to the welcoming, homely atmosphere. Private room & dormitory options with shared showers & bathrooms. Owing to the building's age, the walls are a bit thin & creaky. **$$**

✖ WHERE TO EAT AND DRINK *Map, page 112, unless otherwise stated*

Being a harbour town, the seafood in Otaru is second to none with around 130 sushi shops alone, but there are plenty of other choices too. At the southern end of the canal is a 200m-long street called Sushiya-dōri ('Sushi shop street') which is lined with an assortment of sushi restaurants. You may be pleased to know that Otaru has both beer (w otarubeer.com) and sake (w tanakashuzo.com) breweries.

Sankaku Market 三角市場; 3-10-16 Inahō; \0134 232446; ⏰ 06.00–17.00 daily. Situated just a short hop north from the station, Otaru's small indoor seafood market has vendors offering snow crab, sea urchin & other assorted bounty from the sea which can be bought as is, or eaten in one of the many connected restaurants in the form of sushi, grilled dishes or seafood rice bowls; other stalls sell fresh fruit & ice cream. A bit cramped, so can get busy at w/ends & hols. EM. **$$$$**

Otaru Denuki Koji 小樽出抜小路; 1-1 Ironai; ⏰ varies by establishment. Easy to spot not far from the canal with its small wooden watchtower, this quaint Studio Ghibli-esque complex of tiny sushi, ramen & yakitori joints & other shops is crammed into an enchanting space of narrow alleys which looks quite magical at night. **$$$**

Rin-yū Morning Market [map, page 110] 鱗友朝市; 3-10-15 Ironai; \0134 22 0257; ⏰ 04.00–14.00 Mon–Sat. At the north side of the city in a grey-clad building, this small indoor market has more of a local vibe & is less touristy than Sankaku Market; it's slightly cheaper too. There are 2 restaurants, both offering excellent *kaisendon* (seafood rice bowls). **$$$**

✳ **Yakiniku Jingisukan Tenmeinashi** 焼肉ジンギスカン店名なし; 1-2-6 Hanazono; \0134 21 1129; ⏰ 18.00–midnight daily. Meaning 'the shop with no name', this poky little BBQ restaurant is tucked away down an alley & serves up the finest lamb in Otaru. Only a handful of tables; the super-friendly owner is full of recommendations & does his best with English. EM. **$$$**

WHAT TO SEE AND DO Despite being a small city, there are certainly enough attractions to fill a long weekend, although visits are briefer than that for most.

Otaru Canal (小樽運河) About 10 minutes' walk downhill from the station, Otaru's famous canal is a pleasant place to stroll and is lit up at night by old-fashioned gas lamps, although in fact half of the waterway has been covered up by roads. In the winter it is the venue for the popular Otaru Snow Light Path Festival (see opposite). Throughout the year, Otaru Canal Cruises (w otaru.cc/en; ⏰ 10.00–19.00 daily; day ¥1,800/500, evening ¥2,000/500) operates 40-minute boat rides up and down the canal providing a relaxing way to soak up the views. The cruises run nearly every hour during the day or early evening; the ticket office is at the north side of the canal, just over the bridge. Otaru's iconic old warehouses line the eastern side of the canal, with many having been converted to restaurants, art museums, shops and a brewery (w otarubeer.com; ⏰ 11.00–22.00 daily).

Otaru City General Museum (小樽市総合博物館運河館; Ironai 2-1-20; w city. otaru.lg.jp/docs/2020111400122; ⏰ 09.30–17.00 daily; ¥300/free) Occupying a

Otaru experiences cold and very snowy winters, but despite this the Otaru Snow Light Path Festival (小樽雪あかり の路, Otaru Yuki-Akari-no-Michi; w yukiakarinomichi.org) – established in 1999, and which takes place over ten days each February to coincide with Sapporo Snow Festival – is hugely popular. As evening draws in, hundreds of snow lanterns and candles, which line the path running the length of the canal, are lit by a team of local volunteers, creating a whimsical, romantic atmosphere. The light-up extends to the old Temiya Railway Line pathway which runs roughly north to south through the heart of the city – this was Hokkaidō's oldest railway (dating back to 1880) and now functions as a park-like thoroughfare, with bits of old track and station signs still on show.

small annex facility in one of the old warehouses opposite the canal, the Otaru City General Museum highlights the story of the kitamaebune (trading ships) and the fishing industry, as well as Otaru's natural and human history. Plus an on-site local historian will be happy to answer all herring- and local-history-related questions that may have been causing you sleepless nights. There is a life-size recreation of Otaru's old streets which is quite evocative.

Otaru Art Base (小樽芸術村; Ironai 1-3-1; w nitorihd.co.jp/otaru-art-base; ⏱ May –Oct 09.30–17.00, Nov–Apr 10.00–16.00 daily, though often closed Wed; ¥2,900/1,000 combined ticket) This four-building complex incorporates two art galleries, an excellent stained-glass museum and the former branch of Mitsui Bank, an important cultural property. The combined admission ticket (available online) saves a good chunk of money if visiting all four.

Bank of Japan Otaru Museum (日本銀行旧小樽支店金融資料館; Ironai 1-11-16; w www3.boj.or.jp/otaru-m; ⏱ Apr–Nov 09.30–17.00 Thu–Tue, Dec–Mar 10.00–17.00 Thu–Tue; free) A grand old building dating to 1912 has been converted into a museum on the history of Japanese currency and the banking system. Apart from a basic pamphlet, there is barely any English to explain the displays, but if this is your sort of thing, you'll find it interesting nevertheless.

Sakaimachi (堺町) At the southern end of the canal, this quaint and touristy district of preserved merchants' buildings is chock-full of souvenir shops, glassware stores and sweets emporiums, especially along the main street Sakaimachi-dōri. At the bottom end of the road at the corner of a crossroads is a **steam-powered clock** (apparently one of very few functioning such clocks in the world) which chimes a tune and bellows steam every 15 minutes. It stands in front of **Otaru Music Box Museum** (小樽オルゴール堂; w otaru-orgel.co.jp/en; ⏱ 09.00–18.00 daily; free) – more of a shop than a museum – housed in a brown brick building of 1912 with hundreds of ornate and dainty music boxes on display and for sale.

Otaru Museum (小樽市総合博物館本館; Temiya 1-3-6; ⏱ 09.30–17.00 Wed–Mon; ¥400/free) Up on the north side of Otaru about 20 minutes' walk from the station, the city's main museum is the site of the former railway terminus, and so naturally focuses on Japan's railway history with a collection of miniature and full-size trains (including Hokkaidō's unique snow-plough engines), original station buildings and old infrastructure such as the Thomas the Tank Engine-style turntable.

Old Aoyama Villa (旧青山別邸; Shukutsu 3-63; w otaru-kihinkan.jp; ⏺ Apr–
Oct 09.00–17.00 daily, Nov–Mar 09.00–16.00 daily; ¥1,100/550) Also known as the
'Herring Palace' (にしん御殿, Nishin-goten), this is one of a number of luxurious
houses and villas located on the headland north of the city which belonged to
wealthy fishing families during the herring rush. The Aoyama family began
construction of this villa in 1917, using various expensive woods and traditional
kawara roof tiles, which are not common on Hokkaidō, and filled the interior with
lavish paintings and other refined details, providing a stark show of opulence more
akin to a Kyoto palace. You can wander around inside freely, but if visiting in winter
be sure to wear thick socks as shoes must be removed upon entry and the floors
are bitingly cold. There is also a very good restaurant inside serving traditional
Japanese fare. The villa is a 10-minute drive or a 20-minute bus ride from Otaru
Station (the bus stop is 5mins' walk away).

Nishin Goten (鰊御殿; Shukutsu 3-228; w city.otaru.lg.jp/docs/2020100900596;
⏺ Apr–mid-Oct 09.00–17.00 daily, mid-Oct–Nov 09.00–16.00 daily, closed Dec–
Mar; adult/child over 15/under 15 ¥300/150/free) A little further north along the
cape, this former fisherman's house is what was known as a 'herring mansion'; it was
constructed in 1897 but dismantled and relocated to its current spot perched on a hill
overlooking the bay in 1958. The red-roofed stately building now functions as a small
museum displaying historical artefacts and photos from the old herring industry.

Next door to the herring mansion, the **Otaru Aquarium** (おたる水族館;
w otaru-aq.jp; ⏺ mid-Mar–end Nov 09.00–17.00 daily; ¥1,800/700) is a popular
attraction for families, with dolphin and seal shows. Frequent buses connect JR
Otaru Station to the aquarium and Nishin Goten (¥240). A short walk or drive
beyond the aquarium is an observation deck with great sea views.

Mount Tenguyama (天狗山; w tenguyama.ckk.chuo-bus.co.jp) A 15-minute
drive west inland of Otaru, this pleasant little mountain rises to 533m and offers
excellent night views of the city and bay from the mountain-top observation deck,
with a ropeway (⏺ mid-Apr–early Nov 09.00–21.00 daily; ¥1,600/800 return) for
easy access. The summit area also has a café, gentle walking courses, a zipline, a
bobsleigh slide and even hot-air balloon rides on Saturdays and holidays. In the
winter the ropeway is for skiers and snowboarders as the mountain becomes
Otaru's main ski resort. There are buses twice an hour to the foot of the mountain
from JR Otaru Station (17mins; ¥240).

More serious winter sports fanatics should consider nearby **Kiroro Resort** (キロ
ロリゾート; w kiroro.co.jp), a large ski resort with superb snow and facilities, about
25km out of the city.

YOICHI

Just up the coast 15km from Otaru is the small relaxed coastal town of Yoichi (余市;
population 18,000), an old fishing port and the gateway to the Shakotan Peninsula.
Its beaches attract surfers from autumn to spring, and holidaymakers during the
summer, when in early July there is a big fireworks festival. The fields surrounding
town are full of orchards growing various fruits, with Yoichi known far and wide for
its apple juice, as well as a burgeoning wine scene in recent years. Since the 1940s,
however, Yoichi has been the home of whisky on Hokkaidō; the **Nikka Whisky
Yoichi Distillery** (ニッカウヰスキー余市蒸溜所; w nikka.com/distilleries/yoichi;
⏺ 09.00–15.30 daily; free) is a sprawling site of red-roofed grey brick buildings just

across from the station. Built in 1934, it was the brainchild of Masataka Taketsuru, who learned about whisky making in Scotland, briefly worked for Suntory (helping to establish Yamazaki distillery, Japan's other famous whisky) and set up the first distillery here on Hokkaidō as he thought the area's cool climate, clean water and fertile soil bore similarity to the Scottish Highlands. The museum offers guided (in Japanese, reservation required) and self-guided tours, as well as free whisky tasting, and you can learn all about the whisky-making process and the history of the company, with plenty of information in English.

Virtually next door to the distillery is the futuristic-sounding **Space Dome** (余市宇宙記念館; w spacedome.jp; ⊕ Apr–Nov 09.30–17.00 daily; ¥500/300), a small space museum dedicated to Mamoru Mohri, an astronaut who flew on two NASA space shuttle missions and hails from this town. There is very little English and, although some of the exhibits are fairly interesting, it feels a little dated.

Up on the small hill overlooking the beach is **Yoichi Fisheries Museum** (余市水産博物館; ⊕ Apr–mid-Dec 09.00–16.30 daily; ¥300/100). This old but excellent museum has many exhibits and photos on the history of the town, its fishing heritage, the whisky distillery and the Ainu.

Just down the hill around the corner from the beach is **Shimoyoichi Unjōya** (旧下ヨイチ運上家; ⊕ Apr–mid-Dec 09.00–16.30 daily; ¥300/100), an impressive wooden building built in 1853. Featuring a long, gabled roof and lattice windows, it served as a Matsumae trading post for exchanges with the Ainu – inside is authentically restored, and there are evocative recreations to help imagine the place as it must once have been. Afterwards, head halfway down the beach on Route 228 to **Yoichi Fukuhara Gyojō** (余市福原漁場; ⊕ Apr–mid-Dec 09.00–16.30 daily;

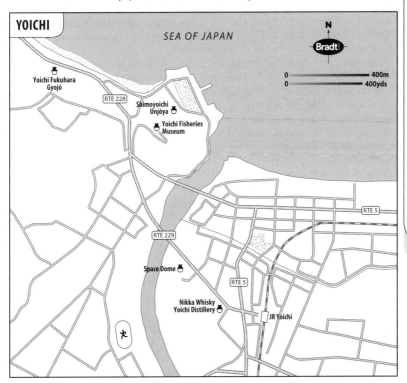

¥300/100), an expansive seaside open-air museum of authentic and wonderfully preserved wooden buildings, crammed full of fishing tools and items from daily life, helping to document the rise and decline of Yoichi's fishing grounds. You can go inside most of the buildings.

Along the coast, at the eastern edge of Yoichi and just off Route 5, is **Fugoppe Cave** (フゴッペ洞窟; ⏰ Apr–mid-Dec 09.00–16.30 daily; ¥300/100), which contains Hokkaidō's best primitive cave art. More than 800 carvings, depicting mostly human figures, have been found at the site, and it is speculated that they were created during the Jōmon period around 2,000 years ago. They were first discovered in 1927 by a rail worker as he was digging a tunnel, with subsequent discoveries accidently made by a schoolboy in 1950 when he came to swim in the sea – it is one of only two caves on Hokkaidō with such art (the other is Temiya Cave a little further east). The carvings are protected by glass and no photography is allowed inside the cave.

SHAKOTAN PENINSULA

The Shakotan Peninsula (積丹岬), to the northwest of Otaru, is a wild and rugged place, a lost world of plunging cliffs and jagged rock pillars, sandy beaches, verdant green mountains and turquoise blue seas. In winter it is a bitterly cold and windy place, but during summer makes for a fantastic road-trip destination, with a full loop on Route 229 which hugs the outline of the coast taking about 3½ hours from Niseko, and perhaps an hour longer from Sapporo (not including stops). On fine weather days the ocean appears almost tropical in colour, and sea kayak trips around rocky bluffs and secret coves to see the famous 'Shakotan Blue' waters up close are highly recommended. There are a few small settlements dotted around the fringes of the peninsula, and some beachside campsites offer sunset views, perfect if you want to get away from it all for a few days.

Travelling anti-clockwise along Route 229 from Yoichi, the first major sight after 10km is a pair of stone pillars, **Ebisu-iwa and Daikoku-iwa** (えびす岩と大黒岩). They are situated just off the shore and said to represent spiritual entities. Ebisu-iwa is the smaller of the two and is the god of fishermen – its narrow base supports such overhead bulk that it looks like it could topple over at any minute; while the larger Daikoku-iwa is the god of wealth. A minor road just before the tunnel leads down to the seafront, and there is parking nearby.

A few minutes up the coast and much further out to sea is a towering 45m-tall sea stack called **Candle Rock** (ローソク岩), so named for its resemblance to a melting candle.

About 13km further on, near the small fishing village of Bikuni (美国) is a scenic promontory called **Cape Ōgon** (黄金岬). A 400m-long footpath leads along the crest of the cape to a viewpoint, from where there are pleasing views of sea and cliffs. This tiny village is the site for the Shakotan Fire Festival – held in the first week of July, the festival involves lively parades of floats, dancing, chanting, and a fire demon who prances through the streets and scarpers through burning piles of tinder.

From Bikuni, Route 229 cuts inland a little, but if you branch off on to Route 913 you can carry on up to **Shimamui Coast** (島武意海岸), a gorgeous wild area boasting sea views, a lighthouse and a human-like sea stack called **Jorōkko-iwa** (女郎子岩), which, according to legend, was the daughter of an Ainu chief who turned to stone as she stood and watched her sweetheart set out to sea without her. Near the end of the road is a car park and a good and reasonably priced seafood restaurant, Rinkō (鱗晃; w rinkou.net; ⊕ mid-Apr–May & Sep–mid-Nov 09.00–16.00 Wed–Mon, Jun–Aug 08.00–17.00 Wed–Mon; $$–$$$); steep steps lead down to a secluded gravel beach framed by rocky buttresses jutting up from the ocean.

Approximately 15km west along the coast is the peninsula's must-see spot, **Cape Kamui** (神威岬), a narrow and stunningly pretty 'dragon's back' headland which juts out into the turquoise waters. This is another place steeped in Ainu legend and was once off-limits to women, as in Ainu folklore it was said to be the place where an Ainu chief's daughter laid a curse after she lost her lover, before then jumping into the sea. From the car park it takes about half an hour to ramble along the up-and-down but well-maintained path to the end of the cape, but be warned that it can often be extremely windy.

Route 229 continues for another 45km, all the way down the western side of the peninsula to Iwanai, offering more in the way of jaunty sea stacks, precipitous cliffs and remote fishing hamlets. While driving is by far the best way to explore the area, there are about four buses a day between mid-April and mid-October from Otaru to Cape Kamui (via Yoichi; 2hrs 20mins; ¥1,810). Chūō Bus (w steikan.chuo-bus.co.jp/en/course/289) also runs one-day bus tours from Sapporo and Otaru which take in most of the main sites on the peninsula, as well as the Nikka Distillery.

If the Shakotan Peninsula whets your appetite for spectacular and remote coastal sea drives, then Route 229 continues for some 120km down the coast all the way to Setana.

IWANAI

A town steeped in history, though you wouldn't necessarily know it, Iwanai (岩内; population 13,000) is one of the oldest settlements in the region; Japanese settlers first came here as far back as 1450 and used it as a seasonal fishing base, meaning that by the time the Meiji government were pushing to colonise the island in the late 19th century, Iwanai was already well established. Accordingly, some of the families who have been living here for generations have developed a distinctive local 'fisherman' accent. Unfortunately, many of the town's old wooden buildings were obliterated by a massive fire in 1954, so Iwanai lacks some of the traditional charm that is befitting of its history, but fishing (along with agriculture) is still one of the main industries here, so it is a good place to sample some sushi – there is a collection of restaurants a few blocks back from the harbour.

There is not a great deal for tourists to do in the town, but art lovers may want to visit the **Kida Kinjiro Museum of Art** (木田金次郎美術館; w kidakinjiro.com; ⊕ Apr–Nov 10.00–18.00 daily; ¥600/free) down at the harbour next to the bus terminal. On display are the works of local artist Kinjiro Kida, whose wonderful paintings are inspired by the landscapes around Iwanai. In fact, there are a number of art galleries in the region. The best is possibly **Nishimura Keiyu Memorial Museum** (西村計雄記念美術館; ⊕ 09.00–17.00 daily; ¥500/100), which – in a striking modern building on a hill just off Route 276 a little way east in the neighbouring town of Kyōwa (共和) – houses a collection of works by Keiyu Nishimura, a prolific local-born abstract painter based in Paris after World War II, famed for his use of soft colours.

On the southern edge of town is **Iwanai Resort** (w iwanairesort.com), a year-round destination offering a small and quiet ski slope with views of the bay and snowcat-skiing in the winter; you can try sea kayaking, camping and hiking during the summer. It also has a small art museum and various accommodation options, including a brewery hotel (w iwanaibreweryhotel.com; $$$).

Famed for its incredible powder snow and world-class skiing and snowboarding, Niseko has become arguably Asia's top winter sports destination, attracting many thousands of visitors from home and abroad each year. Over 15m of light, powdery snow falls on average each season, and the area's multiple connected resorts (page 123) mean there are numerous slopes to choose from, with plenty of options for wilder backcountry runs too.

The Niseko resort area is centred around Mount Niseko-Annupuri to the west; nearby are the two small settlements of **Niseko** (ニセコ; population 5,000) and **Hirafu** (比羅夫; population approx 180), the latter administered as part of the larger **Kutchan** (倶知安; population 15,000), a town-sized city further north which has the area's best amenities and is the main transport hub. Over to the east, the striking conical volcanic form of towering Mount Yōtei (page 125) dominates the region, while the verdant pastures and farmlands all around mean that Niseko has a fertile and productive green season. The area is also blessed with numerous hot springs; one of the great joys of Niseko's winter scene is spending all day on the slopes before revitalising yourself in a piping-hot outdoor bath as darkness falls.

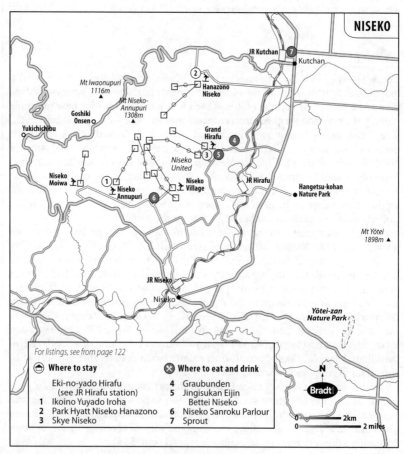

NISEKO

For listings, see from page 122

🍽 **Where to stay**

Eki-no-yado Hirafu
(see JR Hirafu station)
1 Ikoino Yuyado Iroha
2 Park Hyatt Niseko Hanazono
3 Skye Niseko

❌ **Where to eat and drink**

4 Graubunden
5 Jingisukan Eijin
   Bettei Niseko
6 Niseko Sanroku Parlour
7 Sprout

It is not only a winter destination, however, as in recent years Niseko has pushed to become a more year-round resort, with excellent hiking, cycling, camping, rafting, golf and other outdoor pursuits on offer in the relaxed snowless months. Summer can be a good time to visit, in fact, as the place is quiet and prices are more affordable – owing to its stellar reputation and seemingly ever-increasing popularity, during the peak winter season Niseko can be both busy and expensive, and it's advisable to book your accommodation and ski passes well in advance.

HISTORY The Niseko region has been inhabited since at least the Jōmon era, as evidenced by various archaeological finds and a 4,000-year-old stone circle near the Niseko Village ski slopes. The first Japanese settlers arrived at the end of the 19th century from when the area was known as Kaributo, after the group of local Ainu of the same name who lived in the area – in 1964 the name was officially changed to Niseko, which derived from the combined Ainu words Nisekoan Annupuri, meaning something like 'a mountain with a sheer cliff jutting out over a river'. Farmers developed the land around the Shiribetsu River, and from 1861 sulphur mining at Mount Iwaonupuri became a key industry until the mines closed in 1937. In 1904, Niseko became connected to Hokkaidō's nascent railway service, thanks to the building of the line between Otaru and Hakodate, and the proliferation of hot-spring bathhouses garnered interest in the area.

Skiing in Niseko can trace its origins to 1912 when Austro-Hungarian Lieutenant Colonel Theodor von Lerch visited during a trip to Japan to inspect and train Japanese troops; he was an excellent skier and impressed the locals by skiing on Mount Yōtei, inspiring them to take up the sport – statues of the man can now be seen dotted around Niseko. Over the following few decades Niseko gradually developed as a winter sports destination, with the first ski lifts built during the 1960s, followed by more lodges and facilities; the Sapporo Winter Olympics in 1972 only increased interest further.

Up until the 1990s, however, Niseko was relatively unknown outside Japan. During that decade and the 2000s, a handful of Australians arrived and over the years began to help develop the towns and resorts, purchasing properties and setting up businesses, and so turning Niseko into the lively cosmopolitan enclave we see today.

GETTING THERE AND AROUND
By train Niseko is on the JR Hakodate Main Line, with fairly infrequent local and rapid trains between Sapporo and Kutchan (2hrs, ¥2,100), sometimes requiring a transfer at Otaru. This section of the line will be discontinued after the Shinkansen Line opens in around 2030.

JR Kutchan is the principal station with bus and taxi links to the resorts and numerous shops nearby, whereas Hirafu is a tiny, isolated countryside station with no facilities at all (except a no-frills hotel in the station); JR Niseko is a small station with some restaurants and a bathhouse opposite, but is located some distance from the ski resorts.

By bus During the winter there are daily scheduled ski bus services (2hrs 30mins–3hrs; ¥3,000–4,500) from Sapporo (hotels and station) and New Chitose Airport (2hrs 30mins), often stopping directly outside the larger hotels at Niseko's main resorts. Various companies run buses to Niseko including Chūō Bus (w chuo-bus.co.jp), Niseko Bus (w nisekobus.co.jp), White Liner (w goodsports.co.jp/white_eng) and Hokkaidō Access Network (w access-n.jp). Regular shuttle buses and local buses link the main resorts and stations in the winter, but in the summer services are more limited.

By car Niseko is about 95km from Sapporo on Route 230 (toll free), or around 110km on Route 276 (toll free) if coming directly from New Chitose Airport. Both journeys take about 2 hours.

TOURIST INFORMATION

Hirafu Welcome Centre ひらふウエルカムセンター; ⊕ Dec–May 08.30–21.00 daily. Close to the Grand Hirafu gondola and bus terminal, the welcome centre has plenty of English information during the snow season.

Niseko Machi Tourist Information Centre ニセコ町観光案内所; w niseko-ta.jp; ⊕ 09.00–18.00 daily. At JR Niseko Station, packed full of maps, leaflets and bus timetables.

The View Plaza Michi-no-eki on Rte 66 has similar information and caters to drivers.

Town Station Plat くっちゃんまちの駅ぷらっと; ⊕ 10.00–19.00. About 200m down the street east of JR Kutchan Station, has English pamphlets and maps for the Niseko area and beyond. There is a smaller information centre (⊕ 09.00–17.00 daily) in the train station too.

🏠 WHERE TO STAY *Map, page 120*

Each resort has numerous accommodation options nearby, although Hirafu is the only real town with plentiful places to stay right at the foot of the slopes. Kutchan has many amenities but is not an ideal option for skiers who want to access the slopes quickly; while the centre of Niseko town itself (near JR Niseko Station) doesn't have many facilities, and is quite far (15–25min bus ride) from the resort, so doesn't make the best base for powder hounds either. Many hotels and pensions around the Niseko area will provide guests with complimentary shuttle services to the ski resorts and nearest station, so enquire at time of booking.

Park Hyatt Niseko Hanazono パークハイアットニセコ HANAZONO; ✆0136 27 1234; w hyatt.com. A luxury establishment opened in 2022 & located next to the Hanazono resort base chairlift. 11 restaurants, spa, onsen & swimming pool, plus suites with mountain views make this a place to indulge after a hard day on the slopes. **$$$$$**

Skye Niseko Hirafu 1-jō 3-chōme 11-4; ✆0136 55 6414; w skyeniseko.com. Premium & swanky designer ski-in-ski-out apartments right at the foot of the Grand Hirafu slopes. Penthouse suites boast their own hot tubs & panoramic views, while there is an excellent onsen for guests, plus ski rentals on site. **$$$$$**

Ikoino Yuyado Iroha いこいの湯宿いろは; Niseko 477; ✆0136 58 3111; w niseko-iroha.

com. Comfortable, fairly standard hot-spring hotel a tiny scoot from the slopes of the Annupuri resort – think tatami rooms & traditional Japanese dinner & b/fasts. Day visitors can also use the excellent indoor & outdoor onsen, which are some of the best in Niseko (⊕ 12.30–21.00 daily; ¥1,000/500). **$$$$**

Eki-no-yado Hirafu 駅の宿ひらふ; Hirafu, 594-4; ✆080 5582 5241; w hirafu-station.com. Not necessarily one for skiers but a quirky choice for rail fans, as the accommodation here is in the station itself; rooms have been converted into basic hostel-type lodgings, all run by a friendly host. Enjoying a BBQ on the platform as (infrequent) trains roll by is one of the many unique experiences on offer. **$$**

🍴 WHERE TO EAT AND DRINK *Map, page 120*

Hirafu, Kutchan and Niseko Village all have numerous and excellent dining options, and especially in the resorts English is often the default language for menus and restaurants.

Jingisukan Eijin Bettei Niseko ジンギスカンえいじん別邸ニセコ店; Niseko Hirafu, 1-jō 3-chōme 7-2; ✆0136 25 4617; ⊕ 17.00–02.00 daily. Outstanding friendly service & huge slabs

of juicy fresh lamb mark this out as one of the best mutton BBQ places in the area, despite its humble appearance from the outside. There are plenty of other items on the menu, but you can't go wrong with any of the set courses, preferably accompanied by copious amounts of beer or sake. Reservation needed during peak periods. EM. $$$$

Graubunden グラウビュンデン; Niseko Hirafu, 5-jō 4-chōme 2-6; 📞0136 23 3371; 🕐 08.00–17.00 daily. Just off the main road in Hirafu East Village, this ever-popular café can get busy, but does a good line in cakes, breads & desserts, & offers more hearty b/fasts & lunches too. Quaint décor & good service make it a pleasant pitstop whether in the snow or shine. EM. $$$

Niseko Sanroku Parlour ニセコ山麓パーラー; Higashiyama 19-19; 📞0136 55 8918;

🕐 11.00–16.00 Fri–Tue. Hidden among the quiet woods & pensions of Niseko's Higashiyama district, an old metal shipping container has been transformed into a tiny café serving a selection of high-quality sandwiches, venison burgers & cheesecake – well worth tracking down for a quick bite. EM. $$

Sprout Kutchan, Kita 1-jō Nishi 3-chōme 10; 📞0136 55 5161; 🕐 08.00–19.00 Fri–Wed. A popular & invitingly cluttered coffee shop just a short walk down the main street from JR Kutchan Station serving up an excellent choice of beans, beverages & homemade vegan treats. Plenty of comfy seating make it a great spot to chill. EM. $$

WINTER SPORTS With its exceptional deep powder snow, numerous ski runs for all levels and pristine backcountry options, it is no wonder that Niseko has become a top destination for winter sports enthusiasts, particularly from Japan, Australia and neighbouring Asian countries. Niseko is often said to be the second-snowiest resort in the world (after Mt Baker in Washington State, USA), and the long ski season runs from around late November to early May. It also has a distinct international vibe; and English is widely spoken and on signage everywhere.

Niseko's ski resorts are all to be found on the southern and eastern flanks of Mount Niseko-Annupuri (1,308m), with the main tour (going clockwise around the mountain) of Hanazono Niseko, Tokyu Grand Hirafu, Niseko Village and Niseko Annupuri collectively known as **Niseko United** (w niseko.ne.jp/en). At the top of the mountain all four resorts are connected, so it is possible to ski between them, with Niseko United shuttle buses connecting each resort at their bases. The Niseko United All Mountain Pass gives unlimited access to all of the resorts (around ¥8,500/day in peak season; see website) and allows free use of the shuttle bus, or you can just buy a pass for each individual resort (¥6,000–7,000/day).

All resorts have English-language ski schools; and gear rentals, so you can turn up with no equipment, or experience, and get going almost right away. Only experienced and well-equipped individuals should venture off-piste, but there are guided (and helicopter drop-off) tours if you want to make forays into the wild back country – ask at your accommodation for details. Mount Yōtei also attracts hardcore backcountry skiers, despite the very real risk of avalanches.

It is worth checking out what each resort has to do during the summer too, as they all offer a wide range of outdoor activities for even after all the snow has melted.

Hanazono Niseko (w hanazononiseko.com) This family-friendly resort on the northeastern side of the mountain tends to be a bit quieter than the other main ones. It's great for beginners, but also has powder bowls, black, long groomed runs and lots of exciting off-piste tree runs for advanced pow enthusiasts. Variety is the spice of life here, with other winter activities including snow tubing, cat skiing, snowmobiling and snowshoe tours – in the summer you can enjoy the longest zipline in Japan. The restaurants at the base are mostly excellent; and there is a free winter shuttle bus every 20 minutes from 08.00 to 19.00 between Hirafu and Hanazono, or it's 10 minutes by taxi from JR Kutchan Station.

4

Grand Hirafu (w grand-hirafu.jp) Grand Hirafu is the largest of the four resorts, with about a dozen chairlifts and a gondola, a good mix of green, red and black runs, backcountry gates, night skiing and a lively après-ski scene. The village has many restaurants, shops, bars, pubs and clubs to keep you fed and entertained; Upper Hirafu is the area immediately around the base of the resort, with ski-in-ski-out hotels, and many lodges and pensions; Lower Hirafu is a short walk away from the slopes but has numerous accommodation options, from apartments to luxury onsen. The gondola operates all year and whisks sightseers and hikers up the mountain in the summer for stupendous views of Mount Yōtei across the valley. The Hirafu Welcome Centre is the main transport hub at the base of the resort, from where the Niseko United shuttle bus operates throughout the winter, and local buses run in 15 minutes to JR Kutchan Station year-round too.

Niseko Village (w niseko-village.com) Slap-bang between Grand Hirafu and Annupuri, Niseko Village, formerly known as Higashiyama, is the second largest resort on the mountain. It has a dozen green beginner runs, and almost as many red and black trails, two gondolas and six chairlifts, and there is a backcountry gate too. While nowhere near as large or bustling as Hirafu, Niseko Village has some fancy hotels (including a ski-in-ski-out Hilton) and more affordable lodges, plus good dining options. If you don't have a car, though, getting around is a bit more challenging, especially as the buses run to only 20.00. Niseko Village is 30 minutes from JR Kutchan Station by bus, and 6km from Niseko proper.

Niseko Annupuri (w annupuri.info) The westernmost of the main resorts, family-friendly Annupuri is not quite as steep or as busy as the others, and prices are a touch cheaper too. It has a good selection of long beginner and intermediate runs, plus some short, sharp expert trails. At the base of the resort are a small collection of pensions, lodges and hotels, but wining and dining choices are rather limited. It is 45 minutes from JR Kutchan Station by bus and about 8km from the centre of Niseko if driving.

Niseko Moiwa (w niseko-moiwa.jp) A little further around the mountain to the west of the main resorts is Niseko Moiwa, a small and quiet ski resort which is not part of Niseko United and tends to be popular with locals and those seeking a little more seclusion. It has three lifts, family and forest runs, plus longer expert courses, and there are a few hotels, pensions and restaurants near the foot of the slopes.

WHAT TO SEE AND DO The vast majority of visitors come to experience Niseko's long winter skiing season and legendary powder snow, with the resorts open from around late November to early May (page 123). During the summer Niseko is much quieter, but there is still plenty to do. Hikers can spend a day tackling **Mount Yōtei** (see opposite) or ride the Grand Hirafu gondola for a shorter hike to the top of Mount Niseko-Annupuri (1hr 30mins to summit).

Golf, camping, cycling and rafting are all popular summer activities – local operators offer tours or rentals for competitive prices. Hot springs are another draw, and these can be enjoyed throughout the year, although most of them are a short drive out of town. **Yukichichibu** (雪秩父) is a small onsen resort (⊕ 10.00–20.00 Wed–Mon; ¥500/300) tucked away deep in the mountains northwest of Niseko, approximately 30 minutes' drive from Hirafu. Centred around a huge steaming sulphurous lake, some of the resort's outdoor hot springs contain mineral-rich mud which you can slap on and which does wonders for the skin.

MOUNT YŌTEI: THE MOUNT FUJI OF HOKKAIDŌ

Rising majestically above the plains to the east of Niseko, Mount Yōtei (羊蹄山; 1,898m), a towering, beguiling volcano with a beautiful symmetrical cone-shaped form, is visible for miles around (except when it's cloaked in cloud). While called Yōtei-zan by locals, the peak is also known as Ezo-Fuji ('Hokkaidō's Mount Fuji') for its resemblance to Japan's tallest mountain; in the distant past it was known as Mount Shiribeshi, and the Ainu referred to it as Makkarinupuri ('female mountain'). While classed as an active volcano, Yōtei hasn't erupted for around 3,000 years, so the nearby towns around its base are probably in no immediate danger for now.

Skiers and snowboarders in Niseko will have long gazed at Yōtei from the slopes of Mount Niseko-Annupuri directly opposite, while adventurous backcountry skiers sometimes brave the slopes of Mount Yōtei itself and descend into the crater. For us mere mortals, the summer hiking season offers a much better chance of reaching the summit – there are a total of four routes, one on roughly each side of the mountain, to choose from. The two most commonly trodden are: the 6km Kutchan/Hirafu Trail to the west, beginning at **Hangetsukohan Nature Park** (半月湖畔自然公園) not far from Hirafu and taking about 4 hours 30 minutes to climb; and the Makkari Trail, also roughly 6km, to the south, which starts on a forestry road from the **Yōtei-zan Nature Park** (羊蹄山自然公園) – allow 5 hours for the ascent.

Both of these paths have roughly 1,670m of elevation gain, so it is a tough hike by any standards, and all routes to the top are unrelentingly steep – helpfully (depending on how you look at it) they are split into ten stages, so you can easily judge how far you've come, and how far there is to go. The loop path around the summit crater takes about an hour to walk; there is an emergency shelter about 20 minutes below the summit on the western flank.

Locals also claim that you won't need to worry about bears when climbing Mount Yōtei, as there aren't any – apparently the mountain has no natural water sources so no bears live in the area, or at least that's what they say…

About 5km east along Route 58 is **Goshiki Onsen** (五色温泉; w goshiki-onsen. com; ⊕ May–Nov 09.00–20.00 daily, Dec–Apr 10.00–19.00 daily; ¥800/500), a rustic setting of old wooden buildings nestled high up in the mountains which house delightfully soothing and acidic hot baths. There are turquoise-hued outdoor pools nearby too. The road beyond here is blocked by snow in winter, but in summer this is the trailhead for hikes up to the scorched barren summit of the 1,116m-tall active volcano **Mount Iwaonupuri** (イワオヌプリ; 1hr 30mins one way). The small information centre (⊕ Jun–Oct 08.00–17.00 daily) at the trailhead has free hiking maps in English.

RUSUTSU

A picturesque locale situated on the southeast side of Mount Yōtei and north of Lake Tōya, Rusutsu (留寿都; population 2,000) is fast garnering a reputation as a worthy alternative to Niseko for winter sports enthusiasts, with its equally high-quality powder snow, smaller crowds and a wide choice of ski runs. Most of Rusutsu's attractions are part of the sprawling **Rusutsu Resort** (ルスツリゾート; w rusutsu. com), the largest all-season resort on Hokkaidō, with several excellent golf courses, a fun amusement park (⏱ late Apr–mid Oct 09.00–17.00 daily; ¥7,300/6,000 mid-Jul–mid-Aug, ¥5,600/4,500 other times), a waterpark, hot springs and plenty of hotels. As a ski resort it offers well-groomed slopes and fantastic tree runs, with breathtaking views out towards Mount Yōtei, Lake Tōya and the Pacific Ocean. Rusutsu's own shapely landmark, Mount Shiribetsu (1,107m), has ski slopes on its west flanks, while the mountain directly to the south, Mount Isola (994m), has two peaks and offers even more great ski and snowboard options, with an extensive system of lifts and runs.

Rusutsu is a 30-minute drive from Niseko and guests staying at the resort can reserve direct shuttle buses to and from New Chitose Airport (2hrs; **w** rusutsu. com/en/shuttle-bus-winter). There is also a free daily shuttle bus service to and from Sapporo (2hrs) which must also be reserved at least a day in advance online.

SHIKOTSU-TŌYA NATIONAL PARK

The peculiarly non-contiguous Shikotsu-Tōya National Park (支笏洞爺国立公園) covers two main areas, between them encompassing two enormous caldera lakes – Tōya and Shikotsu. The park also includes Mount Yōtei to the west, Jōzankei to the north and the Noboribetsu area (page 129) to the south.

LAKE TŌYA The vast and beautiful Lake Tōya (洞爺湖) is 10km across, roughly circular in shape and has a large island at its centre, while its perimeter has a number of small hot-spring resorts, pleasant campsites and lakeside hotels. Down at the southwestern corner of the lake, Tōyako Onsen is the most touristy and developed shoreside spot and makes a good base for exploring the area. A road runs the 50km or so around the entire circumference of the lake, making for a good sightseeing loop by bicycle or car.

If travelling by train, the nearest station to Lake Tōya is JR Tōya on the JR Muroran Line in the neighbouring seaside town of Tōyako; from there buses run to Tōyako Onsen (25mins, ¥340) almost hourly between 08.00 and 20.00. Dōnan Bus run five services a day between Sapporo and Tōyako Onsen (2hrs 45mins; ¥2,830). By car, Tōyako Onsen is 5 minutes from Abuta-Tōyako Interchange on the Dō-ō Expressway, a drive of roughly 2½ hours from Sapporo (includes tolls).

 Where to stay and eat

The Lake Suite Ko-no-Sumika ザ・レイクスイート湖の栖; Tōyako-onsen 7-1; ☎0142 82 4121; **w** konosumika.com. If you are happier splashing the cash than splashing about in the lake, then indulge yourself for a night or 2 at Tōyako's most luxurious retreat. Sumptuous & stylish rooms come replete with their own private outdoor baths from where you can soak in the incredible views across the lake. Service is exemplary & dinner is a choice of multi-course kaiseki dining or a buffet incorporating only the highest-quality local ingredients. $$$$$

Hydune ハイドゥン; Tōyako-onsen 70-6; ☎080 5835 1085; ⏱ 11.30–17.00 Wed–Sun. Generous-sized succulent hamburgers in freshly made buns are the order of the day at this small but excellent & friendly burger joint. Vegetarian & vegan options, owner speaks great English. EM. $$

What to see and so Tōyako Onsen (洞爺湖温泉) is the main hub for activities, and the waterfront has free *ashiyu* (foot spas) with great views of the lake and distant Mount Yōtei – the lakeside hot-spring hotels have baths which can be used by non-staying guests too.

Year-round sightseeing cruises (**w** toyakokisen.com; 50mins; ¥1,500/750 return) are a relaxing way to see the lake, with boats leaving every 30 minutes. It takes

20 minutes to reach **Nakajima Island** (中島; boats do not stop at the island Nov–early Apr), where you can disembark and enjoy some light hiking through peaceful woods – allow 2 hours for a loop of the island. Visitors should register for hiking at the small nature museum (🕐 09.00–16.00 daily; ¥200/100) next to the jetty, where you can also find the usual plethora of stuffed animals with signs in Japanese. During the warmer months (end of April to the end of October) Lake Tōya hosts nightly fireworks displays on the water, with fireworks cruises (¥1,600/800) offering a closer vantage point; boats depart at 20.30.

Directly behind the town is **Mount Usu** (有珠山; 733m), a knobbly little volcano with steaming vents and an easy but stair-heavy hiking path leading to various observation points (allow 1hr) along the southern rim of the crater. Usu-zan has an explosive recent history, most recently erupting in March 2000. In truth, there are other volcanoes on Hokkaidō which offer more spectacular volcanic vistas, but the views of the lake and surroundings are nice enough.

The mountain is usually accessed via the **Usuzan Ropeway** (有珠山ロープウェイ; w usuzan.hokkaido.jp; 🕐 May–Nov 08.00–18.00 daily, Dec–Apr 09.00–16.00 daily; ¥1,800/900 return); there are restaurants and shops at both the lower and upper stations. Across from the base of the ropeway is an interesting red-tinged lava dome called Shōwa Shinzan (昭和新山; Shōwa New Mountain), one of Japan's youngest peaks and so named because it sprung up from a flat wheat field between 1943 and 1945. The wooden visitor centre explains the history of the mountain and has an eruption experience room.

To reach the ropeway, take one of four buses a day bound for Shōwa Shinzan from Tōyako Onsen (15mins; ¥350); the service seems changeable and may not run at all between January and July, so check locally. Drivers must pay ¥500 to park.

Next door to the ropeway is Shōwa Shinzan Bear Ranch, an extremely depressing zoo which confines bears to purgatory in tiny concrete pits – it is one of the main local attractions here, but you may prefer to avoid it.

LAKE SHIKOTSU

LAKE SHIKOTSU Known as Si-kot to the Ainu, Lake Shikotsu (支笏湖) – a large, deep, pristine caldera lake that lies at the eastern edge of the national park – is much less developed than Lake Tōya, but its closer proximity to Sapporo make it a popular weekend getaway for city folk looking to get closer to nature. Mountains and forest jut right down to the shores of the lake, and there are a number of hotels and wonderfully scenic campsites dotted around its perimeter; during the summer months the water becomes a playground for swimmers, boaters and canoeists.

Shikotsu Onsen (支笏湖温泉), also known as Shikotsu Kohan, is on the eastern side of the lake and is the only place with any kind of facilities; there you can find a visitor centre from where you can rent bicycles, a handful of restaurants and some upmarket hot-spring hotels. Glass-hulled sightseeing boats (w shikotsu-ship.co.jp) leave from the jetty here, and local operators offer canoe, kayak, SUP and even freshwater scuba-diving tours.

Directly south of the lake is an active volcano and popular hike, **Mount Tarumae** (樽前山; 1,041m). If you have a car, then you can drive to the seventh station trailhead (七合目登山口; off Rte 141), located at 660m up the mountainside, for a relatively simple 45-minute plod up to the scorched otherworldly crater rim and bulging lava dome; a loop of the crater takes about 1–2 hours. Tarumae has blown its lid many times in the past 100 years, most recently in 1982, so barring a sudden eruption it makes for a fantastic short hike if the weather is good. Neighbouring **Mount Fuppushi** (風不死岳; 1,102m) has lonelier and longer hiking trails (5–6hrs return), while **Mount Eniwa** (恵庭岳; 1,320m) on the opposite side of the lake is the tallest of the area's volcanic peaks; a steep path on its eastern flank takes 3 hours to climb. Afterwards soak or stay at nearby **Marukoma Onsen** (丸駒温泉), whose outdoor baths are uniquely regulated by the lake via a series of connected channels.

It is best to have your own wheels for getting to and around the lake, although there are a few buses a day from New Chitose Airport (1hr; ¥1,050), stopping at JR Chitose Station en route (45mins; ¥950); the lake is around an hour from Sapporo by car. Since there are no shops or supermarkets anywhere around, stock up on essentials in advance.

DATE

Moving down the coast from Tōyako, the city of Date (伊達; population 34,000) is a place where few visitors stop although it has some historical significance. Originally a Jōmon and then later Ainu settlement, Date was established around the start of the Meiji period and was one of the largest (growing from an initial 220 inhabitants to 3,500 in 14 years) and most successful early Japanese colonies. The first settlers were a large group of mainly samurai families led by Kunishige Date, who headed a branch of the famous Date clan from present-day Miyagi Prefecture. Like many samurai groups, the clan had opposed the Meiji Restoration and so had their land and privileges rescinded, resulting in them moving to Hokkaidō in 1870 to start afresh, with the village (now city) named after them. You can see artefacts and displays related to the Date clan's arrival, and indigenous Ainu and Jōmon-era shell mounds which are to be found all along this coast, at the **Date Museum of History and Culture** (伊達歴史文化ミュージアム; Umemotochō 57-1; w date-museum.jp; ⏰ 09.00–17.00 daily, closed Dec–Feb; ¥300/200). The museum is next to the big michi-no-eki on Route 37 in the centre of the city.

Date is home to one of the oldest and most revered Buddhist temples on Hokkaidō, **Usu-Zenkōji** (有珠善光寺; Usuchō 124; w usu-zenkoji.jp). It is said to have been established in CE826 by the monk Ennin, and was later used for missions to convert the Ainu. The main hall and other Edo-style buildings with their thatched roofs have managed, remarkably, to avoid destruction from the multiple eruptions of nearby Mount Usu, and the whole place seeps with history. Try to catch the cherry blossoms in early May or the colourful hydrangeas in July. The temple is actually closer to Tōyako than Date city proper – look for the turn-off on Route 37 near the Aputa michi-no-eki.

MURORAN

Once Hokkaidō's leading industrial city and still the long-time centre of Japan's steel industry, Muroran (室蘭; population 90,000) is a gritty city with a large natural bay spanned by the impressive Hakucho Bridge, and countless sloping streets which seem to lead down towards the sea – in fact, the name Muroran derives from the Ainu Mo-Ruerani meaning 'bottom of a small slope'. Its harbour is lined with factories, shipyards and oil refineries and is far from pretty during the daytime, but when lit up at night it is transformed into a more beguiling Bladerunner-esque futurescape which attracts Japanese tourists.

Muroran has long been a key city in the development of Hokkaidō. From the late 16th century it was a trading post between the Matsumae clan and the Ainu; in the late 19th century it became an important port on the train–ship link between Sapporo and Hakodate and was designated for the export of coal. The increase in trade and heavy industry made Muroran a target for bombings by American aircraft in the closing days of World War II, when more than 500 people were killed, but the city and its industries recovered in the subsequent decades.

Muroran has never been a touristy place, but it does have some sights to pique the interest of curious visitors. **Muroran History Museum Tonten-kan** (室蘭市民俗資料館とんてん館; Jinyamachi 2-4-25; ⏲ 10.00–16.00 daily, closed mid-Jan–mid-Mar; free) near the north end of the bridge is a good local history museum which, unusually for this type of facility, has lots of detailed English notations. Across the harbour, the headland on the south side of the bridge is **Etomo Peninsula** (絵鞆半島) and is known for its 14km-long stretch of rugged cliffs with numerous scenic beauty spots; these include **Cape Chikyū** (地球岬), where an observation deck looks out over a lighthouse to distant Mount Komagatake on the other side of the bay. Nearby **Itanki Beach** (イタンキ浜) is a gorgeous black-sand beach lined by imposing cliffs, and famed for its 'singing sand' (*narizuna*), so named because the quartz-rich sand squeaks (due to friction between the grains) when you walk on it.

Foodwise, Muroran is said to be the birthplace of curry-ramen but actually is best known for its plethora of charcoal-fuelled yakitori restaurants, which seems apt considering the city's gritty heritage. Muroran in fact has its own variation on the theme, with pork and onion instead of the usual skewered grilled chicken – the city's yakitori joints are located in greatest concentration around Nakajima-Ōdōri a few blocks northwest of JR Higashi-Muroran Station.

It may also come as a surprise that, despite all the shipping and heavy industry, the waters around Muroran are a haven for orcas, dolphins, whales and seals which all congregate in large numbers – pods of Pacific white-sided dolphins can be up to 400 strong. Twice-daily boat tours (**w** star-marine.co.jp; ¥6,600/3,300; 2hrs 30min) to see them up close run from June to August; the company offers harbour, night-time and fishing cruises too.

NOBORIBETSU

By far Hokkaidō's most famous hot-spring resort, **Noboribetsu Onsen** (登別温泉), a rural outpost of the wider Noboribetsu city (登別; population 45,000), is part of Shikotsu-Tōya National Park and can be reached in 25 minutes by bus from JR Noboribetsu Station (1–2 buses per hour; ¥350). Tucked away up in the hills, the small onsen town shot to fame as a health resort for soldiers recovering from the 1904–05 Russo-Japanese War and now has numerous onsen hotels, plenty of restaurants and shops, and makes for a good day trip or overnight stay.

The hotels all allow non-staying guests to sample their mineral-infused baths, and while often a little on the pricey side – around ¥1,000–2,000 – they are generally excellent, and most have a choice of indoor or outdoor pools, with scenic views to boot. The Noboribetsu Gateway Centre (⏲ 08.30–18.00 daily) located inside the bus terminal has a *higaeri-onsen* (day bathing) information sheet in English of all the bathhouses and their prices.

Other than wallowing in a hot-spring bath, Noboribetsu's main attraction is the **Jigoku-dani** (地獄谷) area just a short walk above the town; meaning 'hell valley', this charred landscape is the stomping ground of the *oni* (demon) Yukujin – you'll see statues of his likeness scattered around town – and there are raised boardwalks leading to viewpoints around the gaping crater of steaming fumaroles and sulphuric whiffs. Hiking trails lead a little further uphill in 20 minutes to a small, brilliantly turquoise pond called Okunoyu (奥の湯). Opposite is a large thermally heated pond called Ōyunuma (大湯沼), and its outlet, the Ōyunuma River (大湯沼川), is a baby-blue-hued watercourse which steams and winds its way through the forest;

there are spots where you can sit and dip your feet in its warm waters, so bring a small towel to dry off afterwards. The walk up to the river and around hell valley can be done in an hour, but there is also parking near Okunoyu.

On the east side of town is a ropeway which carries visitors up to a bear park. While we do not endorse visiting the bear park itself, due to the poor conditions in which the animals are kept, entry (fees apply) also grants access to a rather good recreation of an Ainu *kotan* (traditional village; ⏰ 09.30–16.30 daily), with views of nearby Lake Kuttara.

Over to the east of Noboribetsu, **Lake Kuttara** (倶多楽湖) is a stunningly beautiful, little-visited and almost perfectly round crater lake. The steep-sided rim means it remains almost completely untouched by human development, and the waters, fed only by rain, are reputed to be among the clearest in Japan. A small guiding outfit (w paddlestreet.com) offers kayak and SUP board rentals and tours. The lake is a 15-minute drive from Noboribetsu Onsen on the narrow and winding Route 350; there is a car park and viewing spot near the lakeside.

THE HOT SPRINGS OF NOBORIBETSU

It can be a little difficult to know where to begin when it comes to choosing a hot spring to visit, and as most of the baths are connected to hotels you can opt to stay a night if you really want to take it easy and unwind. All of the following have excellent gender-segregated baths for day visitors; and you can usually rent a towel for about ¥300 if you don't have your own.

DAI-ICHI TAKIMOTOKAN (第一滝本館; w takimotokan.co.jp; ⏰ 09.00–18.00 daily; ¥2,250/1,100 09.00–16.00, ¥1,700/825 16.00–18.00) The 'Grand Baths' in this large refined hotel are known as *onsen tengoku*, which literally means 'hot spring heaven', and this is an apt name as the mind-boggling onsen complex (the largest and oldest on Hokkaidō) has 35 baths in total, including enormous indoor baths decked with pastel tiles and fountains, while the outdoor pools look out directly over Noboribetsu's steaming volcanic crater. It's not cheap, but few hot springs offer such variety of mineral-infused waters (acidic, alkaline, sulphuric, salty) or sheer decadence. Last entry for day visitors is 18.00, but you can stay until 21.00, while staying guests can use the baths 24 hours a day.

NOBORIBETSU GRAND HOTEL (登別グランドホテル; w nobogura.co.jp; ⏰ 07.00–10.00 & 12.30–20.00 daily (from 14.30 Mon & Thu); ¥2,000/1,000) Here, lovely indoor and outdoor baths featuring three different types of healing waters overlook beautiful Japanese gardens with a waterfall.

NOBORIBETSU SEKISUITEI (登別石水亭; w sekisuitei.com; ⏰ 11.00–18.00 daily; ¥1,200/600) Day visitors can lie back in a gorgeous large indoor hot spring with relaxing forest views, and there are also saunas, jacuzzis and outdoor wooden pot-shaped baths for a bit of variety.

YUMOTO SAGIRI-YU (湯元さぎり湯; w sagiriyu-noboribetsu.com; ⏰ 07.00–21.00 daily; ¥480/180) The only dedicated public bathhouse in town; its indoor-only baths are clean, pleasant, cheap and popular with locals, but considerably smaller than the fancier ones found in the surrounding hotels.

Halfway up the road to Noboribetsu Onsen on Route 2 is **Noboribetsu Date Jidai Village** (登別伊達時代村; w edo-trip.jp; ⊕ summer 09.00–17.00 daily, winter 09.00–16.00 daily; ¥3,300/1,700), a fun little Edo-themed amusement park featuring a recreated feudal village, a ninja maze and some entertaining historical performances, with enough English around to get by. It is 8 minutes by bus from JR Noboribetsu Station, along the same route as the Noboribetsu Onsen bus.

SHIRAOI

Shiraoi (白老; population 17,000), a small town about 25km up the coast from Noboribetsu and reached in 20 minutes by local train, is most famous for the **Upopoy National Ainu Museum** (ウポポイ民族共生象徴空間; w ainu-upopoy. jp; ⊕ usually 09.00–17.00 daily, until 20.00 in summer; ¥1,200/600), an extensively renovated and sprawling facility reopened in 2020, which is now Hokkaidō's flagship Ainu history museum. It features an open-air replica of a traditional Ainu village on the shores of its own lake, Poroto, and the thoroughly modern main building has excellent exhibits and videos relating to the history and lives of Hokkaidō's indigenous people. There are regular song and dance performances, plus workshops and other cultural experiences, and although it is great that the Ainu finally have a snazzy and clearly well-funded place to showcase their fascinating history and culture, the whole thing has an oddly clinical atmosphere despite the friendliness and enthusiasm of the staff. English signage on displays is abundant; allow at least 2–3 hours to see everything, or longer if participating in all the workshops. The museum is a 5-minute walk from JR Shiraoi Station.

TOMAKOMAI

A gritty industrial port on Hokkaidō's Pacific coast, Tomakomai (苫小牧; population 170,000) is the island's fourth biggest city and was the largest Japanese settlement between Muroran and Cape Erimo during the late 1800s, when it was a village built entirely around herring fishing. The name originates from two Ainu words meaning 'marsh' and 'river from the deep mountains'. There is not a great deal to do in the city, but it has good rail links, is not too far from New Chitose Airport and can be a decent base for exploring this part of the coast.

Located on the eastern side of Idemitsu Culture Park, the **Tomakomai City Art Museum** (苫小牧市美術博物館; Suehirocho 3-9-7; ⊕ 09.30–17.00 daily; ¥300) is a standard local history museum with a model mammoth in the lobby, lots of exhibits on the Ainu and Jōmon people, and temporary art exhibitions too, but not much English. A 15-minute walk south of JR Tomakomai Station is **Tomakomai City Technology Centre** (苫小牧市科学センター; Asahimachi 3-1-12; ⊕ 09.30–17.00 daily; free), a small yet engaging science museum full of interactive displays, various machines and aircraft and an authentic replica of the MIR space station.

The city has two long-distance **ferry ports**. The west terminal (w tomakai.com) is for ferries to and from Sendai and Nagoya; it is 10 minutes by taxi (approx 15mins by bus) from JR Tomakomai Station. The eastern port is some 25km out of town (45mins by bus) but houses the Shin-Nihonkai terminal (w snf.jp) for ferries to and from Akita, Niigata and Tsuruga.

5

Southwestern Hokkaidō

The fishtail-shaped Oshima Peninsula (渡島半島, Oshima hantō) forms the southwestern and southernmost corner of Hokkaidō, and is the closest part of the island to the mainland, separated from neighbouring Aomori Prefecture in northern Honshū by the Tsugaru Strait, which is just 19.5km wide at its narrowest point. Owing to its geography, this area was the first part of the island to be occupied by small groups of ethnic Japanese from around 1400, although it had long been a stronghold of the native Ainu. It took another 400 years or so for the shōgunate to really start developing a more sustained presence here in their efforts to expand Japanese territories north and ultimately take full control of Hokkaidō. As a result, parts of this southern region feel much more 'Japanese' than other areas of the island, especially around the small town of Matsumae, which nestles at the very southern tip of the island. From there the Matsumae clan controlled nearly all trade on Hokkaidō, and also constructed Japan's northernmost and last-ever-to-be-built Edo-style castle; the only one of its kind on Hokkaidō.

The peninsula basically comprises Oshima and Hiyama subprefectures, and the terrain is predominantly forested and mountainous. There are a number of active volcanoes and hot springs, plus a resident population of brown bears which are reputed to be somewhat more aggressive than others on the island. Fishing villages and pockets of farmland are dotted along the narrow coastal belts, with small settlements nestling among the few flat inland river valleys.

MAJOR FESTIVALS IN SOUTHWESTERN HOKKAIDŌ

Kikonai Kanchū Misogi Festival (木古内寒中みそぎ祭り, Kikonai Kanchū Misogi Matsuri) 13–15 January. See page 161.

Ōnuma Hakodate Snow & Ice Festival (大沼函館雪と氷の祭典, Ōnuma Hakodate Yuki to Kōri no Saiten) Early February

Matsumae Cherry Blossom Festival (松前さくらまつり, Matsumae Sakura Matsuri) Late April to mid-May. See page 158.

Esan Azalea Festival (恵山つづじまつり, Esan Tsutsuji Matsuri) Mid-May to early June. See page 154.

Hakodate Port Festival (函館港まつり, Hakodate Minato Matsuri) w hakodate-minatomatsuri.org; 1–5 August

Shikabe Sea & Hot Springs Festival (しかべ海と温泉のまつり, Shikabe Umi to Onsen no Matsuri) w shikabe.jp/event_ideyu; mid-August

Hakodate Christmas Fantasy (はこだてクリスマスファンタジー, Hakodate Kurisumasu Fantajī) w hakodatexmas.com; 1–25 December

The largest city and main gateway to the region is Hakodate, a historic port renowned for its seafood and famous views – it also has direct Shinkansen and ferry connections to the mainland. It is Hokkaidō's third-largest city (including neighbouring Hokuto) and can be reached from Sapporo in about 4 hours by train; if travelling the main east coast route between the two cities (either by rail or by road), you'll be accompanied by sweeping views of Uchiura Bay, alongside the distinctive clean lines of Mount Komagatake and the island-dotted lakes of Ōnuma Park just north of Hakodate. Much of the rest of the peninsula is remote and tricky to reach by public transport, though, so a rental car (or perhaps road bicycle) is the preferred way to explore its many out-of-the-way corners.

HAKODATE

Mention the name Hakodate (函館; population 265,000) to Japanese people and two things will instantly spring to mind – the famous night view from the top of the city's namesake mountain, and its plethora of fabulous seafood. These may be Hakodate's main draws, but the city has much more to offer besides. It is a place steeped in history, with an old district of historical Western-style buildings and hilly cobbled streets that help to give Hakodate a sense of character and cosmopolitan flavour – something that is unique on Hokkaidō. It also serves as a great base for exploring other attractions in the region.

Dominated by the 334m-high Mount Hakodate at its southern end, Hakodate is built on a narrow sandbar, or tombolo, which formed roughly 3,000 years ago and connects the small peak to the main landmass of Hokkaidō proper. A road and ropeway lead up to the peak's summit, from where the unique layout of Hakodate, hemmed in by the ocean on two sides, has become a major tourist attraction (and has in fact been named as one of the 'Three Major Night Views of Japan'; page 53).

Arriving in the downtown area for the first time, there is no mistaking that this is a major port and seaside city – the air is fresh and salty, seagulls squawk in the distance and the smell of seafood wafts down the streets. The fishing in the waters around Hakodate is reputed to be outstanding, with a large variety of marine life such as squid, clams and crab just beyond the harbour walls – this is due to its geographical location, with two separate sea currents and the Tsugaru Strait (page 136) close by.

Most of Hakodate's popular sights and attractions are to be found in the old southwestern end of the city, spread across the lower slopes of Mount Hakodate and up along the narrow isthmus as far as the morning market and JR Hakodate Station. Beyond that, the northern side of town has more of a generic and industrial feel, and apart from the old fortress at Goryōkaku, there are few reasons for tourists to spend much time there. At the eastern edge of the city lies the airport and the popular historic hot-spring district of Yunokawa Onsen. A handy, if slightly rickety tram system connects the northeastern and southern ends of the city.

During the winter months (December to February), many of the old town districts are lit up with thousands of festive lights, and throughout much of December there is a Christmas festival, the Hakodate Christmas Fantasy, which includes a large tree, nightly fireworks and steaming soup stalls lining the streets down in the bay area.

HISTORY Hakodate is defined first and foremost by its unique geography. Mount Hakodate is the remnant of a volcano (now extinct) which formed millions of

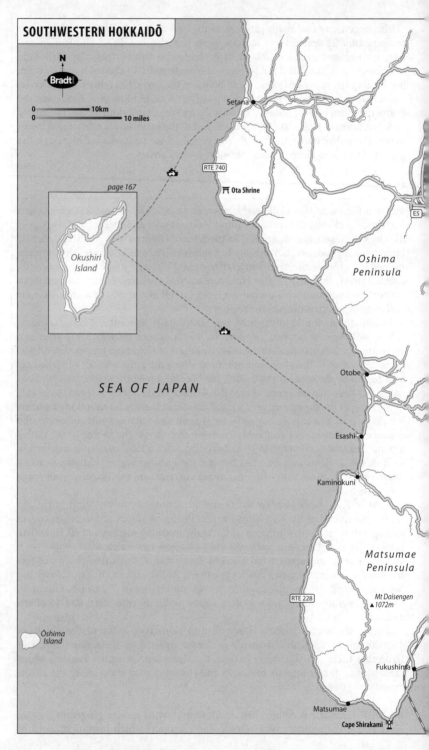

SOUTHWESTERN HOKKAIDŌ

N

Bradt

0 ——— 10km
0 ——— 10 miles

Setana

RTE 740

⛩ Ota Shrine

page 167

Okushiri Island

Oshima Peninsula

E5

SEA OF JAPAN

Otobe

Esashi

Kaminokuni

Matsumae Peninsula

RTE 228

Mt Daisengen
▲1072m

Ōshima Island

Fukushima

Matsumae

Cape Shirakami ⛩

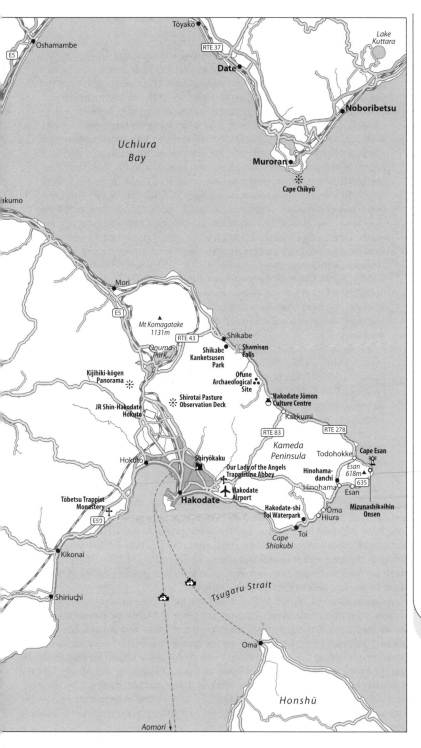

Tōyako

RTE 37

Lake Kuttara

Oshamambe

E5

Date

Noboribetsu

Uchiura Bay

Muroran

Cape Chikyū

akumo

Mori

E5

Mt Komagatake 1131m

RTE 43

Shikabe

Onuma Park

Shikabe Kanketsusen Park

Shamisen Falls

Kijihiki-kōgen Panorama

Ōfune Archaeological Site

Shirotai Pasture Observation Deck

Hakodate Jōmon Culture Centre

JR Shin-Hakodate Hokuto

Kakkumi

RTE 83

RTE 278

Kameda Peninsula

Todohokke

Cape Esan

Hokuto

Shiryōkaku

Our Lady of the Angels Trappistine Abbey

Hinohama-danchi

Esan 618m

635

Hinohama

Tōbetsu Trappist Monastery

Hakodate

Hakodate Airport

Esan

Mizunashikaihin Onsen

E59

Hakodate-shi Toi Waterpark

Ōma Hiura

Kikonai

Toi

Shiriuchi

Cape Shiokubi

Tsugaru Strait

Ōma

Honshū

Aomori

Separating Honshū and Hokkaidō, the Tsugaru Strait (津軽海峡, Tsugaru Kaikyō) connects the Sea of Japan and the Pacific Ocean and is only 19.5km across at its narrowest point. The Tsugaru Current flows eastwards from the Sea of Japan into the Pacific. Early Western (pre-20th century) maps referred to it as the Strait of Sangar, but this name was never used in Japan.

What sets the strait apart from the bodies of water that separate the other main Japanese islands is that it is unusually deep, plummeting to 449m at its deepest point – this has had huge implications on the ecology of northern Japan. In prehistoric times, when the sea level was much lower and land bridges connected most of the Japanese islands to each other and also to mainland Asia, the sheer depth of the Tsugaru Strait meant that Hokkaidō and Honshū remained separated (although some do postulate that they may have been connected at one time, if only for a relatively brief period), meaning few animal species could cross the gap. This resulted in Hokkaidō's very different ecology compared with the rest of Japan, having more in common with the northern environments of Sakhalin and the Kuril Islands (with which it did form land bridges). British naturalist Thomas Blakiston noticed this fact in the late 19th century while living in Hakodate. This faunal boundary – called Blakiston's Line (page 8) – runs along the Tsugaru Strait and marks a significant dividing line, either side of which only certain species are found.

As well as being ecologically important, the Tsugaru Strait is also a crucial shipping lane – not only for Japanese vessels plying the waters between Honshū and Hokkaidō, but for US navy warships and submarines between the Pacific and the Sea of Japan; parts of the strait are designated as international waters allowing for their passage. The entire strait is part of Japan's exclusive economic zone, however.

Currents in the strait are known to be particularly strong, and its worst disaster was the sinking of the *Tōya Maru* train-ferry during a typhoon in September 1954, resulting in the loss of more than 1,000 lives (page 160).

---

years ago, creating a small island; the sandbar on which the city itself is built didn't appear until much later, around 3,000 years ago. Of course, this whole area had long been occupied by the Ainu, and Hakodate probably started off as a small Ainu settlement. From around the 1400s, small groups of Japanese settlers were certainly living in the area, and it is said that the name Hakodate possibly derives from the word for 'box', as a prominent box-shaped mansion, or possibly early fort, was built there by the Japanese in the late 15th century.

As more Japanese moved to Ezo, Hakodate grew from a simple trading post to a more substantial settlement, although the town of Matsumae (some 95km away down the coast) was the region's main centre of trade and governance between about 1600 and 1800. There were regular minor scuffles between Japanese and Ainu groups during this period (mainly over trade) as the Matsumae clan gradually stamped their authority over the region, and particularly over the Ainu, who they gradually began to subjugate. There was one major and bloody revolt by the Ainu in 1669 called Shakushain's War (page 24), and by the Hōei period (1704–11) Hakodate was really beginning to flourish as a fishing port, with more Japanese merchants arriving and temples being built.

The city rose to very notable prominence when in 1802 the shōgunate (central government) decided to take direct charge of affairs in Ezo itself, relinquishing all regional control from the Matsumae clan and shifting the seat of power to Hakodate. This made sense as Hakodate had long been growing as an important fishery, trading and now governing post, aided by the fact that it had a much superior harbour to Matsumae's small wind- and wave-swept inlet.

In March 1854, Commodore Matthew Perry signed the Kanagawa Treaty with officials in Edo (Tokyo); it was a landmark settlement in which the Japanese agreed (under the threat of force) to open up the ports of Shimoda and Hakodate to American trading vessels. On 17 May, Perry's fleet of 'black ships' arrived in Hakodate and remained anchored in the harbour for just under a month. On signing the treaty, Perry had originally requested access to Matsumae's harbour but the shōgunate was reluctant and insisted that Hakodate had the superior port – which, to Perry's great satisfaction, turned out to be the case. However, officials in Hakodate claimed not to have heard the news of the treaty by the time Perry arrived, and so they ordered all the locals to shut themselves inside their homes and not even look out into the harbour at the American ships; shopkeepers were told not to sell any sake to foreign sailors who may come ashore. Local officials did eventually soften their stance and residents began to interact with the foreign visitors, but the Americans were seemingly still not entirely trusted – they later reported seeing no local women out and about during the duration of their visit.

The visit of Commodore Perry was a big turning point for Hakodate, Hokkaidō and arguably Japan as a whole, as it finally opened up the region to significant foreign trade. The 1858 Treaty of Amity and Commerce signed with the USA resulted in five ports (including Hakodate) fully opening for international trade; British and other European powers soon came to orchestrate their own trade agreements too, with Hakodate remaining a key port for the entry of foreign vessels. From around this time, an increasing number of foreign merchants, officials and churchmen came to settle in Hakodate, resulting in the city's various cosmopolitan 'foreigner districts' with their churches, consulates and Western-style architecture which still characterises Hakodate even today.

Fourteen years after the visit of Perry, Hakodate was in the spotlight again, this time during the Battle of Hakodate (page 138), a fairly major conflict and one of the last stands between the old shōgunate's supporters and the new Meiji government forces. While the prolonged main stand-off was centred around the city's Goryōkaku fort, fighting was even more widespread, with battles at other key locations all around southwest Hokkaidō.

On account of it being a narrow and tightly packed city built on a particularly windy promontory, Hakodate has been devastated by numerous, city-wide fires over the years, notably in 1878 and then again in 1879, when huge fires ripped through the city destroying many of the buildings. These were followed by another large fire in 1907 (after which most of the surviving Western-style buildings in the city were built), and another in 1921 which destroyed 4,000 buildings. Then, on 21 March 1934 disaster struck Hakodate yet again in what was later called the 'Great Fire of Hakodate' – a searing blaze that started in a single house ended up burning down about two-thirds of the city's buildings. Fed by strong winds and red-hot floating debris, the fire raged for two days and was one of the worst urban fires Japan has ever seen. It is estimated that around 2,000 people were killed, with nearly 10,000 suffering injuries, and a staggering 145,000 people were made homeless, with many locals never returning to the city.

THE BATTLE OF HAKODATE

Taking place between 4 December 1868 and 27 June 1869, the Battle of Hakodate was a major conflict between the remaining fragmented forces and supporters of the Tokugawa shōgunate (whose 260-year reign over Japan had just come to an end), and the armies of the newly formed Meiji government. It was the final stage of the much broader Boshin War, or Japanese Civil War, during which the Meiji forces overthrew the shōgunate and took up occupation of Edo (Tokyo). Enomoto Takeaki was vice-commander of the shōgunate navy and, refusing to submit to the new rulers, he took his fleet of warships northwards, accompanied by other high-ranking supporters and members of the French military who had helped to train and modernise the shōgunate army, and now felt a sense of loyalty to them.

As the fleet travelled north, it gained ships and additional support, all the while pursued by the imperial army. The rebel army, numbering around 3,000, eventually arrived in southern Ezo (Hokkaidō) in October 1868, overcame the resisting Matsumae forces (who had already pledged allegiance to the new government) and took Hakodate, setting up base in Goryōkaku on 26 October. During the next few weeks, the rebels attacked other government strongholds across southern Hokkaidō, including Matsumae and Esashi and, although victorious, they did lose two vessels near Esashi due to bad weather. On 25 December the rebel army, having eliminated all local opposition, declared themselves leaders of a new Ezo Republic, although the Meiji government of course refused to acknowledge this.

Meanwhile down south, as the imperial army strengthened its fleet of warships, the rebels set up a wall of defences around Hakodate in anticipation of the arrival of government forces. On 20 March 1869, the imperial navy arrived at Miyako in Iwate Prefecture, and in a brave, or perhaps foolish, move the rebels sent three warships to launch a surprise attack on them, in what is known as the Battle of Miyako Bay. The first rebel ship, the *Kaiten*, approached the bay with an American flag hoisted aloft in a cunning ploy to deceive the navy. In the brief few moments before boarding the imperial army's iron-clad flagship, the *Kōtetsu*, the rebels then raised their flag of the Ezo Republic. The attack was short-lived, however, as the *Kōtetsu* soon inflicted huge losses on the rebels (with a newly acquired and recently invented Gatling gun), and the Ezo Republic forces escaped back to Hokkaidō, thoroughly depleted and one ship down.

Unperturbed, the imperial army continued northwards and on 9 April they finally landed on Hokkaidō. Now numbering around 7,000 men, they systematically took hold of rebel outposts, before more prolonged fighting around Hakodate and at Goryōkaku. In early May, the two rival navies did battle off the coast of Hakodate, but the depleted fleet of the rebel navy succumbed within a matter of days. The Ezo Republic leaders finally admitted surrender in June 1869, marking the end of the old feudal regime in Japan.

But the turn of the 20th century was also a prosperous time for Hakodate, with the fishing industry continuing to boom and the inauguration of the Seikan railway ferry, connecting Hakodate to Honshū and making the city more accessible than ever before. Compared with other cities in Japan, Hakodate got off rather lightly during allied raids in World War II; two bombings on 14 and 15 July 1945 destroyed around 400 homes in the west of the city, and a ferry was attacked killing almost all the 400 or so passengers on board.

In recent years, Hakodate has grown as one of Hokkaidō's main tourist spots, welcoming millions of domestic and international visitors in the booming tourism years before the dawn of the Covid-19 pandemic in 2020.

GETTING THERE AND AWAY

By train From Sapporo, Super Hokuto and Hokuto trains (3½/4hrs; ¥8,910–9,440) depart almost hourly for the 318km journey to Hakodate, stopping off at a number of stations en route, including Minami-Chitose (for connections to New Chitose Airport), Tomakomai and Shin-Hakodate-Hokuto.

The Shinkansen runs all the way from Tokyo to its terminus at Shin-Hakodate-Hokuto (4hrs; ¥23,630). The Hokkaidō Shinkansen Line is the northernmost section of the route (until the next section and Sapporo is completed by 2031) and runs between JR Shin-Hakodate-Hokuto Station and Shin-Aomori Station on the mainland in about an hour, with a couple of smaller stops in between, plus a long stretch of tunnel as the train crosses beneath the sea separating the two islands. The grand-sounding Hakodate Line runs between JR Shin-Hakodate-Hokuto and Hakodate stations (20mins; ¥360), along with local trains heading further north.

By air The region is served by Hakodate Airport (函館空港, Hakodate Kūkō; HKD), which lies about 11km east of the city. Domestic routes include daily flights to/from Tokyo (Haneda), Osaka (Itami) and Nagoya, and there are regional flights to Sapporo (New Chitose and Okadama airports) and Okushiri Island. There are also direct international flights between Sapporo and Taipei, Seoul, Hong Kong and Shanghai.

The domestic and smaller international terminals are adjacent to each other and connected, with most shops, restaurants and other services located in the domestic building.

Airport transfers The most popular way to get to and from central Hakodate is by shuttle bus (20mins; ¥450); the 'express line' runs a few times an hour between the airport (bus stop 3) and JR Hakodate Station (bus stop 11), with stops at Yunokawa Onsen, the bay area and other city centre locations. Bus line 96 (35mins; ¥300) and line 5 (50mins; ¥300) also run between the station and airport. Pay on board. There are also buses between the airport and JR Shin-Hakodate-Hokuto Station, and the Ōnuma area. Taxis take about 20 minutes and cost around ¥3,000.

By ferry Hakodate has long been the historical entry point on to Hokkaidō by sea from mainland Honshū, and ferries remain a popular (and affordable) way to get here. There are two main operators plying the waters between Hokkaidō and the mainland's most northerly prefecture, Aomori. Tsugaru Kaikyo Ferry (w tsugarukaikyo.co.jp/global/en) has around eight scheduled sailings every day (3hrs 40mins; ¥2,260–7,230) for passengers and vehicles between Aomori Ferry Port and Hakodate Ferry Terminal. From the terminal it's a 10-minute taxi ride (around ¥1,600) to JR Hakodate Station, and there are buses (30mins; ¥320) to coincide with sailings too.

Tsugaru Kaikyo also runs two ferries per day on the historical route between Hakodate and the small town of Oma (90mins; ¥1,840–3,610) at the very tip of the remote Shimokita Peninsula in Aomori. Prices and schedules for both routes

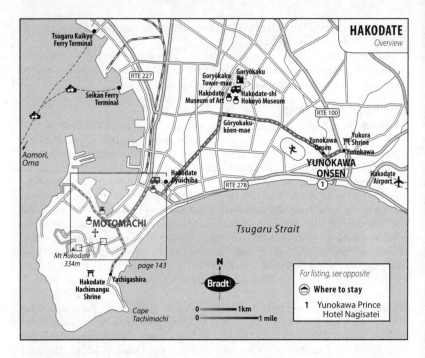

page 143

HAKODATE
Overview

For listing, see opposite

Where to stay

1 Yunokawa Prince
  Hotel Nagisatei

vary depending on season, so it's best to check online. Tickets can be purchased in advance and on the day both in person and online.

Seikan Ferry (w seikan-ferry.co.jp) operates a fleet of slightly smaller ships eight times a day between Aomori and Seikan Ferry Hakodate Terminal (3hrs 20mins; ¥1,800–6,500), from where there are also connections to central Hakodate. Reservations are available online.

By road From Sapporo and the north the E5 Hakodate-shindō ('new road') is the main approach to the city – the bypass branches east and later rejoins the Akamatsu-kaidō, which is the older and slower route into the heart of the city. National Route 228 is the main road west linking the city with Hokuto and towns all along the coast as far as Esashi.

GETTING AROUND
By tram Hakodate's trams date back to the late 19th century, and although the network has been scaled back over the years, they are still a useful way of getting around and for seeing the main sights. A mixture of modern and vintage trams operate on two routes spanning 10.9km, which connect the southern and northeastern sides of the city: Route 2 (red) runs between Yunokawa and Yachigashira, while Route 5 (blue) connects Yunokawa to Hakodate-dokku-mae [143 A1]. Both lines stop at Hakodate-eki-mae [143 D1] (2mins' walk from JR Hakodate Station). In fact, both routes are almost exactly the same, apart from the last three stops after the lines split at Jūjigai [143 B3] (which is a good jumping-off point for Mount Hakodate Ropeway). The popular bay area is a 15-minute walk south of the station along the Kaikō-dōri (開港通り), the main street leading southwest from the station, or can be reached in a few minutes by tram (get off at either Uoichibadori [143 C2] or Jūjigai tram stops).

Trams run every 6–12 minutes (or every 10–20mins after 19.00) and you'll need to wait at designated tram stops which are found on slightly raised island platforms in the middle of the street. Board via the backdoor and take a ticket; press the button when you want to get off, and alight from the front door next to the driver. To pay the fare (¥210–260), check your ticket number on the fare display board and pay the corresponding fee. If you don't have exact change, then use the change machine at the front end of the fare box to exchange your larger coins or bills. You can also use prepaid transport cards such as Suica, Pasmo, Icoca, Kitaca, etc; just tap your card on the reader when you get on and off.

If you plan to use the tram more than twice a day, it's worth buying a one-day tram pass (¥600/300; available from tram drivers, the tourist information centre at JR Hakodate Station and at many hotel front desks) – just scratch off the day, month and year to activate it. There are combined tram and bus passes available too.

By bus The main bus station (Hakodate-eki-mae) is just outside JR Hakodate Station, from where you can catch buses to all the main sights in the city. Tickets, passes and timetables can be obtained from the information desk inside the terminal building. For visitors, the most useful lines are line 1 for Mount Hakodate (Hakodateyama), which goes all the way up to the summit (30mins; ¥400), line 2 for Mount Hakodate Ropeway (11mins; ¥240) and line 3 for the Motomachi/Bay Area (30mins; ¥210; get off at Meijikan-mae). All three leave from bus stop 4. Line 5 runs to Goryōkaku (15mins; ¥240) and Yunokawa Onsen (28mins; ¥260), terminating at the airport.

The one-day KanPass (¥800/400) is good value if you plan to use the bus more than twice a day, and there are combined bus and tram passes as well. Just like the trams, you can use a prepaid card or exact change on buses too.

By road Roads in the city are mostly flat and wide, although the Motomachi area around the foot of Mount Hakodate has many steep and cobbled streets which are not ideal for cyclists. Drivers will find parking is rarely a problem, and away from the main thoroughfares traffic is not an issue (although traffic lights are numerous).

TOURIST INFORMATION There are excellent tourist information centres at JR Hakodate (⊕ 09.00–19.00 daily) and Shin-Hakodate-Hokuto (⊕ 09.00–19.00 daily) stations.

WHERE TO STAY Hakodate has a wide range of accommodation options, mostly concentrated in the city centre near JR Hakodate Station and the morning market. The Yunokawa Onsen district has innumerable hot-spring hotels and ryokan to choose from and is a 30-minute bus or tram ride from the station.

Century Marina Hakodate [143 C1] センチュリーマリーナ函館; 22–13 Otemachi; ☎ 0138 23 2121; w centurymarina.com. Situated right on the harbour within walking distance of the station & Hakodate Morning Market, this new & glitzy hotel evokes the concept of a cruise ship on land. Spacious & comfortable rooms, plus excellent outdoor hot-spring bath on the roof & expansive b/fast buffet. **$$$$**

Yunokawa Prince Hotel Nagisatei [map, opposite] 湯の川プリンスホテル渚亭; 1 chōme 2–25; ☎ 0138 57 3911; w nagisatei. info. Seafront location with relaxing indoor & outdoor hot-spring baths in Yunokawa Onsen. Spacious rooms, including some with private onsen. Excellent Japanese & Western-style food, especially the varied dinner buffet & top-notch desserts. **$$$$**

JR Inn Hakodate [143 C1] JRイン函館; 12–14 Wakamatsuchō; 0138 22 2333; w jr-inn.jp/hakodate. New hotel in a super-convenient location next to the station & 2mins' walk from the morning market. Spotless rooms, & a stylish train station motif in the lobby. Don't miss the outdoor bath or relaxing 12th-floor lounge with great views & free coffee. **$$$**

Hotel Hakodate-yama [143 B3] ホテル函館山; 19–1 Motomachi; 0138 23 7237; w hakodateyama.jp. On the lower slopes of Mt Hakodate at the top of a leafy street, a stone's throw from the ropeway. It has a slightly old-fashioned look & feel, but very kind & attentive staff & comfortable rooms. It also has its own small hot-spring baths. **$$**

OYO Hotel Sharoum Inn 2 [143 D1] ホテルシャロームイン2; 30–19 Wakamatsu-chō; 0138 22 3000; w all-in-well.com. Although this rather dated & shabby-looking hotel has small rooms & little to no AC in summer, it remains cheap & functional, & staff are very polite. Decent b/fast is included, & free rental bicycles available for exploring the city. **$**

✖ WHERE TO EAT AND DRINK

Hakodate is a food-crazed city renowned for its excellent seafood, and the various kinds of *kaisendon* (seafood-topped rice bowls) are a great way to sample all kinds of things in one go. The city was almost built on its squid-fishing industry, and the crab is not to be missed either. Aside from seafood, Hakodate is well known for *shio-ramen* (noodles in a salt-based broth), which has a cleaner, lighter taste than other types of ramen broths.

Hakodate Morning Market (see opposite) is the city's most famous foodie drawcard which lures in tourists, both domestic and foreign, with the promise of a staggering array of freshly caught seafood.

Hakodate Beer [143 C2] (はこだてビール; ⏰ 11.00–15.00 & 17.00–22.00 Thu–Tue), on Kaikō-dōri street in the Bay area of the city, is an industrial-size craft-beer hall, bottle shop and restaurant. Ordering is via a tablet and there are usually six or seven varieties of beer on tap. The brews are pretty good, although the sheer size of the place means it lacks the intimacy of many craft-beer bars. There is an offshoot branch among the Kanemori Warehouses too.

Hakodate Uni Murakami [143 C1] うにむらかみ; 22–1 Otemachi; 0138 26 8821; ⏰ 09.00–14.00 & 17.00–20.00 Thu–Tue. Small, clean & easy to spot with its neat wooden lattice façade, this restaurant next to Hakodate Morning Market specialises in the Hokkaidō delicacy of *uni* (sea urchin). The no-nonsense *uni-don* (sea urchin rice-bowl) is the signature dish, but other options include a mix of *kani* (crab), *ebi* (prawns), *ikura* (fish roe) & other delights. EM. **$$$$**

☀ **Abuya** [143 C1] あぶや; 22–2 Otemachi; ⏰ 08.00–15.00 & 17.00–21.00 Mon–Fri, 07.00–15.00 Sat–Sun. Charmingly ramshackle (half the restaurant seems to be made of plasterboard), but a cosy & super-friendly little place tucked behind the morning market serving a huge variety of seafood. Photos of many of the dishes plastered all over the walls makes it easy to order too. EM. **$$$**

Burger Shop Hotbox [143 D1] 3–11 Matsukazechō; 0138 22 2772; ⏰ 11.30–15.00 & 18.00–20.00, often closed Tue–Wed. Relaxed & trendy burger joint; slightly pricey (especially compared with the McDonald's up the road), but the huge, juicy burgers are in a different league, & the fries are cooked to perfection. Tasty side menu items & beer available too if you really want to go all-out. EM. **$$$**

Cham [143 D1] 茶夢 チャム; 9–15 Donburi-yokochōichibanai; 0138 27 1749; ⏰ 07.00–15.00 daily. Most restaurants in the morning market offer pretty similar fare at similar prices, but this place stands out for its generous portions & side dishes along with its amiable atmosphere. No EM, but the pictures make ordering a breeze. **$$$**

Restaurant Gotōken [143 B3] 五島軒; 4–5 Suehirochō; 0138 23 1106; ⏰ 11.30–14.30 & 17.00–20.00 daily, Jan–Apr closed Tue. Something of an institution in Hakodate's old Motomachi district, Gotōken has a 140-year-old history of serving up Western-style dishes with a slight Japanese twist & is noted for its particularly good line in curries. Immaculate service in stylish faux-European surroundings, it can sometimes get

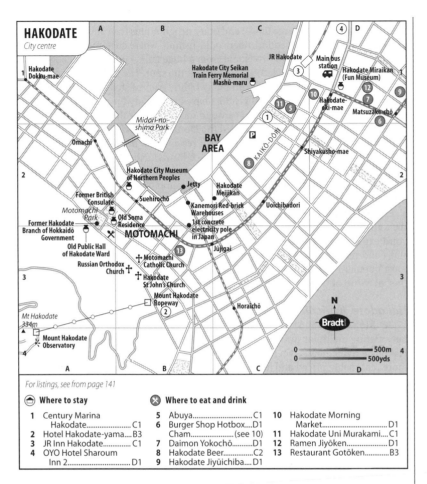

HAKODATE
City centre

Hakodate Dokku-mae
Hakodate City Seikan Train Ferry Memorial Mashū-maru
JR Hakodate
Main bus station
Hakodate Miraikan (Fun Museum)
Hakodate-eki-mae
Matsuzake-chō
Midori-no-shima Park
Omachi
BAY AREA
KAIKO-DŌRI
Shiyakusho-mae
Hakodate City Museum of Northern Peoples
Jetty
Hakodate Meijikan
Former British Consulate
Suehirochō
Kanemori Red-brick Warehouses
Uoichibadori
Motomachi Park
Old Soma Residence
1st concrete electricity pole in Japan
Former Hakodate Branch of Hokkaidō Government
MOTOMACHI
Old Public Hall of Hakodate Ward
Jūjigai
Russian Orthodox Church
Motomachi Catholic Church
Hakodate St John's Church
Mount Hakodate Ropeway
Horaichō
Mt Hakodate 334m
Mount Hakodate Observatory
N
Bradt
0   500m
0   500yds

For listings, see from page 141

Where to stay
1 Century Marina Hakodate......................C1
2 Hotel Hakodate-yama....B3
3 JR Inn Hakodate............C1
4 OYO Hotel Sharoum Inn 2................................D1

Where to eat and drink
5 Abuya...............................C1
6 Burger Shop Hotbox....D1
7 Daimon Yokochō..........D1
8 Hakodate Beer................C2
9 Hakodate Jiyūichiba...D1
10 Hakodate Morning Market...............................D1
11 Hakodate Uni Murakami....C1
12 Ramen Jiyōken.............D1
13 Restaurant Gotōken............B3

busy, & closes early with last orders at 20.00. No EM. $$$

Daimon Yokochō [143 D1] 大門横丁; ⊕ 10.30–midnight but varies by establishment. Not far east from the station, a large torii gate & the welcoming glow of lanterns reveal a rabbit-warren of narrow alleyways & numerous tiny restaurants, most with seating for only 5–15 customers. All kinds of foods are on offer, from yakitori to *nabe* (hotpot) & sushi, but it's best to visit after dark as most of the establishments are closed during the day. It's a great place

to try some hearty dishes & mingle with the locals. $$–$$$

Ramen Jiyōken [143 D1] ラーメン滋養軒; 7–12 Matsukazechō; ☏ 0138 22 2433; ⊕ 11.30–14.00 & 17.00–20.00 Wed–Mon. Popular with locals & tourists alike, this is by far the best place to try Hakodate's signature shio ramen. Cheap & delicious, expect a queue outside the unassuming shop front. No English at all, but the friendly owners will help you out as best they can. Just 6mins' walk east of JR Hakodate Station, on a side street close to the big Maxvalu store. $$

Food markets

Hakodate Morning Market [143 D1] (函館朝市, Hakodate Asa-ichi; Wakamatsuchō 9-19; ⊕ 05.00–15.00 daily depending on store, from 06.00 in winter; $$–$$$$) Situated a block south of the station, Hakodate's famous market is home to more than 200 stalls, vendors and eateries offering all manner of fish, shellfish, crabs (many on view in large tanks) and other delights, plus fruit and vegetables and assorted produce. Some vendors offer squid-fishing, where customers can try their hand at fishing with rods for live squid from a huge tank – once one is caught, it is prepared (as sashimi or grilled) and served on the spot. The indoor 'inner market' is a market in the proper sense, with many tightly packed stalls, jovial sellers, and a general sensory overload. Most vendors have items ready for eating immediately, and there are a few tables and chairs around the market for this purpose.

The north end of the market is called the **Donburi Yokochō Ichiba** (どんぶり横丁市場) and is home to a number of small restaurants, many of which specialise in various varieties of *kaisendon* (seafood rice-bowls). Not all the restaurants have English menus, but there are usually lots of pictures of the dishes to make ordering easier. There are also stalls and some good restaurants in the streets immediately outside the market, especially to the south and west.

Prices in both the market and the surrounding restaurants are aimed slightly at the tourist market, but are not unreasonable, and locals sometimes eat there too. As you'd expect, it opens early and so is a popular place to grab breakfast, with most stalls and restaurants tending to shut up shop by early afternoon – but even the most popular restaurants can be quiet by late lunchtime (although there's a chance they may run out of some items).

Hakodate Jiyūichiba [143 C1] (函館自由市場; Shinkawachō 1-2; ⏰ 08.00–17.30 Mon–Sat; $$–$$$$) Smaller than the more famous morning market, but offering a similar array of fresh seafood, local produce and on-site eateries, Hakodate Jiyūichiba is where restaurant owners and locals shop and so is slightly more reasonably priced and less touristy. The market was established at the end of

CITY OF SQUID

Hakodate has long been a major fishing port and is particularly well known for its squid (*ika*) – in fact, the city's official mascot is a curious half-man, half-alien squid called Ikaaru-Seijin. As you walk around the city, you may notice squid-decorated manhole covers, squid post-boxes (there's one right outside JR Hakodate Station) and there is even a large squid fishing monument down on the waterfront near the red-brick warehouses. Early in the morning, tiny trucks may be spotted trundling up and down the streets, blaring out cries of '*ika, ika*', stopping to sell fresh squid to locals. The Hakodate Port Festival in early August also has daily parades featuring a 'squid dance'.

Unsurprisingly, there is a lot of squid on menus throughout the city, and in the morning market you can try your hand at fishing for live squid from one of the big holding tanks (page 143). Also keep your eyes peeled for places selling squid ink ice cream, which has a startling black colour but a rather mild and sweet umami taste.

Ikkatei Tabiji and a few other restaurants in the morning market offer the slightly disconcerting but famous novelty dish *ika odori-don* (dancing-squid rice-bowl) – a bowl of rice stuffed with seafood and a very fresh cephalopod on top, which writhes around as soy sauce is poured over it. But the squid is not alive – the movement is said to be caused by the squid's muscles reacting to the sodium in the soy sauce, but the 'dance' does seem a slightly undignified final act for the city's favoured mascot!

World War II and moved to its current location in 1951, although was completely rebuilt in 1996 after the building was destroyed in a huge fire the previous New Year's Eve. As you'd expect, mornings are when the market is at its liveliest, and things tend to wind down after lunch. It's a 10-minute walk from the station, or a short stroll from Shinkawa-cho tram stop.

OTHER PRACTICALITIES

Hokkaido Bank 7-18 Hon-cho; `0138 512211; 09.00–15.00 Mon–Fri

Hakodate Central General Hospital 33-2 Hon-cho; `0138 521231

Hakodate Chuo Police Station 15-5 Goryokaku-cho; `0138 540110

Hakodate Chuo Post Office 1-6 Shinkawa-cho; 09.00–19.00 Mon–Fri , 09.00–17.00 Sat–Sun

WHAT TO SEE AND DO

Station area This is Hakodate's 'centre', and when viewed on a map is at the northwestern end of the tombolo where the land starts to narrow, just a stone's throw from the harbour. It's the location of the popular Hakodate Morning Market (page 143), has loads of restaurants and accommodation options, and is a short walk from the attractive bay area with its historic buildings and souvenir shops.

For those with young children, the **Hakodate Miraikan (Fun Museum)** [143 D1] (はこだてみらい館; Wakamatsuchō 20-1, Kiralis Hakodate Bldg, Fl 3; w hakodate-miraiproject.jp/miraikan; 10.00–20.00 daily, closed once a month usually on 1st or 2nd Wed; ¥300) in this area is a great place to while away a couple of hours on a rainy day. Interactive exhibits based on science and technology may interest engineer-minded kids, but the fourth-floor play area is a real fun house, with climbing walls, ball ponds, a bouncy castle and a climbing-net maze suspended from the ceiling.

Bay area Developed as Hakodate's first commercial district in 1869, the historic bay area (ベイエリア) is known for its old buildings and attractive waterfront views. The main landmark is the **Kanemori Red-brick Warehouses** [143 B2] (金森赤レンガ倉庫; Suehirochō 14-12; w hakodate-kanemori.com; 09.30–19.00 daily), constructed in 1887 and originally used as factories and for commercial storage. Rebuilt in 1909 following a huge fire, the seven existing *kuri* (warehouses) have now been converted into restaurants and souvenir shops. The area is lit up at night, giving the cobbled streets an atmospheric glow and making it a popular place to stroll and take pictures.

To the east of the main warehouse area is **Hakodate Meijikan** [143 C2] (はこだて明治館, Kaikō-dōri; Toyokawachō 11-17; w hakodate-factory.com; 09.30–18.00 daily), a large converted red-brick building that once served as the city post office. Today, it houses two floors of unique (and admittedly touristy) gift shops including glassware and music boxes, as well as a teddy bear shop and museum.

For attractions with a more aquatic theme, the catchily titled **Hakodate City Seikan Train Ferry Memorial Mashū-maru** [143 C1] (函館市青函連絡船記念館摩周丸; w mashumaru.com; Apr–Oct 08.30–18.00 daily, Nov–Mar 09.00–17.00 daily; ¥500/250) is the unmistakable blue-and-white ship permanently moored in the harbour to the west of the morning market. Retired from service in 1988, the ferry used to ply the waters between Hakodate and Aomori, and now serves as a museum. Those with an interest in maritime things may enjoy exploring the ship, visiting the bridge and admiring the vessel's late 80s interior décor. There are also short day or night-time cruises around Hakodate Bay on the *Blue Moon* (w hakodate-factory.com/bluemoon; 30–60min duration; ¥500–3,000 pp), a small boat that departs from the jetty opposite the red-brick warehouses.

Finally, on a street corner just south of the warehouses is Hakodate's most underwhelming sightseeing attraction, the **'first concrete electricity pole in Japan'** [143 B2] – honoured with its own bilingual signboard, don't expect massive queues!

Mount Hakodate

Mount Hakodate [143 A4] (函館山, Hakodate-yama) Sitting at the very southwestern end of the city, Mount Hakodate rises to 334m and people flock to see the iconic view from the observatory at the summit – especially at night. The most popular way to reach the summit is by taking the **Mount Hakodate Ropeway** [143 B3] (函館山ロープウェイ; w 334.co.jp; ⊕ late Apr–mid-Oct 10.00–22.00 daily, mid-Oct–late Apr 10.00–21.00 daily; last admission 30mins before closing; ¥1,500/700 return), which whisks people up the mountain in just 3 minutes to admire the splendid vistas both day and night. The service runs every 15 minutes, but is usually most crowded around sunset. The cable car brings you to inside the large **Mount Hakodate Observatory** [143 A4] (函館展望台) at the top of the mountain, which as well as an outdoor viewing platform has restaurants, a gift shop and other facilities. It's also possible to take a **bus** directly to the summit from JR Hakodate Station (⊕ mid-Apr–early Nov; 30mins; ¥400/200 one-way); the road up there is closed to private vehicles between 17.00 and 20.00 and shuts completely between November and April.

If you fancy more of a workout, a number of well-maintained hiking **paths** lead through the woods from the base to the summit (casual footwear is fine in summer), and should take under an hour going up. The main path starts from near the car park at Mount Hakodate Fureai (Information) Centre (函館山ふれあいセンター), which is located up the road from the ropeway, tucked behind Hakodate Gokoku Shrine (函館護国神社) at the start of the mountain road. There are a number of shrines around the foot of the mountain, the most impressive being **Hakodate Hachimangu Shrine** (函館八幡宮), which was established in 1445; the current main hall is 100 years old.

Aside from the sensational views, the west side of the summit is home to the remains of concrete **gun batteries** built during World War II, and some slightly rough and overgrown paths lead to the decaying foundations of the old Ireiyama Observatory.

Motomachi

Motomachi Around the base of Mount Hakodate lies the pretty Motomachi (元町) district, where many foreign traders and officials set up residence after Hakodate opened up to international commerce in 1854. Many of the streets are cobbled and sometimes steep, but if you can handle the gradients then it's a real joy to explore on foot as there is so much interesting architecture and countless historical points of interest (many of which are signposted in English).

Walking west up the hill from Jūjigai tram stop, you'll first come to an area with a number of Western-style churches. The small and very distinctive white-walled, red-roofed Anglican **Hakodate St John's Church** [143 B3] (函館聖ヨハネ教会) was established in 1874; the current cross-shaped building dates back to 1979. Nearby, **Motomachi Catholic Church** [143 B3] (カトリック元町教会) is built in a more traditional Gothic style and has an attractive bell tower. It was reconstructed in 1924 after being burned down in one of the city's many great fires three years earlier. You can also admire the **Russian Orthodox Church** [143 B3] (函館ハリストス正教会) next door, with its teal roof and turrets. All three churches are lit up and look particularly striking at night.

Heading west you'll soon come to **Hachiman-zaka** (八幡坂), a tree-lined, flagstone-paved street with nice views down to the bay; it is the best-known (and most photographed) of Motomachi's many sloping streets. The road leading west from the top of Hachiman-zaka is known for its many shops selling excellent

Hokkaidō soft-serve ice cream, including one store intriguingly called **The Second Most Delicious Ice Cream Melon Bread in the World** [143 A3] (melon bread or *meron-pan* is a popular Japanese sugary bread which doesn't actually contain any melon – it's just shaped like one).

Continuing west you'll arrive in front of the **Old Public Hall of Hakodate Ward** [143 A3] (旧函館区公会堂; Motomachi 11-13; w hakodate-kokaido. jp; ⏰ 09.00–18.00 Tue–Fri, ⏰ 09.00–19.00 Sat–Mon, closes 17.00 Nov–Mar; ¥300/150), a large and impressive colonial-style building with striking blue-grey walls and yellow furnishings. The original town hall burned down in 1907, so the one here today dates to 1910 and was recently renovated. It is still used occasionally for events and is well worth the entry fee to wander through the opulent rooms and halls full of period features, before taking in the magnificent view from the front balcony.

Across the street is **Motomachi Park** [143 A2] (元町公園), a nice green space overlooking the harbour and home to the **Former Hakodate Branch of Hokkaidō Government** (旧北海道庁函館支庁庁舎), a grand 1909 building with four columns abutting the entrance that now houses a tourist information centre (⏰ 10.00–18.00 daily).

Nestled just east of the park is one of Hakodate's frequently overlooked gems, the **Old Soma Residence** [143 A2] (旧相馬邸, Kyū Sōma-tei; Motomachi 33-2; w kyusoumake.com; ⏰ Apr–Nov 09.30–16.30 Fri–Mon; ¥900/300). This elegant Japanese-style wooden house built in 1908 was the former home of Teppei Soma, one of Hokkaidō's most successful merchants, and it contains an intriguing mix of Western-style and Japanese rooms and features, plus a wonderful garden. English audio-guides are available. Next door is the **Former British Consulate of Hakodate** [143 A2] (旧イギリス領事館; Motomachi 33-14; w hakodate-kankou.com/british; Apr–Oct 09.00–19.00 daily, Nov–Mar closes at 17.00), rebuilt in 1913 after the huge 1907 fire; it ceased operations as a consulate in 1934. Set among English gardens, it now houses a small and fairly interesting history museum (¥300/150) covering the story of the consulate, and a shop selling tea and British-themed goods; there is a traditional afternoon tea service too.

Down the hill near the waterfront is the **Hakodate City Museum of Northern Peoples** [143 B2] (函館市北方民族資料館; Suehirochō 21-7; w zaidan-hakodate. com/hoppominzoku; ⏰ Apr–Oct 09.00–19.00 daily, Nov–Mar 09.00–17.00 daily; ¥300/150), which houses a small but nice collection of Ainu artefacts and displays, with some great examples of Ainu clothing and hunting gear; there is an information pamphlet in English available at the front desk and enough English throughout to make it quite informative.

Cape Tachimachi (立待岬, Tachimachi-misaki)
At the very southern tip of the city, this wonderfully scenic area has rugged cliffs and expansive sea views; the old Ainu name for the cape means 'a place to wait and catch fish'. It is a pleasant 15-minute stroll from Yachigashira tram stop to the end of the cape, passing through an old cemetery that houses the grave of Ishikawa Takuboku, a celebrated poet who lived in Hakodate briefly and died of tuberculosis at a young age.

North Hakodate
Though the northern end of the city doesn't have a great many attractions, it is home to one of Hakodate's stand-out historical landmarks: the sprawling fort complex of Goryōkaku. The best way to reach this part of the city is by tram: take any bound for Yunokawa and get off at Gōryokaku-kōen-mae (10mins; ¥250), from where it is a 10-minute walk north. Alternatively take a bus

(5-1, 6-2, 59, 105, 130 or 106 loop 27) from the station and get off right next to the park at Goryōkaku Tower-mae bus stop (15mins; ¥240).

Goryōkaku (五稜郭; w hakodate-jts-kosya.jp/park/goryokaku; inner moat ⊕ Apr–Oct 05.00–19.00 daily, Nov–Mar 05.00–18.00 daily) Arguably Hokkaido's most impressive fortification, and certainly one of the most unique in Japan, Goryōkaku is a sprawling Western-style fort most notable for its five-pronged, star-shaped moat. The name literally means 'five-point fortification', and its design and construction was completed by around 1864 in a joint venture by the scholar Takeda Ayasaburō and a French military officer named Jules Brunet. It was the first Western-style fortification to be built in Japan and was designed to protect Hakodate from any possible attacks by foreign imperial forces, about which there was a growing concern during the 1800s. In reality, it never saw conflict with foreign adversaries but was the stage for the Battle of Hakodate (page 138). The fort eventually fell into disuse as a military facility and was converted into parkland in 1914; this is now a very popular cherry blossom viewing spot in spring (the blooms usually peak around early May).

Although Goryōkaku is designated as a national Special Historic Site, not many original structures remain other than the impressive moat. The beautifully reconstructed **Hakodate Magistrate's Office** (箱館奉行所; w hakodate-bugyosho. jp; ⊕ 09.00–18.00 daily, Nov–Mar closes 17.00; ¥500/250) is the fort's centrepiece, and a jaw-dropping work of wood craftsmanship. Surrounded by pines, the reconstruction work was completed in 2010, and inside are bilingual displays detailing the structure's history and building processes.

To really appreciate Goryōkaku's unique shape and vast layout, it is recommended to take the lift to the top of **Goryōkaku Tower** (五稜郭タワー; w goryokaku-tower. co.jp; ⊕ 09.00–18.00 daily; ¥900/450) situated in the southwest corner of the park. The glass-windowed, 360° observation deck offers fantastic aerial views of the star-shaped fort, plus out over much of Hakodate too. Standing 60m tall, the original tower was built in 1964 to commemorate the centenary of the fort, but was then redesigned and rebuilt much taller (107m) in 2006.

Hakodate Museum of Art (北海道立函館美術館, Hokkaidō Hakodate bijutsukan; Goryōkakuchō 37-6; w artmuseum.pref.hokkaido.lg.jp/hbj; ⊕ 09.30–17.00 Tue–Sun, closed New Year; ¥260/150) Located immediately south of Goryōkaku Tower, this small but stylish museum features permanent collections focused on three areas: art related to southern Hokkaidō; East Asian art and calligraphy; and contemporary works featuring letters and symbols (which includes pieces by the likes of Andy Warhol, among others). There are also seasonal temporary exhibits (additional fee required); check online for the current displays and upcoming schedule.

Hakodate-shi Hokuyō Museum (函館市北洋資料館, Hakodateshi Hokuyō-shiryōkan; Goryōkakuchō 37-8; w zaidan-hakodate.com/gjh/hokuyo; ⊕ Apr–Oct 09.00–19.00 daily, Nov–Mar 09.00–17.00 daily, occasional random closures; ¥100/50) Also going by the catchy name of 'Hakodate City Northern Pacific Fishery's Document Museum', this slightly old-fashioned place next door to the art museum houses an eclectic collection of nautical and natural history displays, with lots of taxidermy animals, historical fishing equipment, a section on the history of whaling and even a fun fishing boat simulator. This museum is often overlooked by visitors, but it has plenty of interest, and all for an absolute bargain-price entry fee.

Yunokawa Onsen and around Yunokawa Onsen (湯の川温泉; w hakodate-yunokawa.jp) is one of Hokkaidō's most famous hot-spring resorts, and certainly one with a long history. A story is told of how in 1653, a young Takahiro (who would later go on to be the ninth head of the Matsumae clan) was sent to the hot spring by his mother, after she received a divine message in a dream that the waters there could heal the disease he had been suffering with. Needless to say, a quick dunk in the hot spring seemed to do the trick, and in later years the Matsumae clan built a shrine there as a nod of appreciation. The original natural spring was apparently nothing more than a lukewarm trickle, and it wasn't until 1886 that a new source of piping hot-spring water was discovered and the area could develop as a resort town.

These days the neighbourhood is crammed with fancy hot-spring hotels and ryokan, some of which have open-air baths with ocean views, plus private options if you really want to splash out; good ones include the upmarket Hotel Banso or Yunokawa Prince Hotel Nagisatei (page 141). There are plenty of more affordable options too, although most of these will be of the communal bath variety. Next to the river near Yunokawa Onsen tram stop are some free ashiyu foot baths.

Also near the tram stop on a small hill is peaceful **Yukura Shrine** (湯倉神社, Yukura-jinja; w yukurajinja.or.jp; free), built by the Matsumae clan in the 15th century; its large red torii gate near the entrance looks particularly striking when there is snow on the ground. Many visitors come here to pray for good fortune, and the shrine's *omikuji* paper fortunes are folded like squid and written in the Hokkaidō dialect, just to make them even more challenging to decipher.

It takes about 30 minutes to reach Yunokawa Onsen by tram from JR Hakodate Station on the Yunokawa Line (¥260 one-way); get off at either Yunokawa Onsen or Yunokawa (the last stop). Buses from the station take 30 minutes (¥300), and there is a direct shuttle bus from the airport (8mins; ¥230). By car it's about 20 minutes from central Hakodate.

Around Hakodate

Shiryōkaku (四稜郭跡) Located about 3km north of Goryōkaku way out on the edge of town, this little-visited site has the remains of a four-cornered (as opposed to Goryōkaku's five) fortification, built in 1869 by the former Tokugawa shōgunate during the Battle of Hakodate (page 138). It wasn't a particularly successful endeavour, however, as it quickly fell to the imperial government forces, and now all that remains are some fairly extensive earthworks and ditches covered in grass. There are lots of signs dotted around, but none in English, so this is one only for real history buffs. There is parking nearby.

Kijihiki-kōgen Panorama Viewpoint (きじひき高原パノラマ展望台, Hijikiri-kōgen-panorama-tenbōdai; ⊕ early Apr–late Nov 08.30–20.00 daily; free) One of the best viewpoints in the region, this new observatory sits at 560m on a high plateau among pastureland, and looks down over the whole of Hakodate to the south, and across to the lakes of Ōnuma Park and shapely Mount Komagatake to the northeast. The night view of the city from here is known as the 'back' view (as opposed to the famous 'front' view from the top of Mount Hakodate) but is equally impressive, if more distant. Access is by car only, around 28km from central Hakodate.

Shirotai Pasture Observation Deck (城岱牧場展望台, Shirotai-bokujō-tenbōdai) This splendid hilltop viewing spot is located well north of the city. From the Nanae Honcho IC, turn off on to the Shirotai Skyline (⊕ closed mid-Nov–late Apr), a winding road up into the hills, which after 8km brings you to an extensive

There are numerous examples of small groups of Christians settling in southern Hokkaidō, especially after the Meiji Restoration when freedom of religion was promulgated. In the Hakodate area there are two Trappist convents; entry to both is prohibited to normal lay folk, but both have nice grounds and European-style architecture to admire (which are probably more of interest to Asian tourists in truth), plus shops to sample some of their excellent handmade produce.

To the east of the city, not far from the airport, **Our Lady of the Angels Trappistine Abbey** (トラピスチヌ修道院; w ocso-tenshien.jp/eng; ⊕ Apr–Oct 08.00–17.00 daily, Nov–Mar 08.00–16.30 daily; free) is an active nunnery and Japan's first female convent, established by eight French women in 1898. It won't take longer than an hour to wander around the gardens and adjacent park, but the ice cream from the 'forest' shop Woods (⊕ May–Oct 08.30–17.10 daily, Nov–Apr 09.00–16.40 daily) is really not to be missed. Local buses run from central Hakodate (35–50mins; ¥300); get off at トラピスチヌ前 bus stop. It is just 10 minutes by bus from Yunokawa Onsen.

Slightly further afield, **Tōbetsu Trappist Monastery** (トラピスト大修道院; Torapisuto-daishūdōin; w trappist.or.jp; grounds ⊕ 24hrs daily; free) is situated roughly halfway between Hokuto and Kikonai in the small seaside town of Tōbetsu (当別). Dating to 1896, this distinctive red-brick monastery is home to cloistered Trappist monks. Visitors can wander the pleasant grounds and up the long tree-lined driveway, and the on-site shop (⊕ 09.00–17.00 (until 16.30 winter) daily) sells the monks' delicious handmade ice cream, jam, butter and biscuits. If you follow the path up through the woods for 20 minutes you will arrive at Lourdes Cave; the 'cave' is nothing more than a fenced-off crack in the cliff with a statue of the Virgin Mary nearby, but there is a viewpoint a bit further on with excellent views across the sea towards Hakodate. Parking is available, otherwise it is a 25-minute walk from JR Oshima-Tōbetsu Station (40mins by train from Hakodate).

hilltop ranch, where during the summer cattle graze happily in the grassy open fields. The observation deck – a concrete building with large bay windows (plus parking, toilets and vending machine) – which opened in 2021, sits at around 500m offering great views down towards the city and coast. If the weather is fine it is a very pleasant drive or even cycle for those with ample leg muscles. If you continue north for 10km you'll arrive down in Ōnuma Park, making it a nice up-and-over route for drivers from Hakodate.

ŌNUMA PARK AREA

One of the most popular day trips from Hakodate, situated just 20km north of the city, Ōnuma Park (大沼公園, Ōnuma-kōen) is a stunning quasi-national park notable for its picturesque lakes and forests which lie at the foot of Mount Komagatake – the distinctively shaped volcano that occasionally spurts into activity and dominates all views in the park. It's a gentle, family-friendly, outdoorsy kind of place, centred around the two main lakes, Lake Ōnuma, and the smaller Lake Konuma – with the former being the major activity hub. The view of Mount Komagatake from the shores of Lake Ōnuma was named as one of the 'New Three

Views of Japan' (page 53) along with Miho-no-Matsubara in Shizuoka Prefecture and Yabakei in Oita Prefecture.

The best place to find out details for activities on offer in the area is the Ōnuma International Communication Plaza (☉ 08.30–17.30 daily) – the fancy name for the fancy tourist information centre located right in front of JR Ōnuma-kōen Station.

GETTING THERE AND AWAY JR Ōnuma-kōen is the main **train** station in the area and is served by limited express trains (30mins; ¥1,270 for a non-reserved seat) which run regularly from Hakodate and then onwards to Sapporo (roughly 4hrs), 300km away. Hakodate is also served by the slower, less frequent, but much cheaper local train (40mins; ¥640).

By **road**, from central Hakodate it's a straightforward zip north along Route 5 (toll-free) reaching Ōnuma Park in about 30 minutes. There is ample space in the large Yukara parking area just south of the main lake. The irregular daily bus 210 from JR Hakodate Station to Ōnuma Park (70mins, ¥750) may also be an option; ask at Hakodate bus terminal for details.

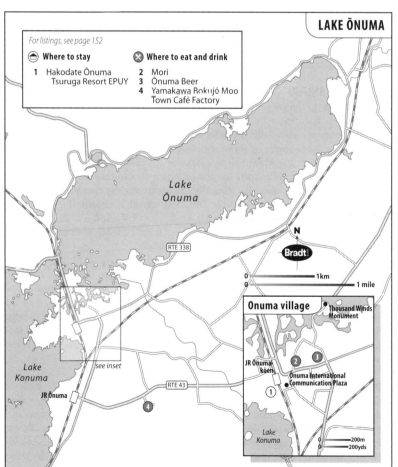

LAKE ŌNUMA

For listings, see page 152

🛏 **Where to stay**
1 Hakodate Ōnuma
   Tsuruga Resort EPUY

🍴 **Where to eat and drink**
2 Mori
3 Ōnuma Beer
4 Yamakawa Bokujō Moo
   Town Café Factory

Lake Ōnuma

RTE 338

N

Bradt

0   1km
0   1 mile

Onuma village

Thousand Winds Monument

JR Ōnuma-kōen

Ōnuma International Communication Plaza

Lake Konuma

0   200m
0   200yds

Lake Konuma

see inset

JR Ōnuma

RTE 43

The small, relaxed village of Ōnuma offers a handful places to stay, including a couple of campgrounds, and numerous food options.

Hakodate Ōnuma Tsuruga Resort EPUY 函館大沼鶴雅リゾートエプイ; 85–9 Ōnumachō; ✆0138 67 2964; w onuma-epuy.com. A fancy hot-spring resort with wonderful outdoor baths, stylish lounges & a bar featuring a full model railway! The rooms are huge, many with private hot springs. Meals are French-style cuisine made from ingredients sourced within 80km, plus there's an excellent on-site bakery. **$$$$$**

Ōnuma Beer 大沼ビール; 208 Ōnumachō; ✆0138 67 1611; ⊕ Apr–Nov 10.00–17.00 Wed–Thu & Sat–Mon, Dec–Mar 10.00–15.00 Wed–Thu, Sat & Mon. Award-winning craft brewery with a friendly atmosphere & decent selection of beers, including IPA & stout. The brewing tanks are visible right next to the bar. Good sausages, plus other tasty pub snacks & light meals are served. Staff speak a little English; EM. **$$$**

Mori 森南店; 1023–10 Ōnumachō; ✆0138 67 2067; ⊕ 09.00–17.00 daily, closed Wed in winter. This small curved-roof cabin near the large car park serves a varied menu of homely & hearty dishes such as yakisoba, fluffy butter potatoes, Japanese curry & fried udon noodles. Cosy wooden interior with wood-burning stove in the corner. Cheap & surprisingly delicious. Lots of photos, so ordering is easy; no EM. **$$**

Yamakawa Bokujō Moo Town Café Factory 山川牧場モータウンカフェファクトリー; 889–14 Ōnumachō; ✆0138 67 4920; ⊕ 10.00–17.00 Fri–Tue. This cute wooden shack with cow décor situated among the fields on the southeast outskirts of town specialises in roast beef sandwiches & milk products from the adjacent farm. Indoor & outdoor seating. The owner studied in the USA & speaks fluent English. **$$**

WHAT TO SEE AND DO

Lake Ōnuma (大沼; w onumakouen.com) At 14km in circumference, this vast lake serves as the centre for activities in the region, with walking and boating being the most popular. Paths meander here and there among the forests and tiny islands on the lake's southern shore, crossing numerous small bridges to lakeside viewpoints of imposing Mount Komagatake in the distance. There are a number of walking courses to follow, the longest of which should take no longer than an hour or so to complete; note that the longer paths are slightly rough underfoot and not suitable for pushchairs or bicycles. The most-visited, if unassuming, viewpoint is the **Thousand Winds Monument** (千の風になって名曲誕生の地), at a spot which is said to have inspired a famous old song. It can be reached in a few minutes by crossing the main bridge to the nearest small island.

During the summer, it is great fun to take a rowing or pedal boat out on to Ōnuma's waters – these can be rented for up to an hour from the kiosks near the shore (¥2,000 for 2 people). There are also almost-hourly motorboat and cruise tours for more extensive views (⊕ 09.00–16.00 daily; prices start at ¥1,320 for adults), lasting between 30 and 60 minutes. In the winter there are also a huge raft of seasonal activities to enjoy, including snowmobiling, snowshoeing and ice-fishing on top of the frozen lake – the tourist information centre (page 151) is the best place to go for organising these.

Mount Komagatake (北海道駒ヶ岳, Hokkaidō-Komagatake) At 1,131m, Hokkaidō-Komagatake (to give it its full name, though it is also occasionally called Oshima-Fuji or Oshima-Komagatake) is a distinctive andesitic stratovolcano and the area's most unmistakable landmark, visible for miles around from almost every direction. Komagatake was once a classic volcanic cone shape (like Mount Fuji) but, following a number of big eruptions from 1640 and up until the latest in 2000, much of the crater collapsed, leaving the peak with the unique sweeping

Hokkaidō Shrine Festival is a traditional Shintō festival with a history of more than 100 years PAGE 91

above
(JK/S)

Kamikawa Shrine in Asahikawa takes on an even more tranquil air in the winter snow PAGE 180

right
(SP/S)

The Hill of the Buddha – a striking work of art and spiritual monument designed by the famous architect Tadao Ando PAGE 107

below
(NP/S)

above
(SP/D)

Asahikawa is the gateway to central Hokkaidō and the wild highlands of Daisetsuzan National Park PAGE 174

below
(SP/D)

Sapporo Beer Museum is the best place for learning more about, and drinking, Hokkaidō's most famous beverage PAGE 103

Hokkaidō has many unique sights, including the Dai Kannon statue in Ashibetsu, which stands 88m tall PAGE 187

above left
(BTS/S)

Cape Sōya, Japan's northernmost point, feels a world away from Tokyo, and even Sapporo PAGE 275

top right
(7M/S)

Abandoned railway stations sometimes find other uses, such as Kōfuku Station near Obihiro, where visitors post tickets on its walls in the hope of being granted bliss and happiness PAGE 218

above right
(CS/D)

Goryōkaku in Hakodate dates to the late Edo period and was built to protect against foreign threats; it is now one of Hokkaidō's premier cherry-blossom-viewing spots PAGE 148

below
(CL/D)

above
(CF/S)

The deep waters of Lake Mashū, arguably Japan's most beautiful lake, are often said to be among the clearest on earth PAGE 247

left
(TS/D)

Venture to Rebun Island for remote coastal scenery and swathes of summer wildflowers PAGE 281

below
(A/S)

Jigoku-dani, or 'hell valley', constantly steams and hisses above the hot-spring town of Noboribetsu PAGE 129

Climbing to the summit of Mount Rishiri is the goal of many visitors to Rishiri Island PAGE 276

above
(DK/S)

Candle Rock is one of many natural spectacles found along the rugged coast of the Shakotan Peninsula PAGE 118

right
(T/S)

There are few better, or wilder, places to hike in Japan than Daisetsuzan National Park PAGE 188

below
(TF)

top
(OP/D)
Few sights are more beguiling than the elaborate courtship dances of red-crowned cranes in the deep winter PAGES 12 & 230

above left
(GA/S)
Steller's sea eagle (*Haliaeetus pelagicus*) PAGE 12

above right
(PS/D)
White-tailed eagle (*Haliaeetus albicilla*) PAGE 12

left
(APA/S)
Blakiston's fish owl (*Bubo blakistoni*) PAGE 12

The magnificent Ezo brown bear (*Ursus arctos yesoensis*) has one of its main strongholds on the Shiretoko Peninsula PAGE 8

right
(SS)

Orca (pictured), dolphins and whales are among the wildlife often spotted close to the shore in the Sea of Okhotsk PAGE 257

below
(NV/S)

Japanese, or Sika, deer (*Cervus nippon yesoensis*) PAGE 10

bottom
(OP/D)

top
(PW/S)

The wonderfully preserved wooden buildings of Abashiri Prison Museum provide a glimpse of inmate life during the Meiji era PAGE 255

above
(TCC/S)

New Year is a time for ritual and shrine visits, and perhaps a drop of *amazake*, sweet sake PAGE 41

left
(SS)

Ainu beliefs and craftsmanship are always deeply intertwined with the natural world PAGE 41

silhouette and pointy dual summits we see today, the highest of which is called Kengamine (剣ヶ峰).

Classed as active, the volcano is open to hikers from June until the end of October (although may close suddenly in the event of increased volcanic activity), with the true summit, Kengamine, frequently officially off-limits. The main hiking route starts from the sixth station parking area (北海道駒ケ根六合目駐車場; 490m) on the mountain's southern flank – parking is free and there are toilets but no other facilities, and spaces can fill up on busy days, so head there early to snag a spot. Note that the road up there is a bit rough and narrow, so take special care if you're in a hire car or are not a confident driver. The hiking trail itself is not particularly difficult although fairly steep and rugged in places; suitable gear and footwear are recommended. It takes about an hour to climb the 2km up to the highest officially accessible point known as Uma-no-se (馬の背; 902m), from where there are outstanding sweeping views for miles around if the weather is fine. Depending on the volcano's current activity status, it may be possible to carry on another hour to the true summit, although the trail becomes steeper and less clearly marked.

If you prefer to approach entirely on foot, then it is 7.8km up to the parking area (around 1hr 40mins) from JR Akaigawa Station. There are also alternative hiking routes on the mountain's opposing flanks.

Mori The town of Mori (森; population 16,000) lies northwest of Mount Komagatake on the shores of Uchiura Bay, and it's the last major settlement before Hakodate (1hr away) if coming from the north. The town's name and kanji character literally means 'forest' – the reason is perhaps not immediately obvious from the centre of the town, but there are plenty of woods along its outskirts. There is not a great deal to see or do, but there are some decent restaurants if you happen to be passing through.

KAMEDA PENINSULA

Directly east of Hakodate and forming the southeastern prong of the Oshima Peninsula, the Kameda Peninsula is little visited by foreign tourists but has a beautiful and fairly remote coastline peppered with fishing villages and some interesting sights. At the far eastern reach of the peninsula lies Mount Esan, one of Hokkaidō's most active volcanoes, set in its own nature park. The main townships of Esan (population 4,500) and Todohokke (population 1,500) were in fact amalgamated into the jurisdiction of Hakodate fairly recently, although they feel far away from the bright lights of the city. The peninsula makes for a good day trip from Hakodate particularly if you have a car, as the public transport options are rather limited.

GETTING THERE AND AROUND Infrequent and slow **buses** ply the route from JR Hakodate Station to Esan (2hrs; ¥1,650) and Todohokke – change for connecting bus at Hinohama-danchi (日ノ浜団地; 2hrs; ¥1,850) – meaning it's certainly possible to visit Esan, hike the volcano and return to Hakodate by bus in one day; a full tour of the peninsula is impossible using public transport. There are also buses from Hakodate to Shikabe (1hr 50mins; ¥1,400) in the north of the region.

Having your own set of wheels opens up the whole area for exploration – Route 278 hugs most of the peninsula's rocky coastline, with only a few minor detours required to see the main sights.

ESAN Lying at the far eastern tip of the Kameda Peninsula is the small town of Esan (恵山) and Esan Prefectural Nature Park, crowned at its centre by Esan (or 'Mount E' as it is sometimes awkwardly written in English), an active stratovolcano rising to 618m. The park boasts some of the best hiking in the Hakodate area, with a number of well-marked paths. The easy 2-hour climb up the mountain's barren slopes (clearly signposted as 'Esan Sanchō 恵山山頂') offers close-up glimpses of steaming sulphur vents, while from the summit there are sweeping sea views south over the strait to Aomori and across to the peaks of Niseko looking northwards. Those taking the bus will need to walk an extra hour or so up the road to the car park and trailhead, so allow 4–6 hours for the return trip.

The park is also well known for its spectacular pink azaleas, which bloom during early summer (peaking from late May to early June) and can easily be seen at the **Esan Azalea Park** (恵山つつじ公園; Esan Tsutsuji-kōen) in the south of the area. The Esan Azalea Festival is held here at the end of May and features stalls and attractions in addition to the impressive blooms and scenic views. The park is a 25-minute walk from the bus stop; if relying on public transport, take a local bus bound for Esan Misaki (恵山岬) from JR Hakodate Station bus stop 6, and get off at Esan Tozanguchi (恵山登山口; 2hrs; ¥1,400). Check the latest bus timetable at Hakodate bus terminal or tourist information centre beforehand. There are a couple of hot-spring hotels in the area, too, where you can bathe or overnight.

Mizunashikaihin Onsen (水無海浜温泉) is a well-known open-air hot spring located right on the rocky shoreline south of Todohokke. The naturally heated pools are accessible only at low tide so it's best to check the tidal schedule before visiting (w tideking.com) – if the tide is in, then everything will be underwater, but if the sea is a long way out, the pools may be shallow and uncomfortably hot! The spring is free to use, and there are toilets and changing rooms nearby – as the pools are mixed bathing, swimsuits are permitted and advisable. If it's not too windy, you may also like to wander around the grounds of **Cape Esan Lighthouse** (恵山岬灯台) not far from the hot springs.

A COASTAL LOOP ON ROUTE 278

This scenic route following Route 278 around the Kameda Peninsula makes for a great one- or two-day driving trip or multi-day cycling route, with splendid sea views and a number of interesting stops en route. The area is also regarded as one of Hokkaidō's best surfing spots and plays host to various surf championships throughout the year. Despite its out-of-the-way location, there are convenience stores, hot springs and places to stay all along the route, so if you have your own wheels it makes for a great little adventure in an area infrequently visited by foreign tourists.

Heading east from Hakodate along Route 278, the road skirts past the airport and then follows the coast for 13km to **Cape Shiokubi** (汐首岬, Shiokubi-misaki), the southernmost point on the peninsula. It's a 1-hour walk up the hill here to **Shiokubi-yama** (汐首山; 290m), a windswept grassy promontory where friendly miniature horses graze (which you can often get close enough to stroke!), plus great views across the Tsugaru Strait and back towards Hakodate. The summit is best reached by walking up the zigzagging access road on its western flank – there are a couple of parking spaces at the bottom of the road.

A short way further along Route 278 you will see a large concrete arch behind some houses to the left – a remnant of the unfinished and never-used Toi Line, a military railway constructed in 1937 but abandoned in 1943 when it was 90% complete.

Four kilometres along the coast from the bridge, the small seaside village of **Toi** (戸井) has a long sweeping beach. A tight left after the second tunnel leads to the car park for **Ikoi-no-oka Park** (憩いの丘公園), a grassy promontory which is another good place to stretch your legs – follow the path for 15 minutes to reach an observatory from where there are views of the small whale-shaped Muino Island just offshore. Back on the 278, the next left inland leads to **Hakodate-shi Toi Water Park** (函館市戸井ウォーターパーク), a standard hot-spring resort and auto-camping ground, with a free site for tents nearby.

Continuing eastwards past the tiny inlet of **Hiura** (日浦), Route 278 ploughs through the hillside to emerge at the harbour village of **Oma** (大澗). But if you take the road to the right just before the tunnel, you can skirt along a narrow lane hugging the coast from where you can spot a number of unique rock formations up along the cliff face. Joining back up with the 278, the route continues along the coast, passing pretty rock bluffs and a couple of sandy beaches. The road then soon cuts north at **Hinohama** (日ノ浜) and heads inland towards the peninsula's northern coast. Before that, however, there is an option to continue east for 4km on road 635 to **Esan** (see opposite), from where you can explore the volcanic wonders of Esan Prefectural Nature Park.

From Hinohama, Route 278 cuts 7km across the peninsula and emerges at the small coastal town of **Todohokke** (椴法華), known for its great surf. It's worth making a small detour right (southeast) for around 4km to where the road ends at Mizunashikaihin Onsen, with the Cape Esan Lighthouse nearby (see opposite).

Back in Todohokke, the upper end of the long sweeping beach has year round breaks and plays host to the annual Hokkaidō Surfing Championships. Just metres from the beach, a small pink shack next to the road is home to **Surfside** (サーフサイド; ◷ 11.00–15.00 Wed–Sun; $$), a casual diner with a cluttered and distinctly 1960s Americana vibe, though the menu surprisingly consists of curries and mostly Japanese dishes, plus excellent cheesecake.

From Todohokke, the road continues northwards and passes through a long tunnel with glimpses of the ocean in places. A river flows above the tunnel, dropping directly into the sea at a waterfall called **Furube-no-otaki** (古部の大滝), but there is almost nowhere to park along the road, so getting out to take a look is difficult. The road continues to hug the coast heading northwest, and about 20km beyond Todohokke you can turn left at **Kakkumi** 川汲 on Route 83 for a direct way through the mountains back to Hakodate (35km).

Otherwise continue north to soon reach **Hakodate Jōmon Culture Centre** (函館市縄文文化交流センター; w hjcc.jp; ◷ 09.00–17.00 (Nov–Mar until 16.30) Tue–Sun; ¥300/150), which looks like a concrete, minimalist art installation from the outside. In fact, the centre is well worth a visit as it houses numerous exquisite treasures from the Jōmon period, including a hollow clay figure which dates back 3,500 years and is the only designated 'national treasure' currently on Hokkaidō. Many of the clay figures and artefacts here came from just up the road at the newly UNESCO-listed **Ofune Archaeological Site** (大船遺跡; w omon-japan.jp; ◷ 09.00–17.00 (Nov–Mar until 16.00) daily; free), which is also worth visiting for its Jōmon-era pit-house dwellings, restored buildings and small museum.

About 10km further up the coast it is easy to miss Shamisen Falls on the left (there is a small parking space nearby), but if you take a right soon after on to coast road 43 you will soon arrive at a michi-no-eki next to **Shikabe Kanketsusen Park** (しかべ間歇泉・かんけつせん; w shikabe-tara.com; ◷ mid-Mar–Nov 09.00–17.00 Mon–Thu, 08.30–18.00 Fri–Sun, Dec–mid-Mar 10.00–15.00 Mon–Thu, 09.00–18.00 Fri–Sun (closed Wed Jan–mid-Mar); ¥300/200). The star attraction here is a huge 15m geyser, which erupts every 10 minutes or so – somewhat surprisingly for a country as geologically active as Japan, geysers are a real rarity. The park also has ashiyu foot baths and there are geothermal steam cookers in the car park for cooking your own lunch.

The sleepy fishing town of **Shikabe** (鹿部) is the largest settlement along this part of the coast with a number of hot springs and places to stay, and from here you can easily visit nearby Ōnuma Park (17km), continue looping northwards around Mount Komagatake towards Mori (27km) or head back to Hakodate (45km) via Route 43.

MATSUMAE PENINSULA

Making up the large southwestern-lying prong of the wider Oshima Peninsula, the Matsumae Peninsula is mostly remote and sparsely inhabited, despite being the southernmost region of Hokkaidō and one of the closest points to mainland Honshū (which lies just 19.5km across the Tsugaru Strait). There used to be a train line connecting Matsumae to Hakodate and beyond, but like a number of small lines on Hokkaidō it was judged to be unprofitable, and was discontinued in 1988. Owing to its proximity to the mainland, the Matsumae Peninsula has been subject to more historical 'Japanese' influence than most other regions of Hokkaidō and was in fact the northern limit of Japan during the Edo period. This rich history is most evident in the town of Matsumae, which is home to the only Edo-style Japanese castle on Hokkaidō, though the whole area's coastline has rather more historical and cultural places of interest than many other parts of Hokkaidō, such as the historical towns of Esashi (page 163) and Kaminokuni (page 166) further north.

MATSUMAE Hemmed in by the sea on one side and mountains to the other, the secluded castle town of Matsumae (松前; population 7,800) may be small, but as the once sole feudal fief and only 'civilised' outpost among the untamed wilds of Hokkaidō, it is a town steeped in history and significance. It is arguably the most traditional 'Japanese' settlement on Hokkaidō, with its ornate castle and cherry-blossom-tree-filled grounds, serene temple district, and various other historic buildings. Matsumae makes for a pleasant (if distant) day trip from Hakodate, or as a stop-off on a broader tour around southern Hokkaidō, and there are a handful of accommodation options if you plan to stay the night. Most of the town's attractions are in a very compact area and can be explored on foot.

History Before the Japanese made firm inroads into the region, the Matsumae Peninsula was a stronghold of the Ainu. Tiny groups of Japanese possibly lived in the area from as early as the 7th century, and medieval documents suggest that they and the Ainu had certainly been co-inhabiting the area since around the 12th century; for many years there was amicable trade between the two. In the early 15th century, the Ando family were forced to settle in Ezo (Hokkaidō), and by around 1430 they had installed the first official Japanese centre of governance there.

As the Japanese gradually sought to exert their influence further in Ezo, a number of outposts were established in the south of the island, and by the late 15th century more than ten castles had been built in the region by various Japanese lords. By around 1600, the Kakizaki clan (who soon renamed themselves the Matsumae clan; page 158) eventually took control of the entire region and established the town of Matsumae (or Fukuyama as it was also sometimes known) as the centre of trade between the Japanese and Ainu, building the castle and other infrastructure. Along with commerce, Matsumae gained much wealth from a very productive herring fishing industry. From their Matsumae base, the clan would attempt to exert their influence over Hokkaidō for the next 200 years or so, until the government later stepped in and moved control from Matsumae to Hakodate in 1802, partly because of the latter's superior harbour.

In 1854 much of Matsumae Castle burned down, but the shōgunate rebuilt it the following year, making it the last Edo-style castle to be built in Japan. By now the government fully controlled Ezo, Hakodate had opened to foreign trade in 1855, and Matsumae, while still being home to many Japanese, lost much of its importance – though it continued to thrive thanks to its still prosperous fishing industry. Almost two-thirds of the town was destroyed in the Battle of Hakodate in 1869 (page 138). However, within a few years most of the town had been restored; visiting in the 1890s, English writer and Explorer A H S Landor wrote that Matsumae was 'the most picturesque of all the towns on Hokkaidō'. The castle burned down and was rebuilt yet again in 1949, and shortly afterwards, in 1953, the ill-fated Matsumae Line was opened – it connected the town to Kikonai, but only operated for a little over 30 years before closing for good in 1988.

Getting there and around There are three direct **buses** a day between Hakodate and Matsumae (3hrs; ¥2,100). Alternatively, there is a much quicker and more frequent bus service every 1–2 hours from JR Kikonai Station (1½hrs; ¥1,300), where both regular **trains** and the Shinkansen stop. If you plan on spending two or three days in the region, it may be worth investing in a 'free pass' bus ticket (2/3 days ¥3,000/4,000), which allows unlimited bus travel on a number of routes between Hakodate, Matsumae and Esashi and is available from Hakodate bus station, the tourist information centres at JR Shin-Hakodate-Hokuto and Esashi stations, and the Misagi-no-sato roadside station near JR Kikonai Station.

By **road**, use Route 228, which mostly hugs the coast as it loops around the peninsula and is the only real way to get in or out of Matsumae. It's 95km from Hakodate, roughly a 2-hour drive.

Where to stay and eat

Onsen Ryokan Yano 温泉旅館矢野; 23 Fukuyama; ☏0139 42 2525; w matsumae-yano. com/english. A short walk from Matsumae Castle, this long-running & slightly dated but clean hotel offers simple Japanese-style tatami rooms. Day visitors may dine at the restaurant & use the hot spring (◷ 15.00–21.00 daily; ¥600, or free for guests), which includes indoor & outdoor baths. $$$$

Ezo Sushi 蝦夷寿し; 249–4 Fukuyama; ☏0139 42 2131; ◷ 12.30–20.30 Tue–Sun. Fantastically fresh sushi made to order right in front of you. Not a lick of English, but you can point at items behind the glass counter or ask for the *nigiri-sushi* set. Situated just east of the castle park, Ezo Sushi is located in an attractive whitewashed building which looks like it could be part of the castle itself. $$$

What to see and do

Matsumae Castle (松前城, Matsumae-shiro; ◷ 09.00–17.00 daily, closed 10 Dec–10 Apr; ¥360/free) Built on a hillside overlooking the town and sea, Matsumae Castle is both the northernmost castle in Japan and the only Edo-style fortification on Hokkaidō. Constructed in 1606 by Yoshihiro Matsumae, the first lord of the powerful Matsumae clan (page 158), the castle's white walls and elegant eaves give it that unmistakably beautiful and classic look of all the great Japanese castles of the period. Like many others, it has been rebuilt a number of times over the years, with the current construction mostly dating to 1961, but it nevertheless remains a

The Matsumae family are synonymous with the history of the Oshima Peninsula and played a key role in the history of Hokkaidō as a whole, though their story starts much earlier when they were known by their original name, Kakizaki. The Kakizaki family were one of a number of Japanese groups based in the Oshima region by the early 16th century, although the powerful Ando clan retained overall control of Wajin (Japanese) territories in both southern Hokkaidō and across the strait on the mainland. The Japanese and Ainu of the Oshima Peninsula generally lived and traded peacefully, although violent conflicts did break out from time to time.

One of the first large conflicts between Wajin and Ainu was Koshamain's War in 1457, which led to several Japanese fortifications being captured by a united Ainu force. Hanazawa, on the west coast of the peninsula, was one of the few Japanese strongholds not to be overrun, defended by a force led by Nobuhiro Takeda, a close associate of the Kakizaki family. By this point the Kakizaki clan oversaw administration of Ezo for the Ando family, who were now mostly based in northern Honshū. Perhaps as a result of his heroic exploits, Takeda was later adopted into the Kakizaki family, and eventually ascended to the top of the tree to inherit full leadership of the family. Takeda died in 1494, but the clan consolidated their power when the Ando family authorised them to take charge of all their affairs in Ezo, and in 1516 the shōgunate granted the Kakizaki the right to claim tax payments from all ships which came to Ezo to trade goods.

Throughout the rest of the 16th century there were a number of minor skirmishes, but also a gradual increase in trade between Japanese and Ainu, with a partial peace deal agreed between the Kakizaki and Ainu: both could earn money from mutual trade, but the Kakizaki (and no other Wajin groups) would have exclusive trading rights with the Ainu, as well as recognise and respect Ainu chiefs. A clear border between Wajin land (which they called Wajinchi or 'Japanese Land') on the Oshima Peninsula and Ainu-controlled land in the rest of Ezo was also agreed. Kakizaki power was consolidated considerably after 1603 when the

truly striking sight when viewed from the surrounding grounds. The inside of the castle keep houses a small museum with only a smattering of English explanations.

In spring (late April to mid-May), large numbers come to participate in Matsumae Sakura Festival, one of Hokkaidō's most famous cherry-blossom festivals which takes place in the adjoining **Matsumae Park** (松前公園). Around 10,000 cherry trees of 250 varieties come into bloom, and visitors can enjoy traditional music and performances, as well as the beautiful views. Entrance to the park is completely free.

For those heading in by bus, the closest stop to the castle and park is Matsushiro (松城), from where it is a 5-minute walk up the hill.

Matsumae Shrine (松前神社, Matsumae-jinja)

Matsumae Shrine (松前神社, Matsumae-jinja) Set back to the north side of Matsumae Park is this shrine with its eye-catching red roof, dedicated to the deity of Nobuhiro Takeda, revered ancestor of the Matsumae clan (see above). A short walk beyond is the beautiful temple district, home to various Buddhist sects, and many of the temples pre-date Matsumae Castle, being among some of the oldest Japanese-style structures on Hokkaidō.

One of the most impressive is nearby **Ryūun-in** (龍雲院), a wooden temple with a remarkable dragon sculpture. It is also known for its white dandelions, which bloom just before the cherry blossoms (around late April).

Tokugawa shōgunate recognised the Kakizaki territory as an official domain, and therefore part of Japan proper. This allowed the Kakizaki to break subservience with the Ando, and with the start of a new era of control they changed their name to Matsumae, sought allegiance from other Wajin groups in Ezo, and Yoshihiro Matsumae (Takeda's grandson) became the first Ezo daimyō (feudal lord) acting as a direct vassal of the shōgunate in Edo (Tokyo).

In 1606 the clan constructed Matsumae Castle, from where they sought to administer their territory and control all trade and movement between the Ainu-held Ezochi (the rest of Hokkaidō) and this tightly run Japanese enclave. The Matsumae clan increased trading across Hokkaidō during the 17th and 18th centuries, establishing ever more remote trading posts in the Ezochi. Unlike other daimyō throughout Japan, whose wealth was chiefly based on rice production, the Matsumae were unable to grow rice because of the harsh climatic conditions, and so relied solely on exploiting Hokkaidō's other natural resources by controlling all trade with the Ainu (who also relayed goods from further afield, such as Russia and China).

In time, the Matsumae came to rely more on money generated by the fishing industry rather than on trade with the Ainu, and this led to an increased number of Wajin in Ezo, which furthered unrest with the Ainu. The shōgunate was also becoming slightly distrustful of the distant and relatively secretive Matsumae, and there was an increasing interest in developing Ezo more directly by the central government. By 1799 the end was nigh for Matsumae dominion, as the government moved into Ezo and took full control of the island in 1807. This was relatively short-lived, however, and Matsumae were granted control of the whole island in 1821, possibly to save the government money amid a lowering of threat from Russian intrusions into Ezo. But the clan had passed their true heyday, and once again relinquished power to the shōgunate in 1854, as Hokkaido was fully incorporated into the newly emerging modern Japan.

Matsumae Feudal Clan Mansion (松前藩屋敷, Matsumaehan-yashiki; ⊕ early Apr–early Nov 09.00–17.00 daily; ¥360/240) This is a large open-air and historically evocative reconstruction of a local township during the Edo era. There are 14 buildings to enter including merchant homes, shops and the Matsumae clan samurai mansion. You can dress up in samurai armour too if you really want to get into the spirit of things; otherwise it's possible to wander around freely and see most things in an hour or two. Don't forget to take off your shoes before entering the buildings or stepping on any tatami!

Cape Shirakami (白神岬, Shirakami-misaki) Around 10km east of Matsumae, this frequently windy spot marked by a red-and-white lighthouse is the southernmost point of Hokkaidō. In truth, there is not much to see or do here, although you can spot Aomori far away across the strait. The Cape Shirakami Observatory Square (白神岬展望広場) has parking, toilets and expansive sea views, and is a short way up the road west of the lighthouse.

FUKUSHIMA The small coastal town of Fukushima (福島; population 4,300) has two main attractions which bring in a decent number of tourists each year, plus a nice sandy beach which is popular with families. The first of these is the

THE SEIKAN TUNNEL

In a country rammed full of examples of remarkable engineering feats, the Seikan Tunnel connecting Hokkaidō to Aomori remains one of the most impressive. Finally opened on 13 March 1988, the tunnel runs for just under 56km, including a 23km-long undersea segment, making it the longest tunnel with an undersea section in the world, although the Channel Tunnel (which is shorter at 50.5km) has a longer undersea section (37.9km). Seikan is also the second-deepest transport tunnel in the world.

Plans for a tunnel beneath the Tsugaru Strait had been mooted since around the early 1920s, with geological surveying first beginning in 1946 (some 42 years prior to the tunnel opening). Efforts were hastened following a terrible disaster in the Tsugaru Strait, when five ferries – including the flagship train-ferry *Tōya Maru* – sank during a typhoon in September 1954, resulting in the deaths of at least 1,153 passengers (the exact number is unknown).

Construction on the tunnel finally began in 1971 and went on for 17 years, but it was a technically challenging project and 34 workers lost their lives in the process. Upon completion in 1988, the total cost of the tunnel ran to ¥1.1 trillion (US$7 billion), around 12 times over the initial budget, though much of that was due to inflation. But, for the first time, Hokkaidō was connected to the rest of Japan by rail, even though the vast majority of people travelling between Tokyo and Sapporo still opted to fly, as it was much quicker (1hr 45mins by air as opposed to around 8hrs by train) and usually cheaper too. Overnight trains to Sapporo from the capital also made use of the tunnel, but with the formation of the Hokkaidō Shinkansen in 2015, the tunnel was converted to dual gauge for use only by high-speed bullet trains, and regular train services on the narrow-gauge Kaikyō Line were ceased (apart from freight trains). At present the Shinkansen runs only as far as Hakodate, but the final extension to Sapporo is scheduled for completion by 2031, meaning it will take just 5, or possibly even closer to 4, hours by rail between Tokyo and Sapporo.

Before the Shinkansen service commandeered full use of the tunnel and regular trains used to ply its depths, there were two stations located deep under the sea at either end: Yoshioka-Kaitei Station on the Hokkaidō side, and Tappi-Kaitei Station on the Aomori end. The former, at 149.5m below sea level, was the deepest underground station in the world. Both stations opened in 1988 and primarily functioned as emergency escape points, although trains did stop there for tourists as each station also housed a museum relating to the tunnel. The service to Yoshioka-Kaitei, however, ended in 2006, followed by Tappi-Kaitei in 2013, to allow preparations for the Shinkansen Line.

Seikan Tunnel Museum (青函トンネル記念館; ⏰ mid-Mar–Dec 09.00–17.00 daily; ¥400/200), commemorating the construction and opening of the nearby undersea tunnel linking Hokkaidō and Honshū (see above). The museum building itself uniquely resembles a section of metallic tunnel pipe, and inside you will find examples of drilling equipment and detailed exhibits and explanations on how the mammoth project was carried out. Unfortunately, there is almost no English, but many of the displays are visual and quite easy to follow. There is another slightly bigger Seikan Tunnel Museum on the other side of the strait in Aomori, which also includes a cable-car ride down to a service tunnel 140m below the sea.

Fukushima is well known as a town that has produced some acclaimed sumo wrestlers, and two of its most famous and successful sons have an entire museum dedicated to them. The **Yokozuna Chiyonoyama and Chiyonofuji Memorial Museum** (横綱千代の山・千代の富士記念館; ⊕ 09.00–17.00 daily; ¥500) contains items and memorabilia related to the pair of legendary wrestlers, along with monitors showing footage of their most famous bouts. Hardcore sumo fans will undoubtedly get a lot out of it, but casual foreign visitors may have a harder time. If you plan to visit both the Seikan Tunnel and sumo museums, then there is a discount ticket available at each location. Fukushima can be reached in about 1 hour by bus from JR Kikonai Station.

SHIRIUCHI There is little reason to stop in Shiriuchi (知内; population 4,600), a fairly nondescript coastal town, apart from perhaps popping into **Komorebi Spa** (こもれび温泉; w shiriuchi.info/threes/index2.html; ⊕ 10.00–20.00 Tue–Sun; ¥350/100) just south of the river. This quiet and very local hot-spring facility has indoor and outdoor baths, a sauna, plus a rarity for an onsen – a small indoor swimming pool. You can also grab a bowl of noodles or a curry from the simple on-site restaurant ($), which serves food until around 14.00.

History buffs may enjoy the small **Shiriuchi Local Museum** (知内町郷土資料館; ⊕ 10.00–16.30 Tue–Sun; free) just off road 228, which displays a real hotchpotch of artefacts including pots and tools from the Jōmon period to more contemporary treasures such as home appliances from the Shōwa era. It's reasonably interesting stuff (if you like that type of thing) with next to no English explanations, but much of it is fairly self-explanatory.

KIKONAI A quiet seaside town located halfway between Hakodate and Matsumae, Kikonai (木古内) doesn't have much in the way of must-see attractions, but does serve as a useful transport hub with the first (or last) Shinkansen stop on Hokkaidō, direct rail connections to Hakodate (1hr), and connecting buses to Matsumae (90mins) and Esashi (80mins). In January, you may be able to catch the Kanchū Misogi Matsuri, the town's traditional Shintō festival (see below).

Perhaps of more interest to rail fans is the **Kikonai Town Museum Ikarinkan** (木古内町郷土資料館いかりん館; ⊕ 09.00–16.00 Tue–Sun; free), which not only explains the general history of the area but has numerous items and displays relating to the disused Esashi Line, along with lots of train-related paraphernalia. There's almost no English, but it is still quite interesting, especially as the museum

> **LOINCLOTHS AT THE READY**
>
> Kikonai's most famous festival, Kanchū Misogi Matsuri takes place over 13–15 January every year and involves four ascetic Shintō practitioners purifying themselves in icy water come sun, rain or (much more likely) snow, in return, it is hoped, for a good harvest later that year. Wearing only loincloths, they undertake this cleansing ritual multiple times throughout each day and night, and on the final day parade down to the seashore and toss themselves – and sacred icons from Samegawa Shrine (佐女川神社) – into the sea at Misogi Beach. Any onlookers splashed by the water are said to be blessed with eternal happiness!

Around 50km off the coast west of Matsumae lies Japan's largest uninhabited island, **Ōshima** (大島). Meaning 'big island', it rises abruptly from the sea like a mirage, covering an area of 9.73km² and measuring around 4km across. It was formed by two overlapping stratovolcanoes and is shaped by their two calderas, with the highpoint of Mount Era (江良岳) reaching 732m, although from the seabed it is almost 2,300m tall. While quiet in recent years, there was a period of dramatic activity around 300 years ago, most notably in August 1741 when a major eruption triggered a huge landslide and tsunami (known as the Kampo Tsunami), devastating the coasts of Hokkaidō, Honshū and even Korea, resulting in almost 1,500 deaths and washing away hundreds of homes. Because of the island's barren terrain and isolated location, it is not ecologically rich, although it is a breeding ground for seabirds such as the streaked shearwater. There is a lighthouse and a helipad on the island, but all visitors require strict governmental approval. Ōshima is also sometimes called Oshima Ōshima or Matsumae Ōshima to differentiate it from other islands of the same name (of which there are many in Japan).

Approximately 38km southeast of Ōshima is its much smaller sibling, **Kojima** (小島), which appropriately enough means 'little island'. At only 1.54km², it is said to be the world's smallest volcanic island and is also uninhabited. It is predominantly grassy and is an important breeding ground for various seabirds including guillemots, gulls and the rhinoceros auklet (a relative of the puffin). The seas around the island have a rich abundance of marine life, and so the area is a popular fishing ground for Matsumae's fishermen – a small harbour for their refuge is the island's only manmade construction. Tourists are not usually permitted to visit either island.

itself was converted from a former elementary school. Next door at the disused Tsuruoka-kōen Station, you can ride a pedal-powered trolley-train along 1km of the old Esashi Line (**w** senro.donan.net; ⊕ late Apr–Nov 10.00–15.00 Sat–Sun; ¥700/400).

In early to mid-May you can catch the bright pink *shibazakura* moss phlox blooms at **Yakushi-yama** (薬師山), a small hill with pleasant views just north of the town (a 10min walk from the station).

MOUNT DAISENGEN (大千軒, Daisengen-dake) A wonderful remote mountain with far-reaching views (on a good day) and high ridgeline meadows of wildflowers, Mount Daisengen (1,072m) is the highest peak in the region and makes for a great day hike for well-equipped walkers. During the Edo period, a gold mine was established on the mountain, and this was the scene of a rather grisly episode in 1639 when 106 unfortunate Japanese Christians were executed there by the Matsumae clan – a result of the Tokugawa shōgunate's brutal crackdown on Christianity.

These days, the mountain is thankfully much more peaceful, with a number of routes leading up to the summit. The easiest and shortest approach is from Matsumae, although it requires a long (32km/1-hour) drive up the winding road 607 (though this was closed at time of writing), arriving at a small car park. From here you can hike the Shindō Course (新道コース) eastwards, following a path up along the ridge to reach the summit in around 2 hours return (5.5km). Don't forget to bring a bear bell or at least sing aloud to avoid any chance encounters. The hike is best attempted from late May to early November when most of the snow will be gone. The Okufutamatato-tozanguchi (奥二股登山口) is the starting point of the long eastern approach on the Shiriuchi Course (知内コース); it has parking spaces and takes around 8 hours return (11km), but with a number of (shallow) river crossings and over 1,000m of ascent, it is only for experienced and fit hikers.

NORTHERN OSHIMA PENINSULA

While the vast majority of visitors to the Oshima Peninsula spend their time in Hakodate or perhaps venture to Matsumae at the southern end of the peninsula, the northern districts of Esashi and Setana see far fewer outside visitors. There are a few things to do in this remote region, and the two townships also serve as the ports for ferries to Okushiri Island.

GETTING THERE AND AWAY
By car The relatively short-lived Esashi Line used to run between Kikonai and Esashi but closed in 2014, so now with no rail connections the only way to reach Esashi is by road. Route 228 hugs the coast all the way around the peninsula from Hakodate to Esashi (155km) and makes for a good road trip as it passes through Matsumae on the way. However, the quickest route from Hakodate is by following Route 227 west through the mountains for 72km to reach Esashi in about 1½hrs.

Setana is another 85km or so up the coast from Esashi, mostly following Route 229. From Hakodate it's a more lengthy 130km, but should take less than 2½hrs following Route 5 as far as Yakumo, and then joining road 42 west all the way to Setana.

By bus It's around 2½hrs from Hakodate to Esashi (5 times daily; 06.00–19.00; ¥1,900 one-way). For Setana it's a bit trickier, as there is usually only one direct bus a day from Hakodate; instead it may be best to take the train to Oshamambe and then transfer to a local bus to Setana. Hakodate bus terminal or the tourist information centres will be able to help with the logistics.

ESASHI The capital of Hiyama subprefecture, Esashi (江差; population 8,000) is one of Hokkaidō's oldest established towns – a small west coast fishing port which began life as an Ainu settlement, and then grew prosperous as Japanese colonists came and developed the herring fishing industry between around 1600 and 1800. During this period the three harbours of Esashi, Matsumae and Hakodate were collectively known as the 'Matsumae Sanso' and were said to have a combined wealth greater than that of Edo (Tokyo). The herring fishing eventually dried up, but many of the well-preserved wealthy merchants' homes can be found along the evocative Inishie kaidō road which runs for 1km through the town.

Esashi plays host to a number of festivals, most notably during the months of July, August and September. The biggest and oldest of these is the Ubagami Danjingu Togyo Festival, held between 9 and 11 August every year, when 50,000 people take to the streets to watch 13 decorated wooden floats being paraded through the town in thanks for plentiful herring catches. Esashi is also famous as the birthplace of

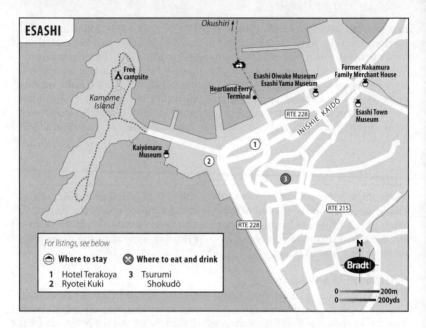

ESASHI

Okushiri

Free campsite

Kamome Island

Esashi Oiwake Museum/
Esashi Yama Museum

Former Nakamura
Family Merchant House

Heartland Ferry
Terminal

RTE 228

INISHIE KAIDO

Esashi Town
Museum

Kaiyōmaru
Museum

①

②

③

RTE 215

RTE 228

N

Bradt

| 0 | 200m |
| 0 | 200yds |

For listings, see below

🏠 **Where to stay**   ❌ **Where to eat and drink**

1 Hotel Terakoya   **3** Tsurumi
2 Ryotei Kuki   Shokudō

Esashi oiwake, a local twist on an old form of folk music called *mago-uta* – lyrics in the Esashi version evoke the region's nature and fishing heritage.

From the port you can take the 2½-hour Heartland ferry over to Okushiri.

 Where to stay and eat *Map, above*

Esashi has plenty of accommodation and restaurant options if you plan to stay over, the majority of which are located close to and just south of the harbour. As well as the excellent local seafood, Nishin soba noodles are one of the town's specialities.

Ryotei Kuki 旅庭群来; 1-5 Ubagamichō; 📞0139 52 2020; w esashi-kuki.jp. Enjoy high-end accommodation at this ultra-modern, eco-conscious (all heat is generated geothermally) & stylish hotel right on the harbour front, with simple yet tasteful rooms, & exquisite organic food using ingredients sourced no further than 25km away. $$$$$
Hotel Terakoya ホテル寺子屋; 26 Ubagamichō; 📞0139 52 0855; w hotel-terakoya. com. Old-fashioned but comfortable rooms, & more spacious than many similar-range business

hotels. It's set price of ¥6,000 pp per night or ¥7,000 including a simple Japanese b/fast. Wi-Fi throughout. Great location for harbour & historic attractions. $$$
Tsurumi Shokudō (Japanese Restaurant) つるみ食堂; 62 Hashimotochō; 📞0139 52 0345; ⏰ 11.00–14.30 & 17.00–20.30 daily. On the main road heading south from the harbour, this unassuming place with 3 wooden pillars at the entrance offers set meals of Japanese comfort food, such as fried prawn, oyster or pork cutlets with rice, ramen, & *kara-age* (fried chicken). $$

What to see and do

Inishie Kaidō (いにしえ街道) One street back from the harbour, the Inishie Kaidō is an old 1km thoroughfare lined by exceedingly well-preserved wooden buildings, including *machiya* townhouses, *shoka* merchant residences and *tonya* wholesale stores. It's a lovely place to stroll and take in the historical ambience; a number of the buildings now function as museums, shops and cafés.

Towards the north end of the street at the crossroads is the large and impressive two-storey **Former Nakamura Family Merchant House** (旧中村家住宅; ⊕ Apr–Oct 09.00–17.00 daily, Nov–Mar 09.00–17.00 Tue–Sun); ¥300/100). Consisting of four connected buildings, the interior looks almost exactly as it did back in its heyday, all built from the wealth the Nakamuras procured from the herring industry. A real time-capsule showpiece and must-see.

Turning southwest at the crossroads and then up the street is **Esashi Town Museum** (旧檜山爾志郡役所; ⊕ Apr–Oct 09.00–17.00 daily, Nov–Mar 09.00–17.00 Tue–Sun; ¥300/100). The attractive building with its Western-style white-and-green façade dates to 1887, and once served as a police station, town hall and government branch office. Worth visiting to check out the period furnishings which have been lovingly restored, it now houses various artefacts spanning the entire history of Esashi. If you've been to any other small regional museums on Hokkaidō, you'll have a good idea of what to expect, although this one pleasingly has lots of English explanations.

Esashi Oiwake Museum/Esashi Yama Museum (江差追分会館・江差山車会館, Esashi Oiwake-kaikan/Esashi Yama-kaikan; ⊕ Apr–Oct 09.00–15.00 daily, Nov–Mar 09.00–15.00 Tue–Sun; ¥500/250)

If you can't make it to the three-day festival held in August, when 13 large and ornate *danjiri* floats are paraded through the streets, then visiting this museum is the next best thing. Here you can see some of the floats on display plus related festival paraphernalia, and you may also catch live performances of Esashi oiwake (the famous local folk music) on stage three times daily. The displays are mostly Japanese-heavy, with smatterings of English here and there, but the floats are interesting to see up close.

Kaiyōmaru Museum (開陽丸記念館, Kaiyōmaru-kinenkan; w kaiyou-maru.com; ⊕ Apr–Oct 09.00–17.00 daily, Nov–Mar 09.00–17.00 Tue–Sun; ¥500/250)

Visitors to Esashi's waterfront will instantly be drawn to the impressive black-hulled sailing ship, masts hoisted upwards, moored over in the west of the harbour. This is an almost exact reconstruction of the ill-fated *Kaiyōmaru*, a Dutch-built warship which was built in 1866, arrived in Japan in 1868, and was intended for use by the Tokugawa shōgunate during the collapse of their reign. However, just over two years after its construction, during the Battle of Hakodate in late 1868, the *Kaiyōmaru* was en route to Esashi when it encountered a blizzard off the coast, ended up stranded and sank. In 1975 a huge salvage operation began, during which time tens of thousands of artefacts were recovered from the wreckage, many now appearing on display in the reconstructed ship (completed in 1990) which serves as an interactive museum. Displayed are a fascinating collection of salvaged objects, ranging from guns, cannons and weaponry to cutlery and assorted personal items. Walking through the galleys and cabins is hugely evocative, with a sizeable mannequin population re-enacting daily scenes from life on the frigate. This is a great place to visit if you like maritime history.

Kamome Island (かもめ島 / 鷗島, Kamome-jima)

West of the harbour and across a narrow sandy isthmus is a grassy hump known as Kamome-jima, named after the Japanese word for 'seagull', which the island is said to resemble when seen from above. The island forms part of Esashi's harbour and so was an important natural feature of the town, especially for fishermen in the past. There are a number of unusual rock forms along its coast, including the Heishi-iwa, to which an old legend that dates back at least 500 years is attached. The legend says that once, when the herring vanished, an old fortune teller woman was given a bottle of magic liquid which she threw into the sea, causing the herring to return. The bottle got wedged in the seabed, turned into rock, and came to represent the deity of the Sea of Japan. A couple of short walking paths run across the island, and on the north side is a nice free campsite with toilets and sunset views.

KAMINOKUNI This small town steeped in history lies 7km down the coast from Esashi, and sits on the banks of the Amano River. One of the ancestors of the Kakizaki (later to become the Matsumae) clan established a fort here in the 15th century, which eventually led to Japanese traders settling in the village. Much later, Kaminokuni (上ノ国) was a former stop on the abandoned Esashi Line.

Out on the western edge of town, **Jōkoku-ji** (上国寺) is said to be the oldest temple structure on Hokkaidō, dating back to the late 1500s. Next door the rustic **Old Sasanami Residence** (旧笹浪家住宅; ⊕ Apr–mid-Nov 10.00–16.00 Tue–Sun; ¥300/100) was built at the end of the Edo period and was the home of the Sasanami family who ran a successful fishing business; it is believed to be the oldest surviving private house on Hokkaidō. A 15-minute walk up the hill behind the temple lie **Katsuyama Castle Ruins** (勝山館跡, Katsuyama-date-ato), built around 500 years ago by Nobuhiro Takeda for the early Japanese colonisers of Hokkaidō, although it is thought that the Ainu peacefully co-existed here too. The extensive grounds and earthworks are dotted with bilingual information boards, and the views down along the coast are splendid. A small museum (⊕ 10.00–16.00 daily; ¥200/100) offers more detailed explanations and exhibits, but can probably be skipped. There is parking next to the museum if you come up by car.

SETANA A remote and quiet fishing port high up on the west coast of the Oshima Peninsula, Setana (せたな町; population 8,500) doesn't see a lot of visitors other than road-trippers and people passing through to catch the ferry to Okushiri. The township itself covers quite a wide and mostly mountainous area along the beautifully wild and rocky coast, but the main settlement lies where the Shiribeshi-Toshibetsu River meets the sea. Lacking in attractions, but with a few decent hotels and restaurants, Setana's most well-known landmarks are the **Sanbonsugi-iwa** (三本杉岩), three pointy 30m-tall rocks jutting just offshore from the long and sandy Sanbonsugi Beach, a few steps north of the harbour.

Adventurous types with their own wheels should head south for 25km along Route 740 to attempt the climb up to **Ōta Shrine** (太田神社, Ōta-jinja) which towers above the coast, near the top of a mountain of the same name. Said to be the steepest approach to any shrine in Japan, the path up there is extremely precarious and crumbly (with the genuine risk of rockfall) and more akin to rock climbing in places, with ropes, ladders and huge metal chains draped down the final near-vertical cliff-face section. The small wooden shrine is hidden inside a cliff-top cave, from where there are outstanding, albeit vertigo-inducing views. The scramble up and down should take around an hour – definitely not one for the faint-hearted!

OKUSHIRI ISLAND

Lying 20km west off the coast of the Oshima Peninsula, Okushiri Island (奥尻島, Okushiri-tō) is relatively small, spanning roughly 11km east to west and 26km north to south at its maximum points. A remote, wind-ravaged outpost with few foreign visitors, the island has a rugged coastline and hilly interior, with extensive beech forests covering over half the land. The population of around 3,000 people reside mostly in the two main towns on the island: Okushiri on the east coast is where the port is located, while Aonae on the southern tip is close to the airport.

It is believed that the first people to occupy Okushiri came from Hokkaidō around 8,000 years ago, and a number of Jōmon-era artefacts have been uncovered on the island. The main industry has always been predominantly fishing, and there was some sulphur mining for a time, although seasonal tourism

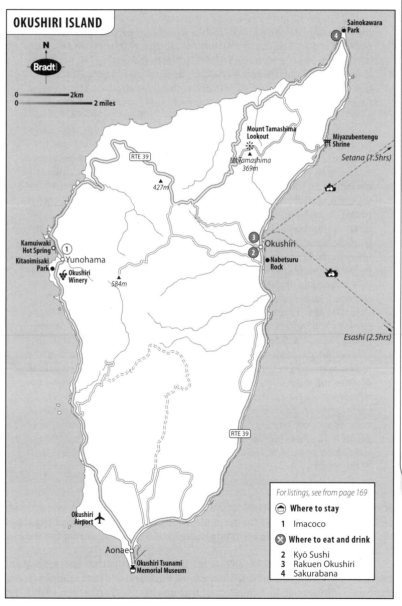

OKUSHIRI ISLAND

N
Bradt

0 ———— 2km
0 ———— 2 miles

Sainokawara Park
④

RTE 39

Mount Tamashima Lookout
Mt Tamashima 369m

Miyazubentengu Shrine
Setana (1.5hrs)

427m

③ ● Okushiri
② ● Nabetsuru Rock

Kamuiwaki Hot Spring ①
Kitaoimisaki Park ● Yunohama
Okushiri Winery
584m

Esashi (2.5hrs)

RTE 39

Okushiri Airport
Aonae
Okushiri Tsunami Memorial Museum

For listings, see from page 169

◒ Where to stay
1 Imacoco

✖ Where to eat and drink
2 Kyō Sushi
3 Rakuen Okushiri
4 Sakurabana

DEVASTATING EARTHQUAKES AND TSUNAMIS

Okushiri has actually suffered from two earthquake disasters in recent history, first in 1983 and then ten years later in 1993, the latter much more deadly, with the resulting tsunami said to be the first tsunami ever recorded on camera.

The 1983 earthquake occurred on 26 May and measured 7.7 in magnitude, but resulted in only two deaths, with the tsunami making landfall around 20 minutes after the initial shake. There would be much less time to escape in the next disaster, however.

At 22.00 on 12 July 1993, a large magnitude 7.7 earthquake occurred off the west coast of Hokkaidō in the Sea of Japan. The epicentre was northeast of Okushiri Island, and after a significant amount of shaking (in two main jolts lasting 20 seconds and 35 seconds), the island was hit just 4 minutes later by a powerful tsunami, with waves rising to a staggering 32m at their highest point on the western side of Okushiri, making it one of the largest tsunamis ever recorded in Japan. The earthquake itself caused the island to subside by up to 80cm, and a landslide triggered by the earthquake crashed into a hotel, killing 29 people. But the greatest damage was caused by the tsunami, particularly in the settlement of Aonae on the southern end of the island. The tsunami actually arrived in a series of three or four major waves spread out over the course of an hour and which completely overwhelmed the island's sea defences, wiping out all the buildings on the southern end of the cape (apart from one monument which still stands today). Those living on the cape had almost no time to evacuate to higher ground, and those who did were greeted by an apocalyptic scene: as the tsunami burst gas lines and smashed boats, causing leaked fuel to burn uncontrollably, fires raged throughout the remnants of town and across the harbour, through the night and into the next morning. The combination of earthquakes, flooding, fires and landslides resulted in carnage, with damage compounded by each subsequent disaster.

It is believed that 165 people lost their lives on Okushiri, the figure rising to 230 in total as the tsunami also reached the shores of Hokkaidō, Honshū, Russia and South Korea. The final bill for the clear-up and building of new sea defences cost the Japanese government somewhere in the region of US$600 million, but the psychological and physical effects of the disaster still loom large over the island. Visitors will see clear evidence of this, especially the concrete sea walls and reinforced cliffs which have been constructed almost everywhere. While the grey ugliness of these defences does detract considerably from the area's natural beauty, in Okushiri of all places it does seem somewhat forgivable, and shows the determination of the authorities to temper the forces of nature in this seismically volatile part of the world.

is now one of the main pillars of the island's economy. Okushiri's empty roads and pleasant scenery make it a great place for cycling and mini-road trips, and the island receives the overwhelming majority of its visitors during the warmer summer months.

Okushiri is perhaps most famous for the huge earthquake and subsequent tsunami in 1993 which completely devastated the island and took many lives, and there are still many vivid reminders of that disaster right across the island. But the island has recovered over the intervening years, and it is a great place to relax, contemplate life and just generally take things slowly for a couple of days.

For visitors arriving by ferry, it's worth popping into the **Okushiri Tourist Information Centre** (奥尻観光情報センター; ⏰ 08.30–17.00 daily) situated in the harbour right next to the ferry terminal; the staff are very friendly and helpful, and can assist with organising activities around the island.

GETTING THERE AND AWAY

By ferry Timetables vary depending on the season, but there are generally one or two car and passenger ferries a day run by Heartland Ferries (w heartlandferry. jp/english), sailing from either Setana (1½hrs; ¥1,700) or Esashi (2½hrs; ¥2,910). Vehicle prices start at around ¥15,000 one-way.

By air There is one flight a day between Hakodate and Okushiri (30mins; ¥9,000 one-way) on a 36-seater aircraft operated by JAL.

GETTING AROUND The best way to get around is by renting a car (bringing one across from the mainland is an option) and there are car rental offices at the port and near the airport.

Okushiri Car Rental 📞0139 72 7210; w oku-shiri.com; ⏰ 08.00–18.00 daily. Located a short walk south from the ferry terminal, 4–8-seater cars are available.

Okushirito Airport Car Rental 📞0139 73 2008; w okushiri-rentacar.jp. Cars & motorbikes for rent; credit cards accepted.

WHERE TO STAY *Map, page 167*
Accommodation is mostly family home-style guesthouses; there are also plenty of campsites all over the island.

✳ **Imacoco** 奥尻ゲストハウスイマココ; 100 Yunohama; 📞0803 237 8988; w okushiri-imacoco. com. Basic but excellent guesthouse with sea views, on Okushiri's west coast. Run by a friendly young family who speak English, it's a great base for coastal hikes, SUP boarding & other outdoor activities, plus the hot spring is just a 1min walk away. **$$**

Shimajikan 島じかん; 189-59 Aonae; 📞090 3397 2766; w unimaru.com; ⏰ closed Nov–Mar. Like most places on the island, Shimajikan offers basic lodgings which are functional rather than fancy; think tatami floors & futons for sleeping. All rooms have AC, TV, fridge & Wi-Fi. Located near the main thoroughfares in Aonae. **$$**

WHERE TO EAT AND DRINK *Map, page 167*
The incredibly clear waters and warm sea currents around Okushiri mean it has long been known for the high quality of its sea urchins (best in July and August) and abalone plus other seafood, while in recent years the locally produced wine has started to garner attention.

Hokkai Sushi 北海寿司; 411-104 Aonae; 📞01397 3 2288; ⏰ from 17.00 daily. Big portions & plenty of seasonal variations are served up at this cosy sushi & seafood restaurant in a fancy-looking Matsumae-style building in Aonae. The special 5-type lunch set (*gentei-go-shoku*) is limited to only 5 servings each day & a bargain at ¥3,000. No EM. **$$$**

Kyō Sushi 叶寿司; 766-11 Okushiri; 📞01397 2 3340; ⏰ 17.00–23.00 daily. Traditional sushi restaurant close to the port with friendly staff, outstandingly fresh seafood & Okushiri wine on the drinks menu. There's both counter & table seating, but they may fill up in the high season. No EM. **$$$**

Rakuen Okushiri 楽園奥尻支店; 794 Okushiri; \01397 2 3480; ⊕ 11.00–14.00 & 17.00–21.00 daily. When you're fed up of seafood, try this excellent ramen & *yaki-niku* (grilled meat) restaurant with a choice of *miso-*, *shio-* (salt) and *shōyu* (soy sauce)-based ramen broths. Near the port, just past the post office; look out for the small yellow-&-red sign next to the door. No EM. $$$

Sakurabana 北の岬さくらばな; 108-Inahō; \01397 2 3630; ⊕ Apr–Oct 08.30–17.00 daily. A seafood restaurant right on the exposed northern tip of the island. In summer try the island specialities of *uni* (sea urchin) & *awabi* (abalone), both of which are in the rare seafood ramen which includes scallops. Most popular, however, is the *uni-don* (sea urchin rice-bowl). No EM. $$$

WHAT TO SEE AND DO Okushiri has a dramatic and rugged coastline, especially on the western side of the island, where the clear waters can be a dazzling hue of turquoise – known as 'Okushiri blue'. A camping and cycling/driving tour around the perimeter of the island is a great way to see the numerous rock formations dotting the coast; allow at least 2 or 3 hours to circumnavigate the 65km of coastal road by car, although it is much better to spread it out over a couple of days.

The most famous landmark on the island is the **Nabetsuru Rock** (鍋釣岩) just a 10-minute walk south of the port; this knobbly rock arch stands 19.5m tall among the waves, mere metres from the shore – best viewed under clear blue skies or at sunrise. Heading north and anti-clockwise from the port, follow Route 39 (the main road around the island) as it hugs the coast and passes through the small settlement of Miyazu (宮津) before scooting past **Miyazubentengu Shrine** (宮津弁天宮), a tiny red shrine perched precariously at the top of a promontory overlooking the ocean, accessed by a set of steep stairs. Pressing on north, **Sainokawara Park** (賽の河原公園) is 10km from the port, on the tip of the cape at the northernmost point of Okushiri. It's a windswept and desolate spot, but a nice place to stroll along the beach and a good option for camping, with toilets on site. Continuing west, the road skirts inland for a while, but if you detour left on to the small road to Miyazu you'll soon arrive at **Mount Tamashima Lookout** (玉島山展望台) which offers excellent views of much of the island.

Back on Route 39, eventually wind down through glorious beech forests to the increasingly rugged western coast, and then south to the tiny settlement of **Yunohama** 湯浜. Here you'll find hot springs, the Okushiri Winery and **Kitaoimisaki Park** (北追岬公園), a cliff-top park home to a number of sculptures and a free, but exposed, campsite. The small **Okushiri Winery** (奥尻ワイナリ; ⊕ 09.30–17.00 daily, closed Sun late Nov–mid-Apr) was established in 2008 and produces a variety of red and white wines (around 50,000 bottles a year), a number of which are only available on site. Warm sea currents mean the local waters don't get quite as brutally frigid as other places further north, which helps with the growing; and perhaps unsurprisingly the wines produced here are said to have a hint of salty sea-breeze to them. In 2015 one of their wines won a national award. Visits to the winery must be booked by telephone one day in advance (your accommodation may be able to help with this), but the shop is open most days and best of all, offers free wine samples. The only dedicated hot-spring facility on the island, **Kamuiwaki Hot Spring** (神威脇温泉, Kamuiwaki Onsen; ⊕ 09.00–21.00 daily; ¥420/160) is located just north of the Okushiri Winery. It looks a bit dated both outside and in, but the authentically retro, rough-around-the-edges ambience is part of its charm. There's a choice of hot baths on two floors; the ground floor one is hotter and mineral-infused. Purchase your ticket from the machine near the entrance and hand it to the staff.

Continuing on the quiet road southwards, it's 14km down the pretty coast to Aonae, passing a number of interesting rock formations along the way.

Aonae (青苗) is the main settlement right at the southern end of Okushiri, and was also the place to suffer most damage from the tsunami. There used to be houses all along the cape, but nearly everything was destroyed during the disaster, and now the Tsunami Memorial Hall is the only building permitted on the southern tip of the peninsula. Aonae has a few restaurants and places to stay, and it's 16km from here back to the port along the 'busiest' stretch of road on the island. The **Okushiri Tsunami Memorial Museum** (奥尻津波館, Okushiri Tsunami-kan; w unimaru. com; ⏰ late Apr–Oct 09.00–17.00 Tue–Sun; ¥520/170), situated on the cape at the extreme southern tip of the island, documents the harrowing events of July 1993 when a devastating earthquake and tsunami ravaged the island and took many lives. The displays and exhibits are moving and informative, with many photos and video footage of the event and its aftermath. Although everything is mostly in Japanese, there is an English information pamphlet available, and the museum is certainly worth an hour of your time. It's sobering to realise that all the homes that used to occupy this exposed spot were completely washed away. The tall plinth at the very tip of the cape was built to commemorate the rescuing of a British warship by the islanders in 1880 when it ran aground nearby; it was one of the only structures on the cape to survive the tsunami.

6

Central Hokkaidō

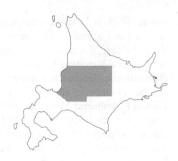

Central Hokkaidō is the island's heartland and a region of startling natural beauty; it is home to the prefecture's second largest city, Asahikawa, from where to the south spread the patchwork-quilt rolling hills and idyllic flower fields of Biei and Furano, which become a riot of colour in the late spring and summer. Travelling through the region, it is difficult not to stop and take photos every few minutes as beautiful vistas reveal themselves around every corner, and there are famous viewpoints galore, including the curious semi-natural wonder of Shirogane Blue Pond. Furano is also famed for its fabulously dry and deep powder snow, making it a superb alternative to Niseko for winter sports lovers. If you scratch under the surface a little, you'll discover that the entire region has quite an artsy, bohemian vibe.

Rising to the east of the lowland picture-book landscapes lies Daisetsuzan; meaning 'great snowy mountains', this spectacular range of volcanic peaks – including Hokkaidō's highest, Asahi-dake – is a vast wild upland area encompassing Japan's largest national park, and it is crisscrossed with hiking trails for those tempted by the beauty and solace of the wilderness. Even in the summer, great swathes of snow remain, and if you're lucky, animals such as brown bear and the elusive pika can be spotted in their secretive alpine domains.

Owing to the geological nature of the region, there are a number of small hot-spring resorts around the perimeter of the park, with the Tokachidake area in particular notable for its spectacular scorched and barren volcanic vistas. To the east where the mountains peter out towards the plains are a couple of great lakes which freeze over in the winter, providing opportunity for ice-fishing and stays in an igloo village, while further out west you can find the once-thriving coal-mining town of Yūbari, now arguably better known for its highly prized and extremely expensive cantaloupe melons. Over to the west, the mighty Ishikari River winds its way through important agricultural regions; here you'll find the remote, secluded and little-visited Sea of Japan coastal towns of Rumoi and Mashike.

MAJOR FESTIVALS IN CENTRAL HOKKAIDŌ

Asahikawa Winter Festival (Asahikawa Fuyu-Matsuri) w asahikawa-winterfes.jp; early February
Sōunkyō Onsen Icefall Festival (Sōunkyō Onsen Hyō-baku Matsuri) w sounkyo.net/hyoubaku; late January to mid-March
Yūbari Fantastic Film Festival (Yūbari Fanta; Yūbari Kokusai Fantasutikku Eigasai) w yubarifanta.jp; late June to early July
Asahikawa Summer (Sanroku) Festival (Asahikawa Natsu-Matsuri) w ccia.or.jp/event/summer-fes; early August

This little-visited region to the north of Sapporo abuts the Sea of Japan on one side and the Ishikari Plain on the other, with the wild and remote Mount Shokanbetsu (1,492m) wedged in between, and it includes much of Sorachi, south Rumoi and northern Ishikari subprefectures. The area is best explored by car, although trains on the JR Hakodate Line bound for Asahikawa provide access along the Ishikari Plain, and from Fukagawa single-carriage 'one-man' trains run another 14km to Ishikari-Numata (although this section is slated for closure by 2026) – the line used to run all the way northwest up to Rumoi on the coast until service was ended in 2023.

Following the Ishikari River upstream from Sapporo, the first major settlement on the plain is the small city of **Iwamizawa** (岩見沢; population 75,000). The main attraction here is **Hokkaidō Greenland** (北海道グリーンランド; w h-greenland. com/park), an old-fashioned theme park with clunky but thrilling rollercoasters, a ferris wheel and haunted house among other things – dated, but great fun for kids. Continuing northwards through these agricultural heartlands, the next major stop is **Takikawa** (滝川; population 37,000). The biggest city in northern Sorachi and one of Hokkaidō's snowiest areas, it is known for its farm produce, namely lamb, Aigamo duck and rice. In February more than 10,000 paperbag lanterns light up town, while yellow canola blankets the fields in mid to late spring. The most exciting attraction here is **Takikawa Sky Park** (スカイミュージアム; w takikawaskypark. jp), where from April to November you can experience a short but exhilarating 10-minute flight above the valley in a glider (¥8,500).

About 24km further north is the tiny farming town of **Hokuryu** (北竜; population 1,600), where over a million sunflowers bloom in July and August and can be viewed easily at the free-entry **Sunflower Village** on the town's outskirts. In the winter, the tiny and quiet local ski slope, with one lift, is a good place for beginners to find their feet.

Heading northwest, the E62 expressway leads in little over half an hour to **Rumoi** (留萌; population 18,000), a small, sleepy enclave of civilisation along this otherwise fairly isolated coastline. The 'Golden Beach' south of the port is presumably named after the sunsets as its sand is almost perversely dull and grey, but the beach is a good swimming and camping spot, with toilets nearby. A harbour city built on herring fishing and, to a lesser degree, mining, Rumoi's quiet streets have a salty air of downtrodden resignation about them (especially now that the train line has closed), but there are a number of places to stay and plenty of good restaurants to sniff out.

Heading back south along Route 231 brings you after 15km to **Mashike** (増毛; population 3,600), a tiny fishing town with its own abandoned railway station (now housing a museum and a stand selling very tasty fried octopus), plus the northernmost sake brewery in Japan, **Kunimare Sake Brewery** (w kunimare.co.jp; ⏰ 09.00–17.00 daily), which houses a small museum space, offers free samples and sells local souvenirs. Around town there are also some other attractive historic buildings and a few excellent sushi restaurants.

The road trip continues southwards along Route 231 down a long stretch of very remote and pretty coastland, passing waterfalls and rocky capes to reach in 40km the small coastal village of **Hamamasu** (浜益), which has a large beach and an adjoining campsite with a Seicomart nearby. Another 30km south is **Atsuta** (厚田), an even smaller fishing village with a seemingly once-thriving but now very quiet morning fish market, a convenience store and a handful of restaurants. From there it is only another hour's drive back to the bustle of central Sapporo.

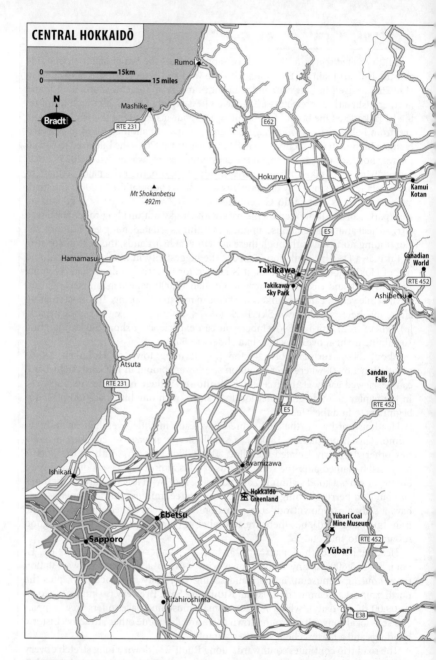

0   15km
0   15 miles

N

Bradt

Rumoi

Mashike

RTE 231

Hokuryu

Kamui
Kotan

Mt Shokanbetsu
492m

E62

E5

Hamamasu

Takikawa

Takikawa
Sky Park

Canadian
World

RTE 452

Ashibetsu

Atsuta

RTE 231

E5

Sandan
Falls

RTE 452

Iwamizawa

Ishikari

Hokkaidō
Greenland

Yūbari Coal
Mine Museum

RTE 452

Ebetsu

Sapporo

Yūbari

Kitahiroshima

E38

ASAHIKAWA

Hokkaidō's second largest city, Asahikawa (旭川; population 333,000) is the capital of Kamikawa subprefecture and a good base for exploring central and northern regions of the island. The city doesn't have a particularly deep history as it was only officially founded in 1922; in fact, despite its substantial population and sprawling urban area,

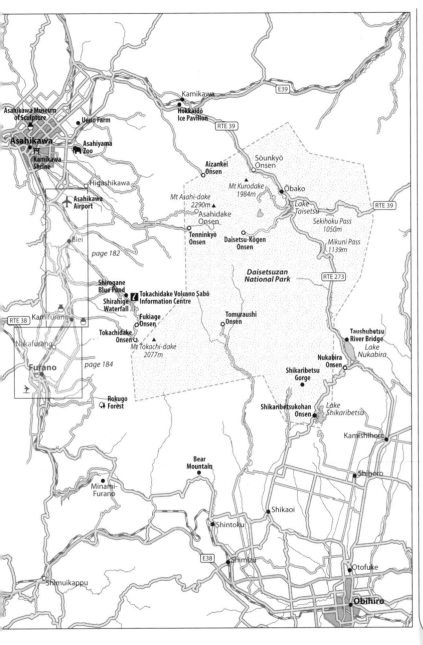

page 182

page 184

Asahikawa has a fairly quiet and relaxed provincial town feel. There are not a great deal of attractions within the city itself, with the wide and pedestrianised Heiwa-dōri shopping street stretching for seemingly miles – it's actually about 15 or so blocks – north from the station, but there are countless hotels and good restaurants within walking distance of this main thoroughfare. The mighty Ishikari River (Hokkaidō's longest) meanders through the heart of the city, while immediately south of the station flows the Chūbetsu River; numerous riverside parks and walkways line both rivers' banks, used and appreciated by locals more than tourists.

Owing to its centralised location near the middle of the island, Asahikawa has an almost continental climate, with temperature extremes similar to those of landlocked cities in Siberia. Winters here are absolutely freezing – the coldest temperature ever recorded in Japan (−41°C) was registered in Asahikawa in January 1902 – with piles of snow and iced-up streets part of the city's make-up for a good third of the year. Summers, by contrast, can be hot and fairly humid, with an average high of around 26°C in July and August.

Don't come to Asahikawa looking for raucous nightlife or high-end shopping – Sapporo is the only city on Hokkaidō that can really offer that – but instead appreciate the more subtle delights of this relaxed and pleasant city, conveniently situated within view of Biei's famous farming landscapes and the distant snow-dappled peaks of Daisetsuzan. The Asahikawa Winter Festival, held for about a week in early February (around the same time as Sapporo's), is Hokkaidō's second biggest winter festival, and includes usually one standout gigantic snow sculpture among myriad smaller ones. The event is spread across two sites in the city; one near the Asahibashi Bridge, the other along Heiwa-dōri.

HISTORY Archaeological evidence suggests that Jōmon people lived in the region well before the Ainu arrived, with the latter naming one of the local rivers Chiu pet, meaning 'river of waves'. However, at some point this was misunderstood as 'Chup pet', which translates to 'sun river' or Asahi-kawa in Japanese. When Japanese colonists first arrived in the fertile Kamikawa Basin at the end of the 19th century, Asahikawa was one of a few small villages established by the tondenhei (page 29), and much like Sapporo, officials planned for it to be the urban centre of a new agricultural area. A railway line was opened in 1898 and, a year after becoming established as a town in 1900, Japan's elite Seventh Army Division was relocated here from Sapporo; Asahikawa would go on to have close ties to the military up until World War II (and today is the headquarters of the Second Division of the Northern Army of Japan's Ground Self-Defence Force). Asahikawa achieved city status in 1922 and was developed on a grid pattern, with the landmark Asahibashi Bridge completed in its current form in 1932. Asahikawa was bombed by American naval aircraft near the end of the war in July 1945, destroying factories and other infrastructure, but the city recovered quickly. In 1966 the airport was built, offering direct connections to Tokyo, and a year later the ever-popular Asahiyama Zoo first opened its doors.

GETTING THERE AND AWAY
By train Two types of limited express train, Kamui and Lilac, run once or twice an hour between Sapporo and Asahikawa (1hr 35mins; ¥5,220). Local trains take twice as long but are roughly half the price. There are also limited express Sōya and Sarobetsu trains to Wakkanai (3hrs 45mins; ¥8,890), and limited express Okhotsk and Taisetsu trains to Abashiri (3hrs 50mins; ¥8,560).

By air Asahikawa Airport (旭川空港, Asahikawa Kūkō; AKJ; w aapb.co.jp) is located about 20km southeast of the city and has multiple daily connections with Tokyo Haneda Airport, plus limited flights to and from Taipei (Taiwan).

The **airport shuttle bus** is timed for every flight and runs between the airport and JR Asahikawa Station (40mins; ¥750), and other buses ply the same route for the same fare. A taxi from the airport to central Asahikawa costs about ¥5,000, otherwise there are numerous car rental agencies at the terminal building.

For listing, see page 178

❌ **Where to eat and drink**

1   Asahikawa Ramen Village

ASAHIKAWA
Overview

Asahikawa Museum of Sculpture

RTE 12

Ishikari

RTE 40

Otokoyama Sake Brewing Museum

JR Chikabumi

Hokuchin Memorial Museum

Kawamura Kaneto Memorial Museum

page 179

JR Shin-Asahikawa

JR Minami-Nagayama

RTE 233

JR Asahikawayojō

RTE 90

N

Bradt

RTE 237

Kamikawa Shrine

Chūbetsu

0   1km
0   1 mile

JR Kaguraoka

By bus The Asahikawa Express bus runs almost every half hour from 07.00 to 21.30 between JR Sapporo and Asahikawa stations (2hrs; ¥2,300); there's a ¥250 discount if you buy a return ticket.

By car Asahikawa is about 130km (1½–2hrs) from Sapporo if using Route E5, also known as the Dō-ō Expressway (toll ¥3,380). If you use toll-free roads, expect the journey to take an extra hour or so.

GETTING AROUND Local buses connect JR Asahikawa Station to some of the city's main tourist attractions – check the bus terminal next to the station for timetables. Many attractions are on the outskirts of the city, so self-drivers have the most freedom. There is ample parking at all points of interest.

TOURIST INFORMATION There is an excellent tourist information centre on the ground floor of JR Asahikawa Station (🕑 Jun–Sep 08.30–19.00 daily, Oct–May 09.00–19.00 daily, closed 31 Dec–3 Jan), and also a useful information desk at Asahikawa Airport (🕑 08.00–20.20 daily).

🛏 **WHERE TO STAY** *Map, page 179*
Asahikawa has many accommodation options, most of them handily concentrated near the railway station or just off the Heiwa-dōri shopping street. There are also some hotels further north, near Tokiwa Park.

Art Hotel Asahikawa アートホテルズ旭
川; 7-jō-dōri 6-chōme; ✆0166 25 8811; w art-
asahikawa.com. The rooms at this distinctive
large white hotel not far from Tokiwa Park are
spacious but have thin walls & are sometimes
uncomfortably warm, plus the décor & facilities are
a little dated. It's also quite a walk from the station.
B/fasts are fantastic, however, offering a wide
choice, & great views across the city. **$$$**

Y's Hotel Asahikawa ワイズホテル旭川駅
前; 9-2-17 Tsuruha Bldg 3F; ✆0166 29 3255;
w yshotel-asahikawa.com. Handily located
next to the railway station & right above the bus

information centre this makes a good base for
those exploring the region by public transport;
self-drivers may want to reconsider as there is no
free parking. Fairly standard but clean rooms &
friendly staff. The lobby is on the 3rd floor. **$$$**

Nine C Hotel Asahikawa 9Cホテル旭
川; 1-jōdōri 9-chōme 92-2; ✆0166 73 3199;
w 9chotel.jp. A great budget option, this modern
hostel-style hotel with chic interior has minimalist
rooms, small & boxy but comfortable, with
bunkbeds, & super-clean shared bathrooms. The
fancy communal area has tables & a sofa area with
a swanky fireplace. **$$**

✕ WHERE TO EAT AND DRINK *Map, opposite, unless otherwise stated*

Sanroku is Asahikawa's main dining and entertainment district; it can be found
about seven blocks up and two west of the Heiwa-dōri shopping street, and is an
area packed with lively izakayas, bars and restaurants.

Asahikawa is best known for its *shōyu* (soy sauce)-based ramen called, fittingly
enough, Asahikawa ramen. The basic toppings are fairly standard fare – pork,
bamboo shoots, eggs and green onions – but the broth tends to have an oily sheen
on top (said to help keep it piping hot) and the noodles are firm, thin and wavy. You
can find the dish at the plethora of ramen restaurants throughout the city, including
at **Furarito** (ふらりーと; w furari-to.net; **$$**), a former fruit and vegetable market on
an old-school narrow alley lit by yellow lanterns; now full of snug little restaurants,
it is found just off 5-jō-dōri. The shopping centre adjacent to JR Asahikawa Station
has a good food court.

Daikokuya 大黒屋; 3-4 Nakadōri;
🕐 16.00–22.30 daily. The striking lattice façade
& mouthwatering umami aromas emanating
from the main store of this popular & cosy
local *jinguiskan* chain draw a steady stream of
customers. Highly rated for good reason, with
many sets & cuts of meat to choose from, the
dishes are all melt-in-your-mouth tender &
juicy with excellent vegetables on the side too.
Reservations recommended, or go early to avoid a
long wait. EM. **$$$**

Asahikawa Ramen Village [map, page 177]
あさひかわラーメン村; Nagayama 11-jō
4-chōme; 🕐 11.00–20.00 daily. 8 of Asahikawa's
most famous ramen restaurants each have a
branch here under the same roof, with some shops

offering half-bowls so you can do a mini ramen
tour. Only a small place, it also manages to have
a gift shop & a small shrine dedicated to ramen.
About 20mins by car or taxi from JR Asahikawa
Station, or a 5min walk from JR Minami-Nagayama
Station. EM. **$$**

Ramen Aoba ラーメン青葉; 2-jō 8-chōme;
🕐 09.30–14.00 & 15.00–17.30 Thu–Tue. Friendly
& unpretentious, with a guestbook for customers
to sign, Ramen Aoba is said to be the birthplace of
Asahikawa-style ramen & the oldest ramen shop in
the city. The menu has 3 main types of broth – opt
for soy sauce for that quintessential Asahikawa
taste. It's a 5min walk from the station up Midoribashi-dōri (Rte 20), 1 block east of Heiwa-dōri
shopping street. EM. **$$**

OTHER PRACTICALITIES

Hokkaido Bank 228-2 Jodori; ✆0166 260141;
🕐 09.00–15.00 Mon–Fri

Asahikawa Municipal Hospital 1-chome 1-65,
Kinseicho; ✆0166 243181

Asahikawa Chuo Police Station 10-chome
6-Jodori, 2231-1; ✆0166 250110

Asahikawa Chuo Post Office 6-chome 6-Jodori,
28-1; ✆0570 943585; 🕐 09.00–19.00 Mon–Fri,
09.00–17.00 Sat, 09.00–12.30 Sun

For listings, see from page 177

Where to stay

1 Art Hotel Asahikawa
2 Nine C Hotel Asahikawa
3 Y's Hotel Asahikawa

Where to eat and drink

4 Daikokuya
5 Furarito
6 Ramen Aoba

Tokiwa Park

Hokkaidō Asahikawa Museum of Art

N

Bradt

0 ___ 250m
0 ___ 250yds

4-JŌ-DŌRI

SANROKU

RTE 12

SHOWA-DŌRI

HEIWA-DŌRI

MIDORIBASHI-DŌRI

MIDORIBASHI-DŌRI

CHUOBASHI-DŌRI

SHINSEIBASHI-DŌRI

MIYASHITA-DŌRI

1-JŌ-DŌRI

JR Asahikawa

Chūbetsu

Asahikawa City Museum

Takasago Shuzo

WHAT TO SEE AND DO

Asahiyama Zoo (旭山動物園; Higashi-Asahikawachō, Kuranuma; w city. asahikawa.hokkaido.jp/asahiyamazoo; ⏲ May–mid-Oct 09.30–17.15 daily, mid-Oct–Nov 09.30–16.30 daily, Nov–Apr 10.30–15.30 daily; ¥1,000/free) Asahikawa's most famous attraction, and one of Japan's better and most visited zoological gardens, Asahiyama Zoo is home to animals such as big cats, giraffes and monkeys, along with cold-climate specialists such as polar bears and penguins. There are many of Hokkaidō's native species to see too. Some enclosures offer unusual and close-up viewing angles from domed windows at ground level, while the penguin pool has a glass tunnel to observe them torpedoing underwater. Wintertime penguin walks draw crowds as the birds waddle along a snowy course for exercise (usually twice daily, at 11.00 & 14.30). It's best to avoid weekends and holidays throughout the year as the zoo can get very busy. From JR Asahikawa Station take bus 41, 42 or 47 (40mins; ¥500); there are usually about two per hour. By car, the zoo is about 30 minutes east of the city centre.

Museums In the **Asahikawa City Museum** (旭川市博物館; Kagura 3-7; w city. asahikawa.hokkaido.jp/hakubutukan; ⏲ 09.00–17.00 daily, closed 2nd/4th Mon Oct–May; ¥350/free), two floors of excellent exhibits showcase the nature and people of Hokkaidō, with many interesting Ainu-related displays (though not much English). It's a 15-minute walk southwest of the station across the river.

Located on the north side of the city, 15 minutes' drive from the station, the **Asahikawa Museum of Sculpture** (旭川市彫刻美術館; Shunkochō 5-7;

w city.asahikawa.hokkaido.jp/sculpture; ⊕ 09.00–17.00 Tue–Sun; ¥450/free) houses an intriguing collection of works by local sculptor Teijiro Nakahara and some associated artists. But if anything it is the grand old Western-style building that really steals the show – dating to 1902 and meticulously restored, it originally served as the officers' social club for the Japanese Imperial Army. The smaller building next door is a museum dedicated to the writer Yasushi Inoue.

Housed in an imposing brown brick building, the **Hokuchin Memorial Museum** (北鎮記念館; Shunkochō, Kokuyūmubanchi; w mod.go.jp/gsdf/nae/2d/hokutin2/top.html; ⊕ Apr–Oct 09.00–17.00 daily, Nov–Mar 09.30–16.00 daily; free) is a military museum which offers free tours (in Japanese) conducted by members of Japan's Self-Defence Force. Displays and artefacts chronicle Asahikawa's rise as a colony for farmer-soldiers to a major city base for the Imperial Army. It's about 15 minutes by bus from JR Asahikawa Station; the nearest bus stop to the museum is Gokokujinja (護国神社).

Situated in Tokiwa Park a short walk west from the northern end of Heiwa-dōri is **Hokkaidō Asahikawa Museum of Art** (北海度立旭川美術館; Tokiwa Park 4046-1; w artmuseum.pref.hokkaido.lg.jp/abj; ⊕ 09.30–17.00 daily; ¥260). This small but functional art gallery features works from local artists and has often-changing visiting exhibits (check website for details). The leafy park grounds have a large pond and are a pleasant place to while away an hour or two on a sunny day.

Established in 1916, **Kawamura Kaneto Ainu Memorial Museum** (川村カ子トアイヌ記念館; Hokumonchō 11; w k-aynu-mh.jp; ⊕ May–Nov 09.00–17.00 daily, Dec–Apr closed Tue; ¥500) is the oldest Ainu museum on Hokkaidō. Though spread across a few buildings, it is small and has a rustic family-run vibe; the founder was an Ainu chief and surveyor who helped lay the foundations of Hokkaidō's railways, setting up the museum after he retired. There are many displays and fascinating period photos offering a glimpse of Ainu life, and occasional music and dance performances and craft workshops are held here. The museum is a 10-minute drive northwest of central Asahikawa, or a 15-minute bus ride (¥190) – from the railway station take bus 24 from stop 14 to Ainu-kinenkan-mae (アイヌ記念館前).

There are two places to visit in Asahikawa devoted to sake. The famous **Otokoyama Sake Brewing Museum** (男山酒造り資料館; Nagayama 2-7, 1-33; w otokoyama.com; ⊕ 09.00–17.00 daily; free) is an award-winning sake brewery on the northern outskirts of the city, with two floors of displays and a shop offering up to three free tasters; you can pay ¥100 to try some of their premium tipples. It is a 2-minute walk from the Nagayama 2-jō 6-chōme (永山2条6丁目) bus stop, or a 20-minute drive from the city centre. About 15 minutes walk east of the station, the historic **Takasago Shuzō** brewery (高砂酒造; Miyashita-dōri 17-chōme; ⊕ 09.00–17.30 daily) has been making sake on the premises since 1909. Inside the attractive building are interesting displays and you can observe the brewing process, plus enjoy free samples of some of their famous dry rice wines such as Kokushi-musō. The well-stocked shop sells sake-flavoured ice cream in the summer.

Kamikawa Shrine (上川神社; w kamikawajinja.com)

Established in 1883, this impressive shrine nestles in a beautiful forest setting, deep within Kaguraoka Park, and a number of deities are said to be enshrined here, including Amaterasu, the famous goddess of the sun in Japanese mythology. It is about 25 minutes' walk (or 5mins by car) southeast of JR Asahikawa Station, crossing the river. A smaller subsidiary shrine of this one can be found in Tokiwa Park on the north side of the city.

Ueno Farm (上野ファーム; w uenofarm.net; ⏰ late Apr–mid-Oct 10.00–17.00 daily; ¥1,000/free) Also known as 'The Gnomes' Garden', this small farm has English-style flower gardens, pretty ponds and some fantastical views, making it a relaxing place to wander around; there is also an on-site café. The farm is located 14km east of the city – it's a 20-minute drive, a 40-minute bus journey (3 buses a day; ¥610), or you can take a train to JR Sakuraoka Station from where it is a 15-minute walk.

Kamui Kotan (神居古潭) This scenic spot at a bridge on a bend in the Ishikari River, way out in the countryside 16km west of the city, is known for its pleasant views and knobbly riverside rock formations. Its name means 'living place of gods' in the Ainu language. Here you can still see evidence of Jōmon-era stone circles, and in addition, the more recent remains of a well-preserved old wooden station, railway tunnels and full-size steam locomotive which were abandoned when the Hakodate Main Line was re-routed in the 1960s. A couple of short circular hiking paths allow you to stretch your legs for an hour or two should the urge take you. Kamui Kotan is reachable in 20 minutes by car on Route 233.

Higashikawa Situated about 15km southeast of Asahikawa, the rural township of Higashikawa (東川; population 8,000) is becoming a fairly hip countryside retreat for outdoorsy and arty types. Dotted around this self-declared 'town of photography', you can find a plethora of trendy organic cafés and restaurants; the centrally located roadside service station 'Higashikawa Michikusakan' (ひがしかわ道草館) is a good place to start as it has an information desk and rental bicycles. It's easiest to explore and reach the locality by car, although there are regular buses (30mins; ¥350) to the service station from JR Asahikawa Station.

KAMIKAWA

A small, isolated town some 45km east of Asahikawa established on the banks of the Ishikari River, Kamikawa (上川; population 4,000) is the gateway to Sōunkyō Onsen in the northern reaches of Daisetsuzan National Park. The town itself has one main attraction, the **Hokkaidō Ice Pavilion** (北海度アイスパビリオン; w icepavilion.com; ⏰ 09.00–17.00 daily; ¥1,200/800), located on the western approach to the town on Route 39. The large, slightly tacky complex building is run by welcoming and energetic staff, and the winter-themed experiences include an ice room, which is chilled down to −41°C, the lowest temperature ever recorded on Hokkaidō and in Japan (in 1902).

Kamikawa is the jumping-off point for buses to and from Sōunkyō Onsen (30mins; ¥890); they run every hour or two and are timed to meet the trains from Asahikawa.

BIEI, KAMIFURANO AND AROUND

BIEI Picturesque rolling hills and a patchwork of fields fill the landscape around the small town of Biei (美瑛; population 10,000), which lies about 25km south of Asahikawa. Many famous television commercials and programmes have been filmed around the region, with some distinctive trees and pretty viewpoints now popular photo spots. The landscapes of Biei are best explored by car or bicycle and the flower fields are at their most colourful from June to October; but everything is transformed into a white wonderland in the winter, when the narrow roads are much trickier to navigate (and some may be impassable). There are regular trains from Asahikawa to Biei on the JR Furano Line (30mins; ¥640).

Outside the tiny town itself there are two main areas to explore. **Patchwork Road** (パッチワークの路), to Biei's northwest, boasts several famous views including the Ken and Mary Tree (ケンとメリーの木; named after characters in the 1972 car advert in which the tree featured), Mild Seven Hill (マイルドセブンの丘; from a cigarette advert) and Seven Stars Tree (セブンスターの木; which appeared on cigarette packaging in 1976). The pyramid-shaped lookout at **Hokusei-no-oka Observatory Park** (北西の丘展望公園; ⊕ 24hrs; free) affords panoramic views over the gentle hills dotted with flower fields and quaint farmsteads and is close to a handful of charming countryside cafés.

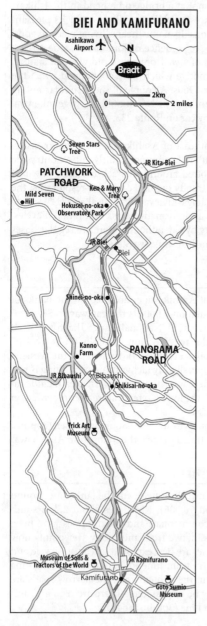

Panorama Road (パノラマロード) is the area south of town and offers a few higher vantage points for wider panoramic views, plus a number of small art galleries tucked away amid the farmland. About 10 minutes' drive south from town is **Shinei-no-oka** (新栄の丘), a free hilltop observatory park with pleasant 360° views of the surrounding hills. Ten minutes' drive further south is **Shikisai-no-oka** (四季彩の丘; w shikisainooka.jp; ⊕ May–Oct 08.40–17.00 daily, Nov–Apr 09.10–16.30 daily; ¥500), a farm with extensive and gloriously colourful flower fields which can be perused on foot or by various forms of transport (for an additional fee) including a trundling tractor bus, self-driven buggies, and snowmobiles in winter. There are a few decent cafés in the immediate vicinity too.

Nearby, on the west side of the small village of Bibaushi (美馬牛), is **Kanno Farm** (かんのファーム; w kanno-farm. com; ⊕ Jun–mid-Oct 09.00–17.00 daily; free), a popular flower farm with very pleasant vistas, with fields of lavender and other vivid blooms and a small shop. It is a good alternative to the much busier Farm Tomita (page 186) in Furano.

KAMIFURANO Situated on the JR Furano Line halfway between Biei and Furano, Kamifurano (上富良野; population 11,000) is a quiet town surrounded by flower meadows and farmland and serves as the gateway to the Tokachidake area. There are a number of restaurants to the southwest of the station, and some rural pensions dotted around the perimeter of the small town.

Goto Sumio Museum (後藤純男美術館; **w** gotosumiomuseum.com; ⏰ Apr–Oct 10.00–17.00 daily, Nov–Mar 10.00–16.00 daily; ¥1,100/550), located among the fields on the eastern edge of town, showcases the remarkable and enormous landscape paintings of the museum's namesake artist, some of which took him decades to complete. There is a good restaurant serving pizza and other Japanified Western-style food on the second floor. Across the other side of town is the curiously named **Museum of Soils and Tractors of the World** (土の館; **w** tsuchinoyakata.jp; ⏰ 09.00–16.00 Mon–Fri; free), which chronicles the history of farming and agriculture in the region, going right back to the pioneer days. The farm tools and tractor collections (the biggest in Japan) are impressive, but the explanations on all the different soil types may leave you scratching your head as there is very little English. Heading north out of town on Route 237 (or on the way in if you have come from Biei) is the **Trick Art Museum** (トリックアート美術館; **w** miyama-ap.com; ⏰ Apr–Jun & Sep–Nov 10.00–17.00 daily, Jul–Aug 10.00–18.00 daily, Dec–Mar 10.00–16.00 Mon–Fri exc holidays; ¥1,300/700), a small and fun facility with lots of quirky artworks featuring visual illusions; friendly staff will advise you on the best angles for selfies. The museum is located within Miyama-tōge Art Park which has a few other random attractions, including a surprisingly large ferris wheel for somewhere so far out in the sticks.

SHIROGANE BLUE POND AND SHIRAHIGE FALLS

Undoubtedly one of Hokkaidō's most famous photography hotspots in recent years, **Shirogane Blue Pond** (白金青い池) is a large pond with mesmerisingly brilliant azure waters. It is manmade and not a purely natural wonder, however, formed by accident as part of a dam-building project in 1988 in order to protect the lowlands of Biei from mudslides should nearby Mount Tokachi-dake erupt again. The startling blue hue of the water is probably caused by white rocks beneath the surface and traces of aluminium sediment which reflects blue light, while the withered larch and birch trees surrounding the pond only add to the mystical atmosphere. The pond is equally spectacular at night when it is lit up for visitors. Entry is free, but parking costs ¥500. There are about five buses a day from JR Biei Station (25mins; ¥550), some of which continue to or from Asahikawa.

After taking your photos, if you drive onwards (or hop on the bus) along Route 966 following the equally blue Biei River upstream for a few minutes, you will arrive at the small, secluded hot-spring resort of **Shirogane Onsen** (白金温泉). There are a handful of hotels, a campground and a restaurant within the woods here, but the main attraction is **Shirahige Falls** (白ひげの滝), a scenic cascade whose name translates to 'white beard waterfall', as the wispy white waters seep from cliffs into the cerulean depths of the river below. A metal truss footbridge offers close-up views.

Just across the bridge and up some stairs is the **Tokachidake Volcano Sabō Information Centre** (十勝岳火山砂防情報センター; ⏰ May–Oct 08.30–17.00 daily, Nov–Apr 10.00–16.00 daily). This free museum (and volcanic shelter!) has some decent videos and displays about volcanology with a good amount of English, so is worth a look if that sort of thing piques your interest.

FURANO

One of Hokkaidō's most popular summer tourist destinations, Furano (富良野; population 22,000) lies in a flat and fertile valley, and is famed for its beautiful flower fields and picturesque rural farming landscapes, backdropped by frequently snow-capped mountains to the east. A city in name, but with the look and feel more akin to a countryside town, Furano is especially known for its glorious lavender fields which start to bloom around late June, peaking in July through to early August. Depending on the season, a wide variety of other colourful flowers decorate the region's meadows and pastures including poppies, lilies, sunflowers and cosmos. Driving along the country roads admiring the idyllic views and stopping for delicious, locally produced cheese and ice cream is a fine way to spend a summer's day.

As it is situated close to the centre of Hokkaidō, Furano has been nicknamed *heso-no-machi* or 'navel town', and in true Japanese style the concept has been grasped with both hands, with a bellybutton festival held in late July (**w** hesomatsuri.com) and a mildly sinister city mascot called Hesomaru – a farmer who likes to look at people's bellybuttons.

HISTORY The area takes its name from the Ainu Fura-nui, which loosely translates to 'foul-smelling place', probably due to the sulphur-heavy smells which emanate from the nearby volcano Mount Tokachi-dake. The first Japanese settlers arrived in

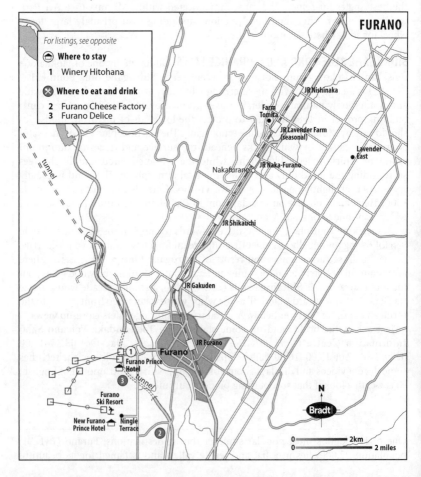

1897 with a railway link to Asahikawa following soon after in 1900. Agriculture has always been and remains a key industry – Furano is Japan's biggest carrot producer, and is also known for onions and sweet Furano melons. The area's flower fields were initially established for the production of fragrant essences and aromatic oils around the end of World War II, but demand dwindled by the 1970s with the prevalence of synthetic scents, so the meadows were commandeered for tourism instead.

GETTING THERE AND AROUND

By train There are numerous trains each day between Asahikawa and Furano (1hr 20mins; ¥1,290). The JR Lavender Express train runs once or twice a day between Sapporo and Furano from June to September (2hrs; ¥5,220) – it is covered by both the JR and Hokkaidō rail passes. The JR Norokko sightseeing train (¥1,290) runs three times daily during the same period between Furano and Biei (with the first and last trains carrying on to Asahikawa) – large open windows allow clear views of the wonderful scenery. This train makes a stop at the seasonal Lavender Farm Station (near Tomita Farm).

By bus From JR Asahikawa Station bus stop 9 there are around eight daily buses to and from Furano (1hr 40mins; ¥880), also stopping at Biei (50mins, ¥620). See w furanobus.jp for details of sightseeing buses and other routes.

By road A rental car is the best way to see the sights in this area. Furano is about 1hr from Asahikawa, and around 2hrs from Sapporo, with the stretch of expressway between Sapporo and Misaka costing around ¥1,500 in tolls. Using local roads, it usually takes around half an hour longer.

WHERE TO STAY AND EAT *Map, opposite*

There are many accommodation options near the ski resort (page 186), and self-drivers are spoilt for choice with countless homely B&B-style pensions dotting the surrounding fields and rural lanes. Furano has many cheese, ice cream and sweet shops – lavender ice cream is a regional speciality in the summer months.

Winery Hitohana Hotel ワイナリーホテル一花; 23-10 Kitanomine; ☎0167 23 8778; w hotel-hitohana.com. A no-frills property, yet understatedly modern & stylish, the Winery Hitohana has spacious rooms & excellent food & drink options. It's close to the ski slopes, & has a shuttle bus service to the station. While it's not the cheapest in class, the friendly staff are more than happy to help with booking tours & activities. **$$$$**

Furano Cheese Factory 富良野チーズ工房; w furano-cheese.jp; ⏰ Apr–Oct 09.00–17.00 daily, Nov–Mar 09.00–16.00 daily. More than just a simple cheese shop, this factory offers free cheese tasting, excellent ice cream & freshly cooked pizza in the restaurant next door. Cheese-, butter- & ice-cream-making workshops (¥1,000) are available – reserve your place in advance by phone or email (see website). **$$**

Furano Delice フラノデリス; w le-nord.com; ⏰ 10.00–17.00 Thu–Mon. Furano Delice is a shop & café famous for its milk pudding in a milk bottle, but also does a good line in cheesecakes & other desserts. There's a pudding vending machine outside for when the craving hits in the dead of night. The elegant café has an outdoor terrace & lovely views. **$$**

WHAT TO SEE AND DO Furano is best known for its beautiful flower and lavender fields, some of which have been developed to cater to tourists, with parking, cafés and other facilities. During the winter season Furano Ski Resort (page 186) is the main reason people flock here. In the woods close to the bottom of the slopes is

Ningle Terrace (ニングルテラス; ⏱ 10.00–20.45 daily, most shops open from noon), a collection of cosy wooden chalets linked by boardwalks where you can browse and purchase locally made handicrafts and refreshments – everything is lit up at night to create a magical atmosphere, especially in the snow.

Farm Tomita (ファーム富田; w farm-tomita.co.jp; ⏱ 08.30–18.00 daily; free)
Probably the most popular sightseeing spot in the Furano region is Farm Tomita, a sprawling site which has some of Hokkaidō's largest and most colourful flower fields, beautifully framed by the Tokachi mountains as a backdrop. The farm is especially famous for its meadows of fragrant purple lavender. It was established in 1903 by Tokuma Tomita, a pioneer originally from Fukui Prefecture, and the farmers started cultivating lavender here in 1958 – tourists began to arrive after 1976 when it featured on a calendar produced by Japanese Rail. The site has various buildings which serve as shops and cafés selling lavender ice cream, freshly cut melon, baked goods, lavender-themed souvenirs and other treats; and visitors are free to wander around the farm and take pictures, making it a nice place to stop for an hour or two. Different varieties of flowers are grown throughout the year (when there is no snow) but it tends to get busy in the peak blooming season of late June to August, when the fields are at their most spectacular. The farm has another, quieter, site named **Lavender East** (ラベンダーイースト; ⏱ Jul only 09.30–16.30 daily; free) about 5km away; there you can find the most extensive lavender fields in Furano (covering 14ha), and you can take a 15-minute ride through the fields on the 'Lavender Bus' (for a small fee), which is in fact a trailer pulled by a tractor.

Farm Tomita is a 5-minute drive (or 20min walk) from JR Naka-Furano Station, but during the summer, the sightseeing Norokko train which runs between Furano and Biei stops at Lavender Farm Station, located just a short walk from the farm.

SKIING IN FURANO

Furano experiences extremely cold and snowy winters and, owing to its location away from the sea, gets some of the lightest, driest and highest-quality powder snow on Hokkaidō. **Furano Ski Resort** (w princehotels. com/en/ski/furano), which is operated by Prince Hotels, is the main skiing hub. The resort began life after around 1912 as a backcountry skiing destination, and has since hosted the Snowboard World Cup multiple times along with other alpine ski events. Today, its 28 courses are spread across two areas in Furano and Kitanomine, just on the west edge of town, and include runs suitable for all levels from beginner to expert and ski schools. Ten lifts operate across the mountain, including Japan's fastest cable car, and on clear days the views of the many peaks of Daisetsuzan way across the valley are fantastic. Both areas have a Prince Hotel (**$$$$**) at the foot of the slopes, so you can literally ski in or out of your accommodation, and there are many other hotels, pensions, hot springs and restaurants super close too for that après experience. There are also cross-country pistes in the area and operators offering backcountry and snowshoe tours, ice-fishing and even hot-air balloon rides.

The resort areas are 2.5km from central Furano, with shuttle buses and taxis available throughout the season, which lasts from about late November to early May, although the best powder is from around Christmas to late March.

For many Japanese people, Furano is synonymous with a popular and long-running (from 1981–2002) television drama called *Kita-no-kuni-kara* (北の国から; *From the Northern Country*). Set around the life of the Kuroita family, who are facing the upheaval of a divorce, the well-meaning father, Goro, returns to his ramshackle and remote childhood home with young son Jun (aged 11) and daughter Hotaru (aged 8), with episodes following the struggles and joys of a young family adapting to countryside living. The distinctive and quirky buildings used in the filming of the series have been preserved and now function as tourist attractions. Most of the sets are located in Rokugo Forest about 15km west of central Furano and include **Goro's Stone House** (⊕ mid-Apr–Sep 09.30–18.00 daily, Oct–Nov 09.30–16.00 daily, closed Dec–mid-Apr; ¥500/300), a fabulously photogenic and rustic cottage – not an essential visit if you've never seen the TV show, but an interesting novelty at the very least.

ASHIBETSU

If you follow Route 38 northwest up the valley out of Furano, passing the picturesque Lake Takisato on the way, in 30km you will reach the remote town of Ashibetsu (芦別; population 14,000). This was once an important coal-mining area, with a population of 70,000 in its pre-World War II heyday. It is now a peaceful agricultural backwater and self-styled 'starry town' due to its dark skies, with a few curiosities for the wayward traveller.

Across the Sorachi River on Ashibetsu's north side is an enormous statue called the **Dai Kannon** (or Hokkaidō Kannon), which seems to gaze out over the town – at 88m high it is the third largest statue in Japan, and the tenth largest in the world (it was believed to be the biggest in the world when it was built in 1989). The park it stands in is now closed to visitors, but even from a distance the Dai Kannon looks striking, especially if there's snow.

Back on Route 38, next to the road-stop near the suspension bridge, is a grey building with three metallic towers – this is the local **museum** (⊕ 09.00–17.30 Wed–Sun; ¥200) which charts the history of Ashibetsu through various well-curated displays and old photos, plus reams of shelves storing a multitude of random historic items; there is almost no English but the collection is interesting to browse.

About 10km north of town on Route 452 and situated in an idyllic valley is a peculiar themed park called **Canadian World** (カナディアンワールド; w canadian-world.com; ⊕ Apr–Oct 10.00–17.00 Sat–Sun & hols only; free). Here the world of Anne of Green Gables has been faithfully recreated, with some period-style buildings you can enter, but there is a half-abandoned melancholy feel to the whole place – the park was clearly built in Japan's prosperous bubble period and is looking a bit dilapidated and rough around the edges now. The park is quite spread out, so you can pay ¥500 to drive your car around if you like.

If, instead of going north, you follow Route 452 south of Ashibetsu, in 22km you will come across a scenic spot called **Sandan Falls** (三段滝). This gushing waterfall is not tall but wide, and flows with impressive gusto over a series of rock steps. It is a short walk from the roadside car park.

Japan's largest national park and the true heart – and roof – of Hokkaidō, Daisetsuzan National Park (大雪山国立公園; w daisetsuzan.or.jp) covers more than 2,300km² of volcanic mountains and untouched upland wilderness. Daisetsuzan (sometimes written Taisetsuzan) translates to 'Great Snow Mountains' and is the name of the mountain range – which includes Hokkaidō's highest peak, Asahi-dake. This is usually the first place in Japan where snow falls (sometimes as early as September), and large perennial snow patches remain throughout the summer. The Ainu name for the area is Kamuy mintara, meaning 'playground of the gods', and the region's unique semi-tundra landscapes and pristine forest ecosystems are home to brown bears and other wildlife, while two of the island's greatest rivers, the Ishikari and Tokachi, have their origins here. There are a few tiny settlements serving as access points dotted around the periphery of the park; Asahidake Onsen in the northwest is the main gateway for the majority of visitors; Sōunkyō Onsen in the north has the most (but still limited) facilities; Tokachidake Onsen in the southwest is the highest in elevation. The eastern and southern sides of the park are the most undeveloped, with a few extremely remote bases for those really seeking to get off the beaten track (page 194).

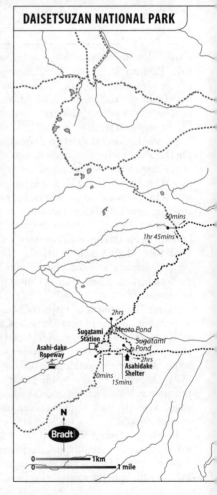

DAISETSUZAN NATIONAL PARK

ASAHIDAKE ONSEN Situated just below the treeline at 1,100m, Asahidake Onsen (旭岳温泉) is a small year-round retreat and the starting point for climbing Mount Asahi-dake, with a ropeway and a handful of hot-spring hotels; most have baths which can be used by non-staying visitors too. In the summer the fresh air and greenery attracts hikers and day-trippers, while in winter everything is buried under metres of snow – perfect for backcountry skiers and snowboarders – and rows of massive icicles hang from the eaves of every building. There are no ATMs or other facilities, though the ropeway has a basic shop and restaurant.

Asahidake Onsen is conveniently accessed by public transport: four buses run daily from JR Asahikawa Station (1hr 30mins; ¥1,800) throughout the year. It is about an hour from Asahikawa by car.

🏠 **Where to stay and eat** Hotels have restaurants for their guests; the ropeway has a restaurant.

Hotel Bearmonte 旭岳温泉ホテルベ アモン; Higashikawa-chō; \0166 97 2325; w bearmonte.jp. Close to the ropeway & renovated

in 2022, this fancy hotel has large spacious rooms & multiple hot-spring baths, including an outdoor one. **$$$$**
Daisetsuzan Shirakabasō 大雪山白樺荘; Higashikawa-chō; ☏0166 97 2246; w shirakabasou.com. This large wooden hostel-style accommodation has basic but clean tatami rooms with futons, shared bathrooms, indoor & outdoor baths & a canteen-like dining hall serving hearty food in hearty portions. The owners are very warm & welcoming. **$$**

What to see and do The main attraction here is **Mount Asahi-dake** (旭岳; 2,290m), Hokkaidō's highest peak and an active volcano – in good weather it is a remarkable sight, and there are numerous hiking trails to suit all levels up and around the mountain. It can be reached by taking the **Asahi-dake Ropeway** (旭岳ロープウェイ; w asahidake.hokkaido.jp/ja; ⊕ summer 06.30–17.30, winter 09.00–16.00; mid-Oct–May ¥2,200/1,500 return, Jun–mid-Oct ¥3,200/1,600 return); the ride takes 10 minutes and operates all year, although service may be suspended in bad weather. Sugatami Station (upper) is situated at 1,600m and from there you can wander along paths passing various ponds and patches of

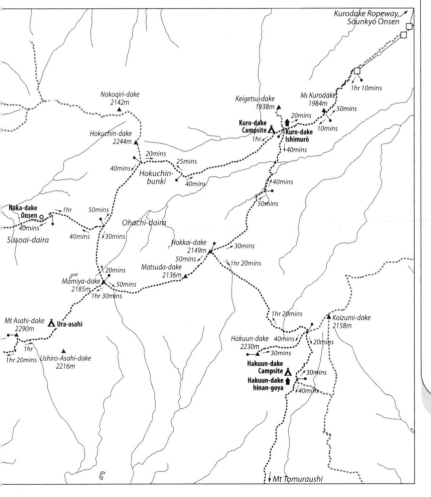

6

There are numerous hiking options in Daisetsuzan, from short, easy courses lasting a few hours to gruelling week-long treks through remote and rough, but spectacular, country. As it is one of the island's prime trekking destinations, almost every tour operator runs guided treks here; Adventure Hokkaido (w adventure-hokkaido.com) is locally based and reliable. The mountains here aren't as high or as steep as ones in the Japan Alps, for example, but the sprawling wilderness, stark, barren beauty and sense of space is unique and even reminiscent in places of the haunting landscapes of Iceland.

Beginners looking for something gentle should start at Asahi-dake Ropeway and walk the small 30–60-minute loop from the upper ropeway station – it offers splendid views of Mount Asahi-dake, natural ponds (which in good conditions reflect the mountain) and you can get up close to the incessantly steaming fumaroles near its base.

A more challenging hike is to the summit of **Mount Asahi-dake** itself. At 2,290m it is Hokkaidō's tallest peak, and the path up there is a steady 2-hour climb from the upper ropeway station. Most people go back the same way, but more adventurous and experienced hikers can continue onwards past the summit and make a long loop back to the ropeway (allow 6–7hrs total). After crossing and steeply descending the backside of the peak (where snow often remains until late in the season), turn left at Mamiya-dake (間宮岳), then follow the path down to Nakadake Onsen (中岳温泉) where you can find a wild open-air hot spring. After soaking your feet, the ropeway is another 2 hours or so along a plateau rich in alpine flowers.

At the other side of the park, another relatively short and straightforward hike begins at Sōunkyō Onsen: take the ropeway and then chairlift from where a 1½-hour climb brings you to the top of **Mount Kurodake** (1,984m).

Experienced hikers can try the classic traverse between Asahidake Onsen and Sōunkyō Onsen – the hike has ropeway access at either end and climbs both Mount Asahi-dake and Mount Kurodake, circumnavigating around the enormous and spectacular Ohachi-daira, Hokkaidō's largest caldera, replete with poisonous gases (don't enter!). With an early start it is possible to complete in a day (8–9hrs), but you can split the route up by staying or camping one night at Kurodake-Ishimuro (黒岳石室; ⏰ late Jun–late Sep; ¥2,000 per night; no reservations, just turn up), a basic stone hut which does not provide meals or sleeping gear, but does sell snacks and drinks.

Further south, Tokachidake Onsen is the base for a couple of tough day hikes through the otherworldly charred volcanic landscapes around the active wildflowers, ending at Sugatami Pond from where you can admire reflections of the rocky peak and see steam bellowing out from cracks beneath the mountain. Well-prepared hikers can carry on up to the summit (see above). The lower ropeway station has a café, storage lockers and a shop, and this is where buses to and from Asahikawa arrive and depart. Backcountry and downhill skiing from the upper ropeway station is possible from December to May for intermediate to advanced skiers.

Next door to the lower ropeway station is **Asahi-dake Visitor Centre** (旭岳ビジターセンター; w asahidake-vc-2291.jp; ⏰ 09.00–17.00 daily), a beautiful building with a large roof and a lovely wooden lattice ceiling. There are lots of interesting multi-lingual displays about the park's flora and fauna and helpful and friendly

Mount Tokachi-dake (十勝岳; 2,077m). From the onsen it takes about 4 hours to arrive at the rocky summit, although the steamy and sulphur-stained Ansei Crater area can be reached in less than 1 hour from the trailhead. The lesser-visited Mount Furano-dake (富良野岳; 1,912m) is known for its wildflowers.

Serious and well-equipped hikers can try the longest and most challenging hike in the park, and arguably one of the best long-distance walks in Japan – the **Daisetsuzan Grand Traverse**. This is a five- to seven-day, 80km north–south trek along the backbone of the park, passing through very remote terrain, from mountain peaks to grassy alpine plateaus, and the sense of wild adventure is hard to beat. There are basic mountain huts (which provide neither food nor sleeping gear) to stay at along the way, and one long stretch near Mount Oputateshike (オプタテシケ岳) requires a night of camping, so you'll need to bring a tent, plus a week's worth of food. At the north end you can start (or finish) from either Asahidake Onsen or Sōunkyō Onsen (or perhaps the even remoter Aizankei Onsen if you're up for a much harder challenge), while the southern start/end point is Tokachidake Onsen. If you only have time for a three- or four-day trek, then consider beginning or finishing around halfway at Tomuraushi Onsen, providing you can time it to match the onsen's short seasonal bus schedule.

The best season for hiking in Daisetsuzan is from around July to late September – any earlier or later and there will likely be snow on the ground. Autumn colours are at their peak in September. You should bring a bear bell (page 9), appropriate footwear, ample snacks and provisions, and good-quality waterproof and warm hiking gear, as even in the summer the weather up on the tops can catch you out (as evidenced in tragic circumstances in July 2009 when eight members of a 15-person guided hiking group succumbed to hypothermia near Mount Tomuraushi-yama). You will probably have to traverse some extensive snow patches on the longer hikes mentioned here, so a pair of simple crampons may come in handy, and portable toilet bags (available in hiking stores) are required at some campsites. Don't forget that you'll need to boil or filter your drinking water too (page 59).

Good paper maps are essential for the more serious hikes. *Asahi-dake: The Heart of the Daisetsuzan National Park* is an excellent all-English map and available to buy online. The best Japanese map is *Daisetsu-zan* 大雪山 (Map No. 3) in the popular Yama-to-kōgen series (山と高原地図), available in hiking stores and most bookshops in Japan.

guides (some of whom speak English); it is also possible to rent snowshoes, poles, hiking boots and skis for making the most of the outdoors.

TOKACHIDAKE ONSEN Situated at the southwestern end of the park and roughly 30km east of Furano, the hamlet of Tokachidake Onsen (十勝岳温泉), consisting of four hot-spring inns (see w kamifurano.jp/rest/spa), nestles at 1,280m halfway up the mountain of the same name. Aside from wallowing in a geothermally heated bath, there is nothing much to do here than hike; the impressive volcanic landscapes around Mount Tokachi-dake are crisscrossed by trails (see above). There are three buses a day running year-round to and from JR Kamifurano Station (45mins; ¥500). With your own transport it takes about 40 minutes from Furano.

Just a few minutes up the road is another tiny hot-spring spot called **Fukiage Onsen** (吹上温泉); here you can find a lovely and free-to-use open-air hot-spring pool (吹上露天の湯). Be warned that it is a mixed-gender bath, so swimwear is permitted and there is no changing room. Just around the corner is a large hot-spring lodge and campground, and 8 minutes' drive further up the road leads to a volcano information centre called **Tokachidake Shelter** (十勝岳望岳台防災シェルター; ⏰ 24hrs daily). A short gravelly walk from the car park is Tokachidake Observatory (十勝岳望岳台), a viewpoint marked by a rock monument – this is also the trailhead for the most direct and popular hiking route up to Mount Tokachi-dake (allow 7hrs return).

SŌUNKYŌ ONSEN Sōunkyō Onsen (層雲峡温泉) is a pleasant, small hot-spring village is nestled in a narrow, 24km-long cliff-lined gorge at the northern end of Daisetsuzan National Park. There are several ryokan with hot-spring baths, and a public bathhouse in the centre of the village. The sumptuous, forested surroundings draw in crowds to marvel at the autumn colours in September and October, while the two-month-long Sōunkyō Icefall Festival is a popular winter event. Just up the valley are two beautiful waterfalls, or keen hikers can take the ropeway to climb nearby Mount Kurodake, which towers above the village. The **Sōunkyō Information Centre** (層雲峡インフォメーションセンター; ⏰ 10.30–17.00 daily) provides useful details for any place in the local area.

To get to Sōunkyō Onsen, you can take a direct bus from JR Asahikawa Station (2hrs; ¥2,140), or catch a train to JR Kamikawa Station (express train 40mins, ¥2,450; local train 60mins, ¥1,290) from where there are buses to Sōunkyō (30mins; ¥890) every hour or two.

🏠 Where to stay and eat *Map, below*

There are a few small restaurants near the centre of the village, plus a couple of convenience stores if you're in a pinch.

Hotel Taisetsu ホテル大雪; Kamikawa-chō, Sōunkyō; ☏ 0165 853211; w hotel-taisetsu.com.

A large, slightly dated hotel, featuring a mix of tatami-floored & Western-style guestrooms. It has

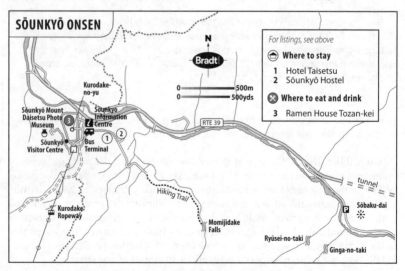

SŌUNKYŌ ONSEN

For listings, see above

Where to stay
1 Hotel Taisetsu
2 Sōunkyō Hostel

Where to eat and drink
3 Ramen House Tozan-kei

Kurodake-no-yu
Sōunkyō Mount Daisetsu Photo Museum
Sōunkyō Information Centre
Sōunkyō Visitor Centre
Bus Terminal
RTE 39
Hiking Trail
Kurodake Ropeway
Momijidake Falls
Ryūsei-no-taki
Ginga-no-taki
tunnel
Sōbaku-dai

a choice of hot-spring baths, including an open-air rooftop one with wonderful views. The restaurant serves buffet-style meals, & the on-site bakery/café sells great breads & coffee. $$$$
Sōunkyō Hostel 層雲峡ホステル; 39 Sōunkyō; \080 2862 4080; w sounkyo-hostel. com. Sōunkyō Hostel has friendly English-speaking staff & a choice of mixed dorm with bunkbeds or private rooms with beds or futons. Showers

only, but guests are given a discount ticket for the nearby onsen. Curry is available for dinner (¥1,500) & there's the option of a ¥500 riceball-based b/fast. $$
Ramen House Tozan-kei ラーメンハウス登山軒; Kamikawa-chō, Sōunkyō; \0165 853005; ⊕ 10.00–22.00. This cosy place serves big bowls of noodles & other homely dishes such as tonkatsu curry. EM. $$

What to see and do There are just about enough attractions here to fill a day or two. Nature lovers shouldn't miss **Sōunkyō Visitor Centre** (層雲峡ビジターセンター; w sounkyovc.net; ⊕ Jun–Oct 08.00–17.30 daily, Nov–May 09.00–17.00 daily; free), a friendly and modern facility next to the ropeway, with plenty of interesting displays about the natural environment, excellent 3D topographical maps (and free paper ones), plus up-to-date information on trail conditions – a multi-lingual guide is available.

Many visitors come to ride **Kurodake Ropeway** (黒岳ロープウェイ; w rinyu. co.jp/kurodake; ⊕ mid-Feb–May 09.00–15.00 daily, Jun–Sep 06.00–18.00 daily, early Oct 06.00–17.00 daily, mid-Oct–early Jan 08.00–16.00 daily, closed Jan–mid-Feb; ¥2,600/1,300 return), which whisks you out of the valley and up the mountain in less than 10 minutes. The lower station has an excellent wood-décor coffee shop with great views on the second floor, run in collaboration with Columbia (the outdoor brand). From the upper station a two-seater chairlift operates in the summer (and for skiers/snowboarders only in the winter; ⊕ 06.30–17.30 daily; ¥1,000/500 return) to deposit you even further up to an altitude of 1,520m – from there it's only a 1½-hour hike to admire the panoramic views from the summit of **Mount Kurodake** (黒岳; 1,984m). A hut and campground lie just beyond the top, and there are more trails leading deeper into the wilds for serious hikers.

Back down in the village, **Sōunkyō Mount Daisetsu Photo Museum** (層雲大雪山写真ミュージアム; w museum.sounkyo-daisetsu.jp; ⊕ 09.00–17.00 Wed–Mon; ¥600) houses a collection of remarkable nature photography from the local area. **Kurodake-no-yu** (黒岳の湯; ⊕ 10.00–21.30; ¥600) is a barebones public onsen near the centre of the village; not a luxurious facility by any means, but it has an indoor and outdoor rooftop bath, a sauna and a cold water pool for rejuvenating your body. There is a free *ashiyu* (foot spa) next door.

Sōunkyō Onsen plays host to two annual **festivals**: the traditional Ainu summer Fire Festival (early–mid-Aug) and the more famous winter Icefall Festival (⊕ late Jan–mid-Mar 17.00–21.30; ¥500). The latter involves ice sculptures crafted from icicles which are illuminated at night, plus other winter attractions.

Close to town are a number of pretty waterfalls. **Momijidaki Falls** (紅葉滝) is reached via a simple 30-minute hike up a trail which offers lovely nature views and starts behind the fire station. About 3km east along the main road up the valley are two waterfalls, **Ginga-no-taki** (銀河の滝; Milky Way Falls) and **Ryūsei-no-taki** (流星の滝; Shooting Star Falls), which both plummet down the 100m-high cliffs. They can be seen by turning off before the tunnel and stopping at the large car park across the river; a steep walking trail behind the gift shop there leads up in 15 minutes to an observation deck called **Sōbaku-dai** (双瀑台). A further 5km up the valley is an interesting columnar riverside rock formation called **Ōbako** (大函), said to resemble folding screens – it's worth a quick stop if you're passing this way.

EASTERN DAISETSUZAN The east side of the national park is remote and relatively undeveloped, but is ripe for exploring if you have your own wheels – scenic Route 273 is a popular road-trip route.

Lake Taisetsu
Route 273 passes alongside the western shore of Lake Taisetsu (大雪湖), a large lake formed by a dam on the Ishikari River. About halfway along there is a car park and toilets but there is in fact not a great deal to do here. Northeast of the lake on Route 39, if heading towards Kitami in eastern Hokkaidō, is **Sekihoku Pass** (石北峠, Sekihoku-tōge). The road rises to its highpoint of 1,050m, where there is parking and a teahouse (🕐 Apr–Oct), but it is not worth coming up here unless you happen to be passing this way. **Mikuni Pass** (三国峠, Mikuni-tōge), Hokkaidō's highest pass, sits at an altitude of 1,139m on Route 273, about 15km south of Lake

---

OFF THE BEATEN TRACK IN DAISETSUZAN

In addition to the more well-known places already mentioned, Daisetsuzan has plenty of secluded spots worth visiting. The first is on the west side of the park at the end of Route 213 – instead of turning off and crossing the bridge over the Chūbetsu River for Asahidake Onsen, carry on along the road for 8km to reach **Tenninkyō Onsen** (天人峡温泉), an almost-forgotten hot-spring resort with just one hotel still in operation. At the end of the road, a 10-minute walk up a trail leads to the gorgeous **Hagoromo Falls** (羽衣の滝), which at 270m high is Hokkaidō's tallest waterfall.

Up in the northwest corner of the park is **Aizankei Onsen** (愛山渓温泉), another tiny hot-spring resort home to a spa and ecolodge (w aizankeionsen. rinyu.co.jp), open from around the end of May until early October. It lies at the end of the narrow and twisting Route 233, about 25km from Kamikawa.

Perhaps most remote of all is **Daisetsu-kōgen Onsen** (大雪高原温泉), located down a 10km-long gravel track which leads into the very heart of the national park. The attractive lodge (w daisetsu-kogen.com) here has indoor and outdoor baths replenished with rejuvenating and slightly sulphuric milky waters (for the use of both day-visitors and staying guests), and if you want to get away from it all, then this is the place as there is no Wi-Fi, mobile phone or TV signal at the property. There is a wonderful 4–5-hour loop hike which takes in a number of nearby scenic ponds, but as this is a brown bear hotspot, hikers should attend a briefing about bears at the adjacent **Brown Bear Information Centre** (ヒグマ情報センター; w higuma-center.com) before setting off. The window for hiking is between 07.00 and 13.00 (return by 15.00); trails are sometimes closed off if there has been lots of bear activity.

Daisetsu-kōgen is open and accessible from around mid-June to early October only, and there is no public transport, although there is a free shuttle bus to and from Sōunkyō Onsen for staying guests.

Deep within the southern realms of the national park is **Tomuraushi Onsen** (トムラウシ温泉), where you can find a big hot-spring hotel (w tomuraushionsen.com), a campground and a trailhead for climbing the remote Mount Tomuraushi, one of Japan's '100 Famous Mountains' (page 81). There is a twice-daily bus (1hr 30mins; ¥2,200) operated by Hokkaidō Takushoku Bus Company (📞 0155 31 8811) running to and from JR Shintoku Station between mid-July and mid-August, and also on select days from late September to early October (reservations are recommended).

Taisetsu. There is an observation deck for admiring the endless ocean of forest and stirring mountain views (the autumn colours are particularly stunning Sep–Oct), and a fabulous cosy coffee shop (⏰ 09.00–17.00 daily) which does remarkable latte art and also serves light meals. Just beyond the pass is **Matsumi Great Bridge**, a shapely marvel of road engineering which snakes and floats above the trees. The pass closes for winter in mid-November.

Lake Nukabira

The artificial Lake Nukabira (糠平湖) in Kamishihoro (上士幌) was formed in 1953 by the construction of a hydro-electric dam. The lake is perhaps best known for **Taushubetsu River Bridge** (タウシュベツ川橋梁跡), a crumbling concrete-arched railway bridge which disappears under rising waters every summer following the snow melt, only to re-emerge by the autumn – hence its nickname of 'phantom bridge'. The arches were built in 1937 and formed part of the disused Shihoro Line which was used for transporting lumber back in the day; at various points along the valley old stations and bits of railway infrastructure can still be seen. The 130m-long bridge is located at the lake's northeast corner, and is a popular photo spot, with most people joining walking tours to view it up close (w guidecentre.jp). It is possible (although not encouraged) to visit independently by walking down a rough forest track for 4km, but there is no parking nearby and you must be wary of bears. If you're really determined, then the escapade can be made a little shorter by borrowing a key for the track's closed gate from Kamishihoro michi-no-eki (reserve the key online: w kamishihoro.info/key) and driving part of the way down. The bridge can also be seen from an observation deck across the lake, just off Route 273, and in winter you can even walk 30 minutes across the lake's frozen surface.

During the winter, Lake Nukabira completely freezes over, and air bubbles formed by various gases rising towards the surface become trapped in the ice, creating an intriguing spectacle. It is also a popular spot for ice-fishing Japanese smelt (*wagasagi*) – you may spot fisherman camped out on the ice when the lake is frozen.

At the lake's southwest corner is **Nukabira Onsen** (糠平温泉). This tiny hot-spring resort has a number of accommodation options, a campground, and Nukabira Gensenkyō (ぬかびら源泉郷), a small and quiet ski slope. **Yumotokan** (湯元館; w nukabira-yumotokan.jp; ⏰ 13.00–19.00 Fri–Mon; ¥1,000) was where the village's original hot spring was discovered in 1919. On the east side of the village you can find the **Higashitaisetsu Nature Centre** (ひがし大雪自然館; w ht-shizenkan.com; ⏰ 09.00–17.00 Thu–Tue) which introduces the ecology and human history of the region via displays, videos and a mixture of taxidermied and model animals (including the extinct Hokkaidō wolf); it also houses a collection of more than 5,000 insects from Japan and abroad, and has a tourist information desk too. Just down the road, the **Kamishihoro Town Railway Museum** (上士幌町鉄道資料館; ⏰ Apr–Oct 09.00–16.00; ¥100) has photos, movies and maps of the now abandoned Shihoro railway during its heyday. Nukabira Onsen can be reached by bus from Obihiro (1hr 45mins; ¥1,330).

Lake Shikaribetsu

Lake Shikaribetsu (然別湖) was formed naturally by a volcanic eruption about 30,000 years ago, and is one of the highest large bodies of water on Hokkaidō at 800m. Beautiful at any time of year, in winter the lake completely freezes over (it is said to be Japan's longest-freezing lake) and becomes a stage for various ice-based activities. At its southwest corner is **Shikaribetsukohan Onsen** (然別湖畔温泉), where you can find a nature centre and slightly dated lakeside hot-spring hotel (see w hotelfusui.com).

From late January to mid-March is the **Shikaribetsu Kotan Festival** (w kotan. jp), when an entire icy igloo village is constructed on the lake's frozen surface. There are ice bars serving cocktails, hotels, a concert hall and an open-air heated bath; you can also try more high-octane pursuits such as snowmobiles, cross-country skiing and snow-rafting (getting pulled along on an inflatable boat). Entry to the village is free, but some activities require a fee.

There are three or four buses a day to Shikaribetsu from Obihiro (1hr 40mins; ¥1,680) and Shintoku (1hr; ¥1,200).

Over to the northwest of the lake on the other side of the mountain is the remote **Shikaribetsu Gorge** (然別峡; Shikaribetsu-kyō). This natural beauty spot lies at the end of the long and winding Route 1088, deep within the woods. There is a secluded and unfussy hot-spring hotel with excellent baths called Shikaribetsukyō Kanno Onsen (然別峡かんの温泉; w kanno-onsen.com; $$$). A little further up the road is a campsite (w shikaoi.net; ⊕ officially open Jul–Sep), from where, if you follow the river upstream, you will discover a number of small, very wild riverside hot-spring pools – they are free to use, mixed-gender and bathing suits are not permitted (although no-one is checking). The nearest pool to the campsite, Shika-no-yu (鹿の湯) is big enough for ten people and has a small changing-room shed, while further upstream (but below the dam) are a number of smaller, wilder ones.

The gorge is about 50 minutes by car from Shintoku, and there is no public transport.

SOUTH OF DAISETSUZAN

SHINTOKU The small town of Shintoku (新得; population 6,000) on the edge of the Tokachi Plain is home to arguably the best and most humane bear sanctuary in the country, **Bear Mountain** (ベア・マウンテン; w bear-mt.jp; ⊕ late Apr–mid-Oct 09.00–16.00 daily; ¥2,200–3,300). Here, native brown bears have been re-homed in a large 15ha natural forest paddock, and visitors can observe them from a glass-windowed observation centre reached by raised open-air walkways, or by riding a bear-watching bus which slowly trundles through the enclosure (the best way to be guaranteed a close view). Entrance fee varies depending which of these you do. Tickets can be purchased online in advance for a slight discount. The sanctuary is part of Sahoro Resort (サホロリゾート; w sahoro.co.jp) which includes a ski area and some fancy hotels. It can be reached in about 1 hour by car from Obihiro, or by taking a taxi from JR Shintoku Station (15mins; ¥3,500).

SHIMUKAPPU The remote village of Shimukappu (占冠; population 1,000) is bounded by the mighty mountains of Daisetsuzan to the north and the Hidaka Range to the south. Despite the relative lack of locals, visitors come in big numbers to enjoy the delights of **Hoshino Resorts Tomamu** (w snowtomamu.jp; $$$$$), a sprawling haven of plush high-rise hotels set incongruously among grassy fields and forested mountains (four of the tallest tower blocks have been refurbished to try to make them fit in better with the natural surroundings – whether they've achieved that is still up for debate). There are countless activities no matter what the season, from skiing and snow buggies and a visit to the ice village in the winter, to tennis and archery in the summer, and year-round guests can use the indoor waterpark (with the biggest indoor beach in Japan). A gondola to the top of the ski resort takes you to the 'Unkai Terrace', an observation deck and café at 1,088m which offers spectacular views above an ocean of clouds if the conditions are right (usually the best chance is early morning).

There are 5-minute shuttle buses to the resort from JR Tomamu Station, and by car it is 1 hour from Furano or 90 minutes from New Chitose Airport.

YŪBARI

A long and narrow city hemmed in by mountains and with the aura of a place that has seen far better days, Yūbari (夕張; population 7,000) was once the centre of Japan's coal-mining industry, when during the late 1950s a peak of 120,000 people lived and worked in the district. However, following the demise of the industry and a couple of major mining disasters in the 1980s, by 1990 all the mines had closed, the population was declining rapidly and in 2007 the city was forced to declare bankruptcy, as the aging population (it was said to be the oldest settlement in Japan) couldn't sustain it. In a further blow, in 2019 the Yūbari branch railway line which connected it to the JR Sekishō Line was permanently closed, depriving the area (although a replacement bus service was introduced). If that all seems a bit depressing (which it undoubtedly is), Yūbari still makes an interesting place to visit, if for nothing more than to examine its many abandoned buildings and imagine how the now empty decaying streets must have bustled back in the day.

At the north end of the valley is the one main attraction which still has a morsel of life to it – **Yūbari Coal Mine Museum** (夕張市石炭博物館; w coal-yubari.jp; ⊕ late Apr–Sep 10.00–17.00 Wed–Mon, Oct–early Nov 10.00–16.00 Wed–Mon; ¥720/440) charts the history of the city and the mining industry through model recreations, photos and videos. It is slightly no-frills, and there is next to no English, but the staff (some of whom are former miners) are enthusiastic.

There are about six buses a day from JR Shin-Yūbari Station to the museum (50mins; ¥830), but because of its spread-out geography, getting around Yūbari is much easier with a car.

MULTI-MILLION-YEN MELONS

In Japan, giving fruit as gifts is big business, with specially grown varieties being highly prized for their taste and exquisite appearance – examples include White Jewel strawberries, Zentsuji square watermelons and Ruby Roman grapes, all of which cost eye-watering prices. But among the most expensive of all fruits in the world is the Yūbari King, a hybrid of two types of sweet cantaloupe which farmers in Yūbari meticulously cultivate for around 100 days in vinyl greenhouses, and when sold brings much-needed money into local coffers. The melons are first planted in February using additional volcanic soil, and by the summer are ready for harvesting when they are categorised into four grades – the best ones being perfectly round, with an attractive green and white netting pattern, while the flesh is deep orange and exceptionally sweet.

The first harvested top-grade melons are sold at a well-publicised auction every year, with a pair bought by a Tokyo-based bidder in 2019 for a record-high price of ¥5 million. More typically the price varies depending on the growing season, but you can sometimes buy a lower-grade Yūbari King for as low as ¥6,000 (around US$40). The fruits have caused such a stir, that for many people, the name Yūbari is now more synonymous with melons than with the city's well-documented economic woes.

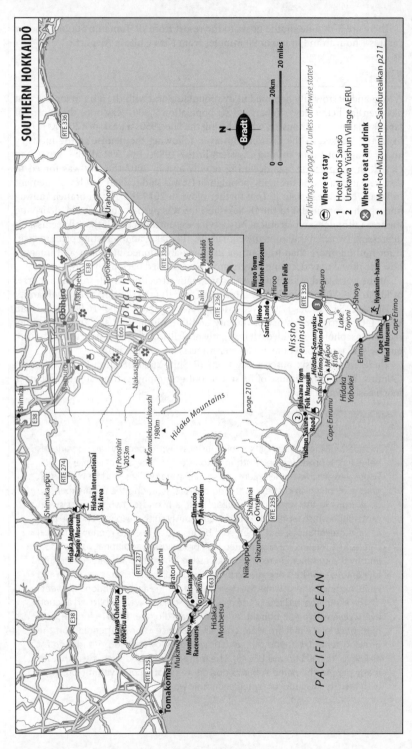

For listings, see page 201, unless otherwise stated

Where to stay
1 Hotel Apoi Sansō
2 Urakawa Yūshun Village AERU

Where to eat and drink
3 Mori-to-Mizuumi-no-Satofureaikan p211

Bradt

N

0 ⸻ 20km
0 ⸻ 20 miles

PACIFIC OCEAN

Tomakomai

Mukawa
RTE 235

Mukawa Chōritsu
Hōbetsu Museum
E38

Mombetsu
Racecourse
Hidaka
Monbetsu
Ohisama Farm
Tomikawa
E63
Nibutani
Biratori
RTE 237

Shimukappu
RTE 274

Hidaka International
Ski Area
Hidaka Mountain
Range Museum
E38

Mt Poroshiri
2053m
Mt Kamuiekuchikaushi
1980m

Dimaccio
Art Museum

Shizunai
Onsen
Shizunai
Niikappu
RTE 235

Hidaka Mountains

page 210

Yūshun Sakura
Road
Santani
Urakawa Town
Folk Museum
Mt Apoi
810m
Hidaka-Sanmyaku-
Erimo National Park
Cape Enrumu
Hidaka
Yabakei

Cape Erimu

Cape Erimo
Wind Museum

Erimo
Shoya
Hyakunin-hama
Cape Erimo

Meguro
RTE 336

Lake
Toyoni

**Nissho
Peninsula**

Hiroo
Santa Land
Hiroo
Funbe Falls
Hiroo Town
Marine Museum

Hokkaidō
Spaceport
Taiki
RTE 236

Toyokoro
E38
Makubetsu

Urahoro
RTE 336

T o k a c h i   P l a i n

Obihiro
E60

Nakasatsunai

Memuro

Shimizu
E38

198

7

Southern Hokkaidō

This region comprises the mountainous and remote Nissho Peninsula (日勝半島, Nisshō-hantō), which juts south of central Hokkaidō's main bulk, and the vast bucolic flatlands of the Tokachi Plain to the east. The peninsula is characterised by its long, frequently fog-engulfed coastline ending at the remote Cape Erimo, while inland rises a central spine of high and lonely mountains known as the Hidaka Range. To the west of these mountains is the rural and relatively little-visited Hidaka subprefecture, a region steeped in history and famed even today as the Ainu heartland, with numerous Ainu settlements dotted all along the coast and up its river valleys. Some of the first Japanese settlers on Hokkaidō also set up camps and fishing villages here, generally living alongside the Ainu, and it has become renowned as the largest horse-breeding region in Japan. The eastern side of the peninsula comprises western Tokachi subprefecture, and provides quite a contrast in terms of landscape, as the Hidaka Mountains roll down towards the sprawling flat and fertile agricultural lands of the Tokachi Plain. Numerous meandering rivers spill out towards the sweeping coast, and the biggest city in the region, Obihiro, lies near the centre of the plain. While included in the 'Southern' section here, Obihiro and the Tokachi Plain are generally classified as the gateway to eastern Hokkaidō.

Both the peninsula's east and west coasts are frequently shrouded in thick swirling sea fog (especially between May and July); this is due to warm spring and summer air passing over the cold Oyashio Current as it flows offshore, with the warmer air cooling and forming into mist – a phenomenon that made this particular stretch of coastline notoriously difficult to navigate for sailors during the early pioneer days. The region's interior is little populated and completely dominated by the Hidaka Mountains (日高山脈, Hidaka-sanmyaku), a vast range of remote mountains which is home to a sizeable brown bear population and generally only attracts the most

MAJOR FESTIVALS IN SOUTHERN HOKKAIDŌ

Obihiro Ice Festival (Obihiro Kōri-Matsuri) w obihiro-icefes.com; late January/early February
Erimo Sea Urchin Festival (Erimo Uni-Matsuri) Late April
Shizunai Shinhidaka Sakura Festival (Shizunai Sakura Matsuri) w sakuranamiki.com/maturi/shizunai-sakura.html; late April/early May
Sarabetsu Plum Festival (Sarabetsu Sumomo-no-Sato Matsuri) Mid-May
Obihiro Flat Plain Festival (Obihiro Heigen-Matsuri) Mid-August
Iwanai Senkyō Momiji Festival (Iwanai Senkyō Momiji-Matsuri) Early October
Obihiro Chrysanthemum Festival (Obihiro Kiku-Matsuri) Late October to early November

hardcore of hikers. These peaks form part of Hidaka-Sanmyaku Erimo National Park, due to be upgraded from quasi-national park status in 2024.

Public transport along the peninsula is rather limited; the JR Hidaka Main Line runs a short distance along the west coast of the peninsula from Tomakomai to Mukawa – it once ran all the way down to Samani, but following storm damage in January 2015 (and further damage from a typhoon later that year) parts of the line were washed away and the service suspended indefinitely. JR eventually decided that repairing the entire line would be too costly and so abandoned it beyond Mukawa. A replacement bus service now runs the length of the coast from JR Mukawa Station. In the east, Obihiro is a medium-sized city with good rail, road and bus connections to other parts of the island. Venture much beyond the city, however, and public transport options on the eastern side of the Nissho Peninsula become quite limited.

HISTORY

The Hidaka Mountains were formed as a result of a collision of the North American and Eurasian continental plates around 13 million years ago. Unlike the majority of Hokkaidō's mountains, which are volcanic in origin, the Hidaka Range was created by tectonic uplift, although these mountains are not thought to be rising any longer. Part of the mantle was thrust up from beneath the earth's crust, meaning that peridotite rocks (igneous rock originating in the mantle) can now been found at the surface, contributing to the Hidaka region's unique geology and ecology, with rare plants prospering due to the uncommon rock and soil conditions – among the Hidaka peaks, jade and other rare stones can be found. Along with its unique geology, the Hidaka Mountains are the only place on Hokkaidō with evidence of former glacial activity.

Humans have been living in the Hidaka region thousands of years, with stone tools dating back over 10,000 years having been excavated in the Saru River basin. Hidaka has long been associated with the Ainu, and their villages once used to dot the river for much of its course. Along the river's middle section at Biratori, even today the population is still predominantly people of Ainu descent, with the highest ratio of Ainu anywhere on Hokkaidō. During the island's colonisation and development phase, Japanese settlers established small fishing and trading posts, often living alongside the Ainu. Both the Ainu and Japanese were reliant on horses for travel and transporting goods due to the tough terrain and lack of good infrastructure, and the Hidaka region developed a strong horse-breeding tradition, now producing about 80% of the country's thoroughbreds. For centuries, one of the main streams of income for locals living on the coast has been the harvesting of Hidaka Konbu (a type of kelp), and this industry continues today, with long lines of seaweed drying in the sun at flat spots along the seashore, usually from around July to September.

HIDAKA AND THE WEST COAST

The present-day Ainu heartland is hemmed by mountains inland and a long coastline dotted with settlements until reaching the windswept Cape Erimo at the peninsula's southern tip.

Tomakomai is one of the main gateways to the region, and so **Tomakomai Tourist Information Centre** (苫小牧観光案内所; ⏰ 09.00–18.00 daily) is a good place to go for bus timetables and other information. It' next to the station, just east of the south exit. **Samani Tourist Information Centre** (様似観光案内所; ⏰ 08.30–8.00 daily) may be useful if exploring the southern end of the peninsula.

GETTING THERE AND AROUND

By train The JR Hidaka Main Line now only runs from Tomakomai to Mukawa (30mins; ¥750). From there you will have to rely on buses to explore further south.

By bus Two companies operate in the region. Dōnan Bus (w donanbus.co.jp) runs buses from Mukawa, Tomakomai and even Sapporo to various towns along the western side of the peninsula, including Biratori, Shizunai (Shinhidaka) and Urakawa. JR Hokkaidō Bus (w jrhokkaidobus.com) operates all the way down to Cape Erimo, with one direct bus per day between the cape and Tomakomai (3hrs 50mins; ¥2,900).

Bus terminals and tourist information centres should be able to provide the most detailed and up-to-date bus schedules.

By road This is one region where having your own wheels really helps. The Hidaka Expressway (E63) runs for 60km down the northwest side of the peninsula as far as Atsuga. From there you can pick up Route 235, which hugs the coast as far as Urakawa, and then Route 336 leads around Cape Erimo up towards Obihiro. There are only two routes that cut inland across the peninsula through the mountains: from between Mukawa and Hidaka, Route 237 heads northeast via Biratori; or further south between Urakawa and Samani you can follow Route 236 for 60km, passing through numerous tunnels over to the eastern side of the peninsula. From Tomakomai to Cape Erimo it is about 180km or 3 hours by road.

WHERE TO STAY AND EAT *Map, page 198, unless otherwise stated*

Biratori Onsen Yukara [map, page 203] び らとり温泉ゆから; Nibutani 92-6, Biratori; ☏0145 72 3280; w biratori-onsen.com. Simple but comfortable rooms in a secluded location. There's a choice of indoor or outdoor hot springs, including an invigorating & highly carbonated bath which is a rarity on Hokkaidō. The onsen restaurant (⊕ 11.00–14.40 & 16.00–20.00 daily) does some good beef dishes using prized local Biratori beef. **$$$$**
Hotel Apoi Sansō ホテルアポイ山荘; Hirau 479-7, Samani; ☏0146 36 5211; w apoi-sanso. co.jp. Understated yet spacious rooms in a mountain resort setting, close to the trailhead for Mount Apoi. Open-air hot springs offer magnificent views & are ideal for a post-hike soak. Guests can enjoy belly-filling kaiseki meals sourced with local ingredients. **$$$**

Urakawa Yūshun Village AERU うらかわ優 駿ビレッジアエル; Nishicha 141-40; ☏0146 28 2111; w aeru-urakawa.co.jp. Deep in horse country surrounded by fields & nature in a beautiful river valley, this large peaceful hot-spring facility offers horseriding & indoor baths with views of pastures & the Hidaka Mountains. Rooms are big & food is of good quality. **$$$**
Tōsenbō 灯泉房; Suehiro 1-70-2, Mukawa; ☏0145 42 5417; ⊕ 11.00–14.00 & 17.00–22.00 Thu–Tue. This local restaurant, a block west of JR Mukawa Station, serves super-fresh sashimi, including the local speciality *shishamo* (when in season). Order the *higaeri-teishoku* set for a little bit of everything. **$$**

MUKAWA This small town near the coast is best known for its *shishamo* (smelt), small fish which are usually eaten grilled or fried whole, often with the roe still intact, and in Mukawa (むかわ) you can also find it served as sushi, a rare delicacy in October and November. The main fishing season is the autumn, and Mukawa hosts a few shishamo-themed events then, including a town race in October and a fish festival in November. Mukawa beef is also highly regarded. The town has a decent number of restaurants and good hot-spring baths next to the Shiki-no-yukata road-stop.

Mukawa township actually extends way inland, and if you follow Route 74 northeast out of town for 35km you will reach the small settlement of

Hobetsu (穂別). Here you can find **Mukawa Chōritsu Hobetsu Museum** (む かわ町立穂別博物館; ⏰ 09.30–17.00 Tue–Sun, closed on some irregular days; ¥300/100), the area's main tourist attraction. It houses simple displays (with little English) of fossils and a number of impressive dinosaur skeletons, including the 'Mukawa Dragon', the nearly complete skeleton of a recently unearthed and previously unknown species which was found locally. A short walk north of the museum is **Hobetsuyagai Museum** (穂別野外博物館; ⏰ 24hrs daily), a rather overgrown but free outdoor exhibit with numerous large models of dinosaurs and prehistoric creatures.

TOMIKAWA The Hidaka region is synonymous with horse breeding and **Mombetsu Racecourse** (門別競馬場; w hokkaidokeiba.net), located just outside the small coastal town of Tomikawa (富川), is Hokkaidō's only municipal racetrack; here you can watch daily races in the afternoon and evening from April to November, and there are restaurants on site too. Just north of the town is **Ohisama Farm** (おひさ ま牧場; w ohisamafarm.com; ⏰ 10.00–16.00 Thu–Tue; ¥500/300) where you can view extremely cute miniature horses up close and feed them carrots – wrap up warm if visiting in winter.

BIRATORI AND INLAND TOWARDS HIDAKA Biratori (平取) is a rural inland region centred around the meandering Saru River and also known as one of the main Ainu heartlands. Follow Route 237 for 17km upstream from Tomikawa passing through the town of Biratori to arrive at the riverside settlement of **Nibutani** (二風谷). This small, remote village has a population of only a few hundred, but around 75% of residents are believed to be of Ainu descent, making it the highest-ratio Ainu settlement in the country. The star attraction here is the **Nibutani Ainu Culture Museum** (平取町立二風谷アイヌ文化博物館; w town.biratori.hokkaido.jp/ biratori/nibutani; ⏰ mid-Jan–mid-Dec 09.00–16.30 daily, exc Mon mid-Nov–mid-Apr; ¥400/150), arguably one of the best museums showcasing Ainu history and culture in Japan. While somewhat smaller and less flashy than the newer (and some say slightly soulless) Upopoy Ainu museum (page 131), this site is more hands-on and has a wonderful collection of Ainu artefacts which you can view up close, including hunting tools and dug-out canoes. There are also dance and craft-making demonstrations. The museum grounds are free to enter and house a faithfully reconstructed kotan (Ainu village) with numerous traditional wooden homes.

Next door to the Ainu Culture Museum on the riverbank is the free-to-enter **Historical Museum of the Saru River** (沙流川歴史館, Sarugawa Rekishikan; ⏰ 09.00–16.30 Tue–Sun, closed New Year; free). Like a hobbit-hole half built underground, it has a nice collection of natural history displays and charts the history of the river and the construction of the Nibutani Dam, a controversial project completed in 1997 which flooded lands sacred to the Ainu. There is very little English.

Across the road from the Ainu Culture Museum (behind the post office) is the **Kayano Shigeru Nibutani Ainu Museum** (萱野茂二風谷アイヌ資料館; w kayano-museum.com; ⏰ 09.00–17.00 daily, reservation required mid-Nov–mid-Apr; ¥400/150). This small private museum houses an interesting collection of artefacts collected by the late Kayano Shigeru (1926–2006), a Nibutani local who was one of the last native speakers of the Ainu language, an author and a master of Ainu folklore and the oral tradition. He rose to prominence as the first Ainu politician to sit in the Diet of Japan, helped set up numerous Ainu language schools and was one of the key figures in pushing through legislation which promoted and protected Ainu culture.

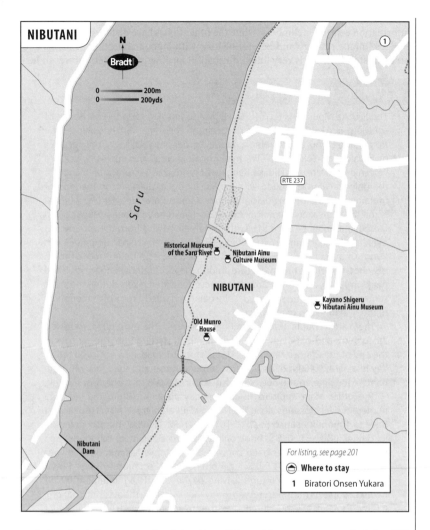

For listing, see page 201

Where to stay

1 Biratori Onsen Yukara

Just a short distance south of the Ainu Culture Museum you can find the **Old Munro House** (旧マンロー邸; year-round; free), an attractive Western-style wooden residence with white walls and a red roof. It was the home of Neil Gordon Munro, a Scottish doctor and anthropologist who lived in Nibutani and dedicated his time to studying, documenting and even filming the Ainu until his death in 1942. The house and gardens are free to view from outside, but only group tours are permitted inside. The tours are free, but must be booked at the museum one month in advance.

HIDAKA Continuing northeast from Nibutani alongside the Saru River eventually brings you to Hidaka (日高), a remote town at the far northern end of the region. Hidden behind the roadside service station you can find the **Hidaka Mountain Range Museum** (日高山脈博物館; w town.hidaka.hokkaido.jp/site/hmc; Apr–Oct 10.00–17.00 Tue–Sun, Nov–Mar 10.00–15.00 Tue–Sun; ¥200/100), a quirky four-storey building with a pointy mountain motif on its roof. The top floor has an observation deck with views towards the mountains; the ground floor serves as an information centre for climbers; while the other floors have displays on the Hidaka Range's unique geology and natural history, with a good collection of fossils and precious stones. There is very little information for English-speakers, however. Just

CLIMBING MOUNT POROSHIRI

The Hidaka Mountains (日高山脈, Hidaka-sanmyaku) form the backbone of southern Hokkaidō, stretching north–south for some 150km down to the tip of Cape Erimo, and forming a natural barrier between the subprefectures of Hidaka and Tokachi. Unlike many of Hokkaidō's mountains, which are volcanic in nature, the Hidaka Range was formed by tectonic uplift, and it is the only place on Hokkaidō with evidence of glacial activity, in the form of moraines and numerous glacial cirques. Mount Poroshiri (幌尻岳; 2,053m) is the tallest peak in the range and also a hyakumeizan (one of Japan's '100 famous mountains'; page 81), with its name deriving from the Ainu words meaning 'huge mountain'. Just below the summit, the Nanatsunuma (Seven Pond) Cirque (七ツ沼カール) is one of Japan's finest cirques and a brown bear hotspot. These mountains are among the most remote and least-visited peaks in Japan, although Poroshiri attracts dedicated hikers during the short summer/early autumn season, despite being regarded as one of the toughest of the hyakumeizan to climb.

There are a couple of routes but neither is easy. The most direct route is a 25km there-and-back approach from the north starting from the car park at the end of the Chiroro-rindō (チロロ林道) forestry road. It's a long and tough day hike with 1,400m of ascent, first through forest and then following the narrow ridgeline up and down over a number of peaks to the highest summit.

The other main approach is a three-day adventure from the west via numerous river crossings along the Nukabira (Biratori) trail – hikers usually first drive to **Toyonuka-sansō** (とよぬか山荘; ☎01457 33568; w horoshiri-biratori. jp; dinner, B&B ¥6,000; $$; book online), an old elementary school deep in the mountains which has been converted into simple accommodation with dorm-style bunkbeds. The following morning you take a shuttle bus for 1 hour to the trailhead (¥4,000 return; leaving 04.00/08.00/10.40, returning 09.30/noon/17.00; seats must be reserved in advance by calling the accommodation). It is then a 7.5km hike up a logging road, from where the path follows the river for 4km, with more than 20 river crossings (usually no more than knee to waist deep, but bring river shoes and walking poles to make the crossings easier, and avoid entirely after heavy rains).

You'll arrive at **Poroshiri-sansō** (幌尻岳山荘; ◷ Jul–Sep; ¥2,000), a remote mountain hut at 950m altitude which also requires advanced reservations (these can also be made online via w horoshiri-biratori.jp). Bring your own food, cooking equipment and sleeping bag as none are provided. You should also bring a portable toilet bag (*keitai-toire*). Most hikers climb the short but gruelling 4km trail to the summit the next day, and return to Poroshiri-sansō for one more night, before making their way back down the river in time for the return shuttle bus on day 3. On a clear day, views from the summit are spectacular, an endless panorama of untouched mountains and sweeping ridgelines the reward for enduring one of Japan's most remote and tough hikes. Don't forget to bring a bear bell (many hikers also carry bear spray; see also page 9), as this is definite brown bear territory.

outside of town to the south is **Hidaka International Ski Area** (日高国際スキー場; w town.hidaka.hokkaido.jp/site/ski; ⏰ late Dec–mid Mar 09.00–21.00 daily; one-day lift pass ¥3,200/2,000), a small, quiet ski resort probably best suited to beginners and intermediate skiers.

NIIKAPPU As you may guess from the huge mural of three galloping horses on the cliff next to Route 235 on the way into Niikappu (新冠), this locality is known for its equine history and especially its thoroughbreds. In the centre of this small town, the distinctive **Record Plaza** (レ・コド館, Recōdo-kan; w niikappu.jp/record; ⏰ 09.00–21.00 Tue–Sun; ¥300/100) with its large observation tower is the town's main landmark and attraction. Part museum and part music library, it houses a huge collection of over 1 million Japanese vinyls; if you find one that piques your interest, you can play it through headphones for free or in a listening booth for a small fee. The observation deck (free entry) has a café, and there is a good service station next door too.

Heading northeast out of town up along the Niikappu River on Route 209 and then Route 71 will bring you in half an hour to the **Dimaccio Art Museum** (太陽の森ディマシオ美術館, Taiyō-no-mori Dimashio Bijutsukan; w dimaccio-museum.jp; ⏰ mid-Jul–late Aug 09.30–16.30 daily, late Aug–mid-Dec & mid-Mar–mid-Jul 09.30–16.30 Thu–Sun, closed mid-Dec–mid-Mar; ¥1,100/300). This excellent and surprisingly rural museum (in an attractive former elementary school) houses works by the esteemed French oil painter Gerard Di-Maccio, the most impressive of which is a huge 9m-by-27m fresco, the largest oil painting in the world. The museum also has a tremendously varied collection of other works including sculptures, ceramics and glassware. The on-site restaurant, Atrantis (⏰ 11.00–14.00 Fri–Sun & hols; $$$), serves tasty pasta dishes.

SHINHIDAKA Located roughly halfway down the peninsula, Shinhidaka (新ひだか) is the most populated township and the economic hub of the entire Hidaka region, focused around the town of **Shizunai** (静内). There are a few hotels and places to eat here, and in May visitors come to see the Nijukken-dōro Cherry Blossom Road (二十間道路の桜並木), an impressively long and straight avenue lined with thousands of cherry trees, a 15-minute drive north of town. A shuttle bus runs from Shizunai to the road during cherry blossom season.

In Shizunai itself, the modern and well-kept **Shinhidaka Town Museum** (新ひだか町博物館; ⏰ 10.00–18.00 Tue–Sun; free) has a modest yet varied collection of local archaeological finds, animal taxidermy and other displays relating to early pioneer life and the Ainu, and is certainly worth a quick visit. A 15-minute drive east of town brings you to **Shizunai Onsen** (静内温泉; w shizunai-onsen.jp; ⏰ 10.00–22.00 daily; ¥500/160), a secluded and unpretentious hot-spring facility deep in the woods. There are saunas and a choice of indoor baths, but no outdoor bath; the restaurant ($) serves light meals. The nearby forest park has camping spots and simple cabins (¥550 per tent, ¥3,300 per cabin; $) – check in at the onsen.

URAKAWA This rural township has a number of minor settlements and more than 200 horse ranches, with the town of Urakawa (浦河) being the main centre of activity. One of the most unique attractions here is **Daikokuza** (大黒座; w daikokuza.com; ⏰ 10.00–19.00 Thu–Tue; ¥1,500/1,000), a tiny Taishō-era cinema established in 1918 which shows an eclectic selection of films (including occasional English-language ones) and where the owner's tabby cat is often

The Hidaka region is one of the top horse breeding regions in the world and produces about 80% of Japan's thoroughbreds. The horse most synonymous with Hokkaidō, however, is the Dōsanko (also known as the Hokkaidō pony or Hokkaidō horse), a native Hokkaidō breed of stocky build, mild temperament and relatively short stature. It probably derives from a type of horse brought over from Korea by fishermen in the 15th century, possibly with a mix of Mongolian blood too. It evolved over the centuries into a strong and reliable workhorse capable of withstanding Hokkaidō's harsh climate, and was used as a pack animal and later for farm work by both the Ainu and early Japanese colonists. It is one of eight surviving native horse breeds in Japan, and the only one that is not critically endangered.

To get a closer feel for southern Hokkaidō's equine culture, the **Breeding Area Hidaka Information Desk** (競走馬のふるさと日高案内所; w uma-furusato.com; ⊕ mid-Apr–mid-Oct 09.00–17.00 Wed–Mon, mid-Oct–mid-Apr 09.00–17.00 Mon–Fri) in Shizunai is the best place to go for information on ranch tours, horse races and also to source local accommodation. Ranch visits must generally be booked in advance – staff at tourist information centres or your accommodation may be able to assist with this.

around to greet you in the lobby. Screenings are four times a day (10.00, 13.30, 16.00, 19.00). It may not be the place to go for cutting-edge sound and visuals, but the retro surroundings have a certain charm. The cinema can be found one block from the seafront just opposite the post office; there are a number of good restaurants in the vicinity too.

Most other spots of interest are in the wide and fertile Hidaka-Horobetsu river valley to the east of the town; simply follow Route 236 inland from the small seaside settlement of **Nishihorobetsu** (西幌別). About halfway up the valley, the **Yūshun Sakura Road** (優駿さくらロード) is a popular cherry blossom spot in the heart of horse country, with plenty of opportunities for photographing both horses and cherry blossom in the same shot. There are a number of notable photogenic trees in the area, the most well known of which is probably the **Urakawa Obake-sakura** (うらかわオバケ桜), one of the largest Ezoyama cherry trees on Hokkaidō. The tree is on private land which is only open to visitors for a couple of weeks from late April – it stands alone in the middle of a wonderfully scenic and open grassy pasture at the northern end of the valley and is a 5-minute walk up a mostly gravel track from the car park.

Returning to the coastal Route 336 and on the eastern outskirts of Nishihorobetsu is **Urakawa Town Folk Museum** (浦河町立郷土博物館; ⊕ 09.00–16.30 Tue–Sun; free). A large arching gate leads to the former elementary school, which now exhibits a vast array of items relating to the human and natural history of the region; it is an Aladdin's cave of Ainu artefacts and stuffed animals, with miscellaneous items piled up in the corridors – certainly worth a visit considering there is no admission fee. There is a small horse museum (⊕ same hours as Folk Museum) in the building next door too.

SAMANI A remote and mostly mountainous township at the southern end of the peninsula, the small coastal settlement of Samani (様似; population 4,400) used to be the southern terminus of the JR Hidaka Line. The coastline here is defined by various jutting rock formations including **Cape Enrumu** (エンルム岬), an impressive plug of rock which overlooks the harbour. An observation platform sits at the top of the cape, and can be reached via a steep 10-minute climb from the car park.

Just west of the harbour, the tiny seaside settlement of Nishimachi (西町) has a small public beach which overlooks Oyako-iwa (親子岩) and three distinctive offshore rocks, with the larger two said to represent parents and the smaller one a child ('*oyako*' literally means 'parents and child'); it is a well-known sunset viewing spot. The beach also has a basic campground which is particularly popular on summer weekends; staff come in the evening to collect the small camping fee. There is a viewpoint overlooking the beach and the harbour from the top of nearby Mount Kannon (観音山), which can be found by following the road up beyond Tōjuin Temple (等樹院).

At the foot of Cape Enrumu is the tiny **Samani Folk Museum** (様似郷土館; ⏲ 10.00–16.30 Tue–Thu; free). It documents the story of Samani from the Jōmon period through to the area's Ainu heyday and its more recent history. There are a number of interesting items on display, though an understanding of Japanese will be needed to appreciate the finer details.

In the centre of town, the now obsolete Samani Station building has been converted into the Samani Tourist Information Centre (様似観光案内所; ⏲ 08.30–18.00 daily), and here you can see pictures of the old train line, as well as shop for souvenirs and gather information on nearby attractions.

East of Samani the skyline is dominated by a band of mountains, which roll in deep from the interior and drop down almost directly into the sea. This area has been designated as the **Mount Apoi UNESCO Global Geopark** (アポイ岳ジオパーク; w apoi-geopark.jp), which grants it protected status due to the rare peridotites (rocks originating in the earth's mantle) and unique alpine flora found here. The geopark actually encompasses a fairly wide area, including the town of Samani itself, but the main focus for visitors tends to be **Mount Apoi** (アポイ岳), an 810m-high mountain which is popular for hiking. The route starts close to the Apoi-dake Geopark Visitor Centre (アポイ岳ジオパークビジターセンター; ⏲ Apr–Nov 09.00–17.00 daily), a modern facility where you can find excellent displays on the geology and ecology of the park. There are a number of amenities nearby; Apoi Sansō has hot-spring baths plus meals and accommodation, and there is a campsite next door too.

Mount Apoi itself is not a particularly difficult hike, with the path to the summit being well trodden and signposted, but is best attempted outside the snowy season. The trail is split into stages, with a small hut and rest point at stage 5, and it should take between 2 and 3 hours to reach the summit from the trailhead. The first half is through forest, and beyond the hut the trail follows the more open ridgeline, with an optional branch leading through the Horoman flower field. There are great views all the way up, although the summit itself is covered in Erman's birch. Strong hikers can continue onwards for 50 minutes or so along the ridge to **Mount Yoshida** (吉田岳; 825m), for even better 360° panoramic views.

Directly to the south of Mount Apoi is a rugged 7km stretch of coastline known as the **Hidaka Yabakei** (日高耶馬渓). This area of rocky bluffs, precipitous cliffs and crashing waves was notoriously difficult to traverse back in the day, although Route 336 now ploughs through to Erimo unimpeded. A number of tunnels have been carved through the rocks here, with a couple of detours possible along the older road which hugs the sea's edge, passing various photographic and geological hotspots, all helpfully indicated by blue-and-white information boards.

ERIMO About 20km down the coast from Samani is Erimo (えりも), the last major settlement before the tip of the cape. Crammed into the limited flat land available between the sea and the mountains, Erimo is a sleepy little town with a handful of restaurant and accommodation options. The **Erimo Folk Museum** (えりも町郷土資料館ほろいずみ; ⊕ 09.00–17.00 Wed–Mon; free) is adjacent to the town hall and is full of the usual Ainu and local history exhibits, as well as displays relating to the fishing and kelp industries. Everything is nicely presented, though there is very little English.

Beyond the town Route 336 soon cuts inland and carries on over to the eastern side of the peninsula, but continue heading southwards along the coast on Route 34 for 12km to reach the remote **Cape Erimo** (えりも岬, Erimo-misaki), the southernmost extreme tip of the peninsula. This desolate and windswept spot has a real ends-of-the-earth feel, although there is a small fishing settlement (known as Erimo-Misaki) nestled on the cape's eastern littoral. The cape is said to be one of the windiest locations in Japan, and its rocky coast is home to the country's largest population of Kuril Seals (also known as harbour seals), an endangered species which can be spotted along the shoreline with their young pups in May and June.

There is plenty of parking space (be careful opening car doors if it's windy!) at the **Erimo Misaki Tourist Centre** (えりも岬観光センター; ⊕ 09.00–16.30 daily), a rather dated building with a slightly overpriced seafood restaurant and souvenir shop, but a good place to take shelter in inclement weather. A short walk from the visitor centre is the distinctive-in-white **Cape Erimo Lighthouse**, a stumpy little structure that shines a warning beacon to vessels out in the dangerous waters around the cape; a bit further beyond it is a good viewpoint looking out over the waves crashing on the reef.

Adjacent to the lighthouse is the **Cape Erimo Wind Museum** (襟裳岬風の館, Erimo-misaki kaze-no-yakata; ⊕ Mar–Apr & Sep–Nov 09.00–17.00 daily, May–Aug 09.00–18.00 daily, closed Dec–Feb; ¥300/200), a curious resthouse-cum-museum-cum-observatory built half underground and approached via a wind-sheltered, spiralling walkway. The large-windowed observatory has fantastic views of the cape's rugged coastline, with free binoculars for spotting seals down below. As well as various exhibits, there's a special indoor wind tunnel where visitors can experience 25m/s winds, which is quite fun if you haven't already been blasted by the actual wind outside. If the weather is reasonable, it's worth taking a walk along the path to the furthest tip of the peninsula as the views of the cliffs and ocean from there are excellent.

THE GOLDEN ROAD

The 33km stretch of Route 336 between Shoya and Hiroo is known as the **Ōgon-dōro** (黄金道路) or 'Golden Road', supposedly on account of the sheer expense of its construction, and for the wealth it was hoped it would bring. This section of coast was once notoriously tricky and treacherous to navigate owing to the many cliffs, landslides, rocky shoreline and frequently torrid weather conditions. There was a rough track here for hundreds of years, providing an overland transport link to the numerous small fishing villages all along the cape, but it was difficult and in 1934 construction of the modern road began. Many sections have been reconstructed and reinforced over the years after incurring damage from rockfall and storms, but it remains an impressive bit of road engineering along one of Hokkaidō's most ruggedly beautiful coastlines.

Following Route 34 north of Erimo-Misaki up the eastern side of the cape, you will soon catch glimpses of **Hyakunin-hama** (百人浜), a vast and mostly desolate sweeping sandy beach, which stretches for nearly 10km and is a place known for its great surfing.

Further up the coast and about 3km inland, almost equidistant between the small fishing villages of **Shoya** (庶野) and **Meguro** (目黒), is **Lake Toyoni** (豊似湖). This nearly perfectly heart-shaped lake became famous after appearing on a Japanese television commercial for biscuits, although its unique form can only be properly seen by drone or helicopter. The lake can be accessed by turning off Route 336 at Meguro and driving about 10km along a gravel forestry road; there is a car park and toilet at the end of the track, and the lake is a short 200m walk uphill from there. It is a secluded nature spot deep in the forest, so be vigilant of bears if you go for a stroll. Meguro itself is home to a former school-cum-restaurant called Morito-Mizuumi-no-Satofureaikan (森と湖の里ふれ愛館; page 211), a great stop-by for its reasonably priced set meals.

THE TOKACHI PLAIN REGION

On the east side of the peninsula's colossal mountainous spine lies the Tokachi Plain (十勝平野). One of Hokkaidō's largest and most prosperous agricultural regions, this vast low-lying plain covers an area of roughly 3,600km², making it the island's second largest expanse after the Ishikari Plain (although both are dwarfed by the Kantō Plain of Tokyo fame). Lying east of the Hidaka Mountains, the land is mostly a patchwork of fields stretching for as far as the eye can see, interspersed with numerous rivers, including the plain's namesake, the Tokachi River.

The area's largest city, Obihiro, which has a few unique cultural and gastronomic curiosities for travellers, sits at the heart of the plain and is one of the main stops along the JR Nemuro Line, which connects eastern and western Hokkaidō. Travelling across the plain, some of the most striking features are the long straight roads, the numerous large farmsteads and the regular rows of tall larch and birch trees planted as windbreaks (to protect crops and stop the light volcanic soils from blowing away). When the first settlers arrived, it was soon realised that the Tokachi Plain would be suitable for grazing, and dairy farming developed alongside large-scale crop growing. The region is a major producer of beans, wheat, potatoes, sugar beet and asparagus, and in the 1960s vineyards for wine making were established – Tokachi Wine (page 219) in Ikeda, east of Obihiro, produces award-winning tipples.

The **Tokachi Tourist Information Centre** (十勝観光情報センター; ⏲ 09.00–18.00 daily) in Obihiro is the best place for information relating to the region.

GETTING THERE AND AROUND
By air Tokachi-Obihiro Airport is a 40-minute bus ride south of Obihiro and has regular flights to Tokyo's Haneda Airport, plus seasonal routes to Nagoya.

By train There is a five-times daily JR limited express train 'Tokachi' between Sapporo and Obihiro (2hrs 40mins; ¥7,790) on the JR Nemuro Line. The 'Ozora' service between Sapporo and Kushiro which runs six times daily also stops at Obihiro.

By bus Highway express buses link Obihiro to other cities; various companies run the 'Potato Liner' to Sapporo (3hrs 40mins; ¥3,840), and Dōhoku operates the 'North Liner' between Obihiro and Asahikawa (3hrs 45mins; ¥3,600). Local and long-distance express buses depart JR Obihiro Station Bus Terminal, with routes

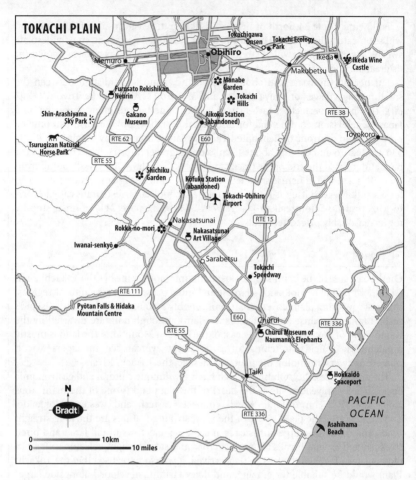

TOKACHI PLAIN

Tokachigawa Onsen
Tokachi Ecology Park
Obihiro
Memuro
Ikeda
Ikeda Wine Castle
Makubetsu
Manabe Garden
Furusato Rekishikan
Nenrin
Tokachi Hills
Shin-Arashiyama Sky Park
Gakano Museum
Aikoku Station (abandoned)
RTE 38
RTE 62
E60
Toyokoro
Tsurugizan Natural Horse Park
RTE 55
Shichiku Garden
Kofuku Station (abandoned)
Tokachi-Obihiro Airport
Rokka-no-mori
Nakasatsunai
RTE 15
Iwanai-senkyō
Nakasatsunai Art Village
Sarabetsu
Tokachi Speedway
RTE 111
Pyōtan Falls & Hidaka Mountain Centre
E60
Chūrui
RTE 336
RTE 55
Chūrui Museum of Naumann's Elephants
Taiki
Hokkaidō Spaceport
N

PACIFIC OCEAN
RTE 336
Asahihama Beach
0 — 10km
0 — 10 miles

covering all the main spots around the city and nearby towns. The Obihiro one-day city bus pass costs ¥900, and there are various passes for the wider Tokachi area (w tokachibus.jp), with routes serving various places around the Tokachi Plain, including Hiroo in the far south (2hrs 20mins, ¥1,910). JR Hokkaidō Bus (w jrhokkaidobus.com) operates a route between Sapporo and Hiroo on the southeastern coast (5hrs; ¥4,720).

By road Obihiro is about a 3-hour drive from Sapporo (using toll roads), about 2 hours 30 minutes from New Chitose Airport, 3 hours from Asahikawa and 2 hours from Kushiro, while it takes about 1 hour to motor down to the southern end of the Tokachi Plain from central Obihiro. The city's streets are wide and generally not congested.

WHERE TO STAY AND EAT For accommodation and restaurant listings in Obihiro, see page 215.

Hotel Arco ナウマン温泉ホテルアルコ; Chūruishishirogane-machi 384-1, Chūrui; ✆0155 88 3111; w hotel-arco.jp. Next to the Naumann's Elephant museum (page 212), the striking &

stylish concrete modernist architecture of this hotel is surprising, although rooms are standard & comfortable tatami-style affairs. Arco also functions as a popular hot-spring facility, with nice indoor & outdoor baths which get much quieter after day visitors retreat. **$$$**

Hotel Taiki ホテル大樹; Kotobuki-dōri 2-18, Taiki; `0155 89 6688; w hotel-taiki.com. Minimalist-style & reasonably priced rooms in this no-fuss hotel on the southern edge of Taiki, but within walking distance of the main dining district. It has its own public bath & the service, like the townsfolk, is friendly. **$$**

Mori-to-Mizuumi-no-Satofureaikan [map, page 198] 森と湖の里ふれ愛館; Meguro 214-6; `0146 64 7722; ⊕ Apr–Oct 10.00–16.00 Thu–Sun. About halfway between Cape Erimo & Hiroo in the tiny fishing hamlet of Meguro, this unique restaurant offers reasonably priced set meals. Its setting in a former school building (which closed in 2006) is rather melancholic, the hallways still almost echoing with the sounds of children, & an old classroom functions as the dining area with the blackboard displaying the day's menu. **$$**

HIROO A small, remote harbour town which draws surfers from afar and where kelp is harvested along the seafront, Hiroo (広尾; population 7,000) has few tourist attractions. But it is perhaps best known for having the curious honour of being the only place in Japan (and the only place outside of Norway) to be officially certified as a 'Santa Land' by the white-bearded man himself…or at least his representatives at the municipal government of Oslo.

The main focus for the festive fun is at **Hiroo Santa-Land** (w santaland.or.jp; free) in Daimaruyama Forest Park (大丸山森林公園), situated on a hillside on the northwest edge of Hiroo town. Don't expect to be dazzled, as in truth it is a small park with a few simple Christmas-themed attractions, including a cabin-style Santa's House where you can buy festive goods. From around the end of October until the New Year illuminations light up the park every evening (16.30–22.00). It all feels slightly cheap and tacky, but it may please small kids and Japanese visitors unaccustomed to the novelty of Christmas. Outside the festive season a few decorations remain in place, and visitors can admire cherry blossom in the spring and azaleas in early summer.

Just north of town right on the seafront is the **Hiroo Town Marine Museum** (海洋博物館; ⊕ late Apr–early Nov 10.00–16.00 Sat–Sun & hols only; ¥330/165), which houses a nice variety of interesting exhibits, historic photos, preserved animals and local history reconstructions, although there is little to no English.

Just beyond the southern limits of town are the **Funbe Falls** (フンベの滝), a tumbling set of waterfalls which plunge from the hillside right alongside Route 336, adjacent to the ocean. Slightly underwhelming in drier spells, the falls look their best in the winter when the cascades are transformed into frozen pillars. There is a layby for parking directly in front of the falls.

TAIKI Located at the southern end of the Tokachi Plain, Taiki (大樹) is an agricultural township of fertile farmland and roadside cheese shops, while also encompassing wild Hidaka peaks to the west and a small slither of coast. The town of Taiki itself sits along the Rekifune River as it meanders down from the mountains and crosses the plains to the sea. In recent years the area has become known as a location for science and space-related initiatives, with a rocket launch site and aerospace research facility at the **Hokkaidō Spaceport** (北海道スペースポート; w hokkaidospaceport.com). Visitors to Taiki can learn about Japan's space history at the spaceport's **Space Exchange Centre SORA** (大樹町宇宙交流センターSORA; ⊕ late Apr–early Nov 10.00–16.00 Sat–Sun & hols only; free), a small and fairly basic facility which nevertheless lets you see some rockets up close and try on a spacesuit; if you get really lucky and time it right, you may be able to witness a rocket launch too. There is not much else to see or do here, although the large white-and-orange-roofed hangar housing who knows what is quite impressive.

South of the space park and a little further down the coast, close to the mouth of the Rekifune River is **Asahihama Beach** (旭浜). Here (and at a few other spots along this stretch of coastline) you can find a number of concrete pillboxes; now weathered and half-buried in sand, these decaying defensive remnants from World War II never saw direct conflict and now stand as lonely angular relics on the beach, creating an especially moody visage when the fog rolls in.

Taiki town doesn't have many attractions, but in the small neighbouring town of Chūrui is the **Chūrui Museum of Naumann's Elephant** (忠類ナウマン像記念館; ⊕ 09.00–17.00 Wed–Mon; ¥300/200) which has models and bones of the prehistoric Naumann's Elephant, a species that once roamed across Japan and was probably hunted by early humans – an almost complete skeleton was discovered here in 1969. Although there is little signage in English, it's worth a quick gander.

SARABETSU A small village surrounded almost entirely by pancake-flat agricultural land, Sarabetsu (更別; population 3,000) is probably best known for the **Tokachi Speedway** (十勝スピードウェイ; w tokachi.msf.ne.jp), which at 5.1km is the second longest course in Japan (after the world-famous Suzuka Circuit in Mie Prefecture). Of the seven international-standard courses in the country, this is the only one where you can drive with a normal driving licence, with the track open to visitors and their vehicles when it is not otherwise in use (¥1,000 pp Sat–Sun; free on non-event w/days). Various domestic races and events are held here throughout the year, including drift championships and a Porsche event in early July.

On the southern edge of Sarabetsu village just off Route 236 is the Sarabetsu Sumomo-no-Sato (さらべつすももの里), a leafy roadside park where *sumomo* (Japanese plums) are grown; it has toilets and a small café, and there is a festival here during peak plum season in May.

NAKASATSUNAI Nakasatsunai (中札内; population 3,900) is another small village set among the patchwork farmland of the Tokachi Plain, although its jurisdiction reaches up deep into the mountains following the Satsunai river valley. It is most well known for a couple of nature-themed art facilities run by Rokkaitei (w rokkatei.co.jp/en), a popular confectioner based on Hokkaidō and famous nationwide for its butter biscuits and white chocolate.

Nakasatsunai Art Village (六花亭アートヴィレッジ中札内美術村; ⊕ late Apr–mid-Oct 10.00–15.00 Sat–Sun & hols only, late Jul–mid-Aug 10.00–15.00 daily; free) is a superb group of art galleries dotted around a small oak wood, situated just off Route 236 between Sarabetsu and Nakasatsunai. The art collections are housed in a variety of interesting and mainly Western-style buildings, and it is very pleasant to wander the grounds between them, admiring the architecture, sculptures and natural scenery. The on-site restaurant, Poroshiri (レストランポロシリ; ↘ 0155 683003; ⊕ May–Oct 11.00–15.00 Sat–Sun & hols only; $$$), serves excellent lunches and desserts, but it can get busy around midday.

Just up the road and closer to Nakasatsunai itself is **Rokka Forest** (六花の森, Rokka-no-Mori; ↘ 0155 631000; ⊕ late Apr–mid-Oct 10.00–16.00 daily; ¥1,000/500), another stylish art facility set in beautiful and expansive natural gardens, with indoor exhibitions showcasing Hokkaidō landscapes among other things. As you'd expect from a place run by a confectionery company, the café here

THE FUKUOKA UNIVERSITY 'WONDER VOGEL CLUB' INCIDENT

One of Japan's most notorious bear-related incidents, and probably the worst one directly involving hikers, took place deep in the heart of the Hidaka Mountains in July 1970, when a group of five university students from Kyūshū were stalked over a number of days by a single large female brown bear. It happened close to Mount Kamuiekuuchikaushi, a very remote peak with a real mouthful of a name (meaning something like 'steep mountain which bears tumble down' in the Ainu language) and which lies along the Hidaka ridgeline.

The incident began when a brown bear appeared at the students' camp and snatched some of their gear. The gear was retrieved, but the bear later reappeared that night and made a hole in the tent. Obviously shaken up, the students switched on their radio to make noise to hopefully deter the bear and took turns to guard the tent through the night. The bear came back early the next morning and completely ravaged the tent, but instead of everyone immediately retreating from the mountain, the group leader sent two members down to call for help. They encountered two other hiking groups and relayed the message, before returning back to the campsite around noon. The students worked to repair the tent, but were forced to flee when the bear returned later in the afternoon. As darkness descended, the bear caught up with the group, killing one of them; and in the panic, another was separated from the group. The rest spent the night in a ravine, but the following morning the bear appeared yet again, killing the 20-year-old group leader – the two remaining members managed to get down from the mountain and alerted the authorities by that evening. A couple of days later a rescue team found two of the victims' savaged bodies, and the following day the bear was shot by a group of hunters, with the body of the third, separated, victim discovered a day after that.

It is believed that things could have turned out differently if the students hadn't retrieved their belongings (bears can be very possessive) and had immediately retreated from the mountain after the first encounter with the bear. In 2019, two more hikers suffered bear attacks on the same mountain, but both survived.

The incident attracted widespread attention, and you can now see the unfortunate brown bear in question and various other items (including a note hastily written before his death by the student who was separated) on display at the Hidaka Mountain Centre (page 214) in the Satsunai River Park up in the mountains above Nakasatsunai.

(⏰ 11.00–16.00 daily) offers all kinds of delightful sweet treats, including cakes and biscuits only available at this site.

Following Route 55 and then Route 111 southwest out of the village, the road takes you upstream alongside the Satsunai River, first passing through typically picturesque and open Hokkaidō farmland and then up a gradually narrowing forested valley. After 20km you'll arrive at **Pyōtan Falls** (ピョウタンの滝), an impressive waterfall formed from an old dam which was destroyed by a flood in the mid 1950s. The falls are part of Satsunai River Park (札内川園地), which also includes the Satsunai River Dam a little further upstream. A bridge in front of the falls serves as a good photo spot and also leads to a car park and the

Hidaka Mountain Centre (日高山脈登山センター; ⊕ Apr–Oct 10.00–17.00 daily; free), a wooden, red-roofed building with a small café, basic shop and excellent displays on the geology and ecology of the mountains, including an impressive 3D topological map of the Hidaka Range. It also houses a stuffed and (now thankfully) placated brown bear which was the man-killing beast involved in the harrowing Fukuoka University 'Wonder Vogel Club' incident (page 213), along with a number of artefacts from that infamous event.

Just beyond the visitor centre is Satsunaigawa Enchi campsite (札内川園地キャンプ場; w satsunaigawacamp.com; ⊕ late Apr–Oct; **$$**; cash only), a popular and spacious campsite close to the riverside with a few ready-set tents and bungalows (for if you don't have your own gear), toilets and showers (for a fee).

OBIHIRO A small city built on a grid layout of wide avenues and long straight streets, Obihiro (帯広; population 165,000) is situated close to the centre of the vast Tokachi Plain and is often seen as the gateway city to eastern Hokkaidō. It is the only designated city in the Tokachi region and its commercial heart, although the city's boundaries also encompass large swathes of rural farmland extending south as far as Tokachi-Obihiro Airport, a 45-minute drive away. The Satsunai River, which flows along the eastern edge of the city, is classified as one of Japan's most pristine rivers, while the much smaller Obihiro River provides a splash of green in the heart of the city.

Obihiro is perhaps best known as the home of *butadon*, a popular rice-bowl dish topped with grilled pork, and it has a reputation also for producing high-quality desserts. The city's most unique non-culinary cultural attraction is the Ban'ei racing held at Obihiro Racetrack (page 217). Obihiro is the only place in the world where this peculiar form of horse racing, evolved from farming traditions, can be seen. The city also plays host to three major festivals throughout the year: a summer festival in August, a chrysanthemum festival at the end of October into early November, and an ice festival around late January or early February.

History Originally a small and remote Ainu settlement going by the name of Opereperekepu, the Obihiro area was first settled by Benzō Yoda and his Banseisha pioneers in May 1883. Within a few years, land for farming had been cleared, horses were introduced, and roads and bridges were under construction. By 1892, Obihiro had its first post office, and in 1905 the Obihiro–Kushiro railway was completed, but it wasn't until 1914 that the first electric lights were installed in the city. From 1932 Obihiro became reachable by air with the opening of Midorigaoka Airport.

In July 1945 the city suffered an air raid as part of the first and only extensive attack on Hokkaidō by American forces during World War II, though damage was negligible. A few years after the war, in 1949 Obihiro University of Agriculture and Veterinary Medicine was established, and it remains the only university in Tokachi subprefecture. JR Obihiro Station was fully rebuilt in 1966 (part of the old tracks can be seen on the north side of the station), and in 2008 Obihiro was designated a 'model environmental city' as a result of extensive tree replanting (a new forest, Obihiro-no-mori, 帯広の森, was established in the south of the city between 1975 and 2004) and other green initiatives. The following year construction of the Meiji Hokkaidō-Tokachi Oval, an Olympic-size indoor speed-skating rink, was completed, although it proved controversial due to the huge expense (around US$30 million) of the project.

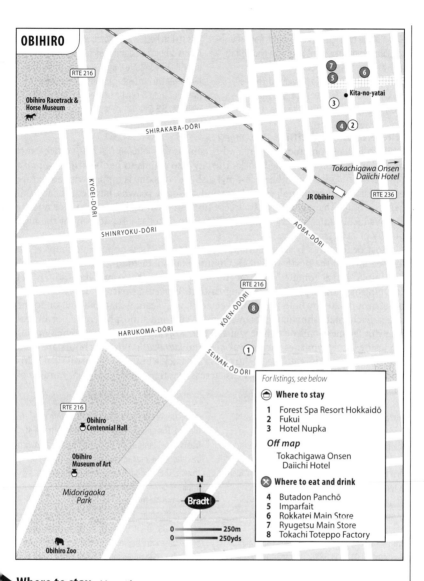

OBIHIRO

RTE 216

Obihiro Racetrack &
Horse Museum

SHIRAKABA-DŌRI

KYOEI-DŌRI

SHINRYOKU-DŌRI

Kita-no-yatai

Tokachigawa Onsen
Daiichi Hotel

JR Obihiro

RTE 236

AOBA-DŌRI

RTE 216

KOEN-DŌRI

HARUKOMA-DŌRI

SEINAN-ŌDŌRI

RTE 216

Obihiro
Centennial Hall

Obihiro
Museum of Art

Midorigaoka
Park

N

Bradt

0 _____ 250m
0 _____ 250yds

Obihiro Zoo

For listings, see below

🛏 Where to stay
1 Forest Spa Resort Hokkaidō
2 Fukui
3 Hotel Nupka

Off map
   Tokachigawa Onsen
   Daiichi Hotel

🍴 Where to eat and drink
4 Butadon Panchō
5 Imparfait
6 Rokkatei Main Store
7 Ryugetsu Main Store
8 Tokachi Toteppo Factory

Southern Hokkaidō   THE TOKACHI PLAIN REGION

7

🛏 Where to stay *Map, above*

Forest Spa Resort Hokkaidō Hotel 森のス
パリゾート北海道ホテル; Nishi 7-jō Minami
19-chōme-1; \ 0155 21 0001; w hokkaidohotel.
co.jp. This refined & long-established hotel is a
15min walk south of JR Obihiro Station. The rooms
& amenities are a little dated, but the service is
top-notch & meals make the most of the region's
finest produce. There's also an on-site onsen &
award-winning sauna. **$$$$**

Tokachigawa Onsen Daiichi Hotel 十勝川
温泉第一ホテル; Tokachigawa Onsen-minami

12-chōme; \ 0155 46 2231; w daiichihotel.com.
Tokachigawa Onsen is a small hot-spring resort
20mins' drive outside of Obihiro. It is one of the
city's most popular hot-spring hotels, which is
open to day visitors too. There is a free shuttle
bus to JR Obihiro Station for staying guests.
$$$$

Fukui Hotel ふく井ホテル; Nishi 1-jō Minami
11-chōme 19-1; \ 0155 25 1717; w fukuihotel.
co.jp. A pretty typical business hotel close to the
station, Fukui is fairly dated but perfectly adequate

215

for a night or two. It has its own direct-from-source hot spring in the basement & serves a good b/fast from a choice of 4 sets. **$$$**

Hotel Nupka Nishi 2-jō Minami 10-chōme 20-3; 0155 20 2600; w nupka.jp. White décor & clean simplicity are the vibe at

this stylish hostel-style hotel, with private rooms & bunkbed dorms; while comfortable, individual rooms are a tight squeeze. Tours in a horse-drawn carriage-cum-drinks bar depart from out front & can be booked via the hotel's website. **$$$**

✕ Where to eat and drink *Map, page 215*

Obihiro has a strong food culture and is famous for *butadon* (豚丼) – a rice-bowl topped with succulent grilled pork. The city also claims to be the origin of *chūka chirashi* (中華ちらし), another rice-bowl dish, but this one is topped with a mixture of almost anything, though typically including squid, prawns, ham, egg, beans and bean sprouts. Thanks to its easy access to fresh farm and dairy produce and its famous local confectionery companies, Obihiro also has a reputation for the high quality of its desserts.

Most of the city's best restaurants – as well as its best hotels and shops – are located around the north side of JR Obihiro Station, including the lively Kita-no-Yatai area. Just 5 minutes' walk north of the station, **Kita-no-Yatai** (北の屋台) is Obihiro's most well-known dining district, a bustling narrow alleyway which hides around 20 tiny hole-in-the-wall eateries, with seating that spills out on to the street. Each establishment has its own unique vibe and atmosphere, and not all deal solely in Japanese cuisine either: you can find Korean, Chinese and French menus alongside local favourites such as *yakiniku* and *kushikatsu*. Business hours are from about 17.00 to midnight. The slightly less ramshackle but equally narrow **Tokachi-no-Nagaya** (十勝乃長屋) directly east across the street houses a similar number of small and cosy establishments.

Butadon Panchō 豚丼のぱんちょう; Nishi 1-jō Minami 11-chōme 19; 0155 22 1974; ⏰ 11.00–19.00 Tue–Sun. In 1933, this historic small restaurant close to the station devised the first butadon – now the city's signature dish. Meat is tender & juicy (you can choose the number of slices), & bowls are served with a smattering of green peas. Come early to beat the queues. EM. **$$$**

Imparfait アン・パルフェ; Nishi 2-jō Minami 9-chōme; 0155 31 8888; w imparfait.jp; ⏰ 10.30–23.00 Tue–Sat, 10.30–20.00 Sun. This shop specialises in creamy puddings served in dinky little jars, with a range of unusual flavours including edamame & rare cheese, although *sakura tamago* (literally 'cherry-egg') is the original. **$$**

Rokkatei Main Store 六花亭帯広本店; Nishi 2-jō Minami 9-chōme 6; 0120 12 6666; w rokkatei.co.jp; ⏰ 09.00–18.00 daily, café 11.00–16.30 daily. One of Hokkaidō's most famous

confectionery brands has its flagship store in Obihiro. The ground-floor shop sells a plethora of treats; most famous are Rokkatei's butter sandwich biscuits, & their caramels have a nice nutty crunch. The 1st floor has a café offering desserts & drinks. **$$**

Ryugetsu Main Store 柳月大通本店; Ōdōri, Minami 8-chōme 15; 0155 23 2101; w ryugetsu. co.jp; ⏰ 08.30–19.00 daily. Another major sweet brand based in Obihiro, its speciality is *sanpōroku*, a German-style ring-shaped *Baumkuchen* with a chocolate coating. **$$**

Tokachi Toteppo Factory 十勝トテッポ工房; Nishi 6-jō Minami 17-chōme 3-1; 0155 21 0101; w toteppo-factory.com; ⏰ 10.00–18.00 daily, café 11.00–17.00 daily. Set in a beautiful park, this is a one-stop shop for cheesecakes & cheeses, along with other delights such as tarts, puddings, ice cream & tiramisu, available in the café or to take out. **$$**

Other practicalities

Hokuyo Bank 12-chome 1-Nishi 2-Jominami; 0155 245181; ⏰ 09.00–15.00 daily

Obihiro Kyoukai General Hospital 5-Higashi 9-Jominami, 2-chome; 0155 226600

What to see and do Not an overtly touristy place, there are nevertheless a few sightseeing spots within Obihiro's city limits, with others spread out among the more rural localities south of the city.

Obihiro Racetrack (帯広競馬場, Obihiro Keibajō; Nishi 13 Minami 9-1; w banei-keiba.or.jp; ¥100) This racetrack hosts the world's only Ban'ei races featuring the Banba, a large breed of workhorse which can weigh over a tonne (double a typical thoroughbred), as they compete to pull a sled weighing between 500kg and 1 tonne along a straight 200m track with two small hills and finishing with a sandy final section. The winner is the first horse to pull the rear end of the sled across the finish line. The races originally started as a competition for workhorses to demonstrate their strength in a tug-of-war, but this then evolved into a 'draft horse festival', which involved the pulling of sleds.

Races are held on Saturdays, Sundays and Mondays, and the track is heated in winter so races can be held year-round, with punters placing bets on the winners. The official website has clear explanations in English of how to buy a betting ticket if you fancy a flutter.

The small on-site **Obihiro Horse Museum** (馬の資料館; w nokyoren.or.jp/horscenter; ⏰ Mar–Nov 10.00–16.00 daily; free) is both a museum and a tourist information centre which explains the history of the horses in agriculture and racing; its collection of historical photographs is quite interesting. Both the racetrack and horse museum are a 20-minute walk west of JR Obihiro Station, or you can simply take a bus to Keibajō bus stop.

Midorigaoka Park (緑ヶ丘公園; ⏰ 24hrs daily) Midorigaoka Park is a large green space in the south of the city, about 25 minutes' walk or a 15-minute bus ride from JR Obihiro Station. It is home to a number of attractions including **Obihiro Centennial Hall** (帯広百年記念館; w museum-obihiro.jp/occm; ⏰ 09.00–17.00 Tue–Sun (closed the day after national hols); ¥380/190), a good museum in the north of the park with plenty of diverse displays covering local natural, industrial, farming and Ainu history, although not much English. The native fauna exhibits include a huge woolly mammoth, while you can also see Japan's oldest earthenware and stone ornaments.

A short stroll south is the **Obihiro Museum of Art** (北海道立帯広美術館, Hokkaidōritsu-Obihiro-bijutsukan; w artmuseum.pref.hokkaido.lg.jp/obj; ⏰ 09.30–17.00 Tue–Sun (closed the day after national hols); ¥210/150), a small facility showcasing modern and contemporary art from a range of Japanese and international artists. The temporary exhibits have featured an interesting roster of artists including Lisa Larson and TeamLab in the past, so it's worth checking to see what's on.

At the southern end of the park is **Obihiro Zoo** (おびひろ動物園; w city.obihiro.hokkaido.jp/zoo; ⏰ late Apr–early Nov 09.00–16.30 daily, Dec–late Feb 11.00–14.00 Sat–Sun & hols only, closed Mar–late Apr & mid–late Nov; ¥420/210), a fairly compact and old place with animals such as tigers, lions, giraffes, bison and even polar bears, and a mini-amusement park full of small, rickety rides. Be aware however that, as in many Japanese zoos, lots of the animals are kept in cramped enclosures with little enrichment.

Around Obihiro Obihiro has a number of popular gardens which make the most of the region's fertile soils and mild summer climate. **Manabe Garden** (真鍋庭園; w manabegarden.jp; ⊕ late Apr–Sep 08.30–17.30 daily, Oct–Nov shorter hrs; ¥1,000/200), situated at the south end of the city, can be reached by bus. It has extensive and very well-maintained botanical and conifer collections spread across numerous themed areas, including a beautiful Japanese garden with koi pond and teahouses, and pretty Western-style gardens. Also keep an eye out for the many Ezo squirrels scurrying about among the trees. The charming on-site café serves excellent cappuccino.

A 20-minute drive southeast of the city, on top of a small knoll is **Tokachi Hills** (十勝ヒルズ; w tokachi-hills.jp; ⊕ late Apr–mid-Oct 09.00–17.00 daily; ¥1,000/400), a scenic farm garden with impressive views, two cafés and a shop selling locally made jams and other produce. The gardens are at their best and most colourful in early summer; you should try the red bean ice cream, a tasty treat on a hot day and much more delicious than it sounds.

Deep in the countryside a 30-minute drive south of Obihiro is **Shichiku Garden** (紫竹ガーデン; w shichikugarden.com; ⊕ late Apr–early Nov 08.00–17.00, early Nov–late Apr 08.00–16.00; ¥1,000/200, free entry in winter). This naturalistic garden famous for its waterlilies was the handiwork of Akiyo Shichiku, a passionate and dedicated woman who ran the place until well into her 90s; although it sometimes struggles to straddle the fine line between wild and manicured, a visit during early summer will reward you with various vibrant blooms in an almost storybook-like garden setting. The café (⊕ 10.00–18.00/19.00; $$) serves light meals, scones and delicately floral rose ice cream.

Also among the farmlands south of Obihiro are a couple of abandoned old train stations which are said to signify 'love and happiness'. **Aikoku Station** (愛国駅跡; free) is associated with romance, as the Japanese characters translate to 'country of love'. The station has been converted into a small railway museum; it is said that if you buy a ticket there, love will surely come (even if a train most certainly won't). An old locomotive engine sits on the tracks outside. It is 30 minutes by bus or 20 minutes by car from central Obihiro.

Representing 'happiness' is the tiny and photogenic **Kōfuku Station** (旧幸福駅; free), a more rustic and rural wooden station located 15 minutes' drive further south. Its walls, both inside and out, are covered by tickets which people purchase and stick up, in the hope of attaining a life of bliss and happiness. You can freely nose around the pair of vintage orange train cars sitting outside the station too. Both stations once served the Hiroo Line until it was discontinued in 1987, and they make nice stop-offs if you are already in the area, but probably aren't worth a special visit unless you're a real train buff.

Way south of Obihiro, where the Hidaka Mountains meet the plain, but just a 15-minute drive from Nakasatsunai, **Iwanai-senkyō** (岩内仙峡) is a pretty nature spot famous for its autumn colours. Easy hiking trails take in the forests and natural beauty of the Iwanai River, with waterfalls and the faded red Senkyo Bridge providing plenty of photo opportunities. A popular *momiji* (maple leaf) festival is held here in mid-October, and there is a campsite nearby plus mountain biking trails.

TOKACHIGAWA ONSEN (十勝川温泉)

Located in Otofuke town, this small hot-spring resort 10km to the east of Obihiro sits on a peat moor on the banks of the Tokachi River. The spring's soft water is naturally infused with botanical minerals and so was revered by the Ainu who called it 'medicine water' due to its healing properties – it is said to be good for a whole range of ailments and for moisturising the skin. As a result, a number of hot-spring hotels (such as Tokachigawa Onsen Daiichi Hotel; page 215) sprang up around town to take advantage, but there is also a free footbath (*ashiyu*) if you don't feel like splashing out. The wide green (white in winter) riverside 'Aqua Park' is a good place to relax and spot cranes on the riverbank. A short drive away on top of the hill above town is an observation platform with nice views of the plains and distant mountains; particularly popular at sunset. To the east, the **Tokachi Ecology Park** (北海道立十勝エコロジーパーク; w tokachi-ecopark.jp; ⊕ 24hrs daily; free) has an impressive visitor centre and is a great place for kids, with large play areas (featuring a climbable 'fluffy dome') and easy walking trails. There is a good campsite too.

IKEDA Ikeda (池田) is a rural and slightly run-down locality 25 minutes by train east of Obihiro with one main landmark – a large mock-European-style concrete 'castle' perched on a hill, within walking distance of the station. This is **Ikeda Wine Castle** (いけだワイン城; w ikeda-wj.org; ⊕ 09.00–17.00 daily, guided tours 11.00 & 14.00 Sat–Sun & hols only; admission free, tours ¥2,000 pp), an ugly grey brute of a building which started as a research facility for wine making in the relatively cool climes of this region, and now offers brief tours plus tasting, with a shop and a good, but slightly expensive, restaurant ($$$–$$$$) on the fourth floor. The building next door is the wine factory, where thousands of bottles of Tokachi Wine are produced each day and all the machinery for wine making is on display.

MEMURO A small sleepy town just west of Obihiro, Memuro (芽室) is replete with long straight roads and a grid-block layout typical of many mid-sized Hokkaidō settlements, and most of its attractions are spread out among the agricultural lands to the south of town.

About 6km southwest of Memuro is the **Furusato Rekishikan Nenrin** (ふるさと歴史館ねんりん; w tokachi-a-muse.jp/center'furusato-center; ⊕ 09.30–16.30 Thu–Mon; free), a fairly interesting museum displaying mostly agricultural tools and machinery used throughout the ages in the region – on the second and fourth weekends every month there are hands-on demonstrations, but don't expect much English.

Not far to the east of Furusato Rekishikan Nenrin and surrounded by fields is **Gakano Museum** (画家の美術館; w gakabi.com; ⊕ 10.00–16.00 Tue–Sun; free). This former elementary school has been converted into an art museum, with the rooms and corridors displaying the colourful paintings of Harumi Muramoto, a friendly local artist who now runs the place and happily chats to visitors.

A little further southwest alongside the Bisei River is the Memuro Ski Area, home to **Shin-Arashiyama Sky Park** (新嵐山スカイパーク; w shin-arashiyama.jp). The small and cheap ski resort (⊕ late Dec–late Mar) has two lifts and a handful of short courses probably best suited to beginner and intermediate skiers, plus a small ski school and good restaurant on site. The area also offers camping throughout the year, and on fine summer days it is worth hiking (or driving) up to the top of the hill where there is a viewpoint overlooking the beautiful patchwork fields of the Tokachi Plain below.

Continuing past the ski resort along Route 55 brings you to the tiny village of Kami-Bisei (上美生), and a short drive west of here leads up a gravel track to the foot of the mountains and **Tsurugizan Natural Horse Park** (剣山どさんこ牧; w dosankomaki.com). This 100ha free-range horse ranch has great herds of Dōsanko, Hokkaidō's stumpy and sweet native horse breed, roaming freely in the vast green pastures among the wooded hills. Three-hour morning and afternoon tours are available (starting from about ¥3,000 pp including a picnic lunch), and visitors can frolic freely with the horses to their heart's content, although it's important to book at least a day ahead.

8

Eastern Hokkaidō

Cut off by the island's mountainous interior and isolated by sheer distance from its biggest cities, the eastern region of Hokkaidō is the very easternmost landmass of all Japan's main islands and almost has the feeling of an independent province separate to the rest of Hokkaidō. In fact in purely geological terms, the region belongs to the Kuril Island arc, a long volcanic belt which sweeps for over 1,000km from Kamchatka in the Russian Far East, all the way along the entire Kuril Island chain and ending in this eastern corner of Hokkaidō. Volcanoes inevitably do form the backbone of the region, but eastern Hokkaidō is also notable for its sheer variety of landscapes, including Japan's largest wetland, vast and fertile agricultural plains, long misty coastlines, stunningly beautiful caldera lakes, wildly untamed peninsulas and three of Hokkaidō's national parks.

Winters here see less snow than the colossal dumps in the more westerly parts of the island, but eastern Hokkaidō has a generally cool climate year-round. The cold Oyashio ocean current flows down from the Bering Sea, causing cooling summer sea fog all along eastern Hokkaidō's Pacific coast, with the stretch of highway all the way from Cape Erimo to Hamanaka known as the 'sea fog road'; the eastern Hokkaidō city of Kushiro is said to have 100 days of fog per year. Further north you can witness one of Japan's true winter marvels, as drift ice floats down across the Sea of Okhotsk, collecting in great white expanses all along the island's northeast coast to the tip of the Shiretoko Peninsula, where it is forced south through the narrow Nemuro Strait which separates Japan from Russian-administered Kunashiri Island. This is the southernmost drift ice in the northern hemisphere, and it forms a creaking mass of icy crust on the ocean's surface making it difficult to know where the land ends and the sea begins, with ice-breaking ships plying the frozen waters during the peak drift-ice months of late January to March.

Owing to its cool conditions and many unique ecosystems, eastern Hokkaidō is also home to some of Japan's rarest and most spectacular wildlife, and is probably the most interesting region in north Japan for keen naturalists to explore. Species

MAJOR FESTIVALS IN EASTERN HOKKAIDŌ

Rikubetsu Shibare Festival (陸別しばれフェスティバル, Rikubetsu Shibare Fesutibaru) w rikubetsu.jp/kanko/event/shibare; early February

Akkeshi Sakura & Oyster Festival (あっけし桜・牡蠣まつり, Akkeshi Sakura Kaki Matsuri) w akkeshi-town.jp/kanko/event/Sakura; late May

Nemuro Saury Festival (根室さんま祭り, Nemuro Sanma Matsuri) Mid-September

Akkeshi Oyster Festival (あっけし牡蠣まつり, Akkeshi Kaki Matsuri) w akkeshi-town.jp/kanko/event/kaki; early October

of note include the graceful and back-from-the-brink red-crowned cranes of Kushiro-Shitsugen National Park, the elusive Blakiston's fish owl (the world's largest living owl species), enormous Steller's sea eagles which can often be spotted perched on blocks of sea ice, a rich abundance of marine life (including orcas, sperm whales and sea otters) and one of the most concentrated populations of brown bear in the world on the Shiretoko Peninsula. But even if you are not an avid wildlife watcher, this endlessly fascinating region has much to enjoy, from fantastic food, numerous natural hot springs, a rich cultural and historical heritage and many down-to-earth and friendly people, with plenty to discover no matter what the season.

KUSHIRO

The largest city on Hokkaidō east of Obihiro, Kushiro (釧路; population 165,000) has long been an important port and lies on the edge of the enormous and ecologically unique Kushiro-Shitsugen wetlands. Sheltered by Hokkaidō's central mountain belts, the city receives roughly a third less snowfall than Sapporo, while its coastal location and effects of sea fog mean the city is much cooler than inland areas during the summer months (with an annual mean of only 6°C) – though Kushiro is still far sunnier than the notoriously foggy Kuril Islands further east. The city's natural harbour at the mouth of the Kushiro River is much less prone to icing over during the winter than many others on Hokkaidō, and so the city developed from an important Meiji-era trading post into the most significant port for fishing and industry in the region.

Stepping out of the retro and slightly 1980s Communist China-looking JR Kushiro Station, it is immediately clear that this is a working-class and unpretentious city – a sprawl of unflashy low-rise buildings and long, straight pot-holed roads, with pavements severely iced over in winter. The wide Kita-dōri main street is lined by nondescript office blocks and a smattering of restaurants and shops; walking southwards brings you in 15 minutes to Nusamai Bridge, the city's main landmark which overlooks the harbour, the Pacific Ocean shimmering away on the horizon. The city boasts a number of art galleries and museums, but most use Kushiro as a hub for visiting Kushiro-Shitsugen National Park, or the slightly further away Akan-Mashū National Park.

HISTORY The first Japanese settlers arrived in Kushiro around 1870, setting up a fishing base and trading post with the Ainu at the mouth of the Kushiro River. In July 1899, the harbour was established as an international trading point with ships from the USA and the UK, and because of its mostly ice-free winters the port grew in importance for both trade and fishing. In the 1920s an undersea coal mine was opened just east of the city, and today the mine remains one of the largest coal mines in the country, although its output has decreased in recent decades (but given a brief boost following the March 2011 Tōhoku earthquake and subsequent nuclear meltdown, after which the government increased its reliance on coal-fired power stations).

During World War II, Kushiro was substantially damaged by US bombers, with hundreds of people (mostly civilians) killed.

Kushiro Airport opened in 1961 and was purposely built at an elevated spot slightly away from the coast so as to minimise trouble with sea fog (although this is still sometimes an issue). The Kushiro Ice Arena is home to professional ice hockey – the Nippon Paper Cranes were the many times All Japan Championship and Asia League champions who (rather aptly) folded in 2019 and have now re-emerged as the East Hokkaidō Cranes.

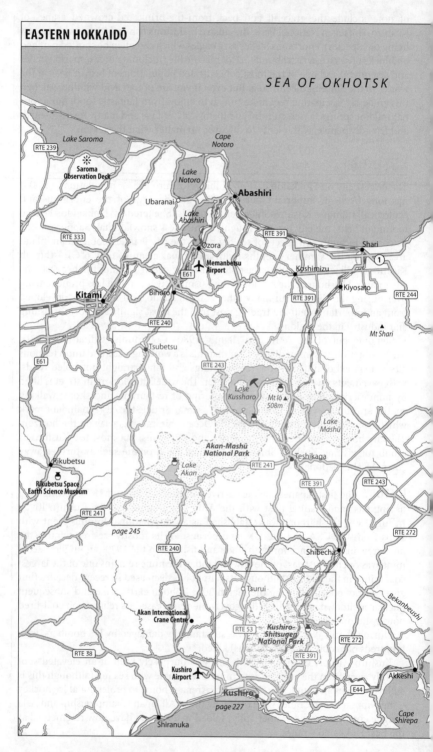

SEA OF OKHOTSK

Lake Saroma

RTE 239

☀
**Saroma
Observation Deck**

*Cape
Notoro*

*Lake
Notoro*

Ubaranai

Abashiri

RTE 333

*Lake
Abashiri*

Ozora

✈ Memanbetsu
Airport

RTE 391

Shari

E61

①

Kitami

Bihoro

Koshimizu

Kiyosato

RTE 391

RTE 244

RTE 240

▲
Mt Shari

Tsubetsu

RTE 243

*Lake
Kussharo*

Mt Iō
508m ▲

*Lake
Mashū*

Rikubetsu

*Akan-Mashū
National Park*

*Lake
Akan*

RTE 241

Teshikaga

🏛
**Rikubetsu Space
Earth Science Museum**

E61

RTE 391

RTE 243

RTE 241

RTE 272

page 245

RTE 240

Shibecha

Bekanbeushi

Tsurui

**Akan International
Crane Centre**

RTE 53

*Kushiro-
Shitsugen
National Park*

RTE 272

RTE 38

RTE 391

RTE 38

**Kushiro
Airport** ✈

Akkeshi

Kushiro

E44

page 227

Shiranuka

*Cape
Shirepa*

page 239

Shiretoko National Park

Mt Iō (Shiretoko-Iō)
1562m ▲

Shiretoko Peninsula

RTE 335

Utoro

RTE 334

RTE 334

Rausu

RTE 335

For listing, see page 240

⊖ **Where to stay**

1   Hotel BOTH

RUSSIA

Kunashiri

Nemuro Strait

Pōgawa Historical Grassland

Shibetsu Science Centre

Shibetsu

Kaiyōdai

RTE 272

Nakashibetsu Airport

Notsuke Peninsula Nature Centre

Todowara

Odaito

Notsuke Peninsula

Nakashibetsu

RTE 224

RUSSIA

Habomai Islets

Betsukai

RTE 243

RTE 221

Hashirikotan

Nemuro

RTE 35

RTE 224

Shunkunitai Wild Bird Sanctuary

Habomai

Lake Fūren

RTE 44

Lake Sunset

Hamanaka

Cape Ochiishi

Kiritappu Wetland Centre

RTE 44

Kiritappu

Biwase

Cape Kiritappu

Cape Azechi

Cape Namida

PACIFIC OCEAN

N

Bradt

0 ——— 10km
0 ——————— 10 miles

8

GETTING THERE AND AROUND

By train Ōzora express trains run six times a day to and from Sapporo (4hrs; ¥9,990), while there are also direct trains north on the Semmo Line to Abashiri (3hrs 15mins; ¥4,070) and east on the Hanasaki Line to Nemuro (2hrs 40mins; ¥2,860).

By air Kushiro Airport (釧路空港; w kushiro-airport.co.jp), also known as Tanchō Kushiro Airport (after the famous local cranes), is 20km northwest of the city and serves the region with daily flights to and from Sapporo (New Chitose and Okadama) and Tokyo (Haneda), plus seasonal flights from Osaka and Nagoya. Airport shuttle buses to central Kushiro (45mins; ¥950) are timed to meet all incoming and outgoing flights; there are also direct airport liner buses to and from Akanko Onsen (1hr 15mins; ¥2,190).

By bus Kushiro Bus (w kushirobus.jp) runs a fairly extensive network of bus routes across the city and to the outskirts, most of which depart from and arrive at JR Kushiro Station.

By road The E30 Dōtō Expressway is the main artery connecting Kushiro to central and western Hokkaidō and loops around the northern edge of the city; from Sapporo it is roughly a 4-hour drive.

TOURIST INFORMATION There is a handy tourist information centre (🕐 09.00–17.30 daily) at JR Kushiro Station with knowledgeable English-speaking staff. Just north of Nusamai Bridge on the corner is a small tourist information office (🕐 09.00–17.00 daily) with maps and pamphlets.

🏠 WHERE TO STAY AND EAT *Map, opposite*

Operating since 1945, **Kushiro Washō Market** (釧路市和商市場, Washō-ichiba; Kuroganechō 13-25; w washoichiba.com/en; 🕐 08.00–17.00 Mon–Sat; $$–$$$$), just a short walk southwest of JR Kushiro Station, is regarded as one of Hokkaidō's top seafood markets. Visitors here can make their own seafood rice-bowl (called *katte-don*) as they walk around – buy a bowl of rice from one of the vendors (the website has a list) and then select what items you'd like to go on top as you peruse the stalls – don't forget to ask for a splash of soy sauce at the end. The market also sells non-seafood products such as fruit and ice cream.

Dormy Inn Premium La Vista Kushiro ドーミーインPREMIUM釧路; 2-chōme 1-1 Kita-Ōdōri; 📞0154 31 5489. In a wonderful location looking over the bridge, river & harbour on Kushiro's main strip, this hotel has simple but comfortable rooms plus complimentary amenities including free ramen & ice cream. There are panoramic city views from the top-floor hot-spring baths. $$$$

Guesthouse Proof Point ゲストハウスプルーフポイント; 4-chōme 4-1; 📞0154 65 5527; w proofpoint946.com. A 15min walk south of the station, this guesthouse has basic dormitory-style rooms or private beds separated by plywood walls & curtain doors. Shared bathrooms, but facilities are good & clean. $$

OTHER PRACTICALITIES

Hokkaido Bank 10-chome 2-1, Kitadori; 📞0154 233111; 🕐 09.00–15.00 Mon–Fri
Kushiro City General Hospital 1-12 Shunkodai; 📞0154 416121

Kushiro Police Station 10-chome 5-1, Kurogane-cho; 📞0154 230110
Kushiro Chuo Post Office 13-chome 2-1, Saiwaicho; 📞0570 034950; 🕐 09.00–19.00 Mon–Fri, 09.00–17.00 Sat, 09.00–12.30 Sun

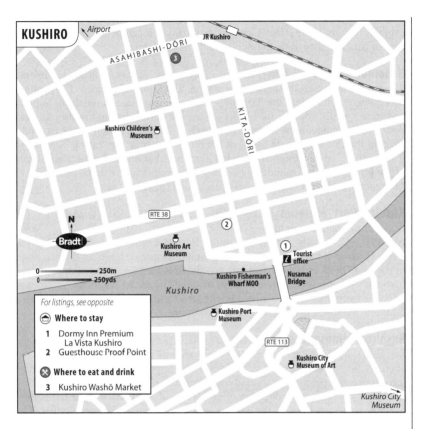

KUSHIRO

Airport

JR Kushiro

ASAHIBASHI-DŌRI

③

KITA-DŌRI

Kushiro Children's
Museum

RTE 38

Bradt

N

②

Kushiro Art
Museum

① Tourist
office

0 ——— 250m
0 ——— 250yds

Kushiro Fisherman's
Wharf MOO

Nusamai
Bridge

Kushiro

Kushiro Port
Museum

RTE 113

For listings, see opposite

Where to stay
1 Dormy Inn Premium
   La Vista Kushiro
2 Guesthouse Proof Point

Kushiro City
Museum of Art

Where to eat and drink
3 Kushiro Washō Market

Kushiro City
Museum

WHAT TO SEE AND DO Most attractions in the city are situated south of the station, so they are listed north to south of there. If you have some time to kill waiting for a train, then the underpass connecting the north and south sides of the station, called the **Kushiro Underground Art Museum** (釧路地下歩道美術館) and decorated with interesting artworks and small paintings, is worth a quick look. Just north of Nusamai Bridge is **Kushiro Fisherman's Wharf MOO** (釧路フィッシャーマンズワーフMOO; Nishikicho 2-4; w moo946.com; ⊕ 10.00–19.00 daily), a large and fairly ugly but popular shopping mall with plenty of restaurants serving local dishes and Japanese staples, plus souvenir shops – the large glass-domed atrium attached to it is an indoor park with trees and benches and is a good place to escape the winter chill.

Kushiro Children's Museum (釧路市こども遊学館; Saiwaichō 10-2; w kodomoyugakukan.jp; ⊕ 09.30–17.00 Tue–Sun; ¥600/120) This strikingly large contemporary glass building about 10 minutes' walk southwest of the station is a great place to while away a few hours if you have children in tow. Across four floors there are loads of interactive exhibits, a giant sandpit, an excellent play area for kids to run and climb around, plus a planetarium (showings four times a day; extra fee of ¥480/120 pp).

Kushiro Art Museum (北海道立釧路芸術館; Saiwaichō 4-1-5; w kushiro-artmu.jp; ⊕ 09.30–17.00 Tue–Sun; ¥460/200) This understated brick-built art museum on the dockside displays the works of local artists and regular temporary exhibitions from some famous international names. It can be found a short walk west of Nusamai Bridge, or 15 minutes south of the station.

Nusamai Bridge (幣舞橋) Nusamai Bridge is Kushiro's main landmark, 15 minutes' walk directly south of the station. This wide bridge spans the Kushiro River where it flows into the harbour – it is a popular place to watch the sunset, and in the winter you can see blocks of ice float downriver out towards the sea. Four female statues on the bridge are said to represent each season. In the riverside park on the east side (north bank) of the bridge is a large sign saying 'Kushiro' – it is another popular photo spot and is illuminated at night. On the south bank of the bridge near the roundabout is a big flower clock and a statue of Takeshirō Matsuura, the famous early explorer of Hokkaidō (page 26).

Kushiro Port Museum (釧路港文館, Kushiro Kōbunkan; Ōmachi 1-1-11; w kushiro-kobunkan.jimdofree.com; ◷ May–Oct 10.00–18.00 daily, Nov–Apr 10.00–17.00 daily; free) The Kushiro Port Museum was built in 1993 as a reconstruction of the former Kushiro Shinbun (newspaper) building; the first floor of the small brick building has a café and displays Meiji-era plans of the city and harbour, while the second floor exhibits materials related to Takuboku Ishikawa, a celebrated young poet who worked briefly for Kushiro Shinbun. The museum is a 3-minute walk west of the bridge on the south side.

Kushiro City Museum of Art (釧路市立美術館; Saiwaichō 4-1-5; w k-bijutsukan. net; ◷ 10.00–17.00 Tue–Sun; entrance fee varies by exhibition, but usually up to about ¥1,000) Located on the third floor of the impressive glass-façaded lifelong learning centre, perched on a small hill 5 minutes' walk south of the bridge, this museum houses a small collection of artworks and hosts well-known temporary exhibits from the likes of the Louvre and some famous Japanese artists. On clear days the views of the harbour and distant mountains from the upper-floor observatory are excellent.

Kushiro City Museum (釧路市立博物館; Shunkodai 1-7; w city.kushiro.lg.jp/museum; ◷ 09.30–17.00 daily, but closed most Mons & irregular Tues; ¥480/110) A full-scale replica skeleton of a woolly mammoth greets visitors at the entrance to this well-appointed museum on the shores of Lake Harutori in the southeast of the city. The first floor is devoted to the natural history of the region, which includes the 38-million-year-old fossilised remains of the Kushiro Tapir, the only known remnant of this species. Other floors focus on Kushiro's human history and archaeology through the Satsumon, Ainu and modern periods; a Chinese-made square mirror dating back to the 1100s was unearthed in the city and is the only one of its kind on Hokkaidō – it probably made its way here through trade with the Okhotsk people. The displays are excellent, although there is hardly any English, but a free multi-lingual audio-guide and text explanations are available from the museum's home page. To reach the museum, take a Kushiro city bus (no. 2, 12, 16, 17 or 55; ¥220) for 15 minutes and get off at Shiritsu-byōin (市立病院) bus stop, from where it is a 5-minute walk through parkland.

KUSHIRO-SHITSUGEN NATIONAL PARK

Situated just to the north of Kushiro and covering 22,070ha, Kushiro-Shitsugen National Park (釧路湿原国立公園) is Japan's biggest wetland and a true wonderland for wildlife lovers. Spread over an area measuring 36km north to south and 25km east to west, this marshy expanse was an enormous ocean inlet until as recently as 6,000 years ago, when it began to silt up and transform into first a delta, then freshwater wetland fed by thousands of underground springs and the many tributaries of the Kushiro River, which meanders towards the Pacific from the volcanic lands of Akan-Mashū National Park further to the north. In the summer the marshes become awash with green and birdsong, while winter sees everything blanketed in snow, with frozen lakes and rivers providing the setting for the elaborate mating rituals of the red-crowned crane, the symbolic bird of Hokkaidō which has somehow managed to bounce back from the brink of extinction.

The eastern side of the park where the Kushiro River flows is lower lying and home to three relict lakes, while the pristine central area is a strictly protected Ramsar site. Much of the park comprises lowland reed marsh, peat bogs and swamp forests of alder, and it is surprisingly hilly in places. There are numerous viewpoints and observatories dotted around the park for spotting wildlife. If you have your own car, then access to these is much easier, but the JR Senmo Line runs through the eastern edge of the park and offers access to the lakes, and buses connect some other locations. During the winter an old-fashioned steam locomotive chugs along the line between Kushiro and Shibecha (page 228), a striking sight and a novel way to see the park. Canoe and kayak tours are another excellent way to appreciate

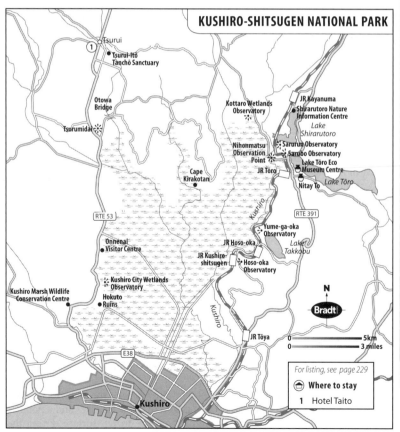

KUSHIRO-SHITSUGEN NATIONAL PARK

Tsurui
Tsurui-Itō Tanchō Sanctuary
Otowa Bridge
Tsurumidai
Kottaro Wetlands Observatory
JR Kayanuma
Shirarutoro Nature Information Centre
Lake Shirarutoro
Nihonmatsu Observation Point
Sarurun Observatory
Sarubo Observatory
Lake Tōro Eco Museum Centre
JR Tōro
Cape Kirakotan
Nitay To
Lake Tōro
RTE 53
Kushiro
RTE 391
Yume-ga-oka Observatory
Onnenai Visitor Centre
JR Hoso-oka
Lake Takkobu
JR Kushiro-shitsugen
Hoso-oka Observatory
Kushiro City Wetlands Observatory
Kushiro Marsh Wildlife Conservation Centre
Hokuto Ruins
Kushiro
N
Bradt
0 ———— 5km
0 ———— 3 miles
JR Tōya
E38

For listing, see page 229
⊖ **Where to stay**
1 Hotel Taito

Two unique sightseeing trains run along the eastern edge of the park to and from Kushiro. Seat reservations are on top of the basic fare, though prices are quite reasonable. You can find more detailed information at w jrhokkaido.co.jp/global/english/travel/tour-train.

The **SL Fuyu-no-Shitsugen** operates in January and February only and runs between Kushiro and Shibecha (basic fare ¥1,290, plus ¥1,680 for compulsory reserved seat ticket). This beautiful black steam train puffs through the snowy landscape and has counter-style window seats in some carriages for unimpeded views and a café-car.

The **Kushiro Shitsugen Norokko** runs from April to October between Kushiro and Tōro (basic fare ¥640, reserved seat ¥840). It is an attractive green engine with one non-reserved carriage, and is a leisurely way to enjoy the scenery.

the environment and get a waterside view of the wildlife – they can usually be done year-round.

GETTING THERE AND AROUND The park is easiest to explore by car, with free parking at nearly every point of interest. Otherwise, the JR Senmo Line connects Kushiro to the eastern side of the park – but be aware that only seasonal sightseeing trains stop at some of the smaller stations. Buses leave from outside JR Kushiro Station to a number of spots in the park, including Kushiro City Wetlands Observatory (ask at the tourist information centre for bus timetables).

WHAT TO SEE AND DO Beginning at Kushiro and first heading northeast, the following points of interest are listed going anti-clockwise in a loop around the national park; all are most easily reached by car, although the first few eastern spots are accessible by train too. Bus tours and guided nature tours are other good options if you don't have your own wheels. Canoe and kayak tours allow you to get closest to nature, while horse trekking is also an option in some areas of the park (such as the pristine and protected Cape Kirakotan) – check at tourist information centres for local operators.

About a 10-minute walk from JR Kushiro-Shitsugen Station is one of the best viewing points in the national park, the **Hoso-oka Observatory** (細岡展望台; ☉ 24hrs daily). This hilltop viewing deck offers expansive views across the wetlands and is notable for its stunning sunsets; there is a car park and visitor centre close by.

Close to the next stop of JR Hosooka Station is the first of the national park's three main lakes, **Lake Takkobu** (達古武湖). A small jetty on the Kushiro River here is used for canoe tours, and on the northeast side of the lake is an auto-camping ground – from there a 2.3km (40mins) nature trail leads through woods, patches of skunk cabbage and up a few steep wooden stairs to **Yume-ga-oka Observatory** (夢ヶ丘展望台), a glorious wood-decked lofty viewpoint with views across the wetlands; if you time it right, you might get an aerial glimpse of a train chugging past too.

If driving, continue northwards on Route 391 (or take the train to JR Tōro Station) to reach **Lake Tōro** (塘路湖), the largest of the three lakes and a popular canoeing spot where ice fishermen camp out on the frozen surface during the winter months. On the western side of the lake is a tiny village with a campsite and the lovely **Lake Tōro Eco Museum Centre** (塘路湖エコミュージアムセンター; w kushiro-shitsugen-np.jp/kansatu/toorodeo; ◷ 10.00–17.00 Thu–Tue; free), a visitor centre with displays on the local ecology. Just across the road is **Nitay To** (ニタイ・ト; w sip.or.jp/~shibecha-museum; ◷ 09.30–16.30 daily; ¥220), a rather good local history museum; the first floor is free to enter, but it's worth paying the entrance fee to see the full collection of stuffed animals, Ainu artefacts and other curiosities. A 600m lakeside trail is a pleasant place to amble and spot wildlife, including ducks, herons and white-tailed eagles which can often be seen soaring overhead. Over in the very northwest corner of the lake are **Sarubo** (サルボ展望台) and **Sarurun** (サルルン展望台) **observatories**; a small parking area and short walking trails climb up to both of these peaceful woodland viewpoints.

Continuing northwards by train or car on Route 391, you will soon arrive at **Lake Shirarutoro** (シラルトロ湖), an important site for migrating geese and swans and a good place for eagle spotting. There is a tiny settlement on the northeast shore, while on the opposite side is the **Shirarutoro Nature Information Centre** (シラルトロ自然情報館; ◷ 09.00–17.00), although it's a bit sad and half-empty.

Route 391 carries on north for Shibecha, but heading back to Lake Tōro you can branch northeast on Route 1060 (known as the Kuchoro-genyatōro-sen; クチョロ原野塘路線), a narrow road which soon becomes a relatively smooth-sailing gravel track. In a few minutes is a small parking area for the **Nihonmatsu Observation Point** (二本松展望地), where a short scramble up a little knoll offers good views across the marshes as far as the factories of Kushiro in the distance. A few minutes' drive further brings you to the **Kottaro Wetlands Observatory** (コッタロ湿原展望台), another fairly lofty viewpoint at the top of some steep wooden stairs.

Turning west on to Route 243 brings you to the arable lands south of the village of **Tsurui** (鶴居; population 2,400), and there are a number of excellent spots here for spotting red-crowned cranes, Otowa Bridge being one of the most famous (page 230). Following Route 53 north leads into the village of Tsurui proper, which boasts a number of accommodation options, including hot-spring baths at the homely **Hotel Taito** (w hotel-taito.com; **$$$**; hot springs ◷ 11.00–22.00 daily).

On the western edge of the marshes are two of the best spots for getting a sense of the wetland environment close up. The first is about 14km south of Tsurui on Route 53 at the **Onnenai Visitor Centre** (温根内ビジターヤンター; ◷ 09.00–17.00 Wed–Mon), from where there are various circular boardwalk courses (10mins–1hr duration) through the marshlands and swamp forests. Continuing a short way further south on Route 53 is the **Kushiro City Wetlands Observatory** (釧路市湿原展望台; ◷ Apr–Sep 08.30–18.00 daily, Oct–Mar 09.00–17.00 daily; ¥480/120 for exhibits), an unusual-looking brick building which boasts a collection of natural history exhibits and views over the forest canopy from the third-floor observation deck. Boardwalks lead for just over 1km (20mins' walk) through the woods to the edge of the wetlands, where a 'satellite observatory' allows for excellent and expansive views across the marshes, before the path loops back to the car park.

Trails also connect to the nearby **Hokuto Ruins** (北斗遺跡; free), where, in this glorious natural landscape, there are wonderful authentic reconstructions of traditional thatched dwellings which you can go inside. A small but good museum (◷ mid-Apr–mid-Nov 10.00–16.00 daily; free) about 10 minutes' walk from the site has earthenware artefacts on display, but no English – there is parking here, and you can borrow bear bells for the walk to the ruins.

The mesmerising courtship dances of the red-crowned crane, and its symbolic status as a species back from the brink of extinction means that nature lovers and photographers from around the world flock to Kushiro-Shitsugen National Park during the winter months to see this natural spectacle – there are few more beautiful sights than these elegant birds leaping and pirouetting in unison in the early morning mists and snow.

The best spots to see them are mostly on the western edge of the park, with the village of **Tsurui** (鶴居) the unofficial tanchō capital of Japan. **Otowa Bridge** (音羽橋) is a short drive south of the village on Route 243 and is one of the most popular locations – on early winter mornings photographers gather on the footbridge here to watch the cranes as they perform elaborate dances in the frigid mists near their roosts in the Setsuri River. There is parking nearby on either side of the river.

A couple of minutes' drive southwest on to Route 53 is **Tsurumidai** (鶴見台), a roadside viewpoint which offers a decent chance of spotting wild tanchō in the snow-covered fields, especially as they flock in at the twice-daily feeding times (usually 09.00 and 14.00).

Over on the eastern edge of Tsurui village is **Tsurui-Itō Tanchō Sanctuary** (鶴居・伊藤タンチョウサンクチュアリ), a wide-open space for viewing cranes, which are enticed to within perfect photographing distance by daily winter feedings (09.00 and 14.00). There is free parking and toilets on site.

Lastly, a 30-minute detour outside the park to the north of the airport on Route 240 leads to the **Akan International Crane Centre** (阿寒国際ツルセンター; ⏰ 09.00–17.00 daily; ¥480/250), a research and feeding facility with crane-related exhibits. The adjacent white-coloured building, part of the crane centre, is the **Tanchō Observation Centre**, and it also offers daily feedings for hundreds of birds through November to March, providing great photography opportunities. There is a small art gallery, a michi-no-eki, a hot spring and a campsite in the area too.

A short distance down the road is the very swanky **Kushiro Marsh Wildlife Conservation Centre** (釧路湿原野生生物保護センター; ⏰ 09.00–16.00 Thu–Tue) which provides care for sick and injured birds of prey, and has an exhibition hall for learning about the area's natural history with some English information too. There are behind-the-scenes tours (13.00 Sat–Sun; conducted in Japanese; ¥800), which allow you to see the birds up close. The centre is accessible by bus from Kushiro.

ALONG EASTERN HOKKAIDŌ'S PACIFIC COAST

CAPE SHIREPA About 40km east of central Kushiro, the little-visited Cape Shirepa (尻羽岬) is a nice detour and short stop-off on the way to Akkeshi, with scenic cliff and ocean views from the wide and gloriously open grassy promontory. To get there, take Route 142 and follow the signs for Chihōmanai (地方学); when you reach the small hamlet turn left at a sign for Shirepamisaki (尻羽岬), and follow the gravel track to a small car park – from there the cape is a short 15-minute walk on a dirt path through rolling clifftop meadows.

AKKESHI Situated around 45km east of Kushiro, Akkeshi (厚岸; population 8,400) is a small fishing town famous for its oysters. The town is sandwiched between Lake Akkeshi, a brackish lagoon where shellfish are harvested, and a broad bay on its west side, with a distinctive red bridge spanning the channel between. The area is part of Akkeshi-Kiritappu-Konbumori Quasi-National Park, and the Bekambeushi River – which feeds into Lake Akkeshi and is considered to be the most pristine major waterway in the whole of Hokkaidō – is home to Japanese huchen (*Parahucho perryi*), also known as the Sakhalin taimen, an enormous type of salmonid, sometimes growing to 2m in length.

In the late 1800s, Akkeshi was the most important settlement on the south coast of Hokkaidō after Hakodate owing to its good harbour and abundant timber, plus natural resources including oysters, fish and seals, and the town grew to include hundreds of Japanese houses, alongside 60 to 70 Ainu huts. Thick sea fogs, however, were a drawback for navigation and hampered its development. But the town remains famous for oysters and clams, while the local Akkeshi single malt whiskies have recently been gaining prominence (w akkeshi-distillery.com). Opposite JR Akkeshi Station at the michi-no-eki (otherwise known as the Akkeshi Gourmet Park 'Conchiglie'), you can sample local oysters and sip drams of whisky both at the same time! Just west of the bridge is **Akkeshi Town Maritime Museum** (厚岸町海事記念館, Akkeshi-chō Kaiji-kinennkan; ⊕ 09.00–17.00 Tue–Sun; free), a decent museum with plenty of maritime artefacts, exhibits and fascinating photos, although next to no English.

If heading east and time allows, then it is worth taking Route 123 south of town and following it along the coast. The road winds past rocky inlets and some glorious viewpoints, including **Cape Namida** (涙岬; about halfway between Akkeshi and Hamanaka), where a short path from the car park leads to an observation deck overlooking dramatic coastal cliffs.

HAMANAKA A small township between Akkeshi and Nemuro, Hamanaka (浜中; population 5,300) itself is a little way inland along the train line and not all that interesting. However, those driving along the scenic coastal road Route 123 will arrive at **Kiritappu** (霧多布), a small fishing settlement on a scenic peninsula of the the same name – it derives from the old Ainu *Ki-ta-p*, or 'place to cut *kaya*' (a kind of silvergrass), and the Japanese name morphed from this, although the kanji characters literally mean 'a lot fog'. The official name of the headland however is Cape Tōfutsu (Tōfutsu-misaki). The town has a hot-spring centre, a handful of restaurants, plus a museum dedicated to the manga and anime Lupin, as the creator Kazuhiko Katō (known by the pen name Monkey Punch) originates from Hamanaka.

Beyond the urban spread, a road loops around the hill-like peninsula, which is green and alive with wildflowers during the summer, and home to some pretty dramatic scenery; from the western side at **Cape Azechi** (アゼチの岬) there are views of cliffs and small islands which are havens for seabirds, while at the far eastern end is **Cape Kiritappu** (霧多布岬), from where a 10-minute walk along a trail from the car park takes you along the narrowing promontory to a lonely viewpoint. There is a basic but nice (and breezy) free campsite just before reaching the cape too.

Immediately inland of Kiritappu is a large wetland area consisting mostly of sphagnum peat bog and an abundance of wildflowers – parts of it are highly protected and regarded as internationally important. The **Kiritappu Wetland Centre** (霧多布湿原センター; w kiritappu.or.jp; ⊕ 09.30–16.00 Wed–Mon) can be found across the marshes on a low hill just off Route 808 (signposted as the 'Marshy Grassland Road'). It has a few decent natural history displays, an information counter (where you can book eco-tours), an on-site café, a kids' playroom full of wooden toys and a shop selling local produce. The second floor offers panoramic views of the wetlands from its large windows, while a short boardwalk course wanders through tussocks of cottongrass and other unusual swamp plants.

A little south on Route 123 is a more extensive 500m-long boardwalk trail at the tiny village of **Biwase** 琵琶瀬; it juts straight and deep into the marshlands and offers the chance of spotting cranes, deer and many types of wildflowers.

Continuing eastwards for Nemuro, you may observe one of the main industries along this part of the coast – *konbu* (kelp) harvesting. Large patches of gravel are used for drying it, with the main season running from July to October. Konbu is commonly used in Japanese cooking and fetches good prices, although the industry is threatened by rising sea temperatures.

NEMURO AND THE NEMURO PENINSULA

Japan's easternmost city, Nemuro (根室; population 25,000) is also one of its most remote, nestled halfway along the windswept Nemuro Peninsula, beyond which just a few kilometres out to sea lie the Russian-administered Habomai Islets at the southern end of the vast Kuril Island chain. This small and gritty city, which has Russian as well as English on its street signs, was founded as a fishery in around 1900 and this remains its key industry today, with the port boasting the largest catches of Pacific saury (*sanma*) in Japan – it is also regarded as one of the best places for sushi in the country.

The peninsula offers some excellent birdwatching opportunities with a number of purpose-built hides dotted here and there, and it is one of the only places in Japan where you have a chance of spotting sea otters. Winters are windy and cold here, as drift ice from the Sea of Okhotsk floats down the channel between Hokkaidō and Kunashiri before passing by this way, and sea fog means conditions remain relatively cool even during summer in this far-flung eastern outpost.

The **Nemuro City Tourist Information Centre** (⏰ 08.00–17.00 daily), is just outside the station and here they will help you with bus schedules, restaurant recommendations and anything else you might need. The website w nemuro-hokkaido.com is also a good source of local information.

GETTING THERE AND AROUND
By train JR Nemuro Station is the terminus of the JR Nemuro Main Line, with the final section between Kushiro and Nemuro called the Hanasaki Line. There are two rapid (Nosappu) trains a day to and from Kushiro (1hr 25mins; ¥2,860) and six local (Hanasaki) trains (2hrs 40mins; ¥2,860). The second-to-last stop, JR Higashi-Nemuro Station, is popular with train buffs as it is the easternmost station in Japan.

By bus Highway express buses operate between Kushiro and Nemuro (2hrs 20mins; ¥2,290). Sightseeing Nosappu bus tours run between May and October (w nemurokotsu.com/tours) and are timed to meet the rapid trains arriving at JR Nemuro Station. Tours loop around the peninsula, stopping at the main points of interest: Course A (2hrs 30mins; ¥3,300/1,650) heads east for Cape Nosappu, while Course B (4hrs 30mins; ¥3,100/1,550) covers the western side (a combined tour ticket is available too). Tickets can be bought from inside the station.

By road Route 44 is the main road between Kushiro and Nemuro with the drive taking about 2 hours. Going via the coastal roads, routes 123 and 142 between Akkeshi and Nemuro take longer but are more interesting.

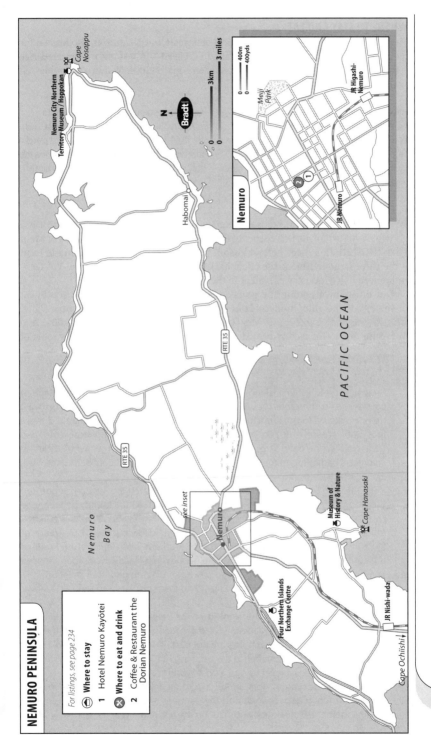

NEMURO PENINSULA

For listings, see page 234

Where to stay
1 Hotel Nemuro Kayōtei

Where to eat and drink
2 Coffee & Restaurant the Dorian Nemuro

Cape Nosappu

Nemuro City Northern Territory Museum / Hoppokan

Habomai

RTE 35

RTE 35

Nemuro Bay

see inset

Nemuro

Four Northern Islands Exchange Centre

Museum of History & Nature

Cape Hanasaki

JR Nishi-wada

Cape Ochiishi

PACIFIC OCEAN

N Bradt

0   3km
0   3 miles

Inset: Nemuro

Meiji Park

JR Higashi-Nemuro

JR Nemuro

0   400m
0   400yds

WHERE TO STAY AND EAT *Map, page 233*

Pacific saury and Hanasaki crab are local delicacies, but Nemuro is also known for its own unique (non-seafood) dish called *escalope* (エスカロップ) – buttered rice topped with sliced pork cutlet and a tasty demi-glace sauce. Nemuro is not blessed with extensive accommodation options.

Hotel Nemuro Kayōtei ホテルねむろ海陽亭; Tokiwachō 2-chōme 24; \ 0153 22 8881; w n-kaiyoutei.co.jp. Unfussy hotel, possibly the best the city has to offer, right in the centre & not far from the station. Kind staff, plain rooms & good food, though the building is showing its age. **$$$**

Coffee & Restaurant the Dorian Nemuro どりあん; Tokiwachō 2-chōme 9; \ 0153 24 3403; ⊕ 10.00–19.30 Wed–Mon. One of the first places to serve Nemuro's local speciality dish *escalope*, this cosy restaurant cooks up warming homely meals & Western-style but still unmistakably Japanese dishes, such as omelette rice. **$$**

WHAT TO SEE AND DO There is not a great deal to do in the city itself, but it is a good base for exploring this corner of the island. On the east side of the city is **Meiji Park** (明治公園), a nice cherry-blossom viewing spot and the site of an old farm – the three large red-brick silos date back to the 1930s are a nod to the Western-influenced dairy industry prevalent in the region.

Out on its own among the grasslands less than 10 minutes' drive southwest of the city is the chic, modern **Four Northern Islands Exchange Centre** (北海道北方四島交流センター; ⊕ May–Oct 09.00–17.00 daily, Nov–Apr 09.00–17.00 Tue–Sun; free). This facility provides a Japan-centric history to the sticky topic of

---

THE KURIL ISLANDS

Known as the Chishima Islands in Japan, this mysterious volcanic archipelago of 56 islands and numerous rocky outcrops stretches for 1,300km from the northeast tip of Hokkaidō to the Kamchatka Peninsula. The Ainu had long inhabited these isles until around the Edo period (1603–1868), when the Japanese extended their claims not only across Hokkaidō but to the Kurils too, with Japanese colonisers beginning to move there in more substantial numbers during the Meiji Era (1868–1912).

In 1855 the Treaty of Shimoda (the first treaty between the Russian Empire and the Empire of Japan) agreed to divide ownership of the Kuril Islands between the two countries. Twenty years later, control of the entire island chain was officially transferred to Japan from the Russian Empire following the 1875 Treaty of St Petersburg, with Japan ceding control of southern Sakhalin in return for all of the Kuril Islands; this treaty was meant to define more clearly the border between Japan and Russia (which had been somewhat murky up until that point). By this time, most of the native Ainu inhabitants had been displaced to Hokkaidō, never to return.

Since World War II and the signing of the Treaty of San Francisco in 1951, the Kurils have been fully administered by Russia. Japan still claims the four southernmost islands, which it says are not part of the Kuril Islands and so are not covered by the agreement, hence the ongoing Kuril Islands dispute between the two countries – they are yet to sign a post-World War II peace treaty.

The name Kuril comes from an Ainu word meaning 'smoky', as the islands are notoriously foggy, especially during the summer (there was once a proposal to rename them the Fog Archipelago). During the rest of the year it is generally windy

the 'Northern Territories', the four southernmost Kuril Islands which have been administered by Russia since the end of World War II but which Japan still claims and sees as part of its territories (see opposite). There are explanations on the history of the islands in Japanese, English and Russian, and some compelling exhibits, so it is a good place to get a (one-sided) handle on the dispute.

From Nemuro, Route 35 runs along the coast for 24km to **Cape Nosappu** (納沙布岬) at the far eastern end of the peninsula, and indeed the country. The eastern-most point of mainland Japan is a suitably desolate place, with a handful of weather-beaten buildings forming the settlement at its tip. Here you can find the **Nemuro City Northern Territory Museum** (根室市北方領土資料館; ⊕ May–Oct 09.00–17.00 daily, Nov–Apr 09.00–17.00 Thu–Tue; free), a facility dedicated to the region's natural and geopolitical history, with more exhibits than the exchange centre, but far less English. The ugly white office-like building next door is called **Hoppokan** (北方館; ⊕ May–Oct 09.00–17.00 daily, Nov–Apr 09.00–17.00 Tue–Sun; free) and is solely dedicated to the territorial dispute, with maps, videos, first-hand accounts from former residents and other exhibits (mostly in Japanese), plus telescopes on the upper floor allowing you to get a close look at the Russian-occupied islands less than 4km away across the water. The big brown arch in the park nearby is said to represent the islands.

From the car park near the tip of the cape it is a short walk to the small, white, stumpy **Cape Nosappu Lighthouse**, the oldest lighthouse on Hokkaidō, dating to 1930. There is a birdwatching hide beyond the lighthouse from where you may spot various seabirds and maybe even minke whales and sea otters, while this spot also

and cold, with long, snowy winters. The northern end of the chain is subarctic and mostly tundra, while the southern end is more temperate with some extensive spruce and larch forests on the larger islands. The Kurils' highest point is the peak of Atlasov at 2,285m; this island at the far north of the chain is a breathtakingly perfect Mount Fuji-esque volcanic cone protruding directly out of the sea – it was lauded for its aesthetic beauty during the Japanese administration of the archipelago.

The four islands closest to the Nemuro Peninsula, Habomai, Shikotan, Kunashiri and Iturup (called Etorofu in Japan), are sometimes referred to as the Southern Kuril Islands and are known in Japan as the 'Northern Territories' (北方領土; *Hoppōryōdo*), where they are also viewed as separate to the Kuril Islands proper. Apart from Habomai, the islands have small human populations (perhaps totalling around 17,000) living in small settlements and serviced by a couple of minor airports. The waters around the islands are extremely rich in marine life owing to the confluence of the Oyashio and Kuroshio currents, and so the area has long been a productive harvesting ground for kelp, salmon, trout, king crab and other species. Prior to World War II, various industries had been established on Kunashiri and Etorofu; these included conifer forestry, mining (gold, silver and sulphur), fishery hatching and some livestock rearing. There are believed to be valuable gas and oil reserves in the area too.

Former Japanese prime minister Shinzo Abe worked to foster good relations with Russia in hope of forging an agreement to return the nearest islands to Japan, but, instead, in recent years Russia has been observed building new military infrastructure on the islands amid the dramatic cooling of Russo–Japanese relations.

witnesses mainland Japan's first sunrise, a not insignificant fact in the 'land of the rising sun'.

Looping back westwards on Route 35 takes you past the fishing port of **Habomai** (歯舞), from where 2-hour nature cruises (w jf-habomai.jp; Nov–Apr at 09.30 & noon daily; ¥7,000/3,000 pp) offer views of rocky islets, marine life and the rugged coast. The most famous spot on the peninsula's southern littoral and just 6km directly south of Nemuro is **Cape Hanasaki** (花咲岬), where you can find a red-and-white lighthouse and the rare and unusual 'Wheel Rocks' (車石). A path from the car park leads to viewpoints where you can observe these wheel-like stone structures, formed from fractured basalt, as waves crash into the shore nearby. If coming by bus, it is a 15-minute walk from the Hanasaki Port bus stop. The small, red-brick **Museum of History and Nature** (歴史と自然の資料館; ◷ 09.30–16.30 Tue–Sun; free) is situated just up the road from the rocks and has some nice displays (including on the little-mentioned Kuril Ainu) plus some rudimentary English.

A little further west and jutting out into the Pacific Ocean at the foot of the peninsula is **Cape Ochiishi** (落石岬). To explore it, follow the road south past Ochiishi Port to where it becomes a gravel track leading to a gate – park here and then follow a trail through forest and wildflowers for 25 minutes to reach an isolated lighthouse on this frequently foggy promontory.

LAKE FŪREN AND NORTH TOWARDS SHIBETSU

LAKE FŪREN To the west of Nemuro Peninsula about 12km drive from Nemuro, Lake Fūren (風蓮湖), a large brackish lagoon, is an important ecological site. In the summer you can see cranes, herons and eagles, while in winter the lake freezes over, and spring and autumn bring large flocks of waterfowl. At the southeast corner of the lake just off Route 44 is a dome-shaped building and budget hotel called **Lake Sunset** (レイクサンセット; w lakesunset.jp) – during the winter here fish are put on the ice to attract eagles and you can pay a small fee to see and photograph the birds up close.

A little further east up the road are the coastal dunes of **Shunkunitai** (春国岱) there is a car park across the small bridge from where you can stroll along boardwalks taking in the sandy shore, forests of Sakhalin spruce and expansive saltmarshes, with a good chance of spotting deer and foxes. The **Shunkunitai Wild Bird Sanctuary** (春国岱原生野鳥公園ネイチャーセンター; ◷ 09.00–17.00 Thu–Tue; free) is a nearby nature centre to learn more about the local ecology.

The northern end of Lake Fūren is notable for the long sandy spit known as **Hashirikotan** (走古丹). It is possible to drive from the turn-off on Route 244 for 13km all the way down to its narrow tip, although the road can sometimes be blocked by drifts of sand or (in winter) snow, and there is nothing much there anyway. About halfway along the spit on the lakeside is a small fishing settlement of the same name, but it is an eerily quiet place any time of year.

BETSUKAI The agricultural town of Betsukai (別海; population 14,000) is located a little inland to the northwest of Lake Fūren, although its jurisdiction stretches a fair way up the coast and includes the tip of the Notsuke Peninsula, its most obvious draw. The small scallop-fishing settlement of **Odaito** (尾岱沼) lies on Route 244 along the coast directly across from the peninsula, and from the harbour sightseeing boats (w aurens.or.jp/~kankousen/; leaving 08.30, returning 10.05; ¥3,200/1,600) sail across Notsuke Bay to Todowara on the Notsuke Peninsula, with a good chance of spotting seals and dolphins on the way, with 30 minutes allowed to stroll around the desolate sandy spit. There are also seal-watching cruises, plus a longer course which sails out into the Nemuro Strait to get a closer look at the nearby, but seemingly ever-out-of-reach, Kunashiri Island.

NOTSUKE PENINSULA (野付半島, Notsuke-hantō) Japan's longest sand spit juts for roughly 26km into the Nemuro Strait and the bay it encloses is a haven for birdlife and coastal flora, with windswept sunken forests, salt, brackish and freshwater marshes, flower meadows and miles of ever-shifting mudflats. The spit (or more correctly, series of spits) is a protected Ramsar site and has been formed by a process called longshore drift, with the hook-shaped spit forming from silt and sediment deposited repeatedly by the action of wind, waves and strong ocean currents. Human habitation of the sand spit dates back to at least the Satsumon period (CE700–1200), judging by archaeological traces of pit dwellings.

A paved road (Rte 950) runs for nearly three quarters of the length of the peninsula and about 15km along is the **Notsuke Peninsula Nature Centre** (野付半島ネイチャーセンター; w notsuke.jp; ⊕ Apr–Sep 09.00–17.00 daily, Oct–Mar 09.00–16.00 daily; free); the ground floor has a shop and café and is the place to book nature tours (including snowmobile-pulled sleigh rides during January to March), while the upstairs has some good nature exhibits. Just beyond the centre, the Todowara boardwalk trail leads in 40 minutes to the tip of a subsidiary spit, or you can instead trundle over there on a tractor bus (¥500/300 one way, tickets available from the small shack outside the centre).

A further 3km on from the nature centre the paved road ends; from there you can walk for 10 minutes to a lighthouse where deer frolic – 5 minutes further along is a nice little birdwatching hide. Kunashiri is clearly visible across the strait and eastern Hokkaidō's distant volcanic peaks provide a beautiful backdrop. Beyond here an increasingly rough gravel track leads all the way to the end of the spit, but it is a very lonely and desolate place indeed. Winters on the peninsula are harsh, bleak and it is almost deserted, while even in the summer there can be a chilling breeze, so wrap up warm whatever the season.

NAKASHIBETSU The largest town in the eastern Hokkaidō region, Nakashibetsu (中標津; population 22,500) is located in the middle of a vast plain of farmlands. The centre of town has plenty of food and accommodation options, and Nakashibetsu Airport (w nakashibetsu-airport.jp) is less than a 10-minute drive north of town. There are daily flights to and from Sapporo (New Chitose) and Tokyo (Haneda), plus seasonal routes to some other cities around Japan.

About a 20-minute drive northwest of the town and an always worthy detour is **Kaiyōdai** (開陽台; ⊕ late Apr–Oct, rooftop all year), a large two-floored observation tower at the crown of a grassy hill, offering a fantastic panoramic vista of the chequerboard plains and distant mountains – the views are so far reaching that it is even claimed that you can see the curvature of the earth from here! Inside is an information centre and a café serving soft-scoop ice cream, while the open-air rooftop is a great place for stargazing (and is accessible all year). There is also a free camping field next door.

SHIBETSU The small harbour town of Shibetsu (標津; population 7,000) halfway along the eastern coast has a few places to stay, including an ocean-side campground near a small beach (swimming prohibited), and the Russian-administered Kunashiri Island is clearly visible across the bay.

8

It's worth detouring to the west side of town for the **Shibetsu Science Centre** (標津サーモン科学館; **w** s-salmon.com; ⊕ May–Oct 09.30–17.00 daily, Feb–Apr & Nov 09.30–17.00 Thu–Tue, closed Dec–Jan; ¥650/200), a large grey building replete with an enormous tower; it functions as a salmon education and breeding facility, and there is plenty to see inside with tanks full of salmonids, hatcheries and other marine creatures and a chance to feed and pet sturgeon.

On the northern edge of the town across the Shibetsu River is **Pōgawa Historical Grassland** (ポー川史跡自然公園, Pōgawa Shiseki-shizenkōen). Humans from the Jōmon to Ainu have been living among these grassy wetlands on the banks of the Pō River for 10,000 years, possibly due to the many literally piping-hot springs here which never freeze even in the depths of winter. This nature park is actually two parks in one – a wetland nature reserve with wooden boardwalks through the marshes, as well as one of Hokkaidō's largest archaeological sites in the nearby forest, where hundreds of Jōmon-era pit dwellings have been excavated. The visitor centre is free to enter, but it's worth paying the ¥330 for entrance to the reconstructed pioneer village and archaeological sites – the fee includes use of rental bicycles to reach the archaeological remains over in the forest about 1km away. At one restored dwelling there you can see rare luminous moss which reflects light with an eerie glow (best in July, but viewable from mid-May to early October).

THE SHIRETOKO PENINSULA

The Shiretoko Peninsula (知床半島) is a rugged, pristine and remote finger of land which protrudes outwards for approximately 70km from the northeast corner of Hokkaidō, separating the Sea of Okhotsk and the Nemuro Strait. It is arguably Japan's wildest wilderness area, with a volcanic and mountainous spine, a deeply forested interior and a mostly undeveloped coastline. Whale-, bird- and bear-watching boat cruises and nature walks are the main activities on the peninsula and should not be missed if the weather is good.

The unique ecosystem here supports Hokkaidō's highest concentration of brown bears (which can often be seen scavenging the shores by sightseers on nature cruises), plus other notable species such as Blakiston's fish owl. The name Shiretoko derives from the Ainu word Sir-etok, which has been translated as 'place where the land protrudes', or the more evocative 'end of the earth', and it certainly feels like a place at the very edge of the known world, with boat tours the only way to reach the tip of the peninsula, as no roads run that far.

A good portion of the peninsula is protected as a national park – **Shiretoko National Park** (知床国立公園) – with most of the same area being listed as a UNESCO Natural World Heritage Site since 2005. During the winter, drift ice in the Sea of Okhotsk envelops the peninsula, before working its way around and into the Nemuro Strait where it floats down towards the Pacific Ocean. The ice brings phytoplankton and makes the waters around Shiretoko a rich feeding ground for marine life, with seals, sea lions, whales, orca and dolphins frequently spotted, depending on the season.

There are two main settlements on the peninsula, Utoro and Rausu, both roughly halfway along each coast and connected by Route 334 and the Shiretoko Pass. Sightseeing boat tours leave from both harbours and are one of the best ways to appreciate the peninsula's topography and wildlife; but if you're feeling adventurous, there are journeys to picturesque lakes, lonely peaks and remote hot springs, with the added thrill of knowing you are deep in bear territory. Shari, though not on the peninsula itself, serves as a gateway to Shiretoko.

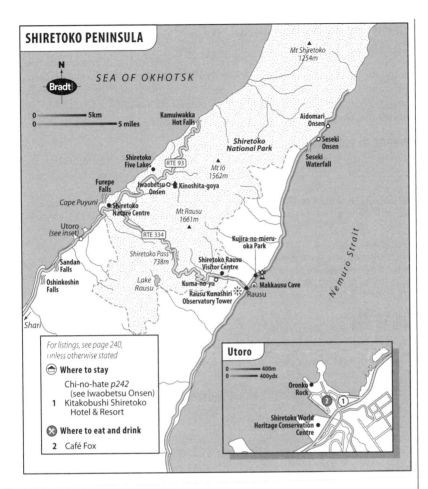

SHIRETOKO PENINSULA

N

Bradt

SEA OF OKHOTSK

Mt Shiretoko
1254m

0 ——— 5km
0 ——— 5 miles

Kamuiwakka
Hot Falls

Aidomari
Onsen

Shiretoko
National Park

Seseki
Onsen

Seseki
Waterfall

Shiretoko
Five Lakes
RTE 93

Mt Iō
1562m

Furepe
Falls

Iwaobetsu
Onsen
Kinoshita-goya

Cape Puyuni

Shiretoko
Nature Centre

Mt Rausu
1661m

Utoro
(see inset)

RTE 334

Kujira-no-mieru-
oka Park

Nemuro Strait

Sandan
Falls

Shiretoko Pass
738m

Shiretoko Rausu
Visitor Centre

Oshinkoshin
Falls

Lake
Rausu

Kuma-no-yu

Makkausu Cave

Shari

Rausu Kunashiri
Observatory Tower

Rausu

*For listings, see page 240,
unless otherwise stated*

🛏 **Where to stay**

Chi-no-hate *p242*
(see Iwaobetsu Onsen)
1   Kitakobushi Shiretoko
Hotel & Resort

✖ **Where to eat and drink**

2   Café Fox

Utoro

0 ——— 400m
0 ——— 400yds

Oronko
Rock

2   1

Shiretoko World
Heritage Conservation
Centre

GETTING THERE AND AROUND

By bus Public transport on the peninsula is fairly infrequent and seasonal. Sharibus (w sharibus.co.jp) operates local services around the peninsula, with altered schedules in summer and winter. The main bus route is between Shari and Utoro Onsen Bus Terminal (60mins; ¥1,650), continuing on to Shiretoko Nature Centre (1hr 10mins; ¥1,800) and Shiretoko Five Lakes (1hr 25mins; ¥2,000). A different bus line connects Utoro and Rausu (50mins, ¥1,380).

From early June to early October and then a short period from mid-January to late March there are direct buses to and from Utoro and Memanbetsu Airport via Abashiri (2hrs; ¥3,500). There are also daily overnight buses to Utoro from Sapporo.

By road Routes 335 and 334 are the main roads on either side of the peninsula; the Shiretoko Pass cuts across and connects Rausu and Utoro in less than an hour, but is closed in winter (early November to late April). Rausu is a 45-minute drive north of Shibetsu, while Utoro is about 35 minutes from Shari or 1 hour 20 minutes from Abashiri. In the winter, the stretch of Route 334 between Shari and Utoro offers some great close-up views of the offshore drift ice.

TOURIST INFORMATION Shiretoko (Utoro) Tourist Information Centre (◷ 09.00–17.00 daily) is located inside the large Utoro-Shirietoko michi-no-eki on the harbourside – it can help with booking boat tours, drift-ice walks and accommodation or transport queries. In **Rausu** there is a tourist information centre (w rausu-shiretoko.com) next to the michi-no-eki there too. The various visitor centres around Shiretoko also have plenty of information and knowledgeable (but not always English-speaking) staff.

🏠 WHERE TO STAY AND EAT *Map, page 239*

The tiny fishing ports of Utoro and Rausu have a number of accommodation and dining options, but Shari is only a 30-minute drive away and offers further choices.

Kitakobushi Shiretoko Hotel & Resort 北こ ぶし知床ホテル&リゾート; Utoro-higashi 172; ☎0152 24 2021; w shiretoko.co.jp. This upscale hotel in Utoro boasts great service, ocean-view rooms with private onsen, a high-quality & varied buffet, & indoor & outdoor public hot-spring baths. Don't miss the lounge, where you can enjoy great views of the harbour while nibbling on free snacks & beer. **$$$$**

☀ **Hotel BOTH** [map, page 222] 106-4 Shari; ☎0152 26 7800; w shiretoko-b.com. Located on the outskirts of Shari about 3km from the station, this Scandanavian-inspired & extremely fancy hostel-like hotel opened in 2023. It features comfortable capsule-style rooms with shared bathrooms, plus more traditional room options. The ground-floor restaurant has a log-burning stove & is a cosy space for guests to unwind. **$**

Café Fox Utoro-higashi 96-5; ☎050 31 888 222; w cafefox.jp; ◷ 11.30–23.00 daily. Casual drinking & dining space down at the harbour in Utoro, serving up *jingisukan* lamb & wild venison. The English-speaking owner also runs boat tours & is a font of local knowledge. **$$**

RAUSU The only settlement of the eastern side of the peninsula, Rausu (羅臼) is a small fishing town looking somewhat forlornly out across the Nemuro Strait towards the Russian-controlled island of Kunashiri. Boat tours leave from the large harbour, where there is also a seafood market.

If you have your own wheels, you can take Route 87 north out of town and drive a fair way up the peninsula, passing sparse fishing settlements and *banya* (fishing huts). Take a right just before the first tunnel and park at the temple – from there it is a short walk to **Makkausu Cave** (マッカウス洞窟) where you can take a look at mesmerising ice stalactites and stalagmites which form during the winter. A little further on about 4km from Rausu, take a narrow road right back on yourself up the hill to **Kujira-no-mieru-oka Park** (クジラの 見える丘公園), a viewpoint near a lighthouse for whale watching in the strait (bring binoculars).

Back on the road, head northwards for 18km to Seseki Waterfall plunging close to the roadside, and carry on for 1km to reach **Seseki Onsen** (瀬石温泉), a natural hot-spring pool on the shoreline which at low tide may be warm enough to bathe in. A short drive further up the road is **Aidomari Onsen** (相泊温泉), a free-to-use no-frills hot-spring bath on the beach, often piping hot. The road comes to an end a little further on at the tiny port of **Aidomari** (相泊), from where bear-watching boats depart in the summer and early autumn.

Heading back to Rausu and venturing inland on Route 334, a quick detour and 5-minute drive up the hill on the south side of the town is **Rausu Kunashiri Observatory Tower** (羅臼国後展望塔; ◷ Apr–Oct 09.00–17.00 daily, Nov–Jan 10.00–15.00 daily, Feb–Mar 09.00–16.00 daily), from where you can get a bird's eye view of Rausu and spy across the waters to those forbidden Russian lands from the tower's indoor and outdoor viewpoints.

Returning to Route 334, it is 3km uphill to **Shiretoko Rausu Visitor Centre** (知床羅臼ビジターセンター; ⊕ Jul–Sep 09.00–17.00 daily, May–Jun & Oct 09.00–17.00 Tue–Sun, Nov–Apr 10.00–16.00 Tue–Sun; free), an excellent modern facility with fantastic exhibits and plenty of English. A short walk behind the centre is **Rausu Geyser** (羅臼間欠泉), one of the rare few geysers in Japan and which erupts with an 8m-high plume every 50–70 minutes – approximate times are posted inside the visitor centre. Close by there is also a campsite, a trailhead for Mount Rausu and the famous **Kuma-no-yu** (熊の湯), a wonderful (and free) outdoor hot spring with separate female and male baths.

About 10km up the winding road is the trailhead for the path to **Lake Rausu** (羅臼湖), a remote body of water reached on a 3–4-hour round trip through pristine marshlands deep in bear country. There is no parking at the trailhead, so you'll have to leave your car at Shiretoko Pass and walk 40 minutes or catch a bus (get off at

HIKING IN SHIRETOKO NATIONAL PARK

The volcanic Shiretoko Range runs most of the length of the peninsula, with three particularly prominent peaks along its spine: **Mount Rausu** (羅臼岳; 1,661m) is the tallest and westernmost, as well as one of Japan's 'famous 100 mountains' and so is the most frequently climbed; **Mount Iō** (硫黄山; 1,562m) – also sometimes called Mount Shiretoko-Iō to avoid confusion with the Mount Iō in Akan-Mashū National Park – lies further along the peninsula and is unusual because it erupts pure molten sulphur (last erupting from December 1935 to October 1936); **Mount Shiretoko** (知床岳; 1,254m) is way out towards the peninsula's tip and rarely visited.

For experienced and well-equipped hikers Mount Rausu is a popular and interesting day hike, with breathtaking 360° views from its rocky summit on a clear day. There are two trails up the mountain. The shorter and most frequently climbed one starts from the northeast side at **Iwaobetsu Onsen**, a hot-spring hotel deep in the forest (page 242) – there is also a much smaller and more basic (no food or bedding) mountain hut called **Kinoshita-goya** (木下小屋; w kinoshitagoya.wordpress.com; ⊕ mid-Jun–Sep; ¥2,500 per night; $) at the trailhead. The hike is 6.6km and takes around 4–5 hours one way (8–9hrs return), passing first through forest, before becoming increasingly steep, rocky and open. There is a longer (9km) and much less frequented trail from the southwest side starting from close to Shiretoko Rausu Visitor Centre. Whichever route you take, the climb is best attempted between June and early October, but expect plenty of snow on the trail if going before mid-July.

A longer and tougher two-day option involves continuing northeast along the range to Mount Iō and finishing at Kamuiwakka Hot Falls; there are a number of small camping spots along the trail and, needless to say, this is one for hardened hikers only.

Also important to keep in mind is that, due to the healthy local bear population, there is an increased (although still unlikely) chance of coming across a bear here compared with other hikes around Hokkaidō – pack a bear bell at the very minimum, check for updates on recent bear sightings at the visitor centres and brush up on advice for bear encounters. Hikers are encouraged to carry bear spray for hikes in Shiretoko too; canisters can usually be rented from the mountain hut or visitor centres for a small fee.

Rausu-ko-iriguchi, 羅臼湖入口), or join a guided tour instead. Be sure to borrow bear spray from the visitor centre beforehand.

The road linking Utoro and Rausu on either side of the peninsula crosses the **Shiretoko Pass** (知床峠), the halfway and highest point on Route 334 at 738m. It is an exceptionally beautiful place at the foot of Mount Rausu, though count yourself lucky if you get clear weather. Owing to the area's topography, conditions may be bright and sunny on one side of the pass, to cloudy and cool on the other. There is a large car park at the top of the pass, but be aware that on account of the brutal winters up here the road has one of the shortest open seasons of any in Japan, usually being closed from early November to late April.

UTORO The small, remote coastal village of Utoro (ウトロ) lies halfway along the Shiretoko Peninsula facing the Sea of Okhotsk, where the whole ocean becomes one frozen white mass in winter. During summer, popular nature-watching boat tours depart from the harbour and offer views of the dramatic coast with its crags and waterfalls, plus the chance of spotting wildlife such as bears and whales. There are a number of operators around the harbour offering various trips including Fox (w cafefox.jp), Aurora (w ms-aurora.com), Godzilla-iwa Kankō (w kamuiwakka. jp) and Dolphin (w shiretoko-kankosen.com); the tourist information centre can help you out too. In the winter you can instead don a dry-suit and join a drift-ice walking tour across the frozen sea – again there are various operators to choose from locally.

Next door to the michi-no-eki is the **Shiretoko World Heritage Conservation Centre** (知床世界遺産センター; ⊕ summer 08.30–17.30 daily, winter 09.00–16.30 Wed–Mon), a marvellous facility with excellent displays about the natural wonders of the peninsula. Visible from afar, **Oronko Rock** (オロンコ岩) is the craggy 60m-tall outcrop at the far end of the harbour; steps lead up to the summit in a few minutes, from where you can get a good aerial view of Utoro, the mountains up behind and the swell of the ocean. There is free parking at the foot of the rock.

A few minutes' drive north of Utoro on Route 334 is **Cape Puyuni** (プユニ岬), a lovely viewpoint overlooking the coast, particularly beautiful at sunset, and then a short distance on from there is **Shiretoko Nature Centre** (知床自然センター; w center.shiretoko.or.jp; ⊕ mid-Apr–mid-Oct 08.00–17.30 daily, mid-Oct–mid-Apr 09.00–16.00 daily exc Wed in Dec), an attractive building with plenty of information on flora and fauna. A short 1km trail leads from there to a good cliff-top viewpoint of **Furepe Falls** (フレペの滝), a waterfall which is fed by groundwater rather than a river and drops almost straight into the sea. The path is gentle and well marked, and you are almost guaranteed to see deer in the grassy lands near the cliffs. You can rent boots from the visitor centre if the ground is snowy.

A turn-off on to Route 93 at the nature centre leads northeast further along the peninsula; in 4km a turning right leads up a river valley for another 4km to **Iwaobetsu Onsen** (岩尾別温泉), a tiny hot-spring spot with two secluded outdoor pools (Sandan-no-yu, 三段の湯; Takami-no-yu, 高見の湯) and a hot-spring hotel called **Chi-no-hate** (知の涯; w iwaobetu.com/onsen; **$$$**). This is also the starting point for hikes to Mount Rausu (page 241).

Back on Route 93 the road scoots along a cliff-top plateau for 5km until a fork left brings you to a big car park at the **Shiretoko Five Lakes** (知床五湖, Shiretoko Goko), a popular beauty spot. Pop into the visitor centre, before strolling along the raised boardwalk and nature trails to admire the picturesque lakes surrounded by forests of fir and oak (guided tours are available in the summer). From here it

is another 11km or so on Route 93 to **Kamuiwakka Hot Falls** (カムイワッカ湯の
滝). Once touted as one of Shiretoko's most secret hidden spots, recent years have
seen many more visitors to this sacred place for the Ainu (which in their language
means the 'Water of the Gods'), where you can climb up a series of four waterfalls in
a naturally heated hot-spring river. The water gets hotter the further upstream you
climb, and the final waterfall used to have a large pool to bathe in, but it has now
been partially filled in due to rockfall.

In previous years, it was possible to explore the falls freely, but since 2023 a
¥2,000 (child ¥500) payment and reservation system is in place (reservations
must be made 1 day in advance; see w goshiretoko.com/kamuywakka for details),
supposedly to improve safety amid the ever-increasing visitor numbers. You can
now either drive or take a shuttle bus (Jul–Aug; 40mins) from Shiretoko Nature
Centre along the gravel road to the falls where you will confirm your reservation
and be given a helmet for the slippery climb up and down the river, accompanied
by a guide. While the reservation and guide system won't be to everyone's taste,
clambering along a warm river in this pristine environment is still a unique

DRIFT ICE

Every year from around late January to early March, drift ice (or sea ice)
arrives on northeast Hokkaidō's Sea of Okhotsk coast, creating a unique
frozen white spectacle rarely seen at these latitudes. Located at roughly
44 degrees north, this coastline is the southernmost limit for drift ice in
the entire northern hemisphere. Known as *ryūhyō* in Japanese, the ice
originates from eastern Russia and the mighty Amur River which flows into
the northwest of the Sea of Okhotsk. Driven southwards by northerly winds
and the East Sakhalin Current, the ice gradually builds up and drifts south
before reaching Hokkaidō's Sea of Okhotsk coast by about late January
or early February. The Shiretoko Peninsula serves as a buffer, drawing ice
to its west to first fill the bay where the city of Abashiri lies. The ice forms
into a white blanket of jostling blocks, rising and falling gently with the
swell. Chunks of ice, ranging from a few centimetres across to ones the size
of cars, scrape along the shore and stretch across the ocean as far as the
horizon. As the ice blocks grind and shunt together, this curious ebbing
frozen landscape creaks and groans, with random ice plinths forming
perches for sea eagles and seals. As the bay fills up, ice eventually drifts
eastwards around the tip of Shiretoko, and is then carried southwards
through the narrow Nemuro Strait and down Hokkaidō's eastern coast.
But the amount of ice can vary greatly from year to year, and has certainly
decreased in recent times. Ice used to drift right around Hokkaidō's eastern
seaboard and then out west, beyond Kushiro on the island's southern coast,
but this is rarely, if ever, seen now.

As well as providing refuge for animals on the surface, the ice is a haven for
underwater life too, notably the tiny clione (also known as sea angels), as well
as other rich micro-plankton which feeds a larger chain of animals including
fish, seals, whales, orca, sea lions and seafaring birds of prey. Icebreaker tours
are popular ways to view the ice and wildlife up close, with boats leaving
from Abashiri and further up the coast at Monbetsu throughout the winter
season; while donning a dry suit and joining a drift-ice walking tour is the
most immersive way to see, feel and hear the ice up close.

experience. It can be very slippery, though, so care is needed. Further downstream where the river reaches the sea it cascades at another waterfall, but this is only visible from tour boats.

A short drive from Utoro on Route 334 heading for Shari you will pass a couple of waterfalls; **Sandan Falls** (三段の滝) is a series of three small waterfalls which can be viewed from an arched bridge next to the road, but the much more impressive **Oshinkoshin Falls** (オシンコシンの滝) a little further on is a 30m-tall waterfall which can be observed from a platform at the end of a short path. Both have roadside parking nearby.

SHARI A small, unpretentious seaside town with views of the distant imposing mountain of the same name, Shari (斜里; population 10,000) serves as a gateway to the Shiretoko Peninsula. The fancy refurbished train station is called Shiretoko-shari and lies on the JR Senmo Line between Kushiro and Abashiri. There is not a great deal to see or do here, but it can serve as a decent base for exploring the region, particularly if you have a car, as accommodation and restaurant options are a little spread out. A 20-minute walk or 5-minute drive from the station is **Shiretoko Museum** (斜里町立知床博物館; w shiretoko-museum.jpn.org; ⏰ 09.00–17.00 Tue–Sun; ¥300/free), an extensive facility with lots of stuffed animals and exhibits on the natural and human history of the region, enjoyable even though it lacks English. A few blocks southeast is an attractive old Western-style building called the **Kita-no-Alpes Museum** (北のアルプ美術館; w alp-museum.org; ⏰ Jun–Oct 10.00–17.00 Wed–Sun, Nov–May 10.00–16.00 Wed–Sun; free), dating back to the founding of the town. Once a family home, it now functions as a kind of museum dedicated to a number of well-known Japanese scholars, with displays of their letters, photos, documents and paintings – even if it's all indecipherable, you can relax with a cup of tea and sip in the nostalgic atmosphere.

AKAN-MASHŪ NATIONAL PARK

One of Japan's most beautiful national parks, Akan-Mashū (阿寒摩周国立公園) is a stunning landscape of steaming volcanoes, verdant boreal forests and picturesque lakes in the heart of eastern Hokkaidō. The area has been entirely shaped by an intense period of volcanic activity which occurred between 200,000 and 30,000 years ago, when great volcanoes formed and collapsed leaving behind the craters and lakes we see today, with subsequent volcanoes and other unusual geological activity such as bubbling mud pools and sulphur springs also distinctive features.

The area around Lake Akan became one of Japan's earliest national parks in 1934, before being expanded to include the Lake Mashū area, and it is best to think of the park as comprised of eastern (lakes Kussharo and Mashū) and western (Lake Akan) areas – they are connected by the scenic 35km long and winding Route 241, a high-pass road which remains open throughout the winter. The closest large town to Akan-Mashū is Teshikaga, just beyond the eastern edge of the national park. There is a limited public transport network in the region, but as no trains or buses connect the eastern side of the park to the west, a car is preferable for thorough explorations.

GETTING THERE AND AROUND
By train The eastern side of the park is served by the JR Senmo Line between Kushiro and Abashiri, with stops at JR Mashū Station (in Teshikaga), Biruwa and Kawayu Onsen – be aware that the latter two stops are rural stations with limited amenities close by, although there are regular buses between JR Kawayu Onsen

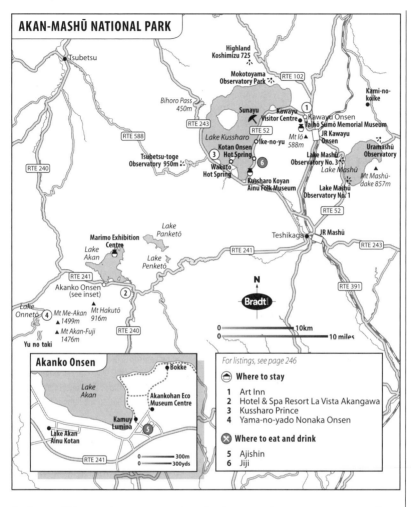

AKAN-MASHŪ NATIONAL PARK

Tsubetsu

Highland Koshimizu 725

Mokotoyama Observatory Park
RTE 102

Bihoro Pass 450m

Sunayu
Kawayu Visitor Centre
Kawayu Onsen
Kami-no-koike
Taihō Sumō Memorial Museum

RTE 243
RTE 52
Mt Iō 588m
JR Kawayu Onsen

Lake Kussharo
Ike-no-yu
RTE 588

Kotan Onsen Hot Spring
Uramashū Observatory

Tsubetsu-toge Observatory 950m
Wakoto Hot Spring
Lake Mashū Observatory No. 3
Lake Mashū

RTE 240
Kussharo Koyan Ainu Folk Museum
Mt Mashū-dake 857m

Lake Mashū Observatory No. 1

RTE 52

Lake Panketō
Teshikaga
JR Mashū

Marimo Exhibition Centre
Lake Akan
Lake Penketo
RTE 241
RTE 243

RTE 241
N
RTE 391

Akanko Onsen (see inset)
Bradt

Lake Onnetō
Mt Me-Akan ▲1499m
Mt Hakutō 916m
0 ———— 10km
0 ———— 10 miles

Mt Akan-Fuji ▲1476m
RTE 240

Yu no taki

Akanko Onsen

Lake Akan
Bokke

Akankohan Eco Museum Centre

Kamuy Lumina

Lake Akan Ainu Kotan

RTE 241
0 ———— 300m
0 ———— 300yds

For listings, see page 246

🛏 **Where to stay**
1 Art Inn
2 Hotel & Spa Resort La Vista Akangawa
3 Kussharo Prince
4 Yama-no-yado Nonaka Onsen

✕ **Where to eat and drink**
5 Ajishin
6 Jiji

Station and Kawayu Onsen proper. From Kushiro it is 1 hour 15 minutes to or from JR Mashū Station; Abashiri is 1 hour 50 minutes away.

By bus Akan Bus (w akanbus.co.jp) operates bus services in the area; schedules are seasonal and often infrequent, so check at a tourist information centre for clarification. From JR Kawayu Onsen Station there is a year-round service to Kawayu Onsen (10mins; ¥290). A summer-only service operates to Lake Mashū and Lake Kussharo; and there is a winter-only service from JR Mashū Station to Lake Kussharo and Kawayu Onsen. The year-round Mashūko Line runs between JR Mashū Station and Lake Mashū (25mins, ¥570).

A two- or three-day (¥2,000/3,000) 'eco bus pass' is available for unlimited use of the area's buses (w eco-passport.net). There are also one-day 'Pirika' sightseeing bus tours covering the three main lakes costing ¥4,000–5,600.

On the west side of the park the Akan Line runs year-round between Kushiro and Akankohan (2hrs; ¥2,750) and Kitami Bus (w h-kitamibus.co.jp) runs a service between Kitami and Kushiro, stopping at Akanko Onsen (1hr 30mins; ¥2,100).

8

By road Akan-Mashū is about a 350km (5hrs) drive from Sapporo, 80km (90mins) north of Kushiro, or 70km (1hr 20mins) south of Abashiri.

By air The park is within easy driving distance of the region's three airports. If using public transport there are direct buses from Kushiro Airport to Akankohan (1hr 15mins; ¥2,190) or you can take a train from Kushiro. From Memanbetsu Airport there are buses to Kawayu Onsen (via Bihoro) or you can take a train from Abashiri. From Nakashibetsu Airport there are buses to Nakashibetsu, where you can change for buses to Teshikaga and other towns.

TOURIST INFORMATION Opposite New Akan Hotel in Akanko Onsen, the large three-storey green-roofed building with a wooden bear head above the door is the tourist information centre (⏲ 09.00–18.00 daily); they can help with booking activities and hotels. The tourist information centre in Kawayu Onsen (⏲ 09.00–18.00 Tue–Sun) has a few English pamphlets but is of more limited use.

WHERE TO STAY AND EAT *Map, page 245*

Art Inn 3-2-40 Kawayu Onsen; e onsengold2@ gmail.com; w artinn.asia/english/onsen/index. html. Art installations litter both inside & out this art gallery-cum-hotel, but one of the main draws is that each of its quirky rooms has a private hot-spring bath. **$$$$**

Hotel & Spa Resort La Vista Akangawa カムイの湯ラビスタ阿寒川; 3-1 Akanchō, Okurushube; ☏0154 67 5566; w hotespa.net/ hotels/akangawa. A fancy hotel in a secluded riverside spot on the outskirts of Akanko Onsen. Some rooms have their own private onsen. Despite the top-end prices, food & service are not quite 5-star, but if you're looking for peace & quiet it doesn't get much better. **$$$$**

Kussharo Prince Hotel 屈斜路プリンスホテ ル; Kussharo Onsen, Teshikaga; ☏0154 84 2111; w princehotels.co.jp/kussharo. Grand, slightly retro lakeside hotel with restaurants, a large hot spring & other facilities. Most of the spacious, unfussy rooms have excellent lake views. **$$$**

Yama-no-yado Nonaka Onsen 山の宿野中 温泉; 159 Moashoro, Ashoro; ☏0156-29-7321; w minkoku.com/yado/top.php?yado_id=7. This is 1 of 2 accommodation choices at the trailhead for Mt Me-Akan, & within walking distance of the beautiful Lake Onnetō. Offers simple tatami rooms, good food & nice rustic sulphur-infused indoor & outdoor hot springs. **$$$**

Ajishin 味心; 1-3-20 Akanchō, Akanko Onsen; ☏0154 67 2848; ⏲ 11.00–13.00 & 18.00–22.00 daily. This great little izakaya in the heart of Akanko Onsen has a cosy atmosphere, generous portions & friendly hosts. Plenty of Hokkaidō specialities are served up including venison & butter scallops, along with staples such as curries, fried chicken & noodle dishes. The Mari Mojito is their refreshing signature drink & a nod to the famous local algae balls. EM. **$$$**

Jiji ぢぢ喫茶; 3-11-1 Kussharo; ☏0154 84 2808; ⏲ 10.00–17.00 daily, irregular holidays. Lovely homely vibes at this lakeside café just across from Kotan Onsen hot spring. It has a limited menu, but the tasty homemade pizzas use locally sourced ingredients & the coffee is good. The friendly owners also run excellent low-key & flexible canoe tours on Lake Kussharo & the Kushiro River. **$$**

Poppotei 1-7-18 Asahi, Teshikaga; ☏0154 82 2412; w poppotei.wixsite.com; ⏲ 10.00–19.00 daily, closed irregularly. Conveniently located next to JR Mashū Station, this welcoming & minimalist-style restaurant serves up quick bites & meals, coffee, dessert & beer, although the specialities are its succulent Mashū pork rice-bowl & Yukimi ramen which is made with a squirt of local milk. The delicious vegetable curry is vegan-friendly. **$$**

WHAT TO SEE AND DO The main draws to the park are its hot springs, hiking and views, while lake-related activities such as boating and fishing are popular too.

Teshikaga The principle town of the region, Teshikaga (弟子屈; population 6,600) derives its roots from the old Ainu settlement name of Tekkaka, although remains from as far back as the Jōmon period have been found in the area. Early Japanese pioneers began mining the sulphur deposits at Mount Iō from 1887 until much of it was depleted, with the mines closing just nine years later, but around the same time more settlers arrived to begin agricultural activities including dairy farming, which remains a key local industry to this day. Over 60% of the township lies within the national park, so it is a good base for exploring the area, with a station and seasonal buses to Lake Mashū and Lake Kussharo. There is not a great deal to do within the town itself, however, and not even all that many places to stay or eat, although Teshikaga ramen has a good reputation and is made using local ingredients.

Lake Mashū Situated northeast of Teshikaga, Lake Mashū (摩周湖, Mashūko) is a stunningly picturesque crater lake which many consider to be the most beautiful lake in Japan, and which is said to have the clearest water of any lake in the world. Its deep, blue waters, which in winter sometimes freeze over completely, are almost untouched by human influence, as the surrounding crater rim slopes down so steeply and deeply to the lakeshore that there is no easy access – unusually, no rivers flow into or out of the lake either. A small island called Kamuishu forms a speck on the surface, although is not always visible due to thick fogs which can often blanket the lake entirely. There is good hiking to be had up to the summit of Mount Mashū-dake (Kamuinupuri) on the eastern side of the lake (page 248).

A couple of observation points for appreciating the outstanding beauty of the place are dotted around the lake. **Lake Mashū Observatory No. 1** (摩周湖第一展望台) is the most popular and the closest to Teshikaga, less than a 10-minute drive away on Route 52. From the large car park (May–Nov ¥500/car, Dec–Apr free) there, it is a short walk to the observation deck – a great stargazing spot – and there are also toilets and a shop/café, which had a bit of a makeover and reopened in 2022 as Mashū Kamuy Terrace (⊕ 08.30–17.00 daily). There are two or three buses a day to the observatory from JR Mashū Station.

Overlooking the west side of the lake 3km further on is **Lake Mashū Observatory No. 3** (摩周湖第三展望台), a free observation point which commands simply jaw-dropping and wide-reaching views when the weather is clear. There is parking just across the road, but no other facilities. The twice-daily, but summer-only, Kussharoko Line bus route stops at both viewpoints. A second observation deck used to exist between one and three, but it is out of use.

Over on the northeast side of the lake, the **Uramashū Observatory** (裏摩周展望台) offers a different perspective from its wooden viewing deck, but with usually far fewer people. There is parking and toilets, and it is a worthwhile stop-off if you happen to be travelling between Nakashibetsu and Kiyosato – the turn-off is clearly signposted and is just before/after the long tunnel on Route 1115, from where it is a 3km drive to the viewing deck at the end of the road.

In the same vicinity about 10 minutes north and just off Route 1115 is a very pretty little pond with startlingly clear, blue water called **Kami-no-koike** (神の子池; 'child of god pond'). The name comes from the fact that the water derives from underground directly from its source of Lake Mashū, the 'god'. There are boardwalks through the woods at the edge of the pond, allowing you to peer down and observe its mysterious depths, where fish swim and dead trees lie in suspended animation. The pond is a 1-minute walk from the parking area 2km along the rough and narrow unpaved forest road.

Akan-Mashū National Park is home to a number of excellent hiking trails, the best of which are listed here.

The Yamap hiking app or Yama-to-kōgen Map No. 1 Rishiri·Rausu (山と高原地図No.1利尻・羅臼) are good map options.

MOUNT MASHŪ-DAKE Also known by its Ainu name of Kamuinupuri, Mount Mashū-dake (摩周岳) is a 857m-tall mountain on the eastern shore of Lake Mashū; it offers fine views of the lake and makes for a good half- or full-day hike. The trailhead is at the car park of Lake Mashū Observatory No. 1, from where it is 7.2km to the summit and takes around 5–6 hours return. There is another approach to the peak from the east, via the wildflower haven of Nishibetsu-dake (西別岳; 799m); the trailhead starts at the Nishibetsu mountain hut which can be reached on an unpaved forest road off Route 150; the hike is about 7.5km one-way.

MOUNT O-AKAN The distinctive conical volcano to the northeast of Lake Akan is Mount O-Akan (雄阿寒岳; 1,370m), another satisfying half-day undertaking. The trailhead is at the end of a short gravel road just off Route 241 near the southeastern corner of Lake Akan. There are lots of steady climbs and a bit of up-and-down over the 6.7km to the summit, which sits on the rim of the vegetated crater – allow at least 6 hours to get there and back.

Kawayu Onsen A small hot-spring village, Kawayu Onsen (川湯温泉) nestles not far from the smoking sulphur-scapes of Mount Iō. The hot springs here are known for their sulphuric and strongly acidic waters – don't bathe for too long! Aside from the baths at various ryokan, you can freshen up at the free footbaths near Kawayu Visitor Centre; and the Onsengawa (hot-spring river) literally steams as it winds through town – a riverside walking path lets you see it up close. Kawayu Shrine has a rare hot-water *chōzuya* (hand-cleansing basin) and is lit up at night. It takes about an hour to walk to Kawayu Onsen (via Mt Iō) from JR Kawayu Onsen Station.

The first stop for most is **Kawayu Visitor Centre** (川湯ビジターセンター; w kawayu-eco-museum.com; ⊕ Apr–Oct 08.00–17.00 Thu–Tue, Nov–Mar 09.00–16.00 Thu–Tue; free). Formerly known as Kawayu Eco Museum Centre, this quietly impressive and stylish facility among the greenery on the western edge of the village has good exhibits, with ample English, about the geological and natural history of the region, and there is also a pleasant café (⊕ 11.00–15.30) on the upper floor. If you plan to do any hiking in the area, then you can rent bear spray and snowshoes here too. From the visitor centre you can walk along the 2.5km Tsutsujigahara nature trail which winds through meadows of alpine flora (including Japan's largest expanse – 100ha – of marsh Labrador tea shrubs, which bloom in a flurry of white flowers from mid-June to late July) to reach Mount Iō in about 1 hour.

At the southern edge of the village is the **Taihō Sumō Memorial Museum** (大鵬相撲記念館; w masyuko.or.jp/sumo; ⊕ 09.00–17.00 daily; ¥420/200), a museum dedicated to Kōki Taihō, a legendary sumo wrestler born in 1940 who rose to become *yokozuna* (the highest rank in sumo) at the young age of 21 and held the record for most tournament victories for many years. He is celebrated as Teshikaga's most famous son (just overlook the fact that he was born in Sakhalin to Japanese and Ukrainian parents, before relocating to Hokkaidō as a child). The museum has

MOUNT ME-AKAN AND MOUNT AKAN-FUJI Mount Me-Akan (雌阿寒岳; 1,499m) is the tallest peak in the national park, one of the hyakumeizan ('100 famous mountains'; page 81), and is a highly active stratovolcano, constantly spewing steam and gas. Together with O-Akan (the 'male' mountain), Me-Akan is considered the 'female' of the pair, although its closest satellite peak is the striking cinder cone of Mount Akan-Fuji (阿寒富士; 1,476m) a little to the south. The upland volcanic scenery is quite spectacular and there are a number of approaches; the most popular trail starts at Nonaka Onsen and heads through the forest up to the craggy crater rim in 3.2km. From there you can either retrace your steps, or instead loop around to Akan-Fuji (which is a 1.1km detour from the main trail) before descending to Lake Onnetō – from the campsite it is another 40 minutes back to Nonaka Onsen. The whole loop takes about 6 hours (add another hour for Mt Akan-Fuji).

There is another longer approach (6.4km) to Me-Akan from a car park on the Furebetsu forest road, way over near Mount Hakutō to the northeast.

MOUNT HAKUTŌ South of Akanko Onsen and beyond the top of the ski resort, Mount Hakutō (白湯山; 916m) offers views of Lake Akan, and has geothermal hotspots which allow tropical mosses to grow here and there. There is a decent viewpoint a short walk from the car park, but the best one below the summit of Mount Hakutō can be reached in just over 1 hour by following a nature trail from the ski resort, passing by some bubbling *bokke* mud pools along the way.

plenty of photos, video footage and paraphernalia for sports fans to enjoy, but don't expect much English.

About 2km south of Kawayu Onsen you can find the amazingly charred and rocky landscape of **Mount Iō** (硫黄山, Iōzan). Known as Atosanupuri in Ainu, meaning the 'naked mountain' – and not to be confused with the Mount Iō on Shiretoko – this volatile little volcano spews gases and steam from over 1,500 fumaroles, and this was the site for sulphur mining which brought railroads and some prosperity to the area in the early pioneer days. From the car park (¥500 parking ticket also valid for parking at Lake Mashū Observatory No. 1) and adjacent visitor centre, a few short trails weave among the otherworldly and odour-filled sulphur fields to see this remarkable geological activity close up. If arriving on foot, Iōzan is a 20-minute walk from JR Kawayu Onsen Station, or 45 minutes from Kawayu Onsen.

Lake Kussharo
Lake Kussharo (屈斜路湖) is the largest crater lake in Japan and the sixth biggest lake of any type, measuring 57km around. In the winter it almost completely freezes over, apart from at spots where thermal vents keep the ice away, so enticing flocks of regal whooper swans to gather – there are a number of free outdoor hot-spring pools dotted around this colossal lake, most of which are maintained voluntarily by locals. An island called Nakajima sits solitarily near the lake's centre, and an outflow in its southeast corner is the head of the Kushiro River.

On the lake's southern shore is the **Wakoto Peninsula** (和琴半島), a fairly substantial protrusion of land with woodland trails for *shinrin-yoku* (forest-bathing), and at its base is a fairly large and free (and piping hot!) outdoor hot-spring pool called Wakoto Hot Spring (和琴温泉露天風呂), with a basic changing room nearby.

Route 52 hugs most of the eastern side of the lake, and in its southeast corner is a tiny lakeside hamlet home to the **Kussharo Kotan Ainu Folk Museum** (アイヌ民族資料館; ⏰ 09.00–17.00 daily, closed Dec–early Apr; ¥420/280), a small museum packed with Ainu-related exhibits and a bit of English. Close by, right on the shore of the lake is **Kotan Onsen Hot Spring** (コタン温泉露天風呂), a wonderfully situated small and free hot-spring pool, also with a simple changing room. It (and you) will be rather exposed, so most people opt to wear a swimsuit – in winter you can watch swans bobbing close by on the lake as you bathe.

A 5-minute drive north is **Ike-no-yu** (池の湯), another pond-like outdoor hot spring in a very pretty spot directly on the lakeshore. This one is not usually boiling hot, and as with most of these rustic wild onsen, there may be a bit of algae and general outdoor grime to contend with. Some 3km further north on Route 52 is **Suna-yu** (砂湯; w sunayu.teshikaga.asia), a unique lakeside beach where you can make your own little sand bath – as you dig deeper the sand gets warmer and hot-spring water seeps up. Swans also gather here during the winter. There is a large car park, toilets, a rest-house (selling ice cream and light meals, and with swan-shaped pedalos for rent), plus a lakeside campsite too.

Over on the west side of the lake are two notable passes. The first, **Tsubetsu Pass** (津別峠), can be reached in about 20 minutes by taking the narrow and winding Route 588 from just past the Kussharo Prince Hotel, then turning north following the signs for the Tsubetsu-tōge Observatory (津別峠展望台; ⏰ 09.00–19.00 daily). This castle-like viewing tower deep in the mountains at about 950m altitude is famous for its views of the *unkai* (sea of clouds), best seen in the early morning. Further north on Route 243 between Teshikaga and Bihoro is the **Bihoro Pass** (美幌峠), the most well-known pass in the region, even though it is about 500m lower than Tsubetsu Pass. It sits on an exposed ridge high above the western shore of the lake and it is a lovely (if twisty) drive up from either direction. Adjacent to the large car park is a michi-no-eki rest-house with a restaurant and shop, and the main viewpoint is a short walk uphill – it is worth the effort as the panoramic views of the lake and surroundings are nothing short of spectacular.

Lastly, on the north side of the lake along Route 102 are a couple of popular viewpoints: **Mokotoyama Observatory Park** (藻琴山展望駐車公園) is nothing more than a parking spot but with excellent expansive views of Lake Kussharo; while a few minutes further north is **Highland Koshimizu 725** (ハイランド小清水725; ⏰ Jun–Aug 09.00–17.00 daily, May & Sep 09.00–16.00 daily, Oct 09.00–15.00 daily, closed Nov–Apr), an observation deck offering panoramic views, plus a shop and restroom facilities. From here it is a very pleasant 1-hour hike on clearly marked paths up to the summit of Mount Mokotoyama (藻琴山, 1,000m) for even more expansive views.

Lake Akan

The western side of the national park is centred around Lake Akan (阿寒湖) and the various volcanoes that surround it. The lake itself is another beautiful crater lake, best known for the curious marimo green algae balls found there (see opposite), with an Ainu marimo festival held every October. The eastern side of the lake is dominated by Mount O-Akan, a shapely volcano which can be climbed in a few hours (page 248), and two more minor lakes (Panketō and Penketō) sit in its shadow. Its sister peak, Mount Me-Akan is part of the spectacular volcanic landscape to the southwest.

The tiny hot-spring resort town of **Akanko Onsen** (阿寒湖温泉; also known as Akankohan, 阿寒湖畔) sits on Lake Akan's southern shore and is the only significant settlement in the area, with bus connections to Kushiro and Kitami.

There are a handful of shops, restaurants and footbaths around town, plus a decent choice of hotels and ryokan, many of which have their own hot-spring baths for staying guests and visitors. Boat cruises (w akankisen.com; ⊕ mid-Apr–Nov 08.00–16.00 daily; ¥2,000/1,040 inc entry to Marimo Exhibition Centre) on the lake leave from the jetty, and take around 85 minutes, stopping off at the small **Marimo Exhibition Centre** on Chūri Island (チュウリ島). In the winter when the lake freezes over, you can partake in a whole range of activities on its frozen surface, ranging from ice-fishing in tents to ice-skating and snowmobiling – tickets can be purchased from the small shack at the lakefront operated by Ice Land Akan (アイスランド阿寒; w koudai-akan.com; ⊕ Jan–Mar).

On the eastern side of town is the **Akankohan Eco Museum Centre** (阿寒湖畔エコミュージアムセンター; ⊕ 09.00–17.00 Wed–Mon), a nice and informative nature centre to learn all about the lake's flora and fauna, with plenty of (stuffed) animal displays and real marimo algae balls bobbing about in tanks; it also offers snowshoe and ski rentals in winter. Nearby, gentle walking trails weave through the forest in 15 minutes to the curious site of bubbling mud pools called *bokke* (ボッケ), a name derived from the popping sound of the mud bubbles. In the evenings, **Kamuy Lumina** (w kamuylumina.jp; ⊕ mid-Apr–mid-Nov approx 18.00–21.00 daily; ¥3,500/1,700) runs unique hour-long night walks which involve lights, sound and projection mapping to tell stories from Ainu mythology as you wave a light stick and follow a course through the forest to the bokke – tickets can be purchased at the boat jetty in Akanko Onsen or at most hotels.

On the west side of the town is **Lake Akan Ainu Kotan** (阿寒湖アイヌコタン; w akanainu.jp/en), a single gently sloping street lined with quaint little shops selling and showcasing Ainu crafts and souvenirs. The whole place feels a bit kitsch and touristy, but not overly so. At the top of the street is a small and well-appointed **Ainu museum** (⊕ May–Nov 09.00–17.00 daily, Dec–Apr 09.00–17.00 Sat–Sun),

GREAT BALLS OF ALGAE

Lake Akan is one of the few places in the world where marimo can be found. These velvety balls of green algae can reach a diameter of +30cm and collect in great numbers in the sunniest shallows of the lake.

The very same algae is in fact found in cold freshwater lakes in some other locations around Japan and other places in the northern hemisphere, but it is only here where it grows to such a remarkably large and round size. This is believed to be because of some very particular and unique conditions at Lake Akan; the water is rich with minerals derived from magma; the shallow (2–3m) and clear waters (particularly around Chūri Island at the north end of the lake) allow marimo to absorb plenty of sunlight for photosynthesis; and perhaps most importantly, strong winds and underwater springs cause a constant flow of water and force the algae to rotate and form into spherical shapes, their movement unhindered on the sandy lake bottom. In years gone by, however, the marimo were threatened by an increase of lake weeds (proliferated by discharge from new tourist businesses) and glass-bottomed sightseeing boats for marimo viewing, which damaged the delicate algae in the process. After the boats were stopped and the water regulated, marimo numbers stabilised and the algae is now strictly protected, ensuring that future generations may still have a chance to witness this rare natural phenomenon.

8

a traditional **Ainu** *poncise* (small house; ⊕ 10.00–21.00 daily; donations) with exhibits on daily life, and behind them an **Ainu Theatre** (Ikor; ⊕ approx 11.00–21.00 daily; ¥1,500/700), which features regular 30-minute performances of Ainu music and dance.

Lake Onnetō At the edge of the national park, below the western flanks of Mount Me-Akan and a short drive southwest of Nonaka Onsen lies Lake Onnetō (オンネトー), a startlingly clear volcanic lake whose waters are often a shade of tropical blue. It is one of the most beautiful spots in the national park, and there are trails around its perimeter, plus a campsite near the southeastern shore.

Nearby is **Yu-no-taki** (湯の滝), a picturesque hot-spring waterfall home to an exceedingly rare geological phenomenon, as it is said to be the only place on the earth's surface where manganese oxide ore can be seen forming in deposits up to 2m thick. The mineral emerges from hot-spring water above the two mossy waterfalls, and the blackish-brown ore is deposited by a microbial process involving bacteria and algae. The falls can be reached by driving or walking to the car park south of the lake, from where a 1.4km (20mins) trail leads to the falls deep in the woods.

RIKUBETSU

Located deep in the island's interior, Rikubetsu (陸別; population 2,400) stakes the claim as Japan's coldest town, with an average daily low temperature of below −20°C in the peak of winter, and it is not uncommon for it to drop well below −30°C. In early February, Rikubetsu holds the two-day Shibare Festival which celebrates the freezing cold with a human cold resistance test, where participants spend the night in an igloo.

The michi-no-eki (Aurora Town 93 Rikubetsu) at the centre of town once served as a railway station on the Furusato Ginga Line; it was finally abolished in 2006 after operations began (under a different name) between Ikeda and Rikubetsu in 1910. It is a real Mecca for rail fans; inside is a rail museum, **Furusato Ginga-sen Rikubetsu Tetsudō** (ふるさと銀河線りくべつ鉄道; w rikubetsu-railway.jimdofree. com; ⊕ late Apr–Oct 09.00–16.00 Thu–Mon; free), where you can experience driving a real diesel train – the 15-minute short course costs ¥2,000 and is for those of primary school age and upwards (preferably at least 130cm tall), while there are much longer (and more expensive, up to ¥60,000) courses for over 18s. Bookings can be made through the website two months in advance, but places often sell out quickly. If driving a train isn't your thing, you can also take a short ride as a passenger on a selection of retired trains (¥300–500). You can also trundle along 400m of track on a pedal-powered contraption (¥300/200) which seats up to five people.

Stargazing fans should drive 10 minutes southeast of the town to **Rikubetsu Space Earth Science Museum** (りくべつ宇宙地球科学館 / 銀河の森天文台; ⊕ Apr–Sep 14.00–22.30 Wed–Sun, Oct–Mar 13.00–21.30 Wed–Sun; daytime ¥300/200 (Apr–Sep until 18.00, Oct–Mar until 17.00), nighttime ¥500/300 (Apr–Sep from 18.00, Oct–Mar from 17.00)). This high-tech facility up in the hills is home to one of the largest telescopes in Japan, and the clear dark skies of central Hokkaidō make this the perfect place for observing the night skies, with the expert and amiable staff zooming in on galaxies and star clusters to give you a spell-binding view of the universe on a big screen (possible during daylight hours too).

KITAMI

Known as Notsukeushi until 1942 and now the largest city in the Okhotsk region, Kitami (北見; population 110,000) is perhaps now best known as an agricultural city with a strong sporting heritage, particularly curling, and a proliferation of yakiniku restaurants. The earliest Japanese settlers are believed to have arrived around 1880, and the town developed considerably after 1911 when a station opened on what was to become the Abashiri Main Line. Despite its large population, Kitami rarely features on the tourist map, although there are a handful of places of note.

Kitami Museum of Science, History and Art (北網圏北見文化センター; Kōenchō 1; w hokumouken.com; ⊕ 09.30–16.30 Tue–Sun; ¥660/free) has a somewhat dated but incredibly varied collection of exhibits including a planetarium, art gallery and historical recreations. It is a 5-minute drive or 25-minute walk northeast of the station. The **Kitami Mint Memorial Museum** (北見ハッカ記念館; Minamiakamachi 1-7-28; w kitamihakka.jp; ⊕ May–Oct 09.00–17.00 daily, Nov–Apr 09.30–16.30 daily; free) is a 5-minute walk south of JR Kitami Station and is a museum dedicated to the production of peppermint, one of Kitami's former key industries, with vintage displays in a well-preserved and quaint Western-style building, but little English. The shop sells countless mint-related products. From the same period, the **Pierson Memorial Museum** (ピアソン記念館; Saiwaichō 7-4-28; w npo-pierson.org; ⊕ 09.30–16.30 Tue–Sun; free) is the former residence of George and Ida Pierson, an American missionary couple who lived here for 15 years during the pioneer days; their house, a 15-minute walk west of the station, has been wonderfully preserved.

ABASHIRI

A small city on the Sea of Okhotsk, Abashiri (網走; population 33,000) is famous for its seafood and drift ice, but for Japanese people the name is perhaps most synonymous with the notorious prison built here in the late 19th century where prisoners were made to work in brutally hard and cold conditions. Nowadays the city has a much more friendly vibe (although winters are still harsh), and with good train, road and even air connections, plus some interesting attractions, Abashiri is one of the main hubs of activity along the remote and mostly fairly desolate Sea of Okhotsk coast.

The city's **tourist information centre** (⊕ 09.00–18.00 daily) is inside the combined michi-no-eki and icebreaker terminal building down at the harbour. Also check w visit-abashiri.jp.

GETTING THERE AND AROUND

By rail Limited express Okhotsk trains run twice daily between Sapporo and Abashiri (5hrs 30mins; ¥10,540), while limited express Taisetsu trains ply the route between Abashiri and Asahikawa (4hrs; ¥8,560). From Kushiro there are direct trains to Abashiri (3hrs 10mins; ¥4,070).

By air Memanbetsu Airport (女満別空港; w mmb-airport.co.jp) is located about 20km southwest of Abashiri. There are daily shuttle buses from the airport for Abashiri (30mins; ¥1,050) and other locations; tickets for the bus can be bought from a vending machine at the airport. There are car rental offices right outside the airport too.

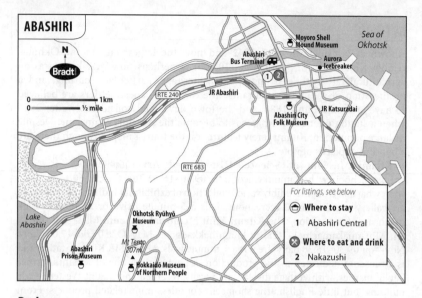

ABASHIRI

N

Bradt

0 —————— 1km
0 —————— ½ mile

Sea of Okhotsk

Moyoro Shell Mound Museum

Abashiri Bus Terminal

Aurora Icebreaker

1 2

RTE 240

JR Abashiri

Abashiri City Folk Museum

JR Katsuradai

RTE 683

Lake Abashiri

Okhotsk Ryūhyō Museum

Mt Tento 207m

Abashiri Prison Museum

Hokkaidō Museum of Northern People

For listings, see below
🏠 **Where to stay**
1   Abashiri Central
❌ **Where to eat and drink**
2   Nakazushi

By bus Sharibus (w sharibus.co.jp) runs routes throughout the region, linking Abashiri to Shari (1hr; ¥1,200) and Utoro (2hrs; ¥2,800). Hokkaidō Chūō Bus (w chuo-bus.co.jp) and Abashiri Bus (w abashiribus.com) operate daily long-distance express buses to and from Sapporo (6hrs; ¥6,800).

By road Abashiri is a 40-minute drive west of Shari on Route 244, a 3-hour 15-minute drive from Asahikawa on the E39 expressway, or 4 hours 30 minutes from Sapporo using the E5 expressway.

🏠 **WHERE TO STAY AND EAT** *Map, above*
Abashiri is known for crabs, salmon and scallops. *Kamaboko*, a steamed, seasoned fish paste formed in a cylindrical shape, usually pink or white, is said to be one of Abashiri's soul foods, and is often served in ramen or *chanpon* (a Chinese-style noodle dish filled with various ingredients). The city was the birthplace of the frozen fish paste cakes called *surimi* (better known as crabsticks).

Abashiri Central Hotel 網走セントラルホテル; 3-chōme 7-7; \0152 44 5151; w abashiririch. com. Decent location halfway between the train station & icebreaker cruise jetty, this functional but dated hotel offers pleasant service, but rooms are showing their age & thin walls mean you may have to tiptoe around. **$$$**

Nakazushi 中鮨; Minami 2-jō Nishi-2-chōme; \0152 43 3447; ⊕ 17.00–23.00 Mon–Sat. Unpretentious but top-drawer sushi restaurant on Abashiri's main street, next door to the Central Hotel – look for the turquoise *noren* (curtain) hanging across the door. No English, but the owner is very welcoming. **$$$$**

WHAT TO SEE AND DO Abashiri forms a fairly sprawling strip along the coast, but luckily most tourist sites are confined to one or two areas, with the harbour and ice-boat tours at one end, and the small Mount Tento – where a number of attractions are located – on the western side.

Around the harbour Starting at JR Abashiri Station, the harbour is a 5-minute drive or 20-minute walk west along Route 490/Route 1083, with the michi-no-eki serving as the terminal for drift-ice sightseeing tours. The **Aurora Icebreaker** (w ms-aurora; ⏲ late Jan–end Mar, 4–7 times daily; ¥4,000/2,000) is a cruiseboat which sails around for about an hour in the frozen waters off Abashiri – riding along as the boat crushes its way through the ice is a remarkable experience, and offers a good chance of seeing magnificent sea eagles perched on their ice plinths as well as other wildlife. It is worth reserving tickets online in advance, as these trips often sell out on the day.

To get a feel for the history of the region, head up the hill a few blocks southwest of the harbour to **Abashiri City Folk Museum** (網走市立郷土博物館; Katsuramachi 1-1; ⏲ 09.00–17.00 (Nov–Apr until 16.00), Tue–Sun; ¥120/60), a stylish old building which, when it was built in 1936, was Hokkaidō's first museum. Inside are lots of incredibly realistic stuffed animals and interesting nature and human history exhibits, starting from Jōmon through to Ainu and modern times, but there's not a lick of English.

For a bit more history, a 4-minute drive or 20-minute walk north and across the bridge leads to **Moyoro Shell Mound Museum** (モヨロ貝塚館; Kita 1 Higashi 2; w moyoro.jp; ⏲ 09.00–17.00 daily (Nov–Apr until 16.00); ¥300/100). This rather small but swanky museum is focused on the intriguing Okhotsk culture shell middens found in the grounds nearby, and displays unusual artefacts and finds from this period. There is very little English, but an audio-guide is available.

The west side of town Over on the western edge of Abashiri is **Mount Tento** (207m), and three of the city's top attractions are found here, with buses running from the station throughout the day.

First is **Abashiri Prison Museum** (博物館 網走監獄; Yobito 1-1; w kangoku. jp; ⏲ 09.00–17.00 daily; ¥1,500/750), a sprawling site featuring relocated historic wooden buildings belonging to the notoriously brutal northernmost prison in Japan. Established in 1890, it first housed political prisoners and rebellious samurai, and operated until as recently as 1984 (when a new prison complex was opened). Prisoners from Hokkaidō's early pioneer days were forced to work on big construction projects, such as the creation of the first road between Abashiri and Asahikawa (nicknamed the Prisoner's Road), although conditions were so unforgiving that many died in the process. The buildings feature life-size reconstructions of inmates in their daily routines, and wandering around is an incredibly evocative experience, especially in the chill of winter. If you want a literal taste of prison life, then the café serves authentic 'prison meals' for lunch.

A short drive up the hill is **Okhotsk Ryūhyō Museum** (オホーツク流氷館; Tentōzan 244-3; w ryuhyokan.com; ⏲ May–Oct 08.30–18.00 daily, Nov–Apr 09.00–16.30 daily; ¥770/550), a museum all about drift ice and the cold-loving wildlife of the region, including tanks full of cliones. There are plenty of items on display with explanations in English, and the top-floor observatory has wonderful views over to Shiretoko.

A short walk from there is the small but very well-appointed **Hokkaidō Museum of Northern People** (北海道立北民族博物館; Shiomi 309-1; w hoppohm.org; ⏲ Jul–Sep 09.00–17.00 daily, Oct–Jun 09.30–16.30 daily; ¥550/free). It showcases the cultures of various northern peoples (not just the Ainu) with colourful displays, lots of English information and is an easy place to while away an hour or so.

Further afield To the west of Abashiri are a number of natural attractions; take Route 76 and follow the turn-off north to reach in 12km the lighthouse at **Cape Notoro** (能取岬), a scenic headland where high cliffs plunge down to the ocean

– in summer the cape is awash in greenery and wildflowers, while winters have a stark frozen beauty, especially if there is ice in the bay.

There are also some large lakes in the vicinity, namely **Lake Abashiri** (網走湖) and **Lake Notoro** (能取湖), both of which freeze over in the winter and are good for ice-fishing. It's a wonderful drive from Abashiri past these lakes – if you come from mid-September to early October, you will see great swathes of red coral grass, especially at **Ubaranai** (卯原内) at the southern corner of Lake Notoro. About 15km further west along Route 239 you will come to **Lake Saroma** (サロマ湖), an enormous expanse of brackish water which is the third largest lake in Japan and the largest on Hokkaidō. It is famed for its scallops (and formerly oysters) and is probably best appreciated from the **Saroma Observation Deck** (サロマ湖展望台), a glorious vantage point high up on a hill on the lake's southern shore (about 1hr 30mins from Abashiri). The road up is narrow and unpaved, and there are steps to climb at the top, but the views (particularly at sunrise) are outstanding. In the winter, the lake freezes and becomes a vast expanse of smooth milky whiteness.

9

Northern Hokkaidō

The far north of Hokkaidō is both the northern extreme of Japan and the final lonely frontier of this island. It is a region of desolate, windswept, rolling landscapes, long empty roads and sweeping coastlines as barren as the hilly interior, where winters are harsh and people are few. The mysterious Russian island of Sakhalin is visible across the sea on clear days.

Close to Cape Sōya, the very northernmost tip of Hokkaidō, the small, gritty port of Wakkanai is every bit the frontier town – Japan's most northerly outpost is the terminus of the JR train line and a city where Russian Cyrillic (as well as Japanese and English) is written on road signs. For many Japanese people who make it this far, it probably feels like a place at the very edge of the known world. Tokyo, and even Sapporo, certainly feel a long, long way from here. But it is also where you can find arguably the best scallops and sea urchins in the whole of the country.

Wakkanai is also the gateway to two of Japan's most intriguing islands: Rishiri, an island formed and dominated by the 1,721m-high pointy mountain at its centre which seems to rise directly out of the sea; and Rebun, with its gentler landscape of grassy hills, scenic coastlines and summer flower meadows. Both lie just a few miles west off the coast and are known for their splendid seafood and unique beauty.

There are three main routes for travelling to and from Wakkanai and Cape Sōya. The most popular central route connects Asahikawa and Wakkanai by rail and Route 40 as both track and road wind inland through open countryside and sleepy backwater towns. A slower west-coast route along the Sea of Japan offers views of two little-visited and tiny islands, Teuri and Yagishiri, both havens for birdlife. Finally, the lonely eastern seaboard route facing the Sea of Okhotsk connects Cape Sōya with the small city of Monbetsu, a hardworking port buffeted by sea ice during the cold winters. But it is the stark barrenness of northern Hokkaidō which gives the region its unique character and an understated solemn beauty, making it feel quite unlike anywhere else in Japan.

THE SEA OF OKHOTSK COAST

The lengthy and lonely stretch between Monbetsu and Cape Sōya is one of Hokkaidō's least-visited areas, where orcas and drift ice swirl offshore in the winter and people living in the small settlements dotted along the coast eke out a living as best they can. The barren beauty and sense of solace here make it great for road trips.

The **Monbetsu Tourist Information Centre** (紋別観光案内所; ⏰ 09.00–17.00 daily) is inside the city's bus terminal; the kind staff will help with any queries.

GETTING THERE AND AROUND Routes 238/239 reach along almost the complete length of the coast; it takes about 3 hours to drive the 180km from Monbetsu

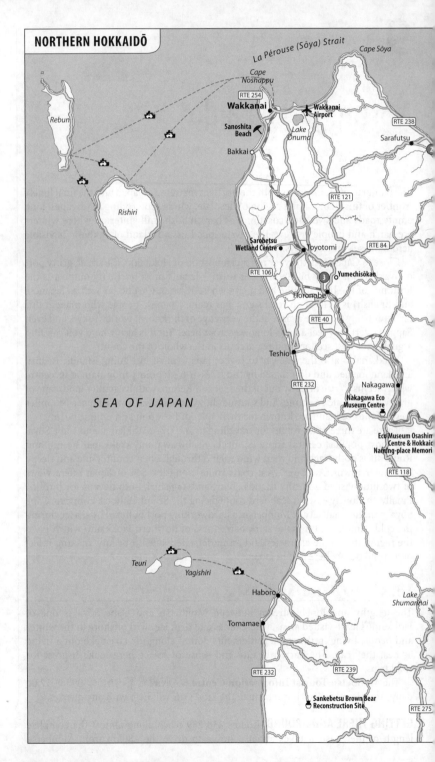

NORTHERN HOKKAIDŌ

La Pérouse (Sōya) Strait

Cape Sōya

Cape Noshappu

RTE 254

Wakkanai

Wakkanai Airport

RTE 238

Rebun

Sarafutsu

Sanoshita Beach

Lake Onuma

Bakkai

RTE 121

Rishiri

RTE 84

Sarobetsu Wetland Centre

Toyotomi

RTE 106

③ **Yumechisōkan**

Horonobe

RTE 40

Teshio

RTE 232

Nakagawa

Nakagawa Eco Museum Centre

SEA OF JAPAN

Eco Museum Osashin Centre & Hokkaic Naming-place Memori

RTE 118

Teuri

Yagishiri

Haboro

Lake Shumarinai

Tomamae

RTE 232

RTE 239

RTE 275

Sankebetsu Brown Bear Reconstruction Site

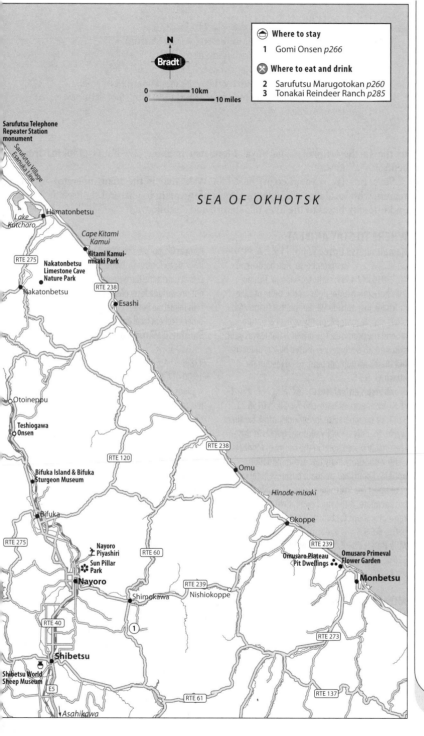

SEA OF OKHOTSK

Where to stay
1   Gomi Onsen *p266*

Where to eat and drink
2   Sarufutsu Marugotokan *p260*
3   Tonakai Reindeer Ranch *p285*

0 ——— 10km
0 ——— 10 miles

Sarufutsu Telephone
Repeater Station
monument

Sarufutsu Village
Esanika line

Lake
Kutcharo
Hamatonbetsu

Cape Kitami
Kamui

Kitami Kamui-
misaki Park

RTE 275
Nakatonbetsu
Limestone Cave
Nature Park

Nakatonbetsu

RTE 238

Esashi

Otoineppu

Teshiogawa
Onsen

RTE 120

RTE 238

Omu

Hinode-misaki

Bifuka Island & Bifuka
Sturgeon Museum

Bifuka

Okoppe

RTE 239

Nayoro
Piyashiri
Sun Pillar
Park

RTE 60

Omusaro Plateau
Pit Dwellings

Omusaro Primeval
Flower Garden

Monbetsu

Nayoro

RTE 275

RTE 239

Shimokawa   Nishiokoppe

RTE 40

1

RTE 273

Shibetsu

Shibetsu World
Sheep Museum

E5

RTE 61

RTE 137

Asahikawa

to the furthest tip of Cape Sōya. Monbetsu is about 2½ hours (140km) from central Asahikawa.

Sōya Bus (w soyabus.co.jp) based in Wakkanai is the main operator in the region, with local routes connecting most of the main towns, and sightseeing buses and intercity buses to the likes of Sapporo and Asahikawa.

🏠 WHERE TO STAY AND EAT

Hamatonbetsu Onsen Wing はまとんべつ 温泉ウイング Hamatonbetsu; Kutcharokohan 40; \0163 42 4141; w hotel-wing.jp. This no-frills hot-spring hotel right on the shore of Lake Kutcharo, just outside Hamatonbetsu (page 264), offers simple rooms & plenty of deer & nature around the premises. The onsen water leaves your skin smooth & slippery & is used by lots of locals, but there's no outdoor bath. Good restaurant attached. **$$$**

Monbetsu Central Hotel 紋別セントラルホテル Monbetsu; Minato-chō 7 1-58; \0158 23 3111; w mombetsu.co.jp/en/index.html. Excellent warm, friendly service welcomes guests at this reasonably priced hotel in the centre of Monbetsu, a city with surprisingly few accommodation options. Rooms are standard business hotel fare – compact & a little worn around the edges – but are adequate, & the food is great with all-you-can-eat scallops for b/fast! Has its own hot-spring baths. **$$$**

Milk Hall ミルクホール Okoppe, Hokko 116-2; \0158 88 2000; w northplainfarm.co.jp; ⊕ 11.00–14.00 Wed–Mon. Part of North Plain Farm in Okoppe, the small restaurant here specialises in local produce, with Japanese-style hamburger sets at lunchtime & ice cream for dessert, but other options include tasty pasta & curry too. The shop sells miniature bottles of milk, yoghurts, cheese & other excellent local dairy products. **$$$**

Sarufutsu Marugotokan [map, page 258] さるふつまるごと館; Sarufutsu 214; \0163 54 7780; ⊕ Apr–Nov 09.00–17.30 daily, Dec–Mar 10.00–17.30 Thu–Tue. Sarufutsu is famed for its scallops & this no-frills place down on the coast just off Rte 238 is one of the best places to eat them; the *hotate-don* (ホタテ丼; scallop rice-bowl) is a thing of wonder: piles of plump, super-fresh shellfish nestled on a bed of fluffy rice. The shop sells scallop-related products too. **$$$**

Umikura う美蔵; Esashi, Misakichō 531-1; \0163 64 7655; w umikura-shop.jp; ⊕ 11.00–14.00 & 18.00–22.00 Thu–Tue. Located a few minutes' drive north of Esashi & overlooking the sea, this striking black-&-white building in the style of a traditional *kura* (storehouse) contains a shop & an excellent restaurant serving seafood sets & ramen. **$$$**

MONBETSU Monbetsu (紋別; population 22,000; also sometimes written as Mombetsu) originated as an Ainu settlement, with its name deriving from the Ainu 'Moupetto', meaning 'calm/quiet river'. During the Meiji era, Japanese people settled in the region and were predominantly involved in fishing plus some agriculture. In 1930 a gold mine was established near the town of Konomai, following the discovery of the largest gold vein in East Asia, and for 40 years the mine brought prosperity to the region.

These days the city is known mostly for its excellent crab (reputed to be the best in Japan) and seasonal sea or drift ice, which arrives along the Sea of Okhotsk coast during February and March and draws in visitors to ride on the city's fleet of small ice-breaking ships (see below). Monbetsu has in fact become a centre for sea ice research, with an international symposium held in the city every year. In February there is a Drift Ice Festival featuring impressive ice sculptures plus an ice maze.

Monbetsu has less precipitation and so receives slightly less snow than many other regions of Hokkaidō during the winter, and can be quite hot (over 30°C) in summer, all due to the influence of the Foehn phenomenon, a dry, warming westerly wind flowing downslope from the nearby mountains. Outside of the popular drift-ice season when Monbetsu is swamped by busloads of tourists, it is a fairly sleepy place, despite being one of the main settlements on Hokkaidō's quiet northeast coast.

What to see and do Unsurprisingly for a port and fishing town, the harbour is Monbetsu's main centre of activity, and probably the place of most interest to visitors, too. The southeast end of the harbour has parkland, a campsite and lots of sprawling car parks, and this is the place to come for icebreaker trips.

Icebreaker **Garinko II** (w o-tower.co.jp; ⏱ 08.00–16.00 daily (or from 05.30 or 06.00 w/ends Feb–Mar); ¥3,000/1,500) The icebreaker *Garinko II* is a bright orange ice-breaking cruise ship which operates from late January to mid-March when the drift ice is at its peak. The vessel's predecessor, the *Garinko*, was the world's first icebreaker cruise ship when it was launched in 1987. The *Garinko II*, which carries up to 195 passengers, sets out from Monbetsu into the vast white frozen ocean, using two large drills on its bow to break through the floating ice. Conditions are usually bitingly cold, so wrap up warm to get a close-up view of the action from the open-air deck on the second floor, from where you may also be able to spot seals lounging on blocks of ice, as well as other wildlife such as Steller's sea eagles. It is a genuinely unique experience, with views more akin to an Antarctic dream than what you'd expect in Japan. However, as the amount of drift ice can vary from year to year, you are not always guaranteed an ice-covered sea, although the cruises still operate (for a slightly reduced fee) even when sea-ice conditions are poor. During the winter there are up to six cruises a day; it is best to book online in advance if possible as tickets often sell out on the day. Drift-ice cruises are also offered on the *Garinko II*'s sister ship, the slightly smaller **Garinko III Imeru** (¥4,000/2,000), which also runs sightseeing, fishing and starry night cruises in the summer.

Next to the icebreaker terminal is the **Okhotsk Tokkari Centre** (オホーツクとっかりセンター; w o-tower.co.jp/tokkaricenter.html; ⏱ 10.00–16.00 daily; ¥200/100), a small open-air facility entered via a big arch where you can see seals up close, with five daily feedings.

Okhotsk Tower (氷海展望塔オホーツクタワー; w o-tower.co.jp/okhotsktower.html; ⏱ 10.00–16.00 daily; ¥500/250) Just east of the icebreaker terminal, you can follow a walkway called the Clione Promenade for 500m along the jetty. There are actually two walkways: the lower one has an attractive drift-ice motif cast on the wall and is the best option in inclement weather as the upper one is very exposed (there is also a free shuttle bus). Both walkways lead to the end of the jetty and the Okhotsk Tower, a slightly dated metallic four-storey structure perched out at sea. The top floor serves as an observation deck, while the bottom floor has an aquarium and is actually beneath sea level with windows allowing you to peer out into the murky ocean depths. The tower also has a café and a 4D cinema showing short marine-related films.

ANGELS OF THE SEA

Commonly known as sea angels, cliones are tiny swimming shell-less sea snails with wing-like appendages, which they flap to propel themselves dreamily through the water. They have mostly transparent bodies, and even the largest of their species reaches only 5cm in length. Despite their graceful appearance, sea angels are carnivores and prey upon another form of sea snail known as 'sea butterflies'.

Sea angels are often associated with the truly frigid oceans around the Arctic and Antarctic, although some of the smaller species inhabit much milder waters, including even equatorial regions. Technically speaking, cliones (or Clionidae) are just one family in the broader Gymnosomata clade which in layman's terms makes them molluscs, and, in slightly less angelic-sounding terms, a type of sea slug.

Okhotsk Sea Ice Museum of Hokkaidō (北海道立オホーツク流氷科学センター; Motomonbetsu 11-6; w giza-ryuhyo.com; ⏰ 09.00–17.00 Tue–Sun; ¥450/150) Just south of the harbour is one of Monbetsu's best-known attractions, the Okhotsk Sea Ice Museum of Hokkaidō. This interesting science facility includes displays on the science behind sea ice, a sub-zero room where you can experience −20°C temperatures year-round, and a slightly macabre 'frozen aquarium' featuring various marine life specimens entombed in ice. You can also marvel at the museum's sea angels or cliones (see above), delicate little sea creatures found in the cold waters of the Sea of Okhotsk. Expect lots of hands-on activities for kids, supremely friendly staff and a decent amount of English too. It's probably just about worth shelling out for the planetarium-style dome theatre (additional fee of ¥450/150, or as a combined ticket with museum entry for ¥750/250) which shows an immersive 15-minute film featuring swooping aerial views of Monbetsu, the coastline and the drift ice from high up in the sky.

Next to the museum is Monbetsu's newest landmark: a realistic 12m-tall orange-and-white crab claw monument, which overlooks the beach.

Okhotsk Sky Tower (オホーツクスカイタワー; w sancho-mombetsu.org/free/okhotskskytower; ⏰ May–Nov 10.00–21.00 daily, Dec–Apr 10.00–18.00 daily; ¥200/100) Up on a hill overlooking the city, near the top of the ski run at the small Monbetsu Ōyama Ski Resort, the Okhotsk Sky Tower is a retro-looking 30m-tall structure which offers excellent panoramic views of Monbetsu and the coast from its glass-windowed observation deck, reachable by lift. The ground-floor rest area has free coffee, and there are plenty of spaces for parking. The tower can be reached by car in less than 10 minutes after turning off Route 239, which skirts the western edge of the city.

Omusaro Primeval Flower Garden On the northwest outskirts of the city, approximately 7km from central Monbetsu, is an area known as the Omusaro Primeval Flower Garden (オムサロ原生花園). This marshy coastal terrace is home to numerous unique wildflowers, generally in bloom from May until September; there are paths to wander along for a closer look. The distinctive roadside **Omusaro Nature View House** (オムサロ・ネイチャー・ビューハウス; ⏰ 10.00–18.00 daily; free) serves as a botanical facility and rest-house right next to the 'garden' and the beach. The first-floor observatory is a good place to view drift ice in the winter, while the ground floor has a shop selling snacks and local souvenirs.

Across the road are the **Omusaro Plateau Pit Dwellings** (オムサロ台地竪穴群; ① 24hrs daily; free). This secluded spot in the woods is where four small Jōmon-era wooden pit houses have been faithfully reconstructed. It is believed that people had lived here for at least 10,000 years, spanning the Jōmon period through to the Ainu. There is a tiny museum displaying recovered earthenware among other things, but perhaps equally interesting are the remains of trenches built by Japanese soldiers during World War II which can also be found at the site.

OKOPPE AND NISHIOKOPPE Buffeting the Sea of Okhotsk, the small town of Okoppe (興部; population 4,000) lies 20km from Monbetsu on Route 239 when travelling north up the coast. It is known mainly for its excellent dairy produce. Beyond the cheese and milk shops there is not a great deal to do in the town, but if you carry on for 20 minutes following Route 239 as it heads inland, you'll arrive at the small out-of-the-way village of Nishiokoppe (西興部), nestled among the hills. The main attraction here is the **Komu Museum of Art** (森の美術館 木夢; w vill.nishiokoppe.lg.jp/komu; ① 10.00–17.00 Wed–Mon; ¥500/100), where you can enjoy hours of hands-on play with hundreds of different wooden toys, puzzles, slides, larger ride-on items, playsets and a wooden ball pond. More akin to a play centre than a museum, children in particular are likely to love it, but even adults can find things to enjoy. Hotel Rimu (**$$$**) next door has a restaurant (**$$$**) and sauna to freshen you up if that's more your thing.

OMU Apart from a bunch of convenience stores and an avant-garde michi-no-eki with an observation tower that looks like a crashed UFO, the little seaside town of Omu (雄武; population 4,500) doesn't have much to entice visitors. But about 10km southeast of the town is **Hinode-misaki** (日の出岬), a tiny peninsula with a good campsite (clean toilets, chalets for rent and hot-spring baths in the hotel next door) and splendid sunrise ocean views. A glass-windowed observatory offers protection from the wind which can often whip up around here.

ESASHI Roughly halfway along the coast between Monbetsu and Cape Sōya, the unassuming harbour town of Esashi (枝幸; population 8,000) is said to have the largest yearly harvest of hairy crabs in Japan. It also has a crab festival (held on the first Sunday in July) with crab-eating contests and a crab lottery. Other than hairy crustaceans, Esashi's main attraction is the **Okhotsk Museum Esashi** (オホーツクミュージアムえさし; ① 09.00–17.00 Tue–Sun, closed last Tue of month; free). This large pink building just off Route 238 looks like a cross between a school and a prison but is actually one of Hokkaidō's best municipal museums, with displays on Esashi's local natural and human history, the Okhotsk culture (including an impressive replica pit dwelling) and much more. It has a great collection of fossils and bones, the stars of the show being a huge orca whale and one of only two complete Desmostylus (an extinct hippopotamus-like mammal) skeletons in the world.

Just north of the town at the end of a small promontory, the unique coastal rock formation of **Usutaibe-senjoiwa** (ウスタイベ千畳岩) is said to look like piled-up tatami mats and was formed by lava cooling quickly into unusual shapes; you can find parking, a campsite and toilets here too.

For the 30km or so from Esashi to Hamatonbetsu, Route 238 follows the coastline, and halfway between the two towns is **Kitami Kamui-misaki Park**

(北見神威岬公園), a pretty beauty spot where you can park up and admire the views. Just past the park, turn right for a short detour around **Cape Kitami Kamui** (北見神威岬), the distinctive mountain-like promontory which juts into the sea. Near the tip of the cape is a black-and-white lighthouse dating to 1962; you can walk right up to it, although it looks most photogenic when viewed from the roadside down below. Joining back on to Route 238 you will occasionally pass a small white building with a red roof – these sombre relics were once railway stations on the now abolished Kōhinhoku Line which ran 30km along the coast between Hamatonbetsu and Kitami-esashi from 1936 to 1985.

HAMATONBETSU Located just inland of the coast near the mouth of the Tonbetsu River, Hamatonbetsu (浜頓別; population 3,800) sits on the shores of **Lake Kutcharo** (クッチャロ湖), a picturesque and sizeable brackish lake famous for its abundant birdlife – more than 300 species have been recorded there. It actually comprises of two lake basins, Konuma and Ōnuma (the latter being largest and closest to town), connected by a narrow channel. The lake is a stopping point for waterfowl such as tundra swans and pintail ducks which can be seen in their thousands during the spring and autumn migrations between Japan and Siberia; during winter it is a haven for white-tail and Steller's sea eagles.

On the lakeside at the far western end of town is a cheap and grassy campsite with gorgeous sunset views (⊕ May–Oct; ¥400/200 pp), a free foot onsen, Hamatonbetsu Onsen Wing (a hot-spring hotel; page 260) and the **Kutcharo Waterfowl Observatory** (クッチャロ湖水鳥観察館; ⊕ 09.00–17.00 Tue–Sun; free), which functions as both a natural history museum (featuring numerous stuffed birds) and a lakeside observation centre – birds and people alike flock here around September, the latter mostly to see the famous masses of whooper swans.

NAKATONBETSU Surrounded by mountains, the small, pleasant town of Nakatonbetsu (中頓別; population 1,500) is roughly 20km down the road from Hamatonbetsu along Route 275. Thanks to its northerly inland location, it is regarded as one of the chilliest towns in Japan, although there is evidence of human activity here from at least the Jōmon period. During the Meiji era, gold dust was discovered in the nearby Tonbetsu River, which along with the government's push for more settlers on Hokkaidō drove the population up to a peak of over 8,000 in the 1920s, with much of the surrounding land cleared for farming and forestry. While the farms still remain, gold rush prosperity never fully materialised. You can learn all about the town's history at **Nakatonbetsu Town Local History Museum** (中頓別町郷土資料館; ⊕ 10.00–17.00 Tue–Sun; ¥120/60), with its good displays ranging from natural history to gold-panning, but next to no English.

On the northeastern edge of town is **Nakatonbetsu Limestone Cave Nature Park** (中頓別鍾乳洞自然ふれあい公園; ⊕ May–Oct 09.00–17.00 daily, closed Nov–Apr; free), a well-maintained forest park with short hiking trails, interesting rock formations and four small caves, the main one of which can be entered for free. Discovered in 1917, the 60m-long cave is quite narrow and has steep steps in places, but is fun to explore – it's best to wear clothes you don't mind muddying – and you can borrow a light and helmet at the cave entrance.

SARUFUTSU The northernmost settlement on the coast before Cape Sōya, Sarufutsu (猿払; population 2,600) is a small village known for its wonderful large scallops (*hotate*), which are well worth hunting down in the handful of local seafood stores and restaurants.

Along this part of the coast, the story recounting the actions of nine brave young women during World War II is widely known, and is often translated in English as 'the tale of nine maidens'.

In 1934 an undersea communications cable was laid off the coast of Hamasarufutsu, a small settlement south of Sarufutsu. This cable stretched from Hokkaidō to Karafuto – the Japanese name for southern Sakhalin, which the Japanese occupied from 1907 to 1949 – allowing for direct communication between the two islands.

On 20 August 1945, just a few days before the full annexation of the island at the end of the Pacific War, Soviet troops arrived in Maoka (now known as Kholmsk), one of the main Japanese administrative centres on Karafuto. As fighting broke out between Russian and Japanese soldiers, the nine female switchboard operators at Maoka post office remained at their stations, even as the Japanese forces began to be overrun and the streets outside were lit up with explosions and gunfire. Valiant and professional to the end, the women completed their work, but rather than surrender or be killed they decided to end their own lives with potassium cyanide. Their last transmission was simply 'Everyone, this is the end. Farewell, farewell.'

There are two monuments in memory of the women – one on the coast at the Sarafutsu Telephone Repeater Station, and another one further north in Wakkanai Park.

A scenic 16km stretch of road running parallel to Route 238 between Hamatonbetsu and Sarufutsu is called the Sarufutsu Village Esanuka Line; it has two particularly long, almost endlessly straight sections flanked by flat fields and – a rarity for Japan – no signs, telegraph poles or other obstructions, making it a popular spot for shooting TV commercials. Just before rejoining Route 238 near Lake Poro, the road passes an inconspicuous monument to Sarufutsu Telephone Repeater Station overlooking the beach (see above). The section of Route 238 heading into Sarufutsu is known as the 'Okhotsk Hotate (Scallop) Road', and just before the village you can't fail to miss the black European-style windmill at Sarufutsu Park (猿払公園). Here you can also find a michi-no-eki, a campsite and Sarufutsu Marugotokan (さるふつまるごと館; page 260), a great, reasonably priced restaurant for trying the area's outstanding scallops.

Directly across the road is a distinctive monument to the victims of SS *Indigirka*, a Russian steamship used for transporting prisoners which ran aground here and capsized in a blizzard in 1939, resulting in the loss of more than 700 lives; most of them were prisoners who were locked in the hold preventing their escape. The majority of the ship's crew, guards and more than 200 fishermen who were also aboard were rescued by Japanese locals, but it remains one of the biggest ever disasters in maritime history.

CENTRAL AREAS AND THE FAR NORTH

The main transport corridor between Asahikawa and Wakkanai follows a mostly central route along the Teshio river valley, home to Hokkaidō's second longest and most northerly major river. Both the JR Sōya Line and Route 40 meander northwards through picturesque agricultural lands and wild hill country. There are a few interesting diversions and places to stay along the way in the various scattered and small sleepy provincial towns.

Drivers can stop off at **Shibetsu Tourist Information Centre** (士別観光協会; ⏱ 10.00–17.00 daily) at the town's newish michi-no-eki to discover more about the area.

GETTING THERE AND AROUND Route 40 is the main artery connecting Asahikawa and Wakkanai – it takes a little under 4 hours by car. Using the parallel-running expressway E5 toll road – which currently goes only as far north as Shibetsu – knocks a bit of time off.

The JR Sōya Line is Japan's northernmost railway line; limited express Sōya and Sarobetsu trains ply the line between Asahikawa and Wakkanai (3hrs 45mins; ¥8,890), stopping at all the major stations in between, continuing on to or from Sapporo, with about three direct services a day.

 WHERE TO STAY AND EAT

Gomi Onsen [map, page 258] 五味温泉; Shimokawa, Panke 2893; ✆0165 54 3311; w gomionsen.jp. You'll find simple tatami & Western-style rooms in an idyllic rural woodland setting at this traditional hot-spring hotel about 6km south of Shimokawa. The onsen features quite rare, carbonated waters & a choice of indoor & outdoor baths. Just up the road is a modern but tiny off-grid luxury cabin (w gurutto-shimokawa. com) for those seeking a more visceral nature retreat. See also page 268. **$$$**

Nakagawa Onsen 中川町公共温泉; Nakagawa 439-1; ✆0165 67 2400; w nakagawa-no-nakagawa.jp. This clean & functional hot-spring hotel (also known as Ponpira Aqua Rizuningu; ポンピラ・アクア・リズイング) can be found among the greenery on the southern outskirts of Nakagawa. It has fairly spacious Western- & Japanese-style rooms & a choice of various indoor baths at the onsen. Reasonably priced, though there is a campsite next door if you want to go even cheaper. See also page 269. **$$**

Restaurant BSB レストランBSB; Bifuka, Ōdōrikita-4-9 5-2; ✆0165 68 7123; w bifukashirakaba-brewery.site; ⏱ noon–22.00 daily. Stylish brick storehouse converted into a brewery on Rte 40 in central Bifuka. It serves a good choice of local IPAs & other hoppy ales, plus there are non-alcoholic options & bottles for sale if driving. The menu focuses on meaty dishes such as beef stew & lamb curry. **$$$**

SHIBETSU Named after the Ainu name for 'great river', Shibetsu (士別; population 19,000) is actually located at the confluence of two rivers, the Teshio River and the Kenbuchi River, and in 1899 it became the last settlement on Hokkaidō to be established by the farmer-soldier colonisers known as the tondenhei (page 29). For this reason, it is also sometimes known as Samurai Shibetsu to differentiate it from another town of the same name in eastern Hokkaidō (page 237). Shibetsu developed as the main agricultural centre in this part of northern Hokkaidō, and today is mostly known for its sheep farming, adopting the playful moniker of *hitsuji-no-machi* or 'sheep town'.

A 10-minute drive west of the town is **Hitsuji-to-kumo-no-oka** (羊と雲の丘; w hitsujitokumo.net), literally meaning 'sheep-and-cloud hill'; it is a bucolic landscape of open fields and rolling pastures, and home to the **Shibetsu World Sheep Museum** (世界のめん羊館; ⏱ Apr–Sep 09.00–17.00 daily, Oct–Mar 09.00–16.00 daily; ¥200/100). At this small facility you can get up close to and feed numerous varieties of sheep (a bag of feed costs ¥100). There are shearing shows, tractor tours and sheepdog trials held here during the summer months too. The restaurant over in the main visitor centre, Hitsujikai-no-ie (羊飼いの家; ⏱ 11.00–15.00 daily), specialises in lamb dishes.

A 5-minute drive southeast of the sheep museum (or a 20min walk southeast of JR Shibetsu Station) is **Shibetsu City Museum** (士別市立博物館; ⏰ 09.30–16.30 Wed–Sun; ¥100), housed in a modern brick building plus an adjacent colonial European-style one. The museum chronicles the interesting human history of Shibetsu and its natural environs, via diverse displays, photographs, fossils and art, although there's scant English. In the grounds nearby is an authentic reconstruction of a wooden house as used by the last of the tondenhei soldiers back in the day – you can pop inside to see what living conditions would have been like for the farmer-soldier colonisers.

LAKE SHUMARINAI A 40-minute detour drive northwest of Shibetsu brings you to Lake Shumarinai (朱鞠内湖; w shumarinai.jp). Covering an area of 24km², this is Japan's largest manmade lake. Formed following the construction of the Uryū Dam in 1943, it lies at the northern end of the tiny backwater town of **Horokanai** (幌加内) and is a popular beauty spot; its numerous wooded islands and fjord-like channels give it the feel of somewhere like Canada or Alaska rather than Japan. Facilities and amenities are all at the southwest corner of the lake, where you can find a visitor centre, observation deck, a large campsite (⏰ May–Nov; ¥600 pp/ night; **$**), log cabins (**$$**) and a hotel (**$$$**). The lake is particularly popular for canoeing and especially fishing, with many anglers coming to catch the Japanese huchen, a critically endangered (though bred for game-fishing) type of large, ancient salmon. You can make an equipment rental reservation and buy a one-day licence for trout and smelt fishing, or ice-fishing in winter (which also includes a ride across the ice on a snowmobile) via the form on the website w en.shumarinai. jp/fishing/trouts/rules; guided fishing and canoe tours are also an option.

NAYORO The Ainu name for this small city is Nay Oro, meaning 'in the middle of the valley'. Nayoro (名寄; population 28,000) first developed as an agricultural trading post on the road to the far north, and as a central railway hub between Hokkaidō's Sea of Japan and Okhotsk coasts, although a number of local lines have now been abandoned. Nayoro is now known for its *mochi-gome* (glutinous rice) production, and the Nayoro basin is the northernmost rice-growing area in Japan.

The main attraction in the city is the small but excellent **Nayoro-shi Kitaguni Museum** (名寄市北国博物館; Midorioka 222; ⏰ 09.00–17.00 Tue–Sun; ¥220/free) which is in Nayoro Park, a 10-minute walk south of the station. At the museum entrance is a monument of a Blakiston's fish owl, a sacred bird to the Ainu, carved across five pillars. Inside you can find a great assortment of artefacts relating to the history of Nayoro including lots of old skiing gear, winter tools and other implements used throughout the ages in this cold and snowy northern region. Perhaps most impressive of all is the grand 'Kamaroki' snowplough steam locomotive, permanently stationed outside on the remains of the now abandoned Nayoro Main Line. Though there is very little English, this museum is well worth a look if you're in the area.

During August don't miss the brilliant fields of yellow sunflowers which stretch as far as the eye can see at **Sun Pillar Park** (北海道立サンピラーパーク; ⏰ 09.00– 18.00 daily; free), with other flowers in other seasons. The park has all kinds of family-friendly attractions throughout the year, including snowshoe rental in winter, and it is also a popular sledging spot. The park is just 10 minutes by car or taxi from central Nayoro.

Thanks to the region's high-quality winter powder, nearby **Nayoro Piyashiri** (名寄ピヤシリスキー場; w nayoro.co.jp/piyashiri) is a well-regarded little ski resort with three lifts, a number of runs, ski school/gear rental, hot-spring hotel and good access, just 9km from the centre of town (there are 5 buses a day from JR Nayoro Station between 1 Dec and 31 Mar).

SHIMOKAWA Taking Route 239 east for 20 minutes from Nayoro, you'll arrive in the tiny town of Shimokawa (下川; population 3,500). Most people don't stop, however, but continue onwards for another 10 minutes to wallow in the waters of **Gomi Onsen** (五味温泉; w gomionsen.jp; ◷ 10.00–21.30 daily; ¥500/300), a well-known, traditional yet unassuming hot-spring hotel, deep in the forest south of the town. It has a choice of indoor and outdoor baths, plus one of only two naturally carbonated spring baths on Hokkaidō (the other is Kyowa Onsen in Aibetsu). The slightly acidic-tasting carbonated water is drinkable (only from the tap – don't glug the bathwater!) and is said to cure various ailments. For accommodation here, see page 266.

BIFUKA The main attraction of Bifuka (美深; population 4,500), a small, quiet valley farming town, is just north up the road at a spot called **Bifuka Island** (びふかアイランド). The 'island' is home to a forest park and was formed in the old cut-off meander of the adjacent Teshio River; it can be accessed by turning off on to the road that leads behind the michi-no-eki. The park has a pleasant, popular campground offering lakeside activities, a fairly standard hot-spring hotel (with no outdoor bath) called **Bifuka Onsen** (びふか温泉; w bifukaonsen.com; for day visitors ◷ 11.00–21.00 daily; ¥450) and one other main attraction, the **Bifuka Sturgeon Museum** (美深チョウザメ館, Bifuka Chōzame-kan; w bifukaonsen.com/sturgeon; ◷ 09.00–17.00 Tue–Sun; free). This small, simple aquarium and breeding facility is home to many specimens of large sturgeon which frequented the nearby Teshio River until the Meiji period (sadly they no longer exist in the wild here), along with other examples of the local river life.

OTOINEPPU Said to be the smallest village on Hokkaidō (at least in jurisdictional terms), Otoineppu (音威子府; population 700) was actually known as Tokiwa (常盤) until 1963, when the name was changed to match the better-known JR Otoineppu Station, a terminus for the Sōya and Tenpoku (the latter now defunct) JR lines. Surrounded by mountains, Otoineppu means 'muddy river mouth' in the Ainu language and is known for its black soba noodles. The area sees frequent temperature extremes, with hot summers and freezing, snowy winters; in fact the village is regularly buried deep under more than 12m of snow, and in 1998 recorded Hokkaidō's second largest ever snowfall for November. Despite (or perhaps because of) its low population, Otoineppu is now promoting village revitalisation projects to bring in new residents and trade, although the station's famous Otoineppu soba stand sadly served its last bowl of noodles in 2022, closing after 90 years of business.

Two train stops south of Otoineppu is **Teshiogawa Onsen** (天塩川温泉; w teshiogawa-onsen.com), an extremely rural hot spring on the banks of the Teshio River. The chalky waters here were first discovered at the beginning of the Taishō period, and the current hotel was built in the late 1980s to make the most of them. Day visitors can bathe for ¥400; there are two indoor baths plus a small outdoor one with views of the river, and although the hotel itself is a bit dated and charmless, it is clean, quiet and offers good food, including Otoineppu's signature black soba noodles. There is a campsite adjacent to the hotel.

In the terminal building of JR Otoineppu Station is the **Tenpoku Line Museum** (天北線資料室; ◷ 09.00–17.00 daily; free), a tiny one-room museum commemorating the Tenpoku railway line which ran from here to Hamatonbetsu and Wakkanai for 75 years, until its discontinuation in 1989. It features a miniature model railway of the station as it would have been back in its heyday, plus plenty of photographs – certainly worth a quick look.

For a quick detour north, drive along Route 275 for 15 minutes to the Old Tanbaya Inn (旧丹波屋旅館), a derelict wooden ryokan which sat alongside the former Tenpoku Line. Built in 1927, this Western-style building is a registered intangible cultural property and seems to be crying out for someone to come and give it a loving refurbishment, but for now it stands empty and is unfortunately not possible to enter.

Back in Otoineppu and leaving the open valley behind, the Teshio River snakes west through hilly country, traced by the Sōya Line along its north bank and Route 40 on the other. At a big bend in the river is the rural hamlet of **Osashima** (筬島), situated in the middle of the Hokkaidō University Nakagawa Experimental Forest. Here you can find the **Eco Museum Osashima Centre** (エコミュージアム おさしまセンター; w bikkyatelier3more.wixsite.com/atelier3more; ⊕ late Apr–late Oct 09.30–16.30 Tue–Sun, closed in winter; ¥300/free), a former elementary school converted into a museum to showcase the works of Asahikawa native and woodcarver Bikky Sunazawa (1931–89); his unique carvings celebrate nature and have nods to Ainu motifs. In the school's former gym is a cosy bar relocated from Sapporo's Susukino district, replete with more of Bikky's woodworks; there is no alcohol on sale but it does offer a good coffee.

Nearby, situated at a secluded riverside spot is the minorly significant, but far from spectacular **Hokkaidō Naming Place Memorial** (北海道命名之地). A large wooden column marks the naming of 'Hokkaidō' by the Meiji-era explorer Takeshirō Matsuura (page 26); he got the idea for the name after listening to a local Ainu elder's stories as he travelled through here. There is also a plaque dedicated to an early governor of Hokkaidō, and although the memorial is far from the most exciting of attractions, the riverside views are quite nice, and the spot marks an important piece of the island's history. Many Hokkaidō natives don't even know about this location, so it may be worth a visit for bragging rights if nothing else. The memorial is signposted and can be found 300m down a gravel road (closed in winter) just off Route 40, close to the bridge turn-off for Osashima.

NAKAGAWA River, road and rail line emerge from the hills into the open plains and the agricultural township of Nakagawa (中川; population 1,500). Since the Meiji period ammonite and dinosaur fossils have been discovered in the area, and the first permanent Japanese settlers arrived in 1896. Thanks to the influence of the Sea of Japan, this region experiences relatively dry springs but wet, turning to snowy autumns.

The main point of interest here is the **Nakagawa Eco Museum Centre** (中川町エ コミュージアムセンター; w city.hokkai.or.jp/~kubinaga; ⊕ 09.30–16.30 Tue–Sun, closed Sat–Sun & hols in winter; ¥200/free), a natural history museum situated in a former junior high school, a short hop across the river from JR Saku Station. While there are some displays relating to the area's anthropological history, the vast majority of exhibits focus on palaeontology, with numerous fossils and dinosaur bones, interestingly juxtaposed with many of the school's original fittings which remain in place. The building next door is yet another of Hokkaidō's many closed-down elementary schools.

Teshio-Nakagawa is the station in the main town, where there are a handful of restaurants and places to stay, most popular of which is Nakagawa Onsen (中川 町公共温泉; also known as Ponpira Aqua Rizuningu, ポンピラ・アクア・リズイング; ⊕ 11.00–19.30 daily; ¥400/200 for day visitors) which has various indoor baths, including a medicinal one with herb-infused waters. For accommodation details, see page 266.

From Nakagawa both the JR Sōya Line and Route 40 gravitate west towards the Teshio Plains and Sea of Japan coast, passing though the districts of Horonobe and Toyotomi (both of which are covered from page 285) before arriving at the end of the line at Wakkanai.

WAKKANAI The capital of Sōya subprefecture, Wakkanai (稚内; population 32,000) is Japan's most northern city, situated right at the upper tip of Hokkaidō, from where the Russian island of Sakhalin is clearly visible on fine days. The pot-holed and windswept streets are befitting of its slightly bleak port-city charm, with the Cyrillic on road signs adding to the distinct frontier vibes. In the winter there are huge dumps of snow and drift ice bobs offshore in Sōya Bay, but only in the very coldest winters does the harbour freeze over. Most visitors use Wakkanai as a base for exploring Rishiri-Rebun-Sarobetsu National Park, as regular ferries depart for the nearby islands of Rishiri and Rebun, and the city is only a short drive from Japan's most northern point of Cape Sōya. Wakkanai was also once one of the few direct Japanese gateways to Russia, but the ferry linking it to Korsakov on Sakhalin is now suspended indefinitely. However, Wakkanai is an interesting place in its own right, with enough distractions to warrant a little exploration. Most of the city's hotels and restaurants, plus the train station (and ferry terminal) are clustered in the central district on the west side of the harbour.

History The name Wakkanai originates from the Ainu Yam-wakka-nay, meaning 'cold water river'. The first Japanese settlers arrived as far back as 1685 when the Matsumae clan established an outpost here and traded with the Ainu. From 1785 onwards, Wakkanai was used as a base for Japanese parties exploring Karafuto (Sakhalin). In 1879 it officially became a 'village', growing to 'town' status in 1901, and finally 'city' in 1949, and remained important as a fishing port.

In May 1911 much of Wakkanai was destroyed as a particularly savage fire incinerated hundreds of houses, the school and a hospital (it was a bad year for fires throughout Hokkaidō). But just two years later the city had been rebuilt, along with a new power plant, allowing the city's first electric lights to be installed. In 1922 Wakkanai was connected by a rail service following the completion of the Tenpoku Line.

Thought to be out of range of American bombers, Wakkanai's harbour was used as a submarine base during World War II, and until the 1960s there were still concrete mooring pens at the north side of the harbour. The famous domed breakwater also functioned as a submarine-repairing facility. Concrete bunkers were also built in the hills surrounding the city.

In 1959 Wakkanai Airport was opened despite Wakkanai being regarded as one of Japan's windiest cities; the nearby hills are one of the few places in the country with wind turbines. Nowadays the city is the venue for the All-Japan National Dogsled Championship, a two-day event in late February which takes place in Wakkanai Airport Park (20mins by car from Wakkanai, next to Ōnuma Birdwatching Observatory).

Getting there and away
By air Wakkanai Airport (w wkj-airport.jp) has scheduled flights with ANA to Tokyo and Sapporo. The airport is about 20 minutes' drive from central Wakkanai, with limousine buses timed for flights (30mins; ¥700). By taxi it costs about ¥4,000.

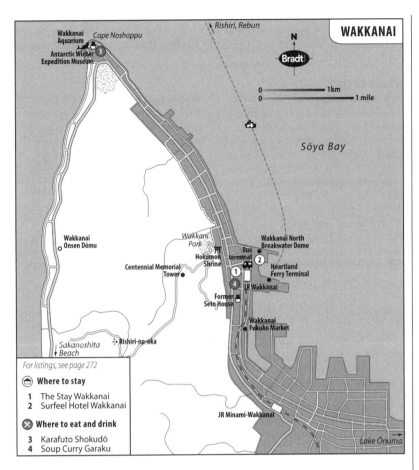

WAKKANAI

↑ Rishiri, Rebun

N

Bradt

Sōya Bay

Wakkanai Aquarium
Cape Noshappu
Antarctic Winter
Expedition Museum

0 ——— 1km
0 ——— 1 mile

Wakkanai
Onsen Dōmu

Wakkani
Park

Wakkanai North
Breakwater Dome

Hokumon
Shrine

Bus
terminal

Héartland
Ferry Terminal

Centennial Memorial
Tower

JR Wakkanai

Former
Seto House

Wakkanai
Fukuko Market

Sakanoshita
Beach

Rishiri-no-oka

JR Minami-Wakkanai

Lake Ōnuma

For listings, see page 272

Where to stay

1 The Stay Wakkanai
2 Surfeel Hotel Wakkanai

Where to eat and drink

3 Karafuto Shokudō
4 Soup Curry Garaku

By train The JR Sōya Line terminates at Wakkanai, the northernmost station in Japan. Limited express Sōya and Sarobetsu trains run between Asahikawa and Wakkanai (3hrs 45mins; ¥8,890), continuing on to or from Sapporo (5hrs 10mins; ¥11,090), with about three direct services a day.

By car Route 40 is the main road between Asahikawa and Wakkanai and takes a little under 4 hours. The parallel running Expressway E5 toll road (which only goes as far north as Shibetsu) makes travel time slightly shorter. The scenic coastal roads – Route 232 on the west coast (3hrs to/from Rumoi), and Route 238 along the east coast (3hrs 30mins to/from Mombetsu) – also eventually reach Wakkanai.

By bus Long-distance buses arrive and depart from the bus terminal right next to the station. Sōya Bus (w soyabus.co.jp) runs services about five times a day between Wakkanai and Sapporo (5hrs 50mins; ¥6,200), plus an overnight bus departing either city at 23.00.

Tourist information The Wakkanai Tourist Information Centre (稚内観光案内所 / 稚内観光協会; ⊕ 10.00–18.00 daily) inside JR Wakkanai Station is a good place for finding out about the locality. The information centre runs a bicycle rental service (1 hr ¥1,000, full day ¥3,000). The ferry terminal also has an information desk.

🏠 Where to stay *Map, page 271*

Surfeel Hotel Wakkanai サフィールホテル 稚内; Kaiun 1-2-2; ☎0162 23 8111; w surfeel-wakkanai.com/en. This very comfortable hotel within walking distance of the train station & ferry terminal has great views of the harbour & bay from the highest floors. The plush lobby, spacious rooms & excellent dining give it a high-end feel, but the price is quite reasonable. **$$$**

The Stay Wakkanai ザステイ稚内; Chūō 2-12-16; ☎0162 73 4610; w thestay.jp. Excellent budget option – though perhaps slightly pricey for a hostel – just across from the station, with a mix of dormitory & private rooms. Friendly staff, spotlessly clean & handy kitchen/washing facilities, but thin walls. **$$**

✖ Where to eat and drink *Map, page 271*

The streets north and west of the station have plenty of dining options, and as a port city, Wakkanai is well known for its excellent seafood; the harbourside **Wakkanai Fukuko Market** (稚内副港市場; Minato 1-6-28; w fukkoichiba.hokkaido.jp) is a good place to start. A 10-minute walk south of the station and adjoining the harbourside michi-no-eki, this indoor market is where you can sample Wakkanai's outstanding fresh (and dried) seafood and shop for souvenirs. Produce is reasonably priced considering the many tourists, plus there are some good restaurants both inside and nearby. Look out for the colourful Gundam-themed (an ever-popular Japanese giant military robot franchise encompassing anime, manga and video games) manhole cover outside (there are supposedly two of these in Wakkanai, plus two each in Toyotomi and Teshio).

❈ **Karafuto Shokudō** 樺太食堂; ☎0162 24 3451; w unidon.net; ⊕ late Apr–early Oct 09.00–15.00 daily. This tan-toned little box-building plastered with signs on Cape Noshappu offers huge, delicious seafood bowls – don't miss the sea urchin. Prices are reasonable considering the volume, freshness & quality which you simply won't find in the big cities. **$$$**

Soup Curry Garaku プチGARAKU; Chūō 3-4-1; ☎0162 73 0325; ⊕ 11.30–15.30 & 17.00–21.00 daily. The cosy Wakkanai branch of this soup curry chain offers big hearty curry bowls packed full of meat, vegetables & flavour which really warm the soul on a chilly night. Cash or online app payment only (no credit cards). EM. **$$$**

Other practicalities

Hokkaido Bank 3-chome 11-10, Chuo; ☎0162 235221; ⊕ 09.00–15.00 Mon–Fri
Wakkanai Municipal Hospital 4-chome 11-6, Chuo; ☎0162 232771; ⊕ 08.30–16.00 Mon–Fri

Wakkanai Police Station 1-chome 6-48, Daikoku; ☎0162 240110
Wakkanai Post Office 2-chome 15-12, Chuo; ☎0570 943719; ⊕ 08.00–19.00 Mon–Fri, 08.00–17.00 Sat, 09.00–15.00 Sun

What to see and do

Wakkanai North Breakwater Dome (稚内港北防波堤ドーム) This huge concrete breakwater at the north side of the harbour is the city's main landmark, and is a little under 10 minutes' walk from JR Wakkanai Station. Completed in 1936 and standing over 13m tall and stretching for over 400m, the overhanging seawall is supported by Roman-style columns, and the structure provides shelter to people walking underneath, along with its main function of protecting the harbour from high waves and savage winter storms. Back when it was built, however, it also functioned as a submarine-repair facility, but the old winching mechanisms were removed a few decades after World War II. Next to the breakwater is a small grassy park from where you can watch ships come and go.

Former Seto House (旧瀬戸常蔵邸; Chūō-ku 4-8-27; ⊕ Apr–Oct 10.00–18.00 daily, closed winter; ¥200/100) Easily missed on a side street halfway between the food market and station, the Former Seto House is a Western-style building with large bay windows and red-brick chimney, in contrast to the interior which is mostly Japanese in style. The property dates back to the Shōwa era and was the former residence of the Seto family, an influential local family who made its fortune in trawler fishing from the late 1940s to the early 1960s. Artefacts from the fishing industry and everyday period items are on display, with free tours (in Japanese) explaining the history in detail; a lot will be lost on non-Japanese speakers but it is interesting to wander around and get a sense of how these wealthy fishing merchants lived.

Wakkanai Karafuto Museum (稚内市樺太記念館; ⊕ Apr–Oct 10.00–17.00 daily, Nov–Mar 10.00–17.00 Tue–Sun; free) On the second floor of Wakkanai Fukuko Market (see opposite), this no-frills facility has lots of displays and photos from the time when southern Sakhalin (Karafuto) was a Japanese territory. There's minimal English, but the photographs provide an interesting window into a region and history little known in the West.

Wakkanai Park Located on a hilltop just west of the harbour, Wakkanai Park (稚内公園) is home to wild deer and a number of attractions; there are good views across to Cape Sōya, and soft-scoop ice cream in the summer. You can drive up there, or it is a 30-minute walk from the station, passing through the grounds of the hillside **Hokumon Shrine** (北門神社), Japan's most northern manned shrine. The park is dotted with monuments including the **Gate of Ice and Snow** (*hyosetsu-no-mon*), a striking 8m-high gate between whose pillars stands the figure of a woman looking towards the heavens, palms exposed, stricken with grief; the monument is dedicated to the Japanese people who had to flee their homes or died on Karafuto at the end of World War II. Bilingual signs explain the particulars of each monument.

The park's centrepiece is the impressive but slightly dated 80m-tall crimson-and white **Centennial Memorial Tower** (開基百年記念塔; ⊕ late Apr–May & Oct 09.00–17.00 Tue–Sun, Jun–Sep 09.00–21.00 daily, closed Nov–late Apr; ¥400/200). It was constructed on the hilltop in 1978 and commemorates the 100-year anniversary of the founding of Sōya Village, the precursor to Wakkanai. Inside there are historical exhibits relating to Wakkanai and Karafuto, plenty of prehistoric excavated goods, Ainu artefacts and interesting period photos, although next to no English. A 360° observation deck on the upper floor offers far-reaching panoramas when it's not murky outside.

The unofficially named Rishiri-no-oka (利尻の丘) is a much wilder hilltop viewpoint reached by following the road southwest past the Centennial Tower, then on to a dirt track; the green hilly landscape and views out to the island of Rishiri are very pleasant on a nice day.

Cape Noshappu At the far northern end of Wakkanai, beyond the hills and army base, Cape Noshappu (野寒怖/ノシャップ岬) juts into the Sōya Strait, marked at its tip with a distinctive red-and-white lighthouse. This flat, windswept promontory is a 10-minute bus ride from JR Wakkanai Station (get off at Noshappu; ノシャップ),

then a 5-minute walk. Deer roam freely in Noshappu Park, and if you're lucky you'll get a glimpse of Rishiri rising over the ocean like a mythical island.

Close to the lighthouse on the western littoral is a tiny park with a dolphin statue – a popular sunset-viewing spot. The pink souvenir store opposite is one of the few places around here open throughout the winter. Right next to the lighthouse is **Wakkanai Aquarium** (ノシャップ寒流水族館, Noshappu kanryū-suizokukan; ⊕ May–Oct 09.00–17.00 daily, Nov & Feb–Mar 10.00–16.00 daily, closed Apr & Dec–Jan; ¥500/100), a small, dated facility showcasing mostly cold-water sealife,

LA PÉROUSE STRAIT

Known in Japanese as the Sōya Kaikyō (Sōya Strait), the La Pérouse Strait is the 42km-wide stretch of water separating the northern tip of Hokkaidō from the southern tip of Sakhalin, while also connecting the Sea of Japan with the Sea of Okhotsk. The strait was named after the French naval officer and explorer Jean François de Galaup, comte de Lapérouse (otherwise known as Lapérouse), who in 1785 was appointed by Louis XVI, the last king of France, to lead an expedition around the world with a particular focus on the Pacific. The aim was to build upon the earlier discoveries of James Cook (who Lapérouse admired greatly) and included completing and correcting maps of the region, establishing new trade links and bolstering French scientific collections and knowledge – one of the applicants for his crew was a 16-year-old Napoléon Bonaparte, although the youngster never made the cut and so remained in France before going on to make his mark in French history.

After visiting among others Chile, Hawaii, California, Alaska, the Philippines and Korea, in 1787 Lapérouse sailed to northeast Asia to explore Oku-Yeso (present-day Sakhalin), where he met the Ainu, who showed him local maps. He then sailed east through what is now known as La Pérouse Strait, skirting past Yezo (Hokkaidō) and on to the Kuril Islands and then Kamchatka. European, and even Japanese, knowledge of the geography of northern Hokkaidō and neighbouring lands was extremely hazy until Lapérouse's visit, so he made significant contributions to that end. The expedition went on to explore Australia and the South Pacific, leaving New South Wales in early 1788 to chart a course to New Caledonia, the Solomon Islands and beyond, but he and his crew were never seen by Europeans again. It is now believed that the expedition became shipwrecked on Vanikoro (an island in the Solomon Archipelago) and most of the crew were violently murdered by the local people; a team in 1964 (and later in 2005 and 2008) examined the wreck of a ship believed to be Lapérouse's flagship vessel, the *Boussole*.

The strait has extremely strong ocean currents which also make it a very fertile fishing ground, and it can be filled with drift ice for periods during the winter. Japan's territorial waters only extend 3 miles (rather than the usual 12) into the strait; this is reportedly to allow US nuclear warships and submarines to transit through without violating Japan's no-nuclear policy in its territory.

There were once talks of constructing a Sakhalin–Hokkaidō tunnel, or even a colossal bridge across the strait, which in theory could have linked Japan to the Trans-Siberian Railway, but the sheer expense, technical difficulty and complicated geopolitics mean that those plans remain a very distant pipe dream.

including seals and penguins. Included in the entry fee is access to the **Antarctic Winter Expedition Museum** (南極越冬隊資料展示コーナー), inside the shuttered white warehouse with a blue roof in the car park behind the aquarium (enter via the left sliding door). It houses an orange snowcat, portable living units and other assorted artefacts from early Japanese Antarctic expeditions.

Route 254, known as Sōya Sunset Road, is the main road running north from Wakkanai right around the cape; relatively scenic in a bleak, northern way, with the sea on one side and rolling hills on the other. Following the road south down the western side of the cape will bring you to **Wakkanai Onsen Dōmu** (稚内温泉童夢; w onsen-domu.com; ⊕ 09.45–22.00 daily; ¥600/300), said to be Japan's northernmost hot springs. This large, unflashy facility has indoor and outdoor baths and is popular with locals and tourists alike. Keep following the road south for 6km to reach **Sakanoshita Beach** (坂の下海水浴場) at the southern end of the cape. This sandy beach hasn't (yet) been ruined by concrete wave breakers and so offers good views of Rishiri, plus is popular for swimming during the peak of summer.

Lake Ōnuma To the east of central Wakkanai (20mins by car) and just west of the airport slightly inland from the coast is Lake Ōnuma (大沼), a large body of water covering an area of 4.6km². It is an important resting place for swans as they make their way south from Siberia during the autumn and again on their return in the spring, and they can be seen in great flocks if you time it right. On the north side of the lake is **Sōya Fureai Park** (宗谷ふれあい公園; w soyafureaikoen.com; ⊕ May–Sep 06.00–22.00, Oct–Apr 08.00–18.00) which has a campground, a visitor centre, an amazing indoor playground and a small ski resort. Nearby on the lakeside is a cosy little log-house with a wood-burning stove; it is a great place to observe the birdlife out on the water.

CAPE SŌYA Roughly 30km northeast of Wakkanai across Sōya Bay, Cape Sōya (宗谷岬, Sōa-misaki) is famous as the northernmost point on Hokkaidō and of mainland Japan, although in fact the small nearby island of Benten-jima is technically Japan's northernmost territory (page 276). The cape is windswept and not particularly spectacular, especially when the weather is rotten (which is often), but on clear days Sakhalin can be seen across the ocean, while tourists, cyclists and bikers pose for obligatory photos next to the triangular 'northernmost point' monument erected there. Everything on the cape is a 'northernmost something', including the public loos which are designated as 'the northernmost toilets in Japan' and nearby is the 'northernmost post-box'. There are a handful of weather-beaten souvenir shops and restaurants close to the car park; and the distinctive blue-pointy-roofed building houses a small **drift ice museum** (⊕ 09.00–17.00 daily; free) with a walk-in winter room to see lumps of drift ice up close and experience minus temperatures even in high summer. It also displays taxidermied wildlife and is home to the 'northernmost gift shop' (selling certificates to prove you visited Japan's most northerly point), and the 'northernmost vending machine'.

Across the road is a small indoor observatory and rest-house. Wander (or drive) a short way up the hill behind to Cape Sōya Park to see a lighthouse, more assorted monuments – the most impressive of these is the **Tower of Prayer**, which resembles a paper crane and commemorates Korean Airlines flight 007, a plane shot down by Russian missiles while en route from New York to Seoul in September 1983 as it accidently infringed on Soviet airspace – and an old naval watchtower, which offers good views of the nearby islands and over the bay towards Wakkanai.

Cape Sōya's hilly, green and pretty interior has free-range cattle pastures and a number of wind turbines, and can be explored by bike or car outside the snowy season – some of the narrow roads appear completely white as they are made from crushed scallop shells. The tiny settlement on the eastern flank of the cape known as **Sōya-misaki** (宗谷岬) has a scattering of houses, minshuku and a small harbour, but Wakkanai offers far more food and accommodation options. Cape Sōya can be reached from Wakkanai by bus (50mins; ¥1,420) or in 30 minutes by car. A return bus ticket saves a bit of money – enquire at Wakkanai Bus Terminal.

RISHIRI ISLAND

Standing in sharp contrast to most of the rolling scenery of northern Hokkaidō, the spectacular island of Rishiri (利尻島, Rishiri-tō; population 5,000) rises abruptly out of the sea, its jagged central volcanic peak, Mount Rishiri (also known as Rishiri-Fuji), at 1,721m tall commanding attention even from the shores of Hokkaidō some 20km away. In the Ainu language Rishiri means simply 'island with a high peak'. The round-shaped island measures just 19km north to south, 14km east to west and 63km in circumference, and its coast is peppered with tiny fishing hamlets and racks for drying kelp, one of the island's prized bounties. A ring road circles Rishiri, which is split into two jurisdictions: Rishirifuji on the east side, and Rishiri-chō on the west. The island's main town and gateway by sea is Rishirifuji-chō on the north coast, although it's better known by the name of its port, Oshidomari; while the second largest is the port of Kutsugata (otherwise known as Rishiri-chō) on the west coast – most of the population live in these two settlements, and life on Rishiri, especially in the long, snowy winter months, requires remarkable resilience. In the past islanders made a living fishing Pacific herring, but stocks have dried up and so the main money-makers now are konbu seaweed and tourism. Many visitors come to drive or cycle around the island, climb Mount Rishiri, or sample the island's rich, creamy sea urchin, which is undoubtedly among the best in the world. While few visitors make it here in the winter, hardcore backcountry skiers can find wild adventure on Rishiri's untamed slopes. Unlike on much of Hokkaidō, brown bear are not found on Rishiri (or neighbouring Rebun), although in 2018 footprints and scat were found on the island as locals speculated that one must have swum over from the mainland; it presumably swam (or got the ferry!) back as no trace of the animal has been detected since.

GETTING THERE AND AROUND

By ferry Heartland Ferry (w heartlandferry.jp) has two to three daily sailings to and from Wakkanai (2hrs; ¥2,660–5,290) and one to three daily sailings to and from Rebun (45mins; ¥980–2,020). Oshidomari on the island's north coast is the main port, but ferries also arrive and depart from the second largest settlement, Kutsugata, on the west coast; from here there is usually one ship a day to and from Wakkanai and Rebun.

By car Rishiri is an excellent road-trip destination, with the 63km loop of the main road around the island taking between 2 and 3 hours. Car rental is somewhat more expensive than over on the mainland, however (perhaps around ¥15,000/day

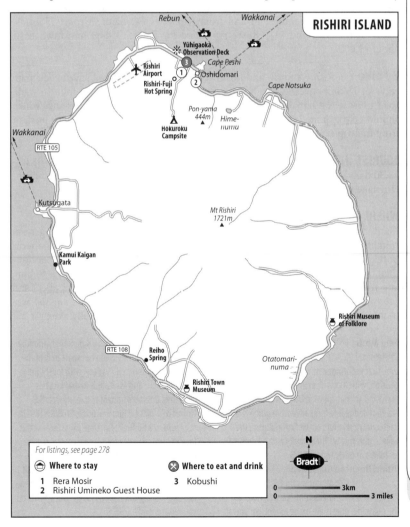

RISHIRI ISLAND

For listings, see page 278

🛏 **Where to stay**
1 Rera Mosir
2 Rishiri Umineko Guest House

🍴 **Where to eat and drink**
3 Kobushi

or ¥5,000 for 3hrs for a small car); there are a number of rental companies opposite the ferry port. Bringing a car over on the ferry from Wakkanai can be expensive, costing a minimum of ¥13,120 one-way for a small vehicle.

By bus Sōya Bus (w soyabus.co.jp) operates local buses along the entire coastal road, with a full loop taking about 1 hour 40 minutes – buses run once every 2–3 hours during summer (3–4hrs outside of that). The 'A Course' goes clockwise around the island, the 'B Course' runs anti-clockwise; either route connects Rishiri's two biggest settlements, Oshidomari and Kutsugata (30mins; ¥760) and the airport. A one-day bus pass costs ¥2,000/1,000 (adult/child).

There are also sightseeing bus tours run by the same company – these typically take between 2 and 4 hours (¥3,000–4,000/1,800–2,000) and stop at all the main sights on the island, with all the information relayed in Japanese.

By air Rishiri Airport is about 5 minutes' drive west of Oshidomari and has daily flights (June to September) to and from Sapporo's Okadama Airport (55mins) operated by ANA and JAL. Buses are timed for flights. A taxi into town costs about ¥2,000.

By bike On Rishiri's north and northwestern coast, a dedicated paved cycle path runs for 25km between Cape Notsuka and Kutsugata. You can then join the main road to cycle the remaining 30km or so to complete the loop of the island, which should take around 7 hours in total. Bicycles can be rented at Oshidomari port, or from many places of accommodation.

TOURIST INFORMATION There is a little tourist information centre (🕐 08.00–18.30 daily) in the Oshidomari port ferry terminal where you can pick up English-language maps and bus schedules, and staff may help with bookings.

WHERE TO STAY AND EAT *Map, page 277*

Many accommodation options on Rishiri are seasonal, typically operating from roughly May to October, and most offer free drop-offs and pick-ups at the ferry port and airport for guests. Foodwise, Kutsugata arguably has better dining options than Oshidomari. Rishiri is known for its outstanding *uni* (sea urchin), as is Rebun, and there are two types, both seasonal: *kita-murasaki uni* (June to September) and *Ezo bafun uni* (July and August). Expect to pay around ¥4,000 for an *uni-don* (sea urchin rice-bowl) at restaurants on the islands – not cheap, but totally worth it.

Rera Mosir レラモシリ; Oshidomari, Sakaemachi-227-5; 📞0163 82 2295; w maruzen. com/tic/oyado/index.html. This comfortable pension, with its own small onsen, serves good seafood & is open all year. Owner Toshi Watanabe is a knowledgeable local adventure guide & offers backcountry ski tours on Mt Rishiri during the winter, plus free trailhead pick-ups and drop-offs for hikers at other times. **$$$**

Rishiri Umineko Guest House 利尻うみね こゲストハウス; Minatomachi-85; 📞0163 85 7717; w rishiriumineko.com. Located right on the quayside, guests are made to feel like one of the family at this welcoming & genuinely friendly place. Guestrooms are clean but spartan & of the tatami-and-futon-style variety, with lovely views of the harbour and Mt Rishiri. Rental bicycles available. Operates from May to early Oct. **$$**

Kobushi こぶし; Honchō-66; 📞0163 82 1891; 🕐 18.30–23.00 Tue–Sun. Dine like a local at this low-key izakaya just off the main coastal road in Oshidomari – lots of fresh seafood fare, meaty things on sticks, fried bits & pieces & cold beer. If completely bamboozled by the all-Japanese menu but open to anything, say *osusume-wa?* ('What do you recommend?'). **$$$**

WHAT TO SEE AND DO A loop of the **'Rishiri Fantastic Road'** (利尻ファンタスティ
ックロード) – the 60km-long road which circumnavigates the island – is the best
way to see Rishiri's main sights and coastal views of beaches, tiny harbours, rocky
bluffs and *konbu* (kelp)-drying racks, with the island's imposing central mountain
an ever-present companion. It can be done on two wheels, by car or by bus in half a
day or so. **Oshidomari** (鴛泊) is the main port and settlement on the island with a
number of places to stay, restaurants, shops and a convenience store, but even so, it
is nothing more than a small sleepy backwater harbour town. There is a hot-spring
facility, **Rishiri-Fuji Hot Spring** (利尻富士温泉; ☺ noon–21.00 daily), a 5-minute
drive (20min walk) uphill from the ferry terminal.

Leaving Oshidomari and heading anti-clockwise, the first point of interest is just
a 5-minute walk away around the north side of the harbour to **Cape Peshi** (ペ
シ岬); a short path leads to the top of this grassy little promontory from where
there are great views of the harbour and Mount Rishiri if the clouds aren't in.
Continuing 1.5km west past the outskirts of town, a short climb up some steps to
the top of another grassy lump leads to **Yūhigaoka Observation Deck** (夕日ヶ丘展
望台), which has splendid views over the sea to Rebun and back across the island,
especially at sunset. There is a small car park nearby.

Back on Route 105, go west for about 10km, passing the airport to arrive at
Kutsugata (沓形), the island's 'second' port, where you will find a few restaurants,
accommodation options and **Rishiri Fureai Spa** (利尻ふれあい温泉; ☺ 13.00–
21.00 daily), a hot-spring facility connected to the adjacent hotel and yet used
mainly by locals.

About 3.5km south of town is **Kamui Kaigan Park** (神居海岸パー; w rishiri-
kamui.com; ☺ 09.00–16.00 daily), a small harbourside spot where you can partake
in sea urchin fishing (and preparation) from a boat tethered to the quay (30–60mins;
¥1,500), possible to reserve online. Back on the road, Route 108 skims southwards
for 6km before passing **Reiho Spring** (麗峰湧水), a natural roadside spring where
you can freely sup on clear spring water – locals can sometimes be seen filling
bottle after bottle. From there, it is another 2.5km to **Rishiri Town Museum** (利
尻町立博物館; ☺ 09.00–17.00 Tue–Sun; ¥200), a small but informative museum
all about the history of the island with some excellent displays, but only the most
perfunctory English information.

From there it is about 7km onwards to **Otatomari-numa** (オタトマリ沼), the
largest body of water on the island, beautifully framed by Mount Rishiri in the
background; wooden walkways allow for a 20-minute looping stroll of the lake
through the luscious Numaura Wetlands, a birding haven. There is ample parking
and a few gift shops and a restaurant here. To the east a narrow lane leads to an
observation point offering another classic view of the mountain – an image which
has been iconically immortalised on the packaging of a famous white chocolate
biscuit brand called Shiroi-kobito ('White Lovers'). There is a campsite and a dark
sandy beach nearby too.

About 3km along in the next seaside settlement is **Rishiri Museum of Folklore**
(利尻島郷土資料館; ☺ May–Jun & Sep–Oct 09.00–17.00 Wed–Mon, Jul–Aug
09.00–17.00 daily, closed in winter; free), a quaint Western-style white-and-red
wooden building housing an old-fashioned museum which charts the island's
history, but once again almost no English. Scooting back up the eastern side of
the island, Route 108 eventually leads in 14km to **Cape Notsuka** (野塚岬);
the large car park here offers another good view of Mount Rishiri, and the
Rishiri cycling lane which leads all the way along the north coast to Kutsugata
starts from (or ends) here. A small monument near the sea is dedicated to

A goal for many serious hikers, climbing to the top of Mount Rishiri (利尻山, Rishiri-zan; 1,721m), also known as Rishiri-Fuji, is one of the main draws to the island – a proper mountain, snow-covered for half the year and encircled by ocean with views as far as Sakhalin on a good day. The northernmost of Japan's '100 famous mountains' (page 81), Mount Rishiri is a long and tiring day hike, with a choice of two routes. The most popular by far is the Oshidomari route, which starts at the **Hokuroku Campsite** (北麓野営場; ⏰ May–Oct; ¥520 pp; **$**) at 220m – it takes about 4–5 hours to reach the summit from the trailhead, passing first through forests of fir and birch, before the views open up as you climb more steeply through flower meadows and then on to the crumbling, rocky-towered summit. There are actually two main peaks: Kita-mine (北峰) has a tiny summit shrine, while the ever-so-slightly-taller Minami-mine (南峰) is closed to hikers for safety reasons. There is an unmanned emergency hut between the eighth and ninth stations (about 90mins from the summit). Allow at least 8 hours to complete the hike, and if you get good weather then count your blessings, as it can be notoriously fickle.

For hikers, the campsite is a good place to stay to get an early start, and also has cabins (from around ¥5,000 per night; **$$**) if you don't have your own tent, while the hot spring down the road is a great place to freshen up post-hike.

The alternative and much less popular route is the Kutsugata Trail which starts from a car park at 420m about 6km up the hill from Kutsugata. It is also a good 4–5-hour walk to the summit, and near the top there are some exposed ridges with a high chance of rockfall, so it is considered much trickier than the other route and one for experienced climbers only.

Hikers should carry a portable toilet bag – these can be bought from the ferry terminal and at some shops on the island – and there are a few wooden 'toilet sheds' along the trails for privacy. Also be warned that, apart from one little spring near the trailhead, there are no water sources on the mountain, so bring plenty of food and drink. The hike is best attempted from around July to October when there will be little snow, although adventurous thrill-seekers may be tempted by a wild winter backcountry descent on skis or snowboard – some local guides and operators offer tours for experienced winter sports enthusiasts. The tourist office at the ferry terminal has decent English-language hiking maps, but the best and most detailed one (although all in Japanese) is Yama-to-kōgen Map.1 Rishiri-Rausu 山と高原地図1利尻・羅臼, available in outdoor shops, some big bookstores and online (it also shows trails on neighbouring Rebun).

If you fancy a shorter and less challenging hike, you can instead climb the much smaller **Pon-yama** (ポン山; 444m), which has fantastic views of Mount Rishiri and can be done in less than 2 hours return – start at the same trailhead at the campsite, and branch off left after about 10 minutes.

Ranald MacDonald (1824–94), a curious American who purposefully became 'shipwrecked' on the shore here in 1848, before being taken and imprisoned in Nagasaki where he taught English to samurai, so becoming the first native-English speaker to teach the language in Japan.

A couple of minutes' drive up the coast is a turn-off for **Hime-numa** (姫沼), a picturesque 1km-wide swamp (or pond) which sometimes offers reflected views of the mountain in its waters. There are short, easy hiking trails among the peaceful woods which loop around the pond in 20 minutes; from there it is only a short hop to the car park, and then a 5-minute drive back to Oshidomari.

REBUN ISLAND

Lying about 52km west of Wakkanai, the small, hilly island of Rebun (礼文島) offers quite a contrast to neighbouring Rishiri's pointed prominence just 10km away. Rebun has a gentler landscape which is luscious and green and cloaked in rare wildflowers during the summer (June to August), the prime time to visit. The island spans 29km north to south but only 8km east to west at its widest point, and near the centre Mount Rebun rises to 490m and is one of a number of good hikes spread across the island. While the wind-battered and remote west coast is full of jagged cliffs and dramatic scenery, the east coast is more serene. The name 'Rebun' derives from the Ainu-language meaning 'in the open sea', and a visit to one of its beautiful but lonely capes only highlights the sense of isolation, although there is plenty of evidence of both Jōmon and later Ainu habitation. Nowadays there are a handful of tiny hamlets dotted around the island which include the main port of Kafuka to the south, with one main road along the island's eastern coast linking them all. Rebun Airport is at the northern end of the island but now no longer serves any scheduled flights, so ferry is the only way to get here. Winters, in contrast to summer, are white and desolate and the island is little visited. Together with Rishiri, it forms part of the Rishiri-Rebun-Sarobetsu National Park, and like Rishiri, the *uni* (sea urchin) from the cold, kelp-rich waters around Rebun is considered world-class. Even if you miss the summer flower blooms, September can also be nice when the swathes of bamboo grass turn golden, and during the warmer months the island offers some truly outstanding hiking.

GETTING THERE AND AROUND

By ferry Heartland Ferry (w heartlandferry.jp) has two to three daily sailings to and from Wakkanai (2hrs; ¥2,960–5,840) and one to three daily sailings to and from Rishiri (45mins; ¥980–2,020). Kafuka is the main port and transportation hub on the island.

By road Driving is an option on Rebun, although car rental is somewhat more expensive than over on the mainland (perhaps around ¥15,000/day for a small car). This, however, can be cheaper than bringing a car over on the ferry from Wakkanai, which costs a minimum of ¥14,770 one-way depending on the size of the vehicle. There are car rental companies opposite the ferry terminal.

By bus Sightseeing tour buses are popular and a convenient way to see all the main sights in around 2–4 hours. Soya Bus (w soyabus.co.jp) has an office near the ferry terminal and tours can be booked in advance online (around ¥3,000–4,000 pp). A tour conductor will relay interesting facts in Japanese as the tour goes along, but you can do as you please at each stop (just don't miss the bus!).

The same company also runs local buses across the island, connecting the main port of Kafuka with Cape Sukoton at the island's northern tip (1hr; ¥1,240), Shiretoko in the south (10mins; ¥320) and Motochi (10mins; ¥460), although buses can be quite infrequent. A one-day bus pass costs ¥2,000/1,000 (adult/

child). English-language bus schedules are available at the ferry terminal; check them carefully.

By bicycle It is possible to rent hybrid electric bicycles (¥3,000/day) and scooters (¥4,500–7,000/day) – you'll need a Japanese copy of your international driver's license – from Cat Rock (🕐 08.00–17.00 daily) just outside the ferry terminal. Some accommodations offer bicycles for rent too.

TOURIST INFORMATION The small tourist information centre (🕐 Apr–Oct 08.00–17.00 daily) inside the Kafuka ferry terminal building has maps and bus schedules. Also check out w rebun-island.jp/en for good information.

🏠 WHERE TO STAY AND EAT *Map, opposite*

Hana Rebun 花れぶん; Tonnai 558, Kafuka; 📞0163 86 1666; w hanarebun.com/english. A 5min walk from the ferry terminal, this is possibly the plushest hotel on the island, with lovely spacious rooms looking out over the ocean towards Rishiri (some complete with their own outdoor private baths), splendid food made from local seasonal ingredients & great service. There is also a fantastic open-air hot spring on the 4th floor. **$$$$**

Momoiwa-sō Youth Hostel 桃岩荘ユースホステル; Kafuka-mura; 📞0163 86 1421; w jyh.or.jp/info.php?jyhno=105; 🕐 Jun–Sep. A real marmite option, this youth hostel in a 150-year-old wooden fishery sits in a stunningly beautiful & isolated spot on the island's west coast, with bunks or tatami mats for sleeping.

The atmosphere is supremely jovial & loud, with singing, dancing & daily organised hikes, but if you value your privacy you might find it a bit overbearing. All is in good heart however & some will love it. Free drop-offs & pick-ups at the ferry terminal. **$$**

Robata Chidori 炉ばたちどり; Kafuka-mura 1115-3; 📞0163 86 2130; 🕐 11.00–20.00 daily, closed irregularly Sep–May. Excellent family-run restaurant a few mins' walk north of the ferrry terminal, focused around *robata-yaki* (charcoal grill), with food cooked at your table. The speciality here is *hokke-no-chanchan-yaki* (ホッケチャンチャン焼き), Okhotsk atka mackerel with miso, although when in season, the *uni-don* (sea urchin rice-bowl) is one of the best around. **$$$**

WHAT TO SEE AND DO The main activities on Rebun involve visiting picturesque nature spots and hiking – there is a useful map of the island's six main hiking courses at w rebun-island.jp/en/trekking. Visitors all arrive at the port of **Kafuka** (香深), the main settlement on the island; here you will find a bunch of accommodation options, a handful of small shops and eateries, a **local history museum** (w rebun-museum.org; 🕐 May–Oct 08.30–17.00 daily; ¥300/150) and a **hot-spring** facility (🕐 noon–21.00; ¥600) with ocean views situated just north of the harbour.

Starting at the far southern end of the island, buses run to the small settlement of **Shiretoko** (知床), where the attractive old wooden school building at **Kita-no-Canary Park** (北のカナリアパーク) was used once as a film set; it offers outstanding views (on sunny days) out towards Rishiri Island. There is a nice little café (🕐 10.00–16.00 Thu–Mon) here too.

On the west side of the hamlet a hiking trail leads northwest into the hills for ever more spectacular views, leading up to a stumpy little lighthouse in 50 minutes, and then gently over ups and downs and through glorious summer flower meadows to reach in another 2 hours **Momoiwa Observatory** (桃岩展望台). This hilltop viewpoint boasts fantastic views of coastal cliffs, green rolling hills and distant Rishiri looming across the ocean. Momoiwa itself is the distinctive and rounded 250m-tall lump of rock directly west, said to resemble a peach. To reach there with less of a hike, approach from the north side instead, by driving in 10 minutes (or take a bus) along the winding Route 765 from Kafuka – it's an easy half-hour walk from the car park.

Heading further north, the **Rebun Forest Course** (礼文林道コース) follows a rough forestry track along the spine of the island, eventually looping east down to the small settlement of Kafukai in about 3 hours of hiking – halfway along this course a path branches west for a lovely 2-hour 30-minute (return) detour down a tranquil grassy valley to **Rebun Falls** (礼文滝), a waterfall which plunges almost directly into the sea.

Kafukai (香深井), which has a bus stop and campsite, is also the start or end point of the **8-Hour Course** (8時間コース), the longest hiking trail on Rebun (although you should probably allow 10 hours to complete it, what with all the photo stops along the way). It mostly hugs the lonely western coast of the island, passing some truly spectacular coastal scenery, and is an excellent hike for those with a full day of provisions and good stamina. About 2 hours out from Kafukai is the isolated spot of **Uennai** (宇遠内), a tiny harbour and collection of weather-beaten shacks on the beach, only reachable by boat or on foot. One of the shacks here used to sell fresh sea urchins and drinks, but sadly no more. The full 8-hour course is possibly easiest if approached from Sukoton in the north, so if not staying nearby, catch the first bus there in the morning from the ferry terminal.

Near the centre of Rebun is the island's highest peak, **Mount Rebun** (礼文岳; 490m), and a 4-hour return hiking course leads to the summit from the tiny fishing hamlet of **Nairo** (内路); buses stop here 20 minutes from the ferry terminal. The peak offers wonderful 360° views of the island and is suitable for reasonably fit hikers.

At the north end of the island is **Lake Kushu** (久種湖), a birding hotspot with a 4km trail looping around it – there is a nice grassy campsite (May–Sep; $) on the northwest shore, and even a tiny ski slope on the east side for anyone who dares visit in the winter. The nearby settlement of **Funadomari** (船泊) has a smattering of pensions and restaurants. Over on the northwest corner of the

REBUN ISLAND

For listing, see opposite

⊖ **Where to stay**
1 Momoiwa-sō Youth Hostel

island is a protruding finger of land with a number of desolate but stunning and windswept capes – the **Cape Tour Course** (岬めぐりコース) is a 4-hour 30-minute hiking trail which starts or ends at Hamanaka (浜中) and visits them all. The northernmost tip and where the road finally ends is **Cape Sukoton** (スコトン岬); there is not a great deal to do here other than take in the barren end-of-the-earth vibes and battle the wind (chilly even in summer) while coach-loads head for the gift shop and toilets. With your own wheels it is easy to visit the nearby and equally desolate **Cape Gorota** (ゴロタ岬), while a 10-minute drive south brings you to **Cape Sukai** (澄海岬), arguably one of the most scenic spots on the island and the best of the three northern capes – a real must-see with its shapely curved bay and stunningly clear waters.

THE NORTHWEST COAST

The main draw here are the Sarobetsu Plains with their rich waterfowl-filled wetland havens, which spill out on to the Bakkai and Wakasakanai coasts – the long-distance Ororon Line with its ever-changing ocean and sunset views is one of Hokkaidō's top driving routes, while the tiny islands of Teuri and Yagishiri are important seabird sanctuaries.

Enjoy the scenery as you make your way up or down the coast – the northern section between Bakkai and Teshio is the western limit of Sarobetsu Plain, which in turn is part of Rishiri-Rebun-Sarobetsu National Park. The long coastline is a delicate ecosystem of lagoons, sand dunes and forests of oak and fir, interspersed with bits of old railway structures from the long-abandoned Haboro Line.

JR Toyotomi Station has a small **tourist information centre** (⊕ 09.00–17.00 daily) for sightseeing information around the Sarobetsu area.

GETTING THERE AND AWAY
By road The scenic road along the northwest coast of Hokkaidō is known as the Nihonkai-Ororon-Line (日本海オロロンライン) and it stretches all the way from Wakkanai down to Rumoi (and beyond) following routes 106, 232 and 239. From Wakkanai to Rumoi it is 175km and takes about 3 hours. It is a splendid, breezy route with the sea on one side and miles of unkempt countryside on the other, dotted with small settlements here and there. It is not a recommended driving route in winter, however, as the conditions can be atrocious.

By public transport The coast is not easily explored by public transport, although it is possible to visit the Sarobetsu Wetlands by taking a train to JR Toyotomi Station (50mins from Wakkanai by local train), from where you can rent a bicycle to reach the Sarobetsu Wetlands Centre in about 25 minutes (1hr walk). Ferries to the tiny islands of Teuri and Yagishiri leave from Haboro, which can be reached by bus from Sapporo (**w** engan-bus.co.jp; 3hrs; ¥4,300) and Asahikawa (2hrs 30mins; ¥3,500); the same company also operates a few other local routes in the region.

 WHERE TO STAY AND EAT

Haboro Onsen Sunset Plaza はぼろ温泉サンセットプラザ; Haboro Kita-3-1 29; ☏ 0164 62 3800; **w** sunset-plaza.com. While not particularly fancy, this large, slightly dated hot-spring hotel in the centre of Haboro has spacious rooms with a balcony for sea & sunset views. B/fasts are good & varied, making use of local fare. The hot-spring water is slightly brown & salty. **$$$**

Teshio Onsen Yūbae てしお温泉夕映; Teshio, Sarakishi 5807-5; ☏ 0163 22 3111; **w** teshiospayubae.com. A standard business-style hotel with fairly large rooms & an excellent

restaurant – the attached hot springs have a faint ammonia whiff, but are very invigorating. Guests can borrow bicycles for free. **$$$**
Tonakai Reindeer Ranch [map, page 258] トナカイ観光牧場; Horonobe, Hokushin 398-1; ✆ 0163 25 2050; w tonakai-farm.com;

⏱ 11.00–16.00 Tue–Sun. After stopping off to feed the reindeer, pop into the farm's on-site eatery, Restaurant Polo (レストランポロポ ロ), which has a varied menu of hearty staples including ramen, tonkotsu & Japanese curry, with set meals available. **$$**

BAKKAI The first settlement after leaving Wakkanai on Route 106 (also known as the Sōya Sunset Road), Bakkai (抜海; population 300) is a fairly grim little place, but the harbour is a good place to spot seals in winter (binoculars may help). A few minutes south of the harbour is Hamayuchi Park (浜勇知園地), a small nature reserve with a freshwater swamp and lots of rare bog plants; there is a rest-house here with rooftop views of Rishiri.

TOYOTOMI The next place down the coast is Toyotomi (豊富; population 3,600), a small town located on the Sarobetsu Plain. At its centre are the Sarobetsu Wetlands, a vast grassy peatland and Ramsar site known for its hundreds of species of rare and beautiful flora including Japanese irises, Siberian lilies and *hamanasu* roses. The best place to learn about the area's unique ecology is a short drive inland at the **Sarobetsu Wetland Centre** (サロベツ原野センター; w sarobetsu.or.jp/swc; ⏱ May–Oct 09.00–17.00 daily, Nov–Apr 10.00–16.00 Tue–Sun; free). Inside there are plenty of natural history exhibits (although not much English), and outside you can stroll along wooden boardwalks to admire the flora and marvel at the sheer flat expanse of the marshlands – useful multi-lingual information boards give you a better idea of what you're looking at.

Back on the Sarobetsu coast and Route 106 continues southwards alongside the Wakasakanai coastal dune forest for 20km; this wall of woods between the wetlands and the sea contains numerous lakes and is home to many tree (Yezo spruce, Mongolian oak) and bird (Japanese snipe, Siberian rubythroat) species. Two of the largest bodies of water in the Sarobetsu wetlands are Penke (ペンケ沼) and Panke (パンケ沼) marshes, the latter of which has a car park and viewing platform on its eastern shore – they are both important wildfowl breeding grounds.

HORONOBE A short way inland and served by the JR Sōya Line, the sleepy little town of Horonobe (幌延; population 2,000) is best known for its reindeer and sake. The **Tonakai Reindeer Ranch** (トナカイ観光牧場; w tonakai-farm.com; ⏱ 09.00–17.00 Tue–Sun; free) just north of town is a rest stop and farm facility where you can feed the reindeer (apparently the only place where they are bred in Japan) and then feed yourself at the good on-site restaurant (see above). There are of course sleigh rides in the winter (¥510/200).

Next door to the farm is a curious facility called **Yumechisōkan** (ゆめ地創館; w jaea.go.jp/04/horonobe/yumechisoukan/index.html; ⏱ 09.00–16.00 daily; free), a research centre for the disposal of nuclear waste – they are currently digging a shaft to 500m in depth for nuclear storage purposes, but as there is almost no English, most of the detailed explanations will be lost on non-Japanese-speaking visitors.

The town of Horonobe itself has a few guesthouses and places to eat clustered around the station.

TESHIO Next stop heading south is Teshio (天塩; population 2,800), a small historic town right on the coast near the mouth of the Teshio River (the second longest on Hokkaidō and fourth longest in Japan), a prime spot for the harvesting of *shijimi* clams. It is believed that humans have been living here for at least 15,000 years, with more than 200 pit-dwellings relating to the Zoku-Jōmon, and later Satsumon and Okhotsk peoples discovered near the river mouth. In the late 18th century an Ainu trading post was opened here by early Japanese colonisers, and the river allowed for further exploration of Hokkaidō's mysterious interior. Later the town prospered with the river as a transportation artery for timber and other produce, in addition to its rich fishing grounds offshore. The lower 150km of the river is unusual in Japan in that it has not been dammed at any point (although alterations have been made in some places to alleviate flooding risk).

Approaching from the north, you'll know when you're getting close to the town from the rows of wind turbines lining the road – one of the few places they can be seen in Japan. Teshio is one of the larger settlements along this coast, but apart from a small local history museum and seaside onsen facility (with a campsite next door), there is not a great deal to do here.

HABORO About 60km (1hr) further down the coast is the next large town of Haboro (羽幌; population 5,700). Once a centre for herring fishing until stocks dried up in 1955, the town had a brief population boom from the 1940s due to nearby coal mining, until the last mine shut in 1970. There is not a great deal to do in the town itself, but there is a small cluster of restaurants to the east of the main road, plus a large michi-no-eki with its own hot springs. Next door is

THE SANKEBETSU BROWN BEAR INCIDENT

Often regarded as the worst bear attack in Japanese history, the Sankebetsu brown bear incident took place at a newly established settlement up in the mountains not far from present-day Tomamae. Over six days in December 1915 a large brown bear attacked a number of households, killing seven people and injuring another three.

Events had begun to unfold a few weeks earlier, when at dawn one mid-November morning a large bear appeared at the Ikeda family home, spooking the horse but taking only some harvested sweetcorn. On 20 November the bear reappeared, so members of the Ikeda family, plus a couple of *matagi* (local hunters) were put on high alert – when the bear appeared once again on 30 November they shot at it, but failed to kill it, but assumed that due to its injuries the bear would not return. However, on the morning of 9 December, the bear suddenly turned up at the Ōta family residence, where it reportedly killed a baby by biting it on the head and then dragged the mother into the forest, with the scene said to have resembled the inside of a slaughterhouse. The next morning a 30-strong team discovered the bear not far away in the forest – they shot at it but it escaped, and the head and legs of the woman were found in the snow nearby. Over the following days, the villagers armed themselves with guns, and a corps of 50 guardsmen went off into the forest to hunt for the bear. It is said that, while they were gone the bear reappeared in the village at night, entering the Miyouke farmstead through a window, before attacking the wife, her children and other villagers taking refuge there, including a pregnant mother who begged the bear to eat her head and not her belly. When the guard corps returned, there were still sounds of movement inside – some proposed setting the house on fire, but in the hope that some victims were still alive, instead the bear was scared out with loud banging. The team at the door misfired and the bear escaped yet again, but two

the northernmost rose garden in Japan, **Haboro Rose Garden** (はぼろバラ園; ⏱ 24hrs daily; free), which reaches its fragrant peak from late June to September, and next to that the **Hokkaidō Seabird Centre** (北海道海鳥センター; w seabird-center.jp; ⏱ Apr–Oct 09.00–17.00 Tue–Sun, Nov–Mar 09.00–16.00 Tue–Sun; free), a modern and well-appointed museum with good exhibits and a decent smattering of English.

Down at Haboro's harbour front is the ferry terminal, from where you can make a crossing to the tiny islands of Yagishiri and Teuri (see below). These islands lie about 25km northwest of Haboro and are little-visited by foreign tourists.

YAGISHIRI AND TEURI ISLANDS
Haboro Enkai Ferry (w haboro-enkai.com) runs daily sailings to Yagishiri and Teuri. There are two ways to reach the islands: by the slow ferry *Ororon 2* (1hr–1hr 45mins; ¥1,600–4,370, no reservations) or by the high-speed boat *Sunliner 2* (35–65mins; ¥2,830–4,360, reservations recommended). Fares vary depending on ticket class and season, with one to three sailings a day from around 08.00 to 15.00. Vessels stop at both islands; it takes 15–25 minutes to sail between Yagishiri and Teuri.

Be warned that the ferries can be cancelled in adverse weather, and there are very limited facilities, shops and restaurants on either island; if you want to visit directly from the big cities there are buses to Haboro from both Sapporo and Asahikawa.

young survivors emerged from the house. By 12 December government officials came to join the hunt, and despite protestations from the victims' families, it was decided for the good of the village to lure the bear back by placing a corpse in one of the houses where a sniper team would wait. From contemporary reports, it appears that the plan half-worked, as the bear did indeed reappear and briefly checked the house, but then scarpered back into the forest. At dawn the following day it was discovered that the bear had ransacked a number of homesteads during the night and had taken winter food stocks. The next day an expert local bear hunter named Yamamoto decided to track down the bear, believing it to be 'Kesagake', a bear that had been blamed for killing three women in previous separate incidents. Familiar with its behaviour, the hunter found the bear and from around 20m away shot it in the heart and head, bringing an end to the saga. The bear turned out to be a male weighing 340kg and measuring 2.7m tall, and had partially digested human remains in his stomach.

While it was undoubtedly a terrifying event, it was sensationalised in later re-tellings which reinforced the idea in the Japanese psyche of bears as fearsome man-eaters – it only later transpired that the bear did not attack anyone until after it had been shot and injured while simply searching for food.

It is possible to visit the location of this grisly incident at the **Sankebetsu Brown Bear Incident Reconstruction Site** (三毛別ヒグマ事件復元地; free), where deep in the woods one of the small, thatched pioneer houses has been reconstructed, complete with a terrifyingly huge model bear looming over it. The site is a 30-minute drive up into the mountains from Tomamae to the end of Route 1049, now nicknamed 'Bear Road' (ベアーロード; closed in winter) – take some insect repellent as the horseflies can be terrible during the summer, and of course, keep a look out for bears…

Yagishiri Island Yagishiri (焼尻島) is the easternmost of the two islands and the first boat stop. Relatively flat and just 4km across and barely 2km wide, it is home to only 160 people plus some small flocks of Suffolk sheep. Once a herring fishery, it is now best known for its peculiar forests of stunted Japanese Yew trees – usually growing to 15m high, the trees on Yagishiri grow only 1m in height and fan outwards, as a result of being pressed down by the wind and winter snow – the best place to see them being on the low hill west of the main settlement.

Yagishiri is a lovely place to cycle, with its yew forests, grassy sheep pastures and splendid views over towards Teuri – rent a bicycle (¥800 for 2hrs, ¥1,000 for one day) from next to the ferry terminal. The main village is on the east side of the island and has a few guesthouses plus a **local history museum** (w town.haboro.lgj.jp/shisetsu/culture/yagishiri-kyoudokan.html; ⏀ May–Sep 09.00–16.00 daily; ¥330/free) inside a lovely old wooden building dating to 1900 – it was once the home of a wealthy fishing family. There is a free campsite with toilets at the southern end of the island.

Teuri Island The island of Teuri (天売島) has an area of 5.5km² and is barely 6km across, with a population of fewer than 300 people. The island's cliff-lined northwest coast is an important breeding ground for many seabirds, including the puffin-like and clumsy-flying rhinoceros auklet, common guillemot, spectacled guillemot and Japanese cormorant, among others. The auklet colony on Teuri is one of the largest in the world with up to 400,000 pairs, and the best time to see them is from around April to mid-August – even if you're not an avid birder, the spectacle and setting is remarkable.

Teuri's only settlement is spread along the east coast of the island. It has a number of homely minshuku and a campsite if you wish to stay over (check w teuri.info/accommodations for listings; advance booking is recommended). and sample the quiet island life, and there are cycle rental shops near the ferry terminal. A road loops around the island, passing a number of cliff-top viewpoints and lighthouses – in the far west is a distinctive shard of rock called **Aka-iwa** (赤岩), and around dusk you can see thousands of birds flock back to their nests after feeding out at sea. If you have good sea-legs, 90-minute boat tours (May–Sep; approx ¥3,000/1,500 pp) around the island, departing from the ferry terminal, allow you to see the birds and cliffs up close.

TOMAMAE A short jaunt 8km down the coast from Haboro brings you to Tomamae (苫前; population 2,700), an inconspicuous fishing town but for the big scary bear statue at the side of the road near the town hall – this relates to Japan's most infamous bear incident which took place in 1915 in the rural backwaters of the district (page 286).

The town's one attraction is the **Tomamae Town Local History Museum** (苫前町郷土資料館, Tomamae-chō kyōdo-shiryōkan; ⏀ May–Oct 10.00–17.00 Tue–Sun; ¥310/100) which charts the lives of the early fishermen and farmers who first settled in the region, including a recreation of the house from the notorious bear attack. The grounds have authentic reconstructions of rustic old wooden dwellings too.

Appendix 1

LANGUAGE

JAPANESE Despite the fact that English is a core subject in schools, and Western influences are to be found everywhere, many Japanese people do not speak or understand English well, so any Japanese you can use and learn will help immensely, as well as please your hosts. Most Japanese people will be delighted and impressed if a foreigner manages to fumble through even a single word of Japanese, so give it a go! Always speak clearly and slowly, and write things down if necessary, as many Japanese people find it easier to read English rather than speaking or listening.

Japanese alphabets Modern Japanese has a famously complex writing system comprised of three different alphabets. *Kanji* (漢字) is a script with Chinese origins. It has tens of thousands of characters (though you really need to know only the 3,000 or so most common ones to be considered fluent), and each one can have multiple pronunciations depending on context or the other characters it is paired with. Even Japanese people often have a hard time reading or writing the less frequently used kanji. *Hiragana* (ひらがな) is a phonetic syllabary (symbols representing syllables) and it has only 46 basic characters. Hiragana is usually attached to the end of kanji to form grammar conjugations, or sometimes represents words with no (or obsolete) kanji readings. *Katakana* (カタカナ) also has 46 basic phonetic characters which are more angular in appearance than the graceful curves of hiragana. It is mostly used to write foreign loan words (such as beer ビール; *biiru*), non-Japanese names, or is sometimes written to provide special emphasis.

If you are keen to learn a little Japanese before your trip, then both hiragana and katakana can be memorised fairly quickly, and they are quite useful for deciphering things like items on restaurant menus.

Grammar Japanese grammar can be quite confusing, with sentences structured back to front for English speakers, with seemingly key information such as pronouns often omitted entirely and no distinctions between singular and plural. There are multiple levels of polite and humble speech, plus the tendency to speak about subjects in an indirect manner.

A Course in Modern Japanese (University of Nagoya Press, 2002) is a good starting point for beginners.

Pronunciation Despite being a notoriously difficult language to master (especially reading and writing), Japanese pronunciation is relatively straightforward – however, if you don't pronounce words close to how a native would, then many Japanese people will struggle to understand what you are saying.

The words and phrases in this appendix have been written in a Romanised form called *romaji*. Vowels with a macron (small bar) over them (such as *ō*) are pronounced the same way as normal vowels, but the sound is held for twice as long. This can completely change the meaning of a word; for example, *kuki* refers to a plant's stem, while *kūki* means 'air'.

The five main **vowel sounds** are:

a as in 'art'
i as in 'ski'
u as in 'flu'
e as in 'bed'
o as in 'old'

Consonants are pronounced almost the same as those in English, apart from:

g as in 'give' if at the start of a word, or a slightly nasal 'sing' if it appears mid-word.
f as in the 'wh' of 'who', made by pursing the lips and blowing gently.
r is closer to an 'l' than an 'r'.

Double consonants in words, such as the double *t* in *matte* (wait), should be pronounced with a slight pause between them.

Useful vocabulary and phrases

	Japanese	Romaji
Basics		
Yes/No*	はい / いいえ	*Hai/iie*
Please	お願いします	*Onegaishimasu*
Thank you	ありがとうございます	*Arigatō gozaimasu*
Sorry	ごめんなさい	*Gomenasai*
You're welcome	こちらこそ	*Kochira koso*

*There are numerous ways to say 'yes' or 'no', and questions are often answered affirmatively simply by repeating the verb or adjective in question. For example, 'Are you hungry?' (お腹空いていますか; *onaka ga suiteimasu ka?*) can be answered with 'Hungry!' (お腹が空いている; *onaka ga suiteiru*).

Greetings and introductions The honorific suffix '*-san*' is often added to the end of people's names when speaking or referring to them, and unless very close, people generally refer to others by their family name, eg: *Takeda-san*.

Hello	こんにちは	*Konnichiwa*
Good morning	おはようございます	*Ohayō gozaimasu*
Good evening	こんばんは	*Konbanwa*
Goodnight	おやすみなさい	*Oyasuminasai*
Goodbye	さようなら	*Sayōnara*
See you again	またね	*Mata ne*
How are you?	お元気ですか?	*O-genki desu ka?*
I'm fine	元気です	*Genki desu*
What's your name?	お名前は何ですか?	*O-namae wa nan desu ka?*
My name is...	名前は...です	*Namae wa...desu*
Where are you from?	どこの出身ですか?	*Doko no shusshin desu ka?*

| I'm from… | …の出身です | …no shusshin desu |
| Cheers! | 乾杯 | Kanpai |

Other useful phrases

Excuse me/I'm sorry	すみません	Sumimasen
Do you speak English?	英語が話せますか？	Eigo ga hanasemasu ka?
I don't understand	わかりません	Wakarimasen
It doesn't matter	気にしないで下さい	Ki ni shinai de kudasai
Can I come in?	はいっていいですか？	Haitte ii desu ka?
I want to go to…	…に行きたいです	…ni ikitai desu
Where's the…?	…はどこですか？	…wa doko desu ka?
Where's the toilet?	トイレはどこですか？	Toire wa doko desu ka?

Shopping

Do you have…?	…ありますか？	…arimasu ka?
This one please	これお願いします	Kore onegaishimasu
How much does this cost?	これはいくらですか？	Kore wa ikura desu ka?
Do you have a cheaper one?	もっと安いのありますか？	Motto yasui no arimasu ka?
Do you have a smaller size?	もっと小さいサイズありますか？	Motto chisai saizu arimasu ka?
Do you have a bigger size?	もっと大きいサイズありますか？	Motto ōki saizuarimasu ka?

Numbers

1	一	ichi
2	二	ni
3	三	san
4	四	shi/yon
5	五	go
6	六	roku
7	七	nana/shichi
8	八	hachi
9	九	kū
10	十	jū
20	二十	ni jū
30	三十	san jū
40	四十	yon jū
50	五十	gojū
60	六十	roku jū
70	七十	nana jū
80	八十	hachi jū
90	九十	kū jū
100	百	hyaku
1,000	千	sen
10,000	一万	icchi-man

Accommodation

| Do you have any vacancies? | 部屋はありますか？ | Heya wa arimasu ka? |
| I have a reservation | 予約してます | Yoyaku shitemasu |

single room	一人	*hitori no heya*
double room	二人の部屋	*futari no heya*
How much is it?	いくらですか？	*ikura desu ka?*
one night	一泊	*ippaku*
boarding only	素泊り	*sudomari*

Eating out

Do you have any tables (now)?	今は空いてますか？	*Ima aiteimasu ka?*
I'd like to make a reservation	予約したいです	*Yoyaku shitai desu*
How many people?	何名様ですか？	*Nan meisama desu ka?*
Do you have any recommendations?	何がおすすめですか？	*Nani ga osusume desu ka?*
May I order please?	注文していいですか？	*Chūmon shi te ii desu ka?*
Do you have any vegetarian dishes?	ベジタリアン料理がありますか？	*Bejitarian ryōri ga arimasu ka?*
I don't eat meat	肉は食べません	*Niku wa tabemasen*
May I have the bill please?	お会計お願いします	*O kaikei onegaishimasu?*
Thank you for the meal	ごちそうさまでした	*Gochisōsama deshita*
breakfast	朝ご飯 / 朝食	*asa-gohan/chōshoku*
lunch	ランチ / 昼食	*ranchi/chūshoku*
dinner	晩ごはん / 夕食	*ban-gohan/yūshoku*
all-you-can-eat	食べ放題	*tabehōdai*
all-you-can-drink	飲み放題	*nomihōdai*
set meal	定食 / セット	*teishoku/setto*
single item	単品	*tanpin*
small/medium/large	小 / 中 / 大	*shō/chū/dai*
chopsticks	はし	*hashi*

Food and drink

beef	牛肉	*gyū-niku*
black pepper	コショウ	*koshō*
bread	パン	*pan*
cheese	チーズ	*chīzu*
chicken	鶏肉	*tori-niku*
crab	カニ	*kani*
egg	卵	*tamago*
fish	魚	*sakana*
fruit	果物	*kudamono*
ice cream	アイス / アイスクリーム	*aisu/aisu-kurīmu*
meat	肉	*niku*
noodles	麺	*men*
octopus	タコ	*tako*
pork	豚肉	*buta-niku*
prawn	エビ	*ebi*
rice	ご飯	*gohan*
salmon	サケ	*sake*
salt	塩	*shio*
scallop	ホタテ	*hotate*

sea urchin	ウニ	*uni*
soy sauce	醬油	*shōyu*
squid	イカ	*ika*
sugar	砂糖	*satō*
tuna	マグロ	*maguro*
vegetable(s)	野菜	*yasai*
beer	ビール	*bīru*
coffee	コーヒー	*kōhī*
green tea	抹茶	maccha
juice	ジュース	*jūsu*
milk	牛乳	*gyūnyū*
red wine	赤ワイン	*aka-wain*
sake	酒	*sake*
tea	紅茶	*kōcha*
water	水	*mizu*
white wine	白ワイン	*shiro-wain*

Hokkaidō-specific words

Within Hokkaidō	道内	*Dōnai*
Person originating from Hokkaidō	道産子	*Dōsanko*
North Hokkaidō	道北	*Dōhoku*
East Hokkaidō	道東	*Dōtō*
Central Hokkaidō	道央	*Dō-ō*
South Hokkaidō	道南	*Dōnan*

Places (manmade) and infrastructure

airport	空港	*kūkō*
aquarium	水族館	*suizokukan*
art gallery	美術館	*bijutsukan*
bank	銀行	*ginkō*
bridge	橋	*hashi*
bus terminal	バスターミナル	*basu-tāminaru*
castle	城	*shiro*
cinema	映画館	*eigakan*
convenience store	コンビニ	*konbini*
dental clinic	デンタルクリニック	*dentaru-kuriniku*
department store	デパート	*depāto*
farm	農場	*nōjō*
ferry terminal	フェリーターミナル	*ferī-tāminaru*
harbour	港	*minato*
hospital	病院	*byōin*
hotel	ホテル	*hoteru*
hot spring	温泉	*onsen*
market	市場	*ichiba*
museum	博物館	*hakubutsukan*
observation deck	展望台	*tenbōdai*
park	公園	*kōen*
pharmacy (drug store)	薬局 / ドラッグストア	*yakkyoku/doraggu-sutoa*
post office	郵便局	*yūbinkyoku*
restaurant	レストラン	*resutoran*

road	道	*michi*
roadside service station	道の駅	*michi-no-eki*
shopping street	商店街	*shōtengai*
shrine	神社	*jinja*
ski resort	スキー場	*sukī-jō*
subway	地下鉄	*chikatetsu*
temple	寺	*tera*
toilet	トイレ / お手洗い	*toire/otearai*
men's toilets	男	*otoko*
ladies' toilets	女	*onna*
tourist information centre	観光情報センター	*kankō-jōhō-sentā*
train station	駅	*eki*
tunnel	トンネル	*toneru*
zoo	動物園	*dōbutsuen*

Geographical features

beach	ビーチ/浜	*bīchi/ hama*
cape	岬	*misaki*
coast	海岸	*kaigan*
field	畑	*hata*
forest	森	*mori*
hill	丘	*oka*
lake	湖	*mizuumi*
marsh	沼	*numa*
mountain	山	*yama*
peninsula	半島	*hantō*
plain	平野	*heiya*
plateau	高原	*kōgen*
pond	池	*ike*
river	川	*kawa*
sea	海	*umi*
summit	山頂	*sanchō*
valley	谷	*tani*
volcano	火山	*kazan*

Animals

bear	クマ / 熊	*kuma*
bird	鳥	*tori*
brown bear	ヒグマ	*higuma*
cat	猫	*neko*
cow	牛	*ushi*
deer	シカ / 鹿	*shika*
dog	犬	*inu*
dolphin	イルカ	*iruka*
fish	魚	*sakana*
frog	カエル	*kaeru*
horse	馬	*uma*
insect	虫	*mushi*
pig	豚	*buta*
sheep	羊	*hitsuji*

If you already have some familiarity with Japanese, you may pick up on some of the more common Hokkaidō-ben words which the locals use:

menkoi	めんこい	rather than the standard *kawaii* (meaning 'cute')
shakkoi	しゃっこい	cold (to the touch)
namara	なまら	instead of *totemo* (an intensifier meaning 'very')
nashite	なして	a casual word meaning 'why?'
-be	-べ	sentence-ending particles (instead of
-besa	-べさ	the standard *deshō*, used when seeking
-beya	-べや	agreement or raising a doubt)
-sho	-しょ	sentence-ending particle also used instead of *deshō*

snake	蛇	*hebi*
squirrel	リス	*risu*
whale	クジラ	*kujira*

Miscellaneous

ambulance	救急車	*kyūkyūsha*
bicycle	自転車	*jitensha*
car	車	*kuruma*
festival	祭	*matsuri*
flower	花	*hana*
foreigner	外国人	*gaikokujin*
Japanese person	日本人	*nihonjin*
police	警察	*keisatsu*
train	電車	*densha*
tree	木	*ki*

AINU There are now almost no native fluent speakers of the Ainu language remaining, but some people of Ainu descent know a few words and phrases, and any efforts to keep the language alive should be encouraged.

Ainu shares some similarities in word order (subject-object-verb) and sounds with Japanese, but it has a more pronounced and quite different pitch-accent system, and none of the long and short vowels of Japanese. Perhaps the best online resource for learning Ainu words and phrases is A Topical Dictionary of Conversational Ainu (w ainu.ninjal.ac.jp/topic/en) by the National Institute for Japanese Language and Linguistics, which has comprehensive word and phrase banks with audio recordings by a native speaker. Here are a few basics:

	Ainu	**Romaji**
Hello	イランクラプテ	*Irankarapte*
Thank you	イヤイライケレ	*Iyairaykere*
What is your name?	エレ ヘマンテ ヤ?	*Ere hemante ya?*
My name is…	カニ アナクネ … クネ	*Kani anakne…kune*
How are you?	エイワンケ ヤ?	*Eiwanke ya?*
Fine, thank you	クイワンケ イヤイライケレ	*Kuiwanke iyairaykere*
Yes	エ	*E*
No	ソモ	*Somo*

Appendix 2

GLOSSARY

ashiyu	hot spring for bathing your feet
daimyō	powerful feudal lords who ruled much of Japan from around the 10th century to the mid 19th century
Edo	the former name for Tokyo
eki	train station
Ezo	the former name for Hokkaidō
izakaya	Japanese-style 'pub' serving food and drink
kaiseki	traditional multi-course dinner composed of seasonal ingredients, noted for its presentation and elegance
kami	deity in the Shintō religion
kamuy	a spiritual or divine entity in Ainu mythology
michi-no-eki	roadside rest stop or service station
minshuku	a family-run Japanese-style bed and breakfast
omikuji	fortunes written on slips of paper, sold at temples and shrines
onsen	hot spring
pension	Western-style family-run accommodation
rotenburo	outdoor hot spring
ryokan	a traditional Japanese inn
sakura	the Japanese word for cherry blossom
shinkansen	bullet train
shokudō	a casual, affordable restaurant serving a variety of dishes
tatami	type of mat used as flooring, usually measuring around 0.9m by 1.8m
tondenhei	military settlers recruited to develop and defend Hokkaidō
torii	gate in front of a Shintō shrine
Wajin	old reference to 'Japanese people'
yakitori	bite-size cuts of grilled chicken served on a skewer
Yakuza	organised crime syndicate

Appendix 3

FURTHER INFORMATION

BOOKS
Literature
Arikawa, Hiro *The Travelling Cat Chronicles* Doubleday, 2018. A heart-warming novel about a cat and his owner, Satoru, as they travel around Japan. The book includes beautiful, vivid descriptions of Hokkaidō's landscape.

Batchelor, John *The Ainu and Their Folk-Lore* The Religious Tract Society, 1901. A classic compendium of Ainu folktales, with notes by a thoughtful contemporary expert who was one of the first (and only) foreigners to live among the Ainu for many decades.

Chamberlain, Basil Hall *Aino Folk Tales* The Folklore Society, 1888. An interesting collection of Ainu folklore, though the introductory and preface notes are certainly of their time.

Chiri, Yukie *The Song the Owl God Sang: the Collected Ainu Legends of Chiri Yukie* (translated by Benjamin Peterson) BJS Books, 2013. A readable collection of Ainu folktales, transcribed for the first time by a native Ainu writer.

Honda, Katsuichi *Harukor: An Ainu Woman's Tale* University of California Press, 2000. Pieced together from original native sources and extensive scholarship, this is a fictional account of an Ainu woman's life on Hokkaidō before Japanese colonisers arrived.

Kayano, Shigeru *Our Land Was a Forest: An Ainu Memoir* Routledge, 1994. A moving personal account of Ainu life on Hokkaidō.

Murakami, Haruki *A Wild Sheep Chase* Vintage, 2002. Authored by one of Japan's most celebrated modern writers, the latter half of this surreal and mysterious thriller is set on Hokkaidō.

Phillipi, Donald L *Songs of Gods, Songs of Humans: the Epic Tradition of the Ainu* Princeton Legacy Library, 1979. A fascinating collection of varied Ainu hero myths, many translated for the first time.

Strong, Sarah M *Ainu Spirits Singing: the Living World of Chiri Yukie's Ainu Shin'Yoshu* University of Hawaii Press, 2011. A detailed study of Chiri's seminal work with well-researched contextual notes and an extended biography on the Ainu writer.

History and society
Fitzhugh, William W *Ainu: Spirit of a Northern People* University of Washington Press, 1999. Now a little pricey and difficult to get hold of, this encyclopaedic and richly illustrated book showcases all aspects of Ainu history and culture.

Hane, Mikiso and Perez, Luis G *Premodern Japan: a Historical Survey* Westview Press, 2014. The second edition of this work is an up-to-date and scholarly study of Japanese history up to the end of Tokugawa rule.

A3

Irish, Ann B *Hokkaidō: a History of Ethnic Transition and Development of Japan's Northern Island* McFarland & Co, 2009. An excellent and comprehensive history of the island, especially from the Meiji era onwards.

Lewallen, Ann-Elise *The Fabric of Indigeneity: Ainu Identity, Gender, and Settler Colonialism in Japan* University of New Mexico Press, 2016. A look at how Ainu and indigenous women craft identity, especially in the face of Japanese colonisation.

Maki, John M *A Yankee in Hokkaidō: The Life of William Smith Clark* Lexington Books, 2003. A well-researched biography of the American adviser who left an indelible mark on the development of Hokkaidō. Currently out of print.

Morris-Suzuki, Tessa *On the Frontiers of History: Rethinking East Asian Borders* Australian National University Press, 2020. An interesting series of essays discussing the nature of borders and boundary-drawing, with a keen focus on the many-times-shifted frontier line between Japan and Russia.

Perry, Commodore M C *Narrative of the Expedition to the China Seas and Japan, 1852–1854* D. Appleton & Company, 1857; Dover, 2000. Fascinating first-hand accounts of Perry's mission to establish diplomatic relations between America and Japan.

Walker, Brett L *A Concise History of Japan* Cambridge University Press, 2015. A splendid, if slightly dry, crash course spanning the entirety of Japan's human history.

Walker, Brett L *The Conquest of Ainu Lands: Ecology and Culture in Japanese Expansion, 1590–1800* University of California Press, 2001. A detailed study of early Ainu and Japanese relations during the Tokugawa era.

Language

Bowring, Richard and Uryu Laurie, Haruko *An Introduction to Modern Japanese* Cambridge University Press, 2004. A thorough introduction to the language in two volumes covering grammar, vocabulary and exercises for typical daily usage.

Bugaeva, Anna (ed.) *Handbook of the Ainu Language* De Gruyter Mouton, 2022. This mighty 700-page tome is the most comprehensive English-language resource on Ainu grammar and history.

Frellesvig, Bjarke *The History of the Japanese Language* Cambridge University Press, 2011. Detailed tracing of the development of Japanese as a language from its early roots to modern form. Heavy going for those with little prior knowledge, however.

Nature and environment

Brazil, Mark *Birds of Japan* Bloomsbury, 2018. The most comprehensive English-language reference guide to Japan's avifauna.

Brazil, Mark *Japan: The Natural History of an Asian Archipelago* Princeton University Press, 2022. Wonderfully well-written guidebook full of excellent colour photos covering Japan's nature and wildlife.

Brazil, Mark *The Nature of Japan* Japan Nature Guides, 2013. An interesting collection of Japan-centric essays and articles concerning a wide range of nature-themed topics.

Brazil, Mark *Wild Hokkaidō* Hokkaidō Shinbun, 2021. Part detailed guidebook, part nature guide and part open love-letter to the natural splendour of eastern Hokkaidō by a long-time resident of the region.

Fukada, Kyūya *One Hundred Mountains of Japan* (translated by Martin Hood) University of Hawaii Press, 2014. Noted mountaineer and writer Kyūya Fukada devised this list of what he considered the country's most noteworthy peaks, presented in 100 short essays.

Totman, Conrad *The Green Archipelago* Ohio University Press, 1998. Although very little relates specifically to Hokkaidō, this is a fascinating study of Japan's environmental policy and land usage over the centuries.

Food

Bird, Winifred *Eating Wild Japan* Stone Bridge Press, 2021. A deep delve into the world of foraging and wild foods in Japan, including a short chapter specifically on traditional Ainu foods.

Goulding, Matt *Rice, Noodle, Fish: Deep Travels through Japan's Food Culture* Hardie Grant Books, 2016. An eminently readable gastro-tour through Japan, with a chapter dedicated to the culinary delights of Hokkaidō.

Travel literature

Bird, Isabella *Unbeaten Tracks in Japan* J Murray, 1905; Dover, 2005. A remarkable account by one of the first Western females to explore Japan's off-the-beaten-track regions (including Hokkaidō) in the late 19th century.

Booth, Alan *The Roads to Sata: A 2,000-mile Walk through Japan* Penguin, 2020. Written in a warm and engaging style, this classic of Japanese travel writing, first published in 1985, chronicles the author's journey across Japan.

Ferguson, Will *Hokkaidō Highway Blues: Hitchhiking Japan* Canongate Books, 2003. Humorous travelogue documenting the author's eventful and character-filled trip hitchhiking his way south to north through the country.

Landor, A H Savage *Alone with the Hairy Ainu; or 3,800 Miles on a Pack Saddle in Yezo and a Cruise to the Kurile Islands* J Murray, 1893. Riveting old-fashioned chronicle from one of the first Westerners to explore Ezo (Hokkaidō) and detail his interactions with the Ainu.

McLachlan, Craig *Four Pairs of Boots* Yohan Publications, 1996. A light-hearted retelling of the author's journey on foot from one end of Japan to the other.

APPS The following apps are all useful for any trip to Japan.

Google Maps Essential app for getting around, with satnav; train times & connections are fairly reliable.

Google Translate Quick, generally accurate translations; the best feature is the camera function for translating signs, menus and any text in real time.

Gurunavi Find something to eat by region, budget and cuisine.

Happy Cow Search for vegetarian and vegan restaurants all over the world.

Japan Official Travel App Loads of information, travel tips and a useful route-finder function.

Maps.me Download maps for the region beforehand to use offline when no Wi-Fi is available.

Navitime Find train routes and travel information.

Yamap Downloadable hiking maps covering the entire country (2 free downloads per month on the free version; for more you need to pay for the premium version), plus recent trip reports.

PODCASTS

Abroad in Japan Popular Youtuber Chris Broad ruminates over the latest happenings from Japan in entertaining 30-minute episodes that are released twice weekly.

Deep Dive from the Japan Times Providing an informative look at recent news stories from the country's leading English-language newspaper.

History of Japan Excellent deep dives into well-known and obscure episodes and figures from the whole gamut of Japanese history.

Japan Eats! Weekly shows delving into the world of Japanese cuisine and touching upon broader themes and Japan-related topics.

The Konnichwa Podcast Bilingual podcast with upbeat hosts; a great resource for learners of Japanese.

WEBSITES
Ainu culture

w **ainutoday.com** A website set up by Dr Kanako Uzawa, an academic of Ainu culture and advocate for Ainu rights, with the aim of sharing Ainu scholarship, advocacy and art.

w **ff-ainu.or.jp** Website of the Foundation for Ainu Culture, a good resource for learning about the Ainu in greater depth.

English-language news

w **japantimes.co.jp**
w **japantoday.com**

Outdoor activities

w **hikinginjapan.com** Comprehensive database of hiking guides for trails right across the country.

w **hokkaidowilds.org** A wonderful and free repository of hiking, cycling, paddling and ski touring routes, plus informative articles relating to Hokkaidō's outdoors.

w **japannatureguides.com** Mark Brazil's excellent website provides information on natural history, birding and wildlife, with information on guided nature tours.

w **japan-skiguide.com** Key information in a clearly presented format for Hokkaidō's best-known resorts.

w **mountainsofhokkaido.com** Extensive and detailed write-ups for hiking many of Hokkaidō's mountains.

w **skiing-hokkaido.com** Up-to-date information on everything related to Hokkaidō's winter sports scene, plus links for buying lift passes at all the major resorts.

Travel and tourism

w **biei-hokkaido.jp/en** A useful site, with some description in English, for the area around Biei and its sites and famous views.

w **en.visit-hokkaido.jp** Official tourism site for Hokkaidō.

w **hakodate.travel/en** Extensive information about Hakodate city and surroundings.

w **jrhokkaido.co.jp/global** Train status, timetable and ticket information.

w **jw-webmagazine.com** Plenty of information and features for destinations all over Japan.

w **kai-hokkaido.com** An online magazine with articles covering various topics related to Hokkaidō.

w **kiyosatokankou.com** Book tours in the vicinity of this eastern Hokkaidō town.

w **nisekotourism.com** A good resource for getting the most out of Niseko.

w **nissho-peninsula.com** Website for Hidaka and southern Tokachi subprefectures.

w **odori-park.jp** Mostly in Japanese but useful for checking events in and around Sapporo's Ōdōri Park.

w **rausu-shiretoko.net** Learn more about Shiretoko's eastern outpost.

w **rebun-island.jp** Discover all about northern Japan's scenic island outpost.

w **visit-abashiri.jp/en** Extensive information in English about the coastal city of Abashiri.

w **visit.sapporo.travel** Official Sapporo tourism website.

w **visitshiretoko.com** A simple website with some information about the Shiretoko Peninsula.

w **visit-teshikaga.com** Promotes tourism and nature in eastern Hokkaidō.

w **visit-tokachi.jp** Information relating to the Tokachi region in southeast Hokkaidō.

Index

INDEX OF ADVERTISERS